RUSSIAN FORMALISM

RUSSIAN FORMALISM

History - Doctrine

VICTOR ERLICH

Third edition

NEW HAVEN AND LONDON
YALE UNIVERSITY PRESS

To the Memory of My Father

Printed in the United States of America by
The Alpine Press, Stoughton, Mass.

Library of Congress catalog card number 80–54220
ISBN 0–300–02635–8

10 9 8 7 6 5 4 3 2 1

CONTENTS

PREFACE

The purpose of this study is to outline the historical development and to present and assess the critical doctrine of Russian Formalism. The term may require some elucidation. What is meant here by 'Formalism' is not the Russian variant of the supranational 'Formalist' trend that asserts itself periodically in artistic creation and in art criticism. The object of inquiry is a more specific and more easily identifiable historic entity. It is a school in Russian literary scholarship that challenged two approaches – social and religiophilosophical – which dominated the discussion of literature in Russia at the beginning of this century and placed the work of literary art in the center of attention. "Russian Formalism" originated in 1915–16; it had its heyday in the early twenties and was suppressed about 1930.

It may seem strange that so short-lived a movement should become the subject of so extensive a study. Perhaps it should be pointed out that the 'death' of Formalism was somewhat premature and at least in part externally induced: the Formalist critics lapsed into silence, not because they ran out of ideas, but because whatever ideas they still had were found undesirable. (Incidentally, the liquidation of Formalism in the Soviet Union and the subsequent campaigns against a totally disarmed 'enemy' would provide a good topic for a case study in Soviet literary politics.) More important still, the achievement of a school of criticism cannot be measured by its life span. The crucial question is not how long the given movement lasted, or was allowed to last, but how well it utilized the period of time which history allotted to it.

Judged by this yardstick, the Russian Formalist school presents a very rewarding field of investigation. A serious student of Russian literature can ill afford to ignore the provocative, if often one-sided, 'practical criticism' which emanated from the Formalist movement. Its theoretical pronouncements, especially those bearing on problems of poetic language, add up to extremely helpful contributions to the present-day debate on the methods and aims of literary scholarship.

A few remarks may be in order with regard to the organization and scope of this monograph. The division of the study into historical and systematic parts can give rise to criticism. The drawbacks of such an arrangement of material are obvious: it entails some repetition, as theory and history inevitably overlap. I felt, however, that this was the only mode of operation which afforded the possibility of arriving at a fairly comprehensive picture of both the evolution and the heritage of Russian Formalism.

Indeed, in order to streamline the organization of the study, it would have been necessary to sacrifice either the historical or the analytical aspects of the argument. It would have been possible to establish briefly the historical frame of reference and then concentrate on the systematic exposition of the Formalist tenets. Such a method, however, could not do justice to the crucial differences beween the successive stages of the Formalist school or to its interaction with the Russian cultural scene of 1915–30. Conversely, one could adopt an opposite course of action – notably, to present Formalist theory in terms of its evolution. But a dynamic account of Formalist doctrine would have a still greater disadvantage. It would fail to sum up, in so many words, the total Formalist contribution to various fields of literary theory, for instance, prosody, stylistics, theory of prose, theory of literary history. It is such a summary that part 2 of this study is intended to provide.

According to the original outline, the work was to deal with the Formalist school in Slavic literary scholarship. This would have included Formalist or quasi-Formalist developments in Czechoslovakia and Poland. In the course of investigation, however, I found it desirable to narrow the initial scope and to focus chiefly on the Russian phase of the subject.

But, if a thorough examination of Western Slavic Formalism could not be attempted here, it proved equally impossible to bypass it altogether. Insofar as the so-called Prague Structuralism and the Polish 'integral approach to literature' were directly influenced by the Russian Formalist movement, both belong clearly in the section of our historical narrative devoted to the aftermath of Russian Formalism. Since both these trends, especially Structuralism, as adumbrated by the Prague Linguistic Circle, represent in many crucial respects the final results of Formalist theorizing, their tenets had to be mentioned in the analysis of the Formalist doctrine as well.

Another matter which deserved an extended treatment but could only be touched upon in this work is the interrelationship between Russian Formalism and New Criticism. I trust that in spite of the brevity and sketchiness of my remarks on the subject I was able to suggest the essential affinities and the no less significant differences between these two schools of criticism.

Since the systematic section of this study is primarily concerned with methodology, more emphasis was placed on theory of criticism than on critical practice, on categories and criteria than on individual literary judgments. Analyses of specific works of literature were invoked chiefly by way of illustrating general principles. Moreover, since I aimed at a comprehensive survey of the Formalist tenets – and these range over a very wide field – I found it necessary to keep the illustrative material to a minimum.

In the course of my work on this book I incurred various debts of gratitude, whether in the form of expert advice or of financial assistance. The debt I owe Roman Jakobson is of a special nature. The standard formula "without whom this work could not have been written" is doubly applicable here. A leading figure in the Formalist-Structuralist movement, he is indeed an important part of my subject. I was fortunate to be able to benefit from his firsthand knowledge of the Formalist school. I am especially indebted to him for such sense of the connection between Formalist methodology and structural linguistics as I was able to glean, and for whatever glimpses of a fertile and hectic era can be found in these pages.

The reissue of a book launched twenty-five years earlier is apt to place the author in somewhat of a quandary. Even if his general orientation has remained the same, his manner is likely to have evolved and his emphasis shifted. Moreover, and no less importantly, when one's subject is a recent and seminal school of thought, the intervening developments are more likely than not to render some of the initial formulations and assessments inadequate, if not obsolete. Hence there exists a nearly inevitable conflict between the temptation to revise and a reluctance to do so in deference to the integrity of the original design.

In a limited way, I had experienced such ambivalence back in 1965 while envisioning the second edition of *Russian Formalism*. After some hesitation, I chose to confine the revisions to what appeared to me an indispensable minimum: since the first printing of this study, owing to the more permissive intellectual climate of the first post-Stalin decade, a number of the leading erstwhile Formalists or near-Formalists, or instance, Boris Eikhenbaum, Viktor Shklovskij, Boris Tomashevskij, and Viktor Vinogradov, have made a visible comeback. I thought it essential to take brief note of their recent contributions and thus bring up-to-date my account of the scholarly careers of the major protagonists of this book.

Fifteen years later, the part of my story which deals with the post-1930 vicissitudes of the Formalists needs no major emendation. The wider repercussions of Formalist literary theory are quite another matter. In fact, what might be called the afterlife of Russian Formalism both in Russia and in the West has by now become so vast a subject that to do it justice would require a more thorough overhauling of the text than I was prepared to undertake. The least I can do at this juncture is to signalize, however briefly, the most relevant neo-Formalist developments and to offer some second thoughts.

Were I writing this book today, I would undoubtedly pause before the achievement of Mikhail Bakhtin, author of the seminal studies of Dostoevsky and Rabelais and an incisive and original literary theorist. Bakhtin, who made his debut in the late twenties only to lapse into enforced obscurity until the sixties, could not be labeled a Formalist. (As a matter of fact, he is rumored to have coauthored the most sustained critique of early Formalism from a quasi-Marxist point of view, *The Formal Method in Literary Scholarship*). But the essentially structural and metalinguistic thrust of his *Problems of Dostoevsky's Poetics* attests to a strong affinity for the mature phase of Formalist theorizing. Since his revival in the sixties, Bakhtin has been increasingly recognized both at home and abroad as one of the key figures within the Structuralist-semiotic ambiance.

The current resonance of Bakhtin's work in the Soviet Union points up a change in the scope and tenor of Russian literary studies since the first two printings of *Russian Formalism*. From the vantage point of 1980, the contrast drawn in the last paragraph of this book between the Formalist contribution and the current state of Soviet criticism appears much too stark. The phrase "tame mediocrity and bleak dogmatism", while still roughly applicable to the bulk of official present-day Soviet criticism, fails to accommodate such distinguished heirs to the Formalist legacy as Lidija Ginzburg, such knowledgeable and perceptive younger literary historians as Sergej Bocharov and Jurij Mann, and last but not least, the literary-historical and theoretical contributions of the Soviet "Neo-Structuralists." I am referring to a group of scholars based respectively in Moscow and at the University of Tartu (Estonia) – namely, Vjacheslav Ivanov, Jurij Lotman, Vladimir Toporov, and Boris Uspenskij – who for nearly two decades now have been engaged in a concerted effort to tackle problems of language, literature, and culture along semiotic lines. Their sophisticated and often highly technical studies in structural poetics hark back to the creative symbiosis of linguistics and literary theory that characterizes both Russian Formalism and Prague Structuralism, even as they take note of recent Western developments in modern communication studies.

Jurij Lotman's brand of structural poetics finds a close counterpart in the concurrent efforts of Roman Jakobson. For some three decades now Jakobson's theoretical statements on "poetics and linguistics", as well as his intricate and wide-ranging textual analysis of individual poems, have tended to center upon the grammatical configurations discernible in poetry. His close readings of poets as disparate as Blok and Cavafy, Baudelaire and Shakespeare, probe the poetic utilization of such grammatical oppositions as masculine versus feminine, plural versus singular, imperfective versus perfective. In documenting painstakingly the complex interaction within a poetic structure of euphony, grammar, and semantics, these formidable exegeses go far to implement the late Formalist notion that no significant dimension of poetic language can be deemed irrelevant either to the poem's overall effect or to its local triumphs.

This important dimension of Jakobson's "American" period brings me to another significant change that has occurred since I wrote this book – a shift in the relative status or visibility of its subject. Back in 1955 Russian Formalism was virtually unknown in the West. By now many of its salient insights, concepts, and terms have been substantially absorbed into our critical discourse. Much of the credit for this is due to the cumulative impact on two generations of Western students of literature of such distinguished representatives and interpreters of the Slavic Formalist-Structuralist tradition as Roman Jakobson, Dmitri Cizevsky, and René Wellek. I would like to think that this book, too, has made some difference.

The relative novelty of my subject is partly responsible, I am sure, for the warm response which *Russian Formalism* has elicited on both sides of the Atlantic. Many reviewers who welcomed my book as the first full-length introduction to a vital school of criticism rightly deplored the virtual inaccessibility of the texts, the importance of which I was urging. Part of the gap, I am glad to say, has since been bridged. Some of the best studies of Boris Eikhenbaum, Viktor Shklovskij, Boris Tomashevskij, and Jurij Tynjanov have now been translated or reproduced. A large-scale edition of Jakobson's selected works is under way. Moreover, the Western student of criticism has now at his disposal valuable and representative selections from Russian Formalist writings ranging from *Readings in Russian Poetics* (1971) through the two-volume *Texte der russischen Formalisten* (1969–72) to *Théorie de la littérature: textes des formalistes russes réunis* (1965). The latter anthology, edited by the resourceful and prolific literary historian and theorist Tzvetan Todorov, can be said to have made history – in any event, history of criticism – as it played a significant role in orienting French critical discourse toward poetics and semiotics.

French criticism had been rather slow in responding to the Structuralist impulse. Until the late fifties, it was, in the main, gracefully resistant to theorizing. Yet the next decade witnessed a major shift toward methodology. An increasing recoil on the part of the heterodox French critics from urbane eclecticism of traditional literary history, the belated discovery of the remarkable pioneer of new linguistics Ferdinand de Saussure, the impact of Lévi-Strauss's structural anthropology on the entire range of French "sciences humaines," and last but not least, the increasing awareness, through the good offices of Todorov, of the Russian Formalist legacy – all these converged to turn Paris of the 1960s into a lively center of literary Structuralism.

Some ten years ago I had occasion to watch these stirrings at close range. My feelings, I must confess, were, and have since remained, decidedly mixed. To see a vital body of critical theory and practice, victimized by Soviet thought control and hamstrung by the language barrier, receive at long last the recognition it amply deserved was intensely gratifying. So were the sophistication, the inventiveness, and the intricacy of textual analysis to be found in Roland Barthes, Gerard Genette, and the best of Tzvetan Todorov. At the same time, some of the methodological pronouncements that issued from this high-powered group seemed curiously disappointing.

As will be mentioned below, one of the distinct advantages of the earlier Prague variant of Structuralism over Formalism lay in its clear recognition that literature cannot be reduced to language since it comprises elements or dimensions, such as plot, which are transposable into other systems of signs – for example, film. The corollary of this insight was a view of poetics as an integral part of an emerging science of signs, semiotics, rather than a branch of linguistics.

In the light of this advance, Roland Barthes's almost casual reference, in an introduction to the 1966 symposium on narrative fiction, to "the identity of language and literature" may well appear regressive. Elsewhere this brilliant and mercurial man of letters pushed his thesis about the "intransitive" (self-contained?) nature of poetic discourse so far as to describe literature at some point as a "tautological activity." His much touted distinction between "writerly" (traditional) and "readerly" (modern) writing came dangerously close to denying any intersubjective meaning to the latter and could be easily construed as an invitation to unbridled "readerly" subjectivity. Indeed, one of the curious features of much critical writing spawned by Paris Structuralism is that at times it manages to be at once technical and arbitrary, esoteric and trivial. Time and again, as in Barthes's elaborate dissection of a marginal Balzac novel, *Sarrasine,* the expenditure of ingenuity and sophistication would prove incommensurate with the relative weight of the text under discussion.

The more systematic forays into the theory of narrative by Claude Brémond, J. A. Greimas, and Tzvetan Todorov were heavily indebted to Viktor Shklovskij as well as to an important late Formalist study, the *Morphology of the Folktale* (1928) by Vladimir Propp. Propp's methodological contribution lay in evolving a remarkably economical typology of the Indo-European fairy tale by reducing the seeming multiplicity of its plots to the limited number of underlying narrative patterns. The taxonomic efforts of the French scholars seemed to me less rewarding. Diagramming human behavior as enacted in fiction – including the psychological novel where, in contradistinction to the fairy tale, so much depends on the complexity and elusiveness of human motive – in such terms as "task", "contrast", "trap" or "trickery", and "violation", did not strike me as particularly illuminating. I sensed in this mode of schematization an excessive proclivity for what might be called operational platitudes, a danger to which Todorov's early studies are not altogether immune. For instance, in his discussion of the masterly eighteenth-century French novel, *Liaisons dangereuses* by Chaderlos de Laclos, Todorov describes the siege laid by the resourceful libertine Valmont to the fetching Madame Tourvel as an attempt to effect a change from the active voice, "to love", to the passive voice, "to be loved" – a rather benign account this of a cunning seduction scheme and a dubious instance of the "structuraliste" compulsion to translate every aspect of human behavior into linguistic terms.

It is this latter-day brand of what a keen observer of the recent French cultural scene has called "linguicity" – an awkward term but, perhaps, not inappropriately so – that may account for the airless, claustrophobic quality of much present-day French intellectual discourse, whether of the structuralist or the "poststructuralist" ("deconstructionist") variety. Let me make, in haste, an essential distinction. It is one thing to recognize the centrality of language to literature, indeed to culture. It is quite another to enthrone language as the only legitimate frame of reference – let alone the ultimate reality – to contrive a ritual dance of "signifiers" in a vacuum. "The absence of a transcendental signified," declares leading contemporary French philosopher Jacques Derrida, "stretches the play of signification to infinity."

To pursue the implications of so heady a pronouncement would clearly lead me too far afield: as so much current French literary theory shades off into arcane philosophizing, its initial connection with the Formalist impulse is becoming increasingly tenuous. It is high time that I return, before closing, to the endeavors which can be directly traced back to that impulse.

Back in 1955 I hailed the Prague revision of Russian Formalism as a way out of the methodological impasse in which early twentieth-century literary scholarship had found itself, as a conception of literature that would enable the critic to "connect" style and word view, verbal texture and moral vision. Twenty-five years later I see no reason to rue this sanguine endorsement, but I am inclined to qualify it. There is no question that in the most significant studies produced within this tradition – most notably, in Roman Jakobson's studies in the "grammar of poetry and the poetry of grammar" – much headway has been made in what might be called the microdimension of the issue. Sound and meaning as elements of verse – and more broadly, texture and import – have been correlated time and again at the level of a single line or stanza. At the level of a poetic text such connections have been less compelling. Typically, a meticulous linguistic description of the poem would be followed by a sound and perceptive overall interpretation. But more often than not, only some elements of the latter could be shown to depend on, or derive from, the former. Jakobson's structural analyses of poetic touchstones are an impressive demonstration – indeed, a celebration – of the shaping power of language and of the poem's adeptness at dramatizing this power, of revealing and proliferating the multifarious verbal patterns. Yet, as I. A. Richards pointed out in an otherwise admiring response to Jakobson's analysis of a Shakespearean sonnet, only some of the patterns which a linguist's keen eye can discern in a poem are aesthetically "operative" or, to put it differently, germane to the poem's overall thrust.

How does one distinguish between the patterns which are "operative" and those which are not? I do not presume to offer, on the run, a satisfactory answer to this taxing question. All I wish to suggest here is that such a distinction cannot be made on strictly linguistic grounds.

Nor can predominantly linguistic perspectives on literature enable a literary scholar to undertake the task which appeared to me years ago to lie well within the province of Structuralist methodology – that of probing such connections as may obtain between the organization of the poetic "message" and the mode or modes of structuring experience uniquely available to poetry.

Yet, in all fairness to the subject of this book, one could hardly envision such a problematic had it not been for the pathfinding efforts of men like Roman Jakobson, Jan Mukařovsky, and Jurij Tynjanov. By the same token, the perspective – at once potentially comprehensive and centrally literary – opened up by Czech Structuralism would not have been so readily available to the leaders of the Prague Linguistic Circle as it was if the Russian Formalists in their day had not had the pluck to be extravagantly lopsided, creatively outrageous.

Finally, if in our assessment of this brilliant team, impatience with their excesses and immaturities is largely offset by an abiding sense of intellectual gratitude, this fact is only partly due to the saliency of the questions they asked and the cogency of many of the answers they offered, and in no smaller measure to the sheer concentration in the ranks of the Formalist movement of critical talent, zest, and wit. Few serious students of Russian literature, whatever their methodological persuasion, will fail to place Jurij Tynjanov's *Dostoevsky and Gogol,* Boris Eikhenbaum's *Young Tolstoy,* or Roman Jakobson's "On the Death of Vladimir Majakovskij" among the finest achievements of twentieth-century criticism.

V.E.

New Haven, Connecticut
October 1980

PART I

HISTORY

I. THE FORERUNNERS

1

The Formalist School occupies a distinctive place in contemporary Russian literary scholarship. Throughout its brief yet tempestuous course Russian Formalism provoked vehement controversy; its emergence was a defiant challenge to the critical tenets and procedures of its immediate predecessors, and its decline represented a hasty retreat before the onslaught of victorious successors.

The bitterness of the conflict and the apparent lack of continuity between the Formalist School and rival critical trends may easily give rise to the notion that Formalism was merely a curious but inconclusive and fortuitous episode, a marginal fact of the history of literature in twentieth-century Russia. This view appears the more plausible since it is generally believed that Russian literary criticism always tended to sacrifice formal analysis to ideological considerations. A contemporary British student of Soviet literature writes: "... it is noticeable even from the early days of Russian literary criticism, that political and social considerations tend to predominate, and that a work of art is judged by its social and political message in the first place and for its formal qualities only later or not at all." [1] Likewise, a Russian critic considers the "disregard of external form for the sake of significant content" [2] as an essential component of the Russian literary tradition.

Were this premise to be accepted, the Formalist School would have to be treated as a deviation from the main current of Russian critical thought and evaluated, depending on the historian's particular bias, either as a healthy reaction against the 'traditional' obsession with social significance, or as an irresponsible escape from social issues which a 'genuine' Russian critic would never fear to face.

The truth of the matter is that the popular theory about the traditional

---

[1] George Reavey, *Soviet Literature Today* (London, 1946), p. 105.
[2] P. K. Gruber, *Don-Žuanskij spisok Puškina* (Petrograd, 1923), p. 8.

anti-esthetic bias of Russian literary criticism is a gross oversimplification. The 'disregard of the outward form for the sake of significant
content' is merely one of the trends in Russian criticism, however
momentous and influential. Formalism was, it is true, the first critical
movement in Russia which attacked in systematic fashion the problems
of rhythm and meter, of style and composition. But the interest in literary
craft was not in itself a novel phenomenon in Russian critical thought,
nor was it necessarily a product of foreign influences. While the affinity
between Russian Formalism and similar developments in Western literary
scholarship cannot be denied, the spokesmen of the new critical school
could point to a rich indigenous tradition of form-consciousness going
back as far as the Middle Ages.

An attempt to bolster this thesis with sufficient historical evidence
would lie outside the scope of this study. Suffice it here to cite several
pertinent but often forgotten facts. In the eighteenth century critical
controversy centered around problems of prosody and language rather
than those of ideology. Likewise, the criticism of Puškin's time, including many pronouncements of the master himself, was predominantly esthetic. As recent research has shown, [3] contemporary reactions
to Puškin's poetry reveal more attention to questions of genre and style
than to that elusive 'wisdom' of Puškin with which some twentieth-
century Russian critics have been so concerned. [4]

Even Belinskij, the father of Russian social criticism, was not unaware
of formal considerations. Whatever the shortcomings of this gifted if
somewhat erratic critic, he was not guilty of that crudely didactic
approach to literature which is often ascribed to him. Indeed, it was
not until the second half of the nineteenth century that Russian literary
criticism, journalistic and academic alike, fell under the sway of social
utilitarianism.

Several factors were responsible for this development. One of these
was the challenge to the 'genteel' aristocratic tradition presented by
a new cultural formation: the plebeian intelligentsia (raznočincy). Its
spokesmen, the 'men of the sixties', entered Russian literature in a
rebellious and defiant mood. Their first impulse was to reject the
cultural heritage of the leisured classes. No wonder that esthetic considerations were discarded as a luxury, as a part of the obsolete and
hateful patrician way of life.

[3] See especially Viktor Žirmunskij, *Bajron i Puškin (Iz istorii romantičeskoj
poèmy)* (Leningrad, 1924).
[4] See below, chapter III, p. 53.

Neither Dobroljubov, to whom critical endeavor was primarily a vehicle for high-minded journalism, nor Pisarev, who in his famous article "Puškin and Belinskij" [5] scoffed at the frivolous irrelevancies of *Evgenij Onegin,* could have much use for formal analysis of literary works. These pundits of civic criticism looked at the creative writer with the stern, distrustful eye of a prosecutor. The defendant had to prove his innocence, or more exactly, justify his right to exist by an explicit and 'progressive' social ideology. With literature seen chiefly as a medium of political propaganda, the problem of form could be of interest to the critic only insofar as it had a bearing on the effectiveness and lucidity of the message presumably embodied in the work.

'Pisarevism' (*pisarevščina*) was not, to be sure, the last word of the Russian radical intelligentsia. As the 'sound and fury' of the 1860's abated, the *raznočincy* developed some of the tolerance of maturity. On the other hand, the process of rapid democratization had drawn into its orbit many an aristocratic intellectual. Thus, the boundary between the two social groups became increasingly fluid. The excesses of esthetic nihilism – this, to paraphrase Lenin's famous expression, 'infantile disease' of Russian criticism – gave way to a more sober and discriminating view of literature.

And yet the emphasis on the message, the tendency to account for literature in terms of political ideas, was to remain a salient feature of Russian literary studies for years to come. This applies not only to the frankly ideological criticism of such Populist writers as Mixajlovskij or Ivanov-Razumnik, but to the more academic contributions of the literary historians as well. Not a few scholarly studies in the field, particularly those dealing with nineteenth-century literature, are marked by a purely external approach to the object of inquiry. More often than not they seem to confound, in Šklovskij's phrase, the history of Russian literature with the history of Russian liberalism.

One of the most typical products of this methodological fallacy is Skabičevskij's popular *History of Contemporary Russian Literature.* [6] Another prominent literary historian of the late nineteenth century, the more cultivated and erudite Pypin, [7] sees in literature primarily a manifestation of social thought. His definition of literary history comes perilously close to reducing the works of literature to the status of

---

[5] *Russkoe Slovo* (St. Petersburg, 1865), no. 4.
[6] A. M. Skabičevskij, *Istorija novejšej russkoj literatury* (several editions during the 1890's).
[7] A. M. Pypin, *Istorija russkoj literatury* (St. Petersburg, 1913).

historical documents, of subsidiary material for the adjacent disciplines. "The history of contemporary literature . . . does not confine itself to works of pure art and draws within its sphere contiguous manifestations of collective thoughts and emotions, studying these works of literature as it does as a material for national or social psychology." [8]

These tenets were not merely an offshoot of the Pisarev tradition. Other forces were at work here – philosophical as well as political ones. While the European intellectual scene was dominated by positivism, regarding natural science as the only *bona fide* type of scientific inquiry, and causal determinism as the only legitimate frame of reference, the notions of purpose or function were bound to be discarded as relics of medieval mysticism. With the structural analysis of literature thus made impossible, the genetic method had its heyday. Taine's theory of art or the *Kulturgeschichtliche Schule* in German philology focused the attention of the scholar not on the literary work itself, but on "that which lies at the bottom of this work and manifests itself in it". [9]

Another potent factor in the preoccupation of the Russian literary historian with 'social thought' was the plight of imaginative literature in nineteenth-century Russia. Since political censorship often made explicit criticism of the regime well-nigh impossible, the tasks of upholding individual rights and of exposing social evils fell largely to the creative writer. The literary artist had at his disposal numerous devices of indirection, prone to elude the watchfulness of the literal-minded censor. But poetic ambiguity is a double-edged weapon. The elliptic 'Aesopian language' used by the writer not infrequently impaired the effectiveness of the 'subversive' message; a subtle hint which evaded the censor's red pencil was likely to go unnoticed by the reader as well. The poetic parable had to be deciphered, the half-concealed idea had to be stated more explicitly, whenever the political atmosphere made possible temporarily a modicum of plain speaking. This was clearly the responsibility of the literary critic, more specifically of the student of modern Russian literature. It was thus that the ideological exegesis of nineteenth-century Russian poetry and fiction became the paramount concern of A. Skabičevskij, A. Pypin, D. Ovsjaniko-Kulikovskij [10] and many other leading literary scholars of the time.

[8] *Ibid.*, p. 33.
[9] Hermann Paul, *Grundriss der germanischen Philologie* (Strassburg, 1891), I, iii.
[10] D. Ovsjaniko-Kulikovskij, *Istorija russkoj intelligencii* (Moscow, 1908); *Istorija russkoj literatury 19 veka*, edited by D. Ovsjaniko-Kulikovskij (Moscow, 1809), 5 vols.

With the study of contemporary Russian literature heavily slanted toward journalism or the history of ideas, formal analysis had to go somewhere else. It was in domains further removed from the 'burning' social issues that literary scholars of the last decades of the nineteenth century produced their most fruitful insights into the problems of literary craft. I have in mind the comparative study of literature and folklore as well as the philosophy of language, more specifically the stimulus which these disciplines received from the work of A. Potebnja and A. Veselovskij.

2

The attempt of Aleksandr Potebnja (1835-1891) to tackle the problem of poetic language deserves special mention here. The affinity between this pioneering venture of one of Russia's most distinguished philologists and the subsequent Formalist theorizing was considerably greater than the Formalist spokesmen have ever cared to acknowledge. This apparent lack of intellectual gratitude may be attributed to the cavalier treatment of recognized authorities which was so typical of Russian Formalism. Such an observation, however, does not tell the whole story. The disparaging account of 'Potebnjanism', found in the articles of Šklovskij, [11] though not entirely inaccurate, seems to indicate that the Formalist theoretician derived his notion of Potebnja's doctrine from second-hand versions rather than from original texts.

The group of Potebnja's disciples who after their teacher's death set out to popularize his theories in a collective volume entitled *Problems of the Theory and Psychology of Art* [12] were often guilty of canonizing precisely the most vulnerable and least original facets of Potebnja's heritage. Entirely too much emphasis was laid in these exegeses on the antiquated psychological conceptions which the Russian scholar borrowed from the German philosopher Herbart and on Potebnja's equally derivative theory of imagery.

The aspect of Potebnja's approach to poetry which seems most relevant here was his determination to describe the nature of poetic creation in linguistic terms. Following the lead of the great German linguist and philosopher, Wilhelm von Humboldt, Potebnja argued that "poetry and prose are linguistic phenomena".[13] Poetry was seen

[11] See "Potebnja" and "Iskusstvo kak priëm", *Poètika* (Moscow, 1919).
[12] *Voprosy teorii i psixologii tvorčestva*, 8 vols. (Petrograd-Xar'kov, 1907–1923).
[13] Quoted by V. Xarciev in his paper "Elementarnye formy poèzii", *Voprosy teorii i psixologii tvorčestva*, 1907, I, 199.

here [14] as one of the two basic modes of apprehending reality, of acquiring knowledge "through the agency of the word".[15]

This raises a broader problem which indeed loomed very large in Potebnja's writings – that of the relation between thought and language. In dealing with this question Potebnja veers away from the Hegelian tradition which otherwise exerted considerable influence on his thinking; he postulates a mutual inadequacy between the word and the idea. For one thing, he points out, language is not the only mode of objectifying ideas. "Thought can dispense with words. Is not that which is expressed in musical tones, in graphic forms, or in colors, also thought?" [16] Moreover, inasmuch as thought and language do constitute co-extensive notions, they are fundamentally at cross purposes. Thought tends, as it were, to subjugate the word, to reduce it to the status of a handmaiden, a mere tag, to cut down the range of its functions to that of pure denotation by establishing a point-to-point correspondence between term and meaning. Language, on the contrary, strives for the supreme autonomy of the verbal sign, for the actualization of the potentialities inherent in its complex semantic structure, in its connotative richness.

It is here that poetic creativity enters the picture. For, according to Potebnja, it is in the work of poetry that the 'ideal' of language – the emancipation of the word from the tyranny of the idea – comes closest to realization. Poetry is a powerful defense mechanism used by the 'word' in order to vindicate its autonomy in the face of 'hostile' pressures. It is language *par excellence,* language at its most creative.[17] Conversely, each manifestation of speech activity, such as the coining of new words, may be conceived of as a poetic act. Each word, taken separately, may be regarded as a work of poetry.[18] ". . . The word is art, more exactly, poetry." [19]

According to Potebnja, the process of inventing names for unfamiliar phenomena is effected by abstracting from the object to be named a property which it shares with a group of objects already designated. Thus, to quote one of Potebnja's disciples, "from the standpoint of

[14] It goes without saying that the terms 'poetry' is used here in the generic, Aristotelian sense.
[15] A. Potebnja, *Iz lekcij po teorii slovesnosti* (Xar'kov, 1894), p. 99.
[16] *Iz lekcij po teorii slovesnosti,* p. 127.
[17] This tendency to equate poetry with linguistic creativity bears considerable resemblance with such twentieth-century developments as B. Croce's esthetic doctrine and Vossler's 'neo-idealistic school'.
[18] *Iz lekcij po teorii slovesnosti,* p. 113.
[19] A. Potebnja, *Mysl' i jazyk* (Xar'kov, 3rd ed., 1926), p. 149.

their derivation, all the words we use are tropes".[20] Eventually, under the impact of linguistic and social change, the original meaning of the word is forgotten or relegated to the background; its figurative core is no longer perceived. The trope turns into a 'faded metaphor' as the word gradually 'shrinks' and from a vivid image becomes a mere 'emblem'.[21]

In the light of this theory poetry is not so much a distinct type of verbal behavior as a quality or power which language bears within itself and which is operative in varying degrees of intensity at several levels of speech-activity. Potebnja does not hesitate to identify this quality as the 'symbolism of language,' i.e. imagery: "Symbolism of language may be regarded as its poetic value."[22]

As in most nineteenth-century esthetic doctrines, the preoccupation with imagery entailed here considerable emphasis on such characteristics as 'vividness' and 'concreteness'. It was indicated above that to Potebnja 'poetry' and 'prose' – i.e., roughly, imaginative literature and science – were two forms of cognition. The difference between them, Potebnja argued in his *Lectures on Literary Theory,* lies not in the goals pursued, since both types of discourse aim at the ordering of experience, at 'generalizations', but in the methods employed. While science works with homogeneous material, poetry brings together, through the agency of the metaphor, phenomena belonging to different spheres of experience. While science deals in general concepts, poetry "gives a specific answer to a specific question".[23] The former asserts; the latter exemplifies.

It is hardly necessary to point out that the proposition "poetry is thinking in verbal images" [24] was neither novel nor uniquely Potebnja's. Already Aristotle had hailed the 'command of the metaphor' as the crucial test of the poet's power.[25] In modern times, the belief in the "inevitability of imagery", to use J. L. Lowes' expression,[26] became the cornerstone of the romantic theory of poetry.

Moreover, it is doubtful whether such traditional antitheses as concrete vs. abstract, image vs. concept, synthetic vs. analytic could provide an adequate basis for differentiating between poetry and prose *qua*

[20]   A. Gornfel'd, "Poèzija", *Voprosy teorii i psixologii tvorčestva,* 1907, I, 200.
[21]   Cf. *op. cit.,* p. 203.
[22]   A. Potebnja, *Mysl' i jazyk,* p. 134.
[23]   *Iz lekcij po teorii slovesnosti,* p. 75.
[24]   *Voprosy teorii i psixologii tvorčestva,* 1907, I, 200.
[25]   Aristotle, "Poetics", *Criticism,* ed. by M. Schorer (New York, 1948), p. 213.
[26]   Quoted in Cecil Day Lewis, *The Poetic Image* (New York, 1947), p. 135.

'linguistic phenomena'. Nor was the distinction attempted by Potebnja furthered by the notion of the poetic image implicit in his writings. Potebnja's keen awareness of the kinship between poetry and myth [27] did not save him from the rationalistic fallacy of overemphasizing the cognitive, not to say the didactic, aspect of imagery. The view of the trope as an explanatory device, as a mental shortcut, substituting "small intellectual units for a heterogeneous mass of ideas" [28] was largely misguided. As the Formalist critics of Potebnja subsequently pointed out,[29] the function of the image in poetry is of an entirely different nature; it lies not in bringing closer to us the unfamiliar, but, on the contrary, in 'making strange' the habitual by presenting it in a novel light.[30]

And yet, there is much in Potebnja's heritage that anticipates some of the crucial Formalist insights. Whatever their shortcomings, Potebnja's pioneering studies had the distinct merit of focusing on the problem of poetry as a *sui generis* mode of discourse. Potebnja's insistence on the need for a close alliance between the study of language and literary scholarship found its sequel in the linguistic or semiotic orientation of Slavic 'Formalist' poetics. By the same token, the view of poetic creation as a liberation of the Word, as a release of its multiple potentialities can be said to have foreshadowed one of Formalist's basic tenets: notably, the thesis that poetry is sign-oriented verbal behavior.[31]

3

While Potebnja was thus inquiring into the semantic dynamics of poetic speech, another outstanding Russian scholar set out to evolve, along quite different lines, a system of scientific poetics. This was Aleksandr Veselovskij (1838–1906), Russia's foremost authority on comparative literary history.

The point of departure of Veselovskij's work in the methodology of

---

[27] See especially the chapter on 'Myth' in *Iz zapisok po teorii slovesnosti* (Xar'-kov, 1905), pp. 397-407, and the discussion of symbolism in Slavic folk poetry (*O nekotoryx simvolax v slavjanskoj poèzii*, Xar'kov, 1860).
[28] *Iz lekcij po teorii slovesnosti*, p. 97.
[29] See below, chapters IV and X, p. 76 and 175 respectively.
[30] Some of Potebnja's strictures on the function of the image come dangerously close to Herbert Spencer's ill-fated notion of the economizing of mental energy as the supreme law of 'psychological hygiene', operative at all levels of spiritual endeavor (*Philosophy of Style*, New York, 1880).
[31] See below, chapter X, pp. 181–186.

literary research was his desire to establish literary history as a distinct intellectual discipline, with closely defined aims and methods. Hence his insistence on the necessity of defining the actual subject of literary scholarship, his recurrent attempts to answer the question: what is literature? Time and again Veselovskij reverts to this fundamental query. And, characteristically, with each new answer the frame of reference shifts substantially.

The first definition of literature found in Veselovskij is the broadest and the least satisfactory. In the "Report from a Trip Abroad" (1863),[32] no attempt was made to distinguish between cultural history and the history of literature. The latter is defined as "the history of education, culture, social thought as mirrored in poetry, in science and in life".[33] The anti-esthetic bias of the sixties makes itself felt in the disparaging remarks about Ševyrëv's [34] 'undue preocupation' with *belles lettres*, as well as in the petulant assertion that "the times of treatises on rhetoric and poetics have irretrievably passed".[35]

Seven years later Veselovskij restated his conception of literary scholarship in a somewhat modified form. The definition is still perilously broad: once again the history of literature is declared to be "the history of social thought insofar as it manifests itself in the philosophical, religious and poetic currents and is embodied in words".[36] But this time an essential qualification is introduced: "If (and this seems to be the case) it is poetry that should receive the special attention of the literary historian, the comparative method is likely to open new vistas within this narrower field of inquiry." [37]

It was in one of Veselovskij's last methodological utterances that the need for sharply delimiting the province of literary scholarship is clearly recognized.[38] In an apt phrase which foreshadows the Formalist attacks on traditional literary history,[39] Veselovskij likens the latter to a "no man's land (*res nullius*) where there comes a'hunting the cultural historian along with the esthetician, the philologist and the stu-

---

[32] "Iz otčětov po zagraničnoj komandirovke", *Istoričeskaja poètika*, pp. 386–397.
[33] *Ibid.*, p. 397.
[34] A noted Russian critic, author of the scholarly *Istorija russkoj slovesnosti* (Moscow, 1859–1860).
[35] *Istoričeskaja poètika*, p. 388.
[36] *Ibid.*, p. 52.
[37] *Ibid.*, p. 54.
[38] A. N. Veselovskij, "Iz vvedenija v istoričeskuju poètiku", *Istoričeskaja poètika*, pp. 53–72.
[39] Roman Jakobson, *Novejšaja russkaja poèzija* (Prague, 1921), p. 11.

dent of social ideas".[40] In order to remedy this chaotic situation it is necessary to differentiate between creative literature and 'writing' in the broader sense of this word (*slovesnost'*). "Literary history is the history of social thought as mirrored in imaginative poetic (*obrazno-poètičeskij*) experience and in the forms embodying this experience. History of thought is a broader term; literature is only one of its manifestations."[41]

V. Peretc, a prominent Russian historian and theoretician of literature, is essentially correct in describing the evolution of Veselovskij's conception of literary study as a gradual shift from cultural history to historical poetics.[42] It is true that even in the last definition the study of literature is classified as a subdivision of the history of social thought, but the principal emphasis here is on the distinctive features of poetry, on the "evolution of poetic consciousness and its forms".[43]

This far-reaching modification of the initial premises was testimony to the intellectual flexibility and integrity of a scholar who, refusing to accept uncritically the axioms of nineteenth-century *Kulturgeschichte*, tirelessly re-examined them in the light of the evidence accumulated in the course of research. It is probable, however, that his continuous grappling with basic methodological problems prevented Veselovskij from settling down at a sufficiently early stage to what would have proved under any circumstances a colossal task – that of working out a comprehensive scheme of universal literary evolution. The grandiose structure remained unfinished. But its impressive fragments – voluminous works in comparative literary history and folklore and, particularly, the pioneering studies in historical poetics [44] – contain many penetrating insights into the 'forms of poetic consciousness'.

B. Engelhardt points out correctly in his thoughtful monograph [45] that Veselovskij's approach to the art of poetry was more 'static' and less psychological than that of Potebnja. To Veselovskij imaginative literature was not the 'continuous activity of the spirit', the dynamic process of image-making, of apprehending reality. It was fundamentally a sum-total of literary products, which can be assessed and corre-

---

[40]   *Istoričeskaja poètika*, p. 53.
[41]   *Ibid.*
[42]   See V. N. Peretc, *Iz lekcij po metodologii istorii russkoj literatury* (Kiev, 1914), pp. 205–206.
[43]   *Istoričeskaja poètika*, p. 53.
[44]   "Tri glavy iz istoričeskoj poètiki", 1899; "Iz istorii èpiteta", 1895; "Poètika sjužetov", 1897–1906.
[45]   Boris Engelhardt, *Aleksandr Nikolaevič Veselovskij* (Petrograd, 1924).

lated without reference to their creators or, for that matter, their consumers. Nor is the work of literature the ultimate unit of investigation in Veselovskij's 'inductive poetics'. The literary monument is dissected into recognizable objective components – ideological concepts, narrative schemes, poetic devices, consecrated images. The latter in turn can easily be reduced, for the purposes of comparative analysis, to a limited repertory of general types – of traditional literary "formulae, persistent motifs which are handed down from generation to generation" [46] and which reappear time and again in the literature and folklore of various ages and countries. It is not invention but tradition, not individual creativeness but supra-personal limiting factors which hold the center of the stage in Veselovskij's conception of world literature. "A gifted poet", he conceded, "may by chance hit upon this or that motif, produce imitators, create a school of writers which will follow in his footsteps", but seen in "a larger historical perspective, these minor details of fashions, schools and personal influences are hardly discernible in the broad alternation of the socio-poetic demand and supply." [47]

Consequently, the main concern of the literary historian is not with assessing the unique contributions of individual writers, but with spotting the migratory poetic 'formulae', accounting for their appearance in various ethnic milieus, and, last but not least, tracing them through all vicissitudes back to the starting point, to the "epic past, or even farther back to the myth-making stage". [48]

The preoccupation with genealogy which this formulation seems to imply was largely abandoned by the Formalist theoreticians. Otherwise, however, they received many valuable stimuli from Veselovskij's studies in poetics. This is particularly true of his last work, the unfinished *Poetics of Plots* (1897–1906). [49] The key concepts of this study – the notion of the 'motif' as the 'simplest narrative unit' and the 'plot' as complex 'cluster of motifs', though not accepted without reservations, were widely utilized in Formalist studies on the composition of prose fiction or the folktale. [50] More important still, the treatment of the plot (*sjužet*) as a compositional rather than a purely thematic category, implicit in Veselovskij's argument, rested on an essential distinction

---

[46] *Istoričeskaja poètika*, p. 51.
[47] *Ibid.*, p. 69.
[48] *Ibid.*, p. 47.
[49] "Poètika sjužetov", *ibid.*, pp. 493–597.
[50] Cf. Viktor Šklovskij, *O teorii prozy* (Moscow, 1925); V. I. Propp, *Morfologija skazki* (Leningrad, 1928) (see chapter XIII of this study, pp. 239–243; 249–250).

between the theme of the literary work and the plot, i.e., the artistic organization of the subject matter.

The affinity between Veselovskij's poetics and Formalist literary theory is not confined to specific definitions or classifications; it has to do with general emphases as well. The concern of the author of *Historical Poetics* with the components of the literary work – with artistic devices and their clusters, literary genres, or, as he put it himself, with the peculiar "media which poetry has at its disposal",[51] was a long step toward the morphological analysis which was to become the watchword of twentieth-century poetics. Veselovskij's insistence on studying the poetry rather than the poet, the objective structure of the literary work rather than the psychic processes underlying it, found its sequel in the avowedly anti-psychological orientation of early Formalism. Even Veselovskij's tendency to discount the role of the individual in literary history has its counterpart in some of the Formalist manifestoes.[52]

Yet, for all his awareness of literary techniques, Veselovskij could never free himself from the prevalent mechanistic notion of poetic form as a mere superstructure or by-product of the 'content'. His overall scheme of literary evolution bears the distinct imprint of this fallacy.

Having dispensed with creative genius as a major factor, Veselovskij had to seek the causes of literary change either in the inner dynamics of the poetic forms or in extra-literary determinants. (I purposely omitted the most rewarding but obviously a too modern hypothesis – that of an interaction between literature and society.) Actually, however, it was only the latter course that was open to Veselovskij; the former clearly implied a concept completely alien to his methodology – that of the work of art as a structure *sui generis* with its own laws of integration.

The prime mover of the 'evolution of the poetic consciousness' had to be located outside the province of literature, the more so since the purely literary components, the 'formulae', were found to be fundamentally constant. "In the poetic forms which we inherit there is a certain regularity generated by the socio-psychological process." [53] In the "alternating combinations of these forms with regularly changing social ideals", it is the 'ideals' that call the tune and undergo substantial changes from one period to another, according to ascertainable socio-

---

[51]　*Istoričeskaja poètika*, pp. 71–72.
[52]　Cf. Osip Brik, "T. n. formal'nyj metod", *Lef,* No. 1 (1923).
[53]　*Istoričeskaja poètika*, p. 317.

logical laws. Traditional images, endowed as they are with considerable elasticity and with almost universal applicability, are only slightly modified so as to 'accommodate' the new world-view clamoring for literary expression.[54]

This implied a clear-cut division of powers between the essentially static 'form' and the dynamic 'content'. The comparative literary historian, argued Veselovskij, ought to ascertain "how this new life-content, this element of *freedom,* riding the wave of each new generation, penetrates the old images, these forms of *necessity*" (italics mine, V.E.).[55] Literary evolution becomes a corollary of the evolution of *Weltanschauung,* the periodical shifts of social ideology.

It is not difficult to see how such an extraneous approach would vitiate Veselovskij's suggestive discussions of Greek lyric poetry or the medieval epic tradition. These valuable contributions to sociological poetics [56] suffer from a simplified notion of the causal relationship between the poetic form and the 'life-content'.

Veselovskij's explorations of literary craft were thus hampered by what some modern critics call the Genetic Fallacy. It was the task of literary theorists more alive to the inner dynamics of poetic art, even though lacking Veselovskij's formidable scholarly equipment, to pursue further some of the crucial insights suggested by his invaluable studies.[57]

The pioneering efforts of Potebnja and Veselovskij failed to influence to any substantial degree the direction of literary scholarship in late nineteenth-century Russia. Formal considerations were still largely overshadowed by concern with the writer's ideology. There were, at the turn of the century, a few critics, like S. Andreevskij or N. Straxov, who were willing to discuss such 'untimely' problems as the future of rime or the structure of Puškin's verse.[58] There were even fewer literary historians who, like D. Ovsjaniko-Kulikovskij, managed to combine a psycho-ideological approach to current literary production with a lively interest in questions of linguistic poetics. Most students of literature were too busy deciphering actual or imaginary messages to pay much attention to the involved and 'academic' arguments of Potebnja

---

[54] *Ibid.*
[55] *Ibid.*
[56] We shall revert to this concept in chapter VI of the present study (pp. 114–116), in conjunction with the Marxist-Formalist controversy.
[57] See below, chapter XIII, pp. 239–250.
[58] S. Andreevskij, *Literaturnye očerki* (St. Petersburg, 1902); N. Straxov, *Zametki o Puškine i drugix poètax* (Kiev, 1897).

or Veselovskij. They were too strongly influenced by the prevalent notion of form as something purely external and secondary to realize the need for a rigorous analysis of plot structure or style. Moreover, the run-of-the-mill literary historian was none too eager to venture into a new field of inquiry such as the study of poetic language; he was perfectly satisfied to leave it to the linguist.

The latter, however, was in no hurry to undertake the task. The so-called neo-grammarian school which held sway in European linguistics at the end of the last century, and was particularly firmly entrenched at Moscow University,[59] had little use for such esoteric pursuits as inquiries into the nature of poetic discourse. This doctrine instructed the linguist to address himself primarily to the most 'natural', 'artless' types of speech; the folk dialects were on the top of the linguist's priority list, with even the standard language relegated to a secondary position. No wonder that the study of poetic diction, presumably an artificial, hothouse plant, was looked upon as a luxury which the student of language, digging painstakingly for the 'primary' facts, could ill afford.

The first decade of this century was a turning point in the development of Russian critical thought. The problems of literary craft found themselves all of a sudden in the center of the critic's attention. This upsurge in the field of poetics was due only to a very limited degree to the efforts of the academie literary scholar or philologist. The reawakening of interest in the theory of poetry – especially, in the study of versification – was closely bound up with a new flowering of Russian poetry itself, brought about by the advent of Symbolism.

[59]   The school of Professor F. Fortunatov which for several decades completely dominated Moscow linguistics was, perhaps, the most orthodox stronghold of the neo-grammarian doctrine in Europe.

II. APPROACHES TO FORMALISM

From the 'Forest of Symbols' to the 'Self-Valuable Word'

1

The emergence of the Symbolist movement raised conspicuously the level of poetic craftmanship in Russia. Verse writing, which had been overshadowed by prose fiction since the mid-nineteenth century, staged a triumphant comeback. The flat and anemic poetry of Nekrasov's progeny gave way to Valerij Brjusov's Parnassian mastery of form, to the lush euphony of Konstantin Bal'mont and, above all, to the irresistible verbal magic of Aleksandr Blok. And in the wake of this poetic revival came a renascence of verse study, a concentrated effort to attack the problems of poetic technique from the viewpoint of the Symbolist School.

This close interrelation between creative practice and literary theory was not in itself a novel phenomenon in the history of Russian letters. Since the eighteenth century each literary school had had its critical spokesmen who attempted to justify theoretically and to raise to the status of immutable laws the current exigencies of esthetic sensibility. In the Symbolist era, however, this alliance of the artist and the theoretician took on the form of organic symbiosis. It is the poet rather than the professional literary scholar who now assumed the lead in exploring the secrets of the creative laboratory.

The principal impetus behind the Symbolists' collective venture into the study of poetics is to be sought in the artistic creed, and, ultimately, in the underlying philosophical tenets of the movement which they represented.

Russian Symbolism, in the words of one of its chief spokesmen, "could not be, and did not want to be, merely art".[1] It aspired to become an integrated world-view, a philosophy, more exactly, a metaphysics. While Verlaine, Laforgue, and Mallarmé were primarily

[1]   Vjačeslav Ivanov, *Borozdy i meži* (Moscow, 1916), p. 137.

concerned with evolving a new form of poetic expression, their Russian counterparts grappled with 'ultimate' questions in a forthright attempt to find a way out of the *fin-de-siècle* spiritual impasse.

The Symbolist movement was the swan song of that part of the Russian intelligentsia which was drawn from the gentry or upper middle class. It was the product of a culture which achieved a high degree of intellectual and esthetic sophistication only to find itself faced with the prospect of inevitable extinction. As the historical cataclysm of revolution drew nearer, the world of the Symbolist poet began to crumble. The "ever-present sense of catastrophe",[2] pervading the verse of Aleksandr Blok, the greatest poet of the period, injected into the writings of this doomed generation a note of tragic urgency. The intensity of creative endeavor and of speculative pursuits, instead of being paralyzed or dampened by the anticipation of the impending disaster, was raised to an almost feverish pitch.

In the rarefied atmosphere of Vjačeslav Ivanov's famous 'Tower', where in the years 1905–1910 the literary and intellectual elite of Petersburg used to foregather every Wednesday evening, the conversation, combining French 'esprit' and German 'inwardness', probed with equal zest into Oscar Wilde and Nietzsche, into Eleusinian mysteries and Neo-Kantian philosophy. Under the eye of a kindly though rather elusive host, bold and extravagant syntheses were attempted – efforts were made to wed Dionysus to Christ, to reconcile Solov'ëv's spiritualist philosophy with Rozanov's sexual mysticism.[3] In these unique gatherings there was some room, to be sure, for snobbish preciosity, for blasé estheticism seeking new trills in pseudomystical flirtations with the 'Absolute'. But it can hardly be doubted that the main participants of the Symbolist symposia brought to them a genuine, indeed a desperately earnest, search for the meaning of life, for a satisfying set of values, however 'private' or esoteric.

An important aspect of the *Weltanschauung* toward which Russian Symbolism was groping was its attitude toward language. The symbolist's antipode and predecessor, the positivist, had been concerned almost exclusively, with the informative or – to use the terms of Ogden and Richards – the referential function of language. During the period of 'realism' the emphasis was always on the object, never on the word itself. The latter was seen merely as the medium for transmitting thought, a pointer, a pure denotation. The texture of the verbal sign

[2] Aleksandr Blok, *Sobranie sočinenij* (Leningrad, 1932–36), VII, 95.
[3] A. Belyj, "Vospominanija o Bloke", *Èpopeja*, 1922, No. 1.

seemed largely irrelevant. 'Form' was regarded as the mere outward garb of the 'content' or – in a work of imaginative literature – as a purely external embellishment with which one could dispense without any appreciable damage to communication.

Symbolist poetics made a deliberate effort to do away with the mechanistic dichotomy of form and content. As Ivanov put it in one of his later essays, "the present split between the sound of the word and its meaning, glossed over by the schematism of rationalist thought, must be recognized, unmasked and rejected".[4] Ivanov's concept of the organic unity of sound and meaning was inextricably bound up with an essentially esoteric notion of poetic creation. To the Symbolist theoretician, poetry is a revelation of ultimate Truth, a higher form of cognition, a 'theurgy',[5] capable of bridging the gap between empirical reality and the 'Unknown'. The poetic word is seen as a mystical Logos, reverberating with occult meanings. The metaphor, one of the poet's basic devices, is elevated from a mere figure of speech to a Symbol, the function of which is to "express the parallelism of the phenomenal and the noumenal",[6] to reveal the latent correspondences between the world of the senses, the 'realia,' and the superior or transcendental reality, the 'realiora'.[7] The "macrocosm", wrote Ivanov, "is reflected in each microcosm, in the same way in which the sun is reflected in each drop of rain." [8] And as the sensitive reader strained himself beyond the 'microcosm' of the poetic image toward its 'deeper' meaning, the perception of the visible symbol ushered in the intuition of the invisible 'substance'.

But, if one may say that in Symbolist poetry the sign blends with the object, the reverse is equally true: the object is conceived as merely a sign, 'nur ein Gleichnis' (Goethe). The word as we know it appears to the eye as a mysterious code to be deciphered. Nature itself is, to quote Baudelaire's famous sonnet, "Correspondances", a 'forest of symbols', where each individual 'tree' embodies an element of a higher reality. The unity of sign and object, postulated by Ivanov, is thus vindicated: "Form becomes content, content becomes form." [9]

---

[4] Vjačeslav Ivanov, "O novejšix teoretičeskix iskanijax v oblasti xudožestvennogo slova", *Naučnye izvestija*, 1922, II, 16.

[5] "The Symbolist", wrote Blok in a revealing article, "is first and foremost a theurgist (*teurg*), that is, a possessor of occult knowledge," ("O sovremennom položenii russkogo simvolizma", *Apollon*, 1910, No. 8, p. 22).

[6] *Borozdy i meži*, p. 134.

[7] *Ibid.*

[8] *Ibid.*, p. 212.

[9] *Ibid.*

In the light of this theory the relationship between the 'signifier' and the 'signified' was no longer arbitrary and conventional; it became intimate and organic. The word did not merely refer or point to a recognizable object, an identifiable thought-content. It suggested rather than designated, it evoked the otherwise inexpressible by uniquely apt combinations of sounds, by 'verbal magic'. Thus a direct correspondence was established between the texture of poetic language and its elusive referent. In order to decipher the latent message, it was necessary to pay close attention to the poet's 'words, rhythms, images'[10] – to the metrical pattern, the euphonic devices, and the mechanism of the metaphor. In short, it became imperative to concentrate on the problems of poetic form.

It was fortunate indeed for the study of Russian verse that two leading theorists of Symbolism – Andrej Belyj and Valerij Brjusov – were at the same time remarkable and conscious practitioners of the literary craft. Their intimate knowledge of and vivid interest in the problems of poetic technique tempered to a considerable extent their insistence on the esoteric nature of poetry. Moreover, a certain degree of intellectual discipline which both Belyj and Brjusov had managed to acquire during their student years prevented them from bogging down in unbridled irrationalism or the sterile impressionism of a Bal'mont.[11]

Particularly significant was the contribution made by Andrej Belyj. In an essay bearing the characteristic title "Lyric Poetry as Experiment",[12] Belyj challenged the popular notion that a literary artist could dispense with systematic study of poetic technique. "While a composer", he complained, "who grapples with the theory of counterpoint is a common sight, a poet engrossed in the problems of style and metrics is looked upon here as a kind of monster." [13] Spurning this prejudice, Belyj plunged into what he called "comparative morphology of rhythm",[14] in an effort to discover the 'empirical laws' of verse structure. The first result of this challenging attempt was a series of studies on the evolution of Russian iambic tetrameter from Lomonosov

[10] Valerij Brjusov, *Izbrannye stixotvorenija* (Moscow, 1945), p. 218.
[11] K. Bal'mont's essay, "Poetry as Magic" (*Poèzija kak volšebstvo*, Moscow, 1915), an impressionistic poem about poems, verges constantly on the oracular and favors questionable metaphors such as "Vowels are women, consonants are men."
[12] "Lirika kak èksperiment", *Simvolizm*, pp. 231–285.
[13] *Simvolizm*, p. 237.
[14] See the study "Sravnitel'naja morfologija ritma russkix lirikov v jambičeskom dimetre", *Simvolizm*, pp. 331–395.

up to the Symbolist period, published in Belyj's celebrated book *Simvolizm* (1910).[15] These highly competent analyses of Russian lyrical poetry were undoubtedly a distinct advance over the obsolete procedures of school metrics.

Belyj was the first among modern students of Russian verse to focus attention on the phenomenon of rhythmical variations. He understood full well that total conformity to the metrical norm, or, to quote L. Abercrombie,[16] "a perfectly regular succession of accents", is neither possible nor desirable in 'accentual' verse. Belyj demonstrated by means of painstaking rhythmical analysis that even a seemingly 'regular' verse, such as Puškin's iambic tetrameter, cannot dispense with metrical interruptions; time and again one finds in Puškin 'half-stresses', where one is led to expect full metrical accents. These departures from the scheme, insisted Belyj, are too frequent to be regarded as exceptions. They constitute too organic a part of the actual rhythmical flow of many poetic masterpieces to be dismissed as occasional, formal deficiencies. The evocative power of the poem is not impaired, indeed it is enhanced by metrical irregularities which lend to the verse the quality of rhythmical suppleness and variety.

The close connection between these strictures and the creative practice of the Russian Symbolists is all too obvious. Even though the latter never went so far as some of their French counterparts in advocating and cultivating 'free verse', they loosened up considerably the 'syllabo-accentual' canon established by Lomonosov and perfected by Puškin. Such masters of Russian Symbolism as Brjusov, Blok, and Zinaida Gippius, evolved a purely accentual type of verse, the so-called *dol'nik,* where the number of the syllables between stresses varied from one line to another.

Belyj's obvious bias, and his tendency to regard the artistic methods of the Symbolist School as the only acceptable approach, lent an unduly dogmatic quality to his treatment of the meter-rhythm dichotomy. In the eyes of the fiery champion of the 'new verse', transgression of the rule became the rule; violations of the canon were canonized. 'Irregular' verse was hailed as intrinsically superior to regular. Rhythm, defined in purely negative terms as the "symmetry in deviations from meter",[17] was found to be 'better' than meter. This insistence on the

---

[15] See "Opyt xarakteristiki russkogo četyrexstopnogo jamba", and "Sravnitel'naja morfologija ritma russkix lirikov v jambičeskom dimetre", *Simvolizm.*
[16] Lascelles Abercrombie, *Poetry: Its Music and Meaning* (London, 1932), p. 21.
[17] *Simvolizm,* p. 397.

basic antinomy of meter and rhythm was more pronounced in one of Belyj's latest works, *Rhythm as Dialectics*.[18] In this erratic study, a unique attempt to combine the Symbolist theory of poetry with Marxian dialectics, scientific definitions give way increasingly to emotionally over-charged value judgements. Meter is scornfully referred to as the 'sclerosis of the tissue', while rhythm is described glowingly and vaguely as the "principle of metamorphosis and growth".[19]

Belyj's normative interpretation of the basic prosodic concepts vitiated to a certain extent his concrete analyses of rhythm as well. In his study, "Attempt at a Description of the Russian Iambic Tetrameter", he tends to judge the rhythmical richness of a poem by the frequency of deviations from the metrical scheme or, more exactly, by the number of missing accents. Brjusov, who in general exhibited more caution and common sense in tackling specific problems of Russian versification, called attention to the inadequacy of this procedure. In his thoughtful review of Belyj's *Symbolism*,[20] Brjusov correctly objected to appraising verse structure on the basis of an arbitrarily chosen component. Frequency of 'half-stresses', he pointed out, is not necessarily an asset. Missing accents become a factor of rhythmical gracefulness and ease "only if they occur in felicitous combinations with caesuras and with other elements of verse",[21] if this is not the case, they may, on the contrary, give the impression of clumsiness.

And yet, in spite of their deficiencies Belyj's studies in versification were an important milestone in the development of Russian scientific poetics. The effort to trace the evolution of a metrical pattern through a century of Russian verse writing was a long step toward the concrete, historical study of Russian verse, and it markedly influenced subsequent studies in the field. Instead of mechanically superimposing an abstract, a priori scheme upon a heterogeneous body of literature, Belyj carefully distinguished between the actual realizations in different periods of Russian verse writing of a given metrical pattern. He painstakingly described the peculiar rhythmical tendencies exhibited by Russian iambic tetrameter in the late eighteenth century, the Puškin era and the second half of the nineteenth century.

In his efforts to ascertain the unique rhythmical timbre of individual

[18]   Andrej Belyj, *Ritm kak dialektika i 'Mednyj vsadnik'* (Moscow, 1929). For a more detailed discussion of *Rhythm as Dialectics* see Victor Erlich, "Russian Poets in Search of a Poetics", *Comparative Literature*, Winter 1953.
[19]   *Op. cit.*
[20]   Valerij Brjusov, "Ob odnom voprose ritma", *Apollon*, 1910, No. 11.
[21]   *Ibid.*, p. 58.

poets or literary groupings, Belyj came close to the historical relativism of later Formalist verse study. He seemed to be aware that each literary school had its own 'poetics,' that is, its own set of artistic devices. In rhythmical terms, this meant a peculiar way of modifying or violating, if one will, the prevailing metrical canon.

The procedure of reconstructing the 'poetics' of an individual master or of a literary school stood Belyj in good stead in his few ventures into the study of artistic prose. His brilliant re-evaluation of Gogol' found in the collection of essays, *Lug zelënyj* (Green Meadow),[22] was followed more than twenty years later by a comprehensive and penetrating analysis of Gogol's literary craft.[23]

In his attempt to confer on poetics the dignity of an exact science, Belyj did not hesitate to apply statistical techniques to the study of Russian verse. He used this procedure for the first time in *Symbolism*.[24] The rhythmical peculiarities exhibited by the poets under discussion are illustrated here by geometrical figures and graphic charts, showing the distribution of accents, the position of caesuras and the so called interverbal pauses in the lines. A technique of painstaking sound-recording (*sluxovaja zapis'*), devised by Belyj himself and perfected subsequently by the concerted effort of his disciples,[25] was a distinct improvement over the loose metaphors and glittering generalities about the 'music of verse' which posed only too often as actual descriptions of verse rhythm. Belyj's 'statistical methods', though substantially modified, were put to good use by the Formalist students of verse, such as B. Tomaševskij and R. Jakobson.

While the usefulness of graphic representation of various rhythms is not to be denied, Belyj, with his characteristic bent for exaggeration, tended to overrate the importance of his 'invention'. As Žirmunskij correctly observed in his review of Belyj's *Rhythm as Dialectics*,[26] the Symbolist theorist seemed to forget that in the study of versification charts and figures were merely auxiliary devices, purely conventional

---

22 Andrej Belyj, *Lug zelënyj* (Moscow, 1910).
23 Andrej Belyj, *Masterstvo Gogolja* (Moscow, 1934).
24 It would be inaccurate to regard Belyj's charts and figures as completely new phenomena in the study of versification. Statistical techniques were used in the metrical analyses of ancient verse long before Belyj wrote his *Symbolism*. The latter work, however, is apparently the first attempt to apply these methods to the study of Russian verse.
25 I am referring here to the 'Kružok Ritmistov' (Rhythmists' Circle) founded by Belyj in 1910.
26 Viktor Žirmunskij, "Po povodu knigi *Ritm kak dialektika*", *Zvezda*, 1929, No. 8.

ways of presenting one's findings. He seemed all too often to proceed
on the assumption that there exist in poetry immanent laws of 'mathematical dialectics'. Algebraic symbols, Žirmunskij observed, acquire in
Belyj's writings an autonomy of their own, when the critic embarks
upon elaborate mathematical operations, the results of which hardly
warrant the effort they entailed.[27]

Valerij Brjusov shared Belyj's belief that the practitioner of the
literary craft could ill afford to neglect its theory. "Poetic technique",
he insisted, "can and must be studied." [28]

More sober and level-headed than Belyj, Brjusov avoided the vagaries
of his brilliant comrade-in-arms. Deeply steeped as he was in Russian
and West European literary tradition, Brjusov was at the same time
keenly aware of the new currents in poetry as well as in the study of
verse. He eschewed the purely acoustic approach to verse and emphasized the close connection between the phonic, semantic and grammatical aspects of poetic language. Brjusov was one of the first Russian
students of verse to insist on the importance of 'interverbal pauses'
(which the Formalists were to rechristen 'word-boundaries') as a factor
in verse rhythm.

In assessing concrete phenomena of Russian versification Brjusov
steered clear of the dogmatism which marred some of Belyj's critical
studies. Not unlike Belyj, but more consistently, he appraised rhythmical devices within a proper historical context, that is, within the
framework of a particular prosodic system. A good example of this
wholesome historicism is provided by his provocative review of V.
Žirmunskij's study, *Rime, Its History and Theory*.[29] Brjusov's discussion of the imperfect rimes of modern poets is particularly apposite.
He objected to V. Žirmunskij's definition of the imperfect rime as a
product of 'decanonization' of the classical rime. This purely negative
description struck him as inadequate. Revolutions in literature, he
insisted, have laws of their own. Thus, it would be more rewarding
to speak about a new system of rimes, about the emergence of a new
canon rather than about the disintegration of the old.

[27] Tomaševskij, likewise, cautioned against giving too much credence to statistical data. "A statistical operation", he insisted, "cannot yield meaningful results
unless it is preceded by a preliminary classification of the phenomena investigated." (See *O stixe*, Leningrad, 1929, p. 76). Otherwise it is bound to remain a
"harmless though tiresome mathematical exercise". Not infrequently data arrived
at after a painstaking count can be traced to purely statistical factors, such as the
law of probability, and thus are irrelevant to the purpose of the investigation.
[28] Valerij Brjusov, *Opyty*, quoted by Tomaševskij, *O stixe*, p. 320.
[29] Valerij Brjusov, "O rifme", *Pečať i revoljucija* (1924), I.

Less satisfying were Brjusov's ventures into general verse theory: *A Brief Course of Prosody* (1919) and *The Foundations of Prosody* (1924).[30] These erudite treatises are vitiated by terminological confusion and weighed down by obsolete concepts derived from Greek and Latin metrics, scarcely if at all applicable to Russian verse. As Roman Jakobson correctly pointed out,[31] Brjusov was unduly preoccupied with prosodic phenomena practically nonexistent in Russian verse, such as syncope, while paying surprisingly little attention to crucial problems of the Russian accent.

2

Some of the studies cited above did not appear in a book-form until the second decade of this century. (Belyj's *Symbolism* was published in 1910, Ivanov's *Furrows and Boundaries* in 1916.) By that time the Symbolist tide was already receding. After a brief, if luxuriant flowering Russian Symbolism found itself challenged by new literary forces.

One of these trends was called Acmeism. A group of young poets gathered about the literary magazine *Apollon*,[32] including Nikolaj Gumilёv, Anna Axmatova, Osip Mandelstam, set out to chart a new course in Russian poetry. Their notion of poetic art was modelled on Gautier rather than on Verlaine or Mallarmé. The Acmeists scorned the mystical vagueness of Symbolism, its vaunted 'spirit of music'. They strove for 'Apollonian' clarity and for graphic sharpness of outline. The poets of *Apollon* were more interested in the sensory texture, the 'density' of things,[33] than in their inner soul, or, to use Ivanov's terms again, in 'relia' more than in 'realiora'. And, as they sought to bring closer to earth the poet's subject, the Acmeists tended to reduce the gap between poetic idiom and cognitive speech. The sobered verse of Gumilёv and Axmatova went a long way toward discarding the esoteric allusiveness and studied ambiguity typical of Symbolist poetry. And yet, for all its vocal opposition to Symbolist esthetics, Acmeism was essentially an outgrowth of Symbolism – a Symbolist heresy, as it were. Gumilёv may have pushed beyond Brjusov in many respects, but he

---

[30] Valerij Brjusov, *Kratkij kurs nauki o stixe* (Moscow, 1919); *Osnovy stixovedenija* (Moscow, 1924).
[31] Roman Jakobson, "Brjusovskaja stixologija i nauka o stixe", *Naučnye izvestija*, 1922, II.
[32] *Apollon*, St. Petersburg, 1910–1917.
[33] See Osip Mandelstam (Mandel'štam), "Utro akmeizma", quoted from N. L. Brodskij and V. L'vov-Rogačevskij, *Literaturnye manifesty* (Moscow, 1929), p. 45.

remained within the limits of the same poetic tradition and the same social pattern.

A much more vehement and perhaps more momentous assault was launched on Symbolism by the rising Futurist movement. The watchword of the disgruntled artistic Bohemians who rode onto the Russian literary scene on the wave of the Futurist offensive was a complete break with the 'stifling past'. The Futurists declared war on all the idols of respectable society – on 'common sense and good taste'.[34] With a sweeping gesture they repudiated all authorities, all established standards – social, ethical, esthetic. In the notorious manifesto bearing the characteristic title, "A Slap in the Face of Public Taste" (1912),[35] the signatories – D. Burljuk, V. Xlebnikov, A. Kručënyx, V. Majakovskij – called defiantly for "throwing Puškin, Dostoevskij, and Tolstoj overboard from the steamer of modern times",[36] and they proudly announced their "uncompromising hatred for the language used hitherto".[37] The subsequent Futurist declarations insisted on the poet's right to revolutionize the vocabulary, syntax and subject-matter of verse, to do away with any and all literary conventions – from the worn out 'sentimental' themes of love and romance to the 'obsolete' rules of grammar.[38]

The Futurist manifesto-writers made it amply clear that their sweeping indictment of the Russian literary heritage was meant to apply to the recent past as well. In fact, some of the most savage blasts of Futurist rhetoric were aimed at the Symbolist masters, contemptuously referred to as genteel and degenerate epigons.[39] Symbolism had been the poetry of apocalyptic forebodings, anguished soul-searching, and the tortured calm before the storm. Now, as the historical pandemonium half-hopefully, half-fearfully anticipated by Blok and Belyj was about to break loose, the subdued quaver of the Verlaine-like 'autumnal violin' was bound to be drowned out by the deafening drumbeat of Vladimir Majakovskij. It was the Futurist rebel – irreverent, boisterous, uninhibited – who was fit and eager to speak in and for the storm. Shunning prettiness and 'harmony', he managed to recapture

---

[34] N. L. Brodskij and V. L'vov-Rogačevskij, *op. cit.*, pp. 77–78.
[35] "Poščečina obščestvennomu vkusu", Moscow, December 1912. See *Literaturnye manifesty*, pp. 77–78.
[36] *Ibid.*, p. 77.
[37] *Ibid.*, p. 78.
[38] "Slovo kak takovoe", 1913, "Sadok sudej", 1914, *Literaturnye manifesty*, pp. 78–82.
[39] *Literaturnye manifesty*, p. 77, p. 82.

in his uncouth, staccato verse, freed from metrical fetters, the 'polyphonic noise' [40] of the turbulent era. "We have invaded", boasted Majakovskij, "the love whispers of the cozy porches with the thousand-foot step of the ages. These are our rhythms – the cacophony of wars and revolutions." [41]

This is not to say that the Futurist notion of poetry was in all respects at variance with Symbolist esthetics. The champions of Russian Futurism shared their prodecessors' distaste for realistic art and an abiding belief in the superior evocative power of the poetic word. Belyj had contrasted the 'dead emblems' of conceptual language with 'living' poetic images,[42] and Velemir Xlebnikov likewise drew a sharp distinction between poetic and 'everyday' (bytovoj) discourse.[43] Moreover, the Futurist slogan of 'shaking loose the syntax',[44] may be indirectly traced to Mallarmé's painstaking attempts to substitute rules of poetic euphony for those of logic. But, if the Futurists were at one with the Symbolists in postulating an essential difference between poetic and prosaic speech, they were far apart in their notions of the nature and function of language.

The theorists of Russian Symbolism, as indicated above, valued the word not for its own sake, but for what it suggested. In Symbolist poetics, to quote Majakovskij's acute remark, "the accident of alliteration was presented as organic affinity, as indissoluble kinship".[45] The poetic Logos was seen as an esoteric allusion. The pattern of imagery, rhythm or verbal orchestration was supposed to reveal the underlying pattern of the 'higher' reality.

Futurist poetics unequivocally discarded the Baudelairian theory of correspondences. It had as little use for mystical as for social 'messages'. To Kručёnyx of Xlebnikov, the poetic word was neither a vehicle of rational thought nor a glimpse of the 'other world'. It was not, as Ivanov suggested in his essays quoted above, a reminiscence of mankind's mythical youth,[46] but, on the contrary, a "creator of myths";[47]

---

40   Marinetti's expression.
41   Vladimir Majakovskij, *Sobranie sočinenij* (Moscow, 1928–1933), III, 18.
42   "Magija slov", *Simvolizm,* pp. 429–448.
43   Velemir Xlebnikov, *Sobranie proizvedenij* (Leningrad, 1933), V, 229.
44   *Literaturnye manifesty,* p. 79.
45   Vladimir Majakovskij, *Polnoe sobranie sočinenij* (Moscow, 1939–1947), II, 476.
46   Vjačeslav Ivanov, *Borozdy i meži,* pp. 130–132.
47   *Literaturnye manifesty,* p. 79. One should add that the theory about the linguistic genesis of myths did not originate with Futurism. This hypothesis was advanced by a number of nineteenth-century anthropologists and linguists (see

it was a primary fact, a self-sufficient and self-valuable entity.[48] Poetic speech became an end in itself rather than a medium for conveying ideas and emotions. "We, the Futurist poets", declared the manifesto called *Word as Such,*[49] "thought more about the Word than about the Psyche, mercilessly abused by our predecessors. Let us rather live by the word as such than by our own experiences." And David Burljuk, one of the most belligerent spokesmen of early Russian Futurism, did not hesitate to denounce "all this talk about content and spirituality" as "the greatest crime against genuine art".[50]

This aggressive anti-psychologism may strike one as inconsistent with the position taken by the recognized leader of Western European Futurism, F. T. Marinetti. In his famous *Technical Manifesto of Futurist Literature*, Marinetti insisted that the principal aim of the new poetry was to express the modern sensibility in the language of the mechanical age. The new poetic diction, freed from the delaying devices of conventional grammar, such as adjectives, adverbs, punctuation, was to become, in a phrase of Altenberg, the "telegraphic language of the soul".[51]

There is indeed a significant difference of general emphasis between the esthetics of the Italian Futurist and that of the Russian Futurists. Marinetti laid his principal stress on modern themes. Modern poetry, he maintained, must throb with the pulse of the huge metropolitan centers. It will "sing great throngs, brought into motion by work, pleasure or revolt ... greedy railroad stations, which swallow smoking snakes, factories hanging under the clouds on the ropes of smoke".[52] ... It will glorify the advent of the new, industrial age.

For the spokesmen of pre-revolutionary Russian Futurism, subject matter was a minor consideration. "Genuine novelty in literature", wrote Kručënyx, "does not depend upon content. ... A new light thrown on the old world may produce a very interesting interplay." [53]

E. Cassirer, *Language and Myth,* New York and London, 1946); in Russia the problem of the relation between myth and language was tackled by Aleksandr Potebnja in his studies cited above, *Iz zapisok po teorii slovesnosti* and *O nekotoryx simvolax v slavjanskoj narodnoj poèzii.*

[48] The above is the rough equivalent of the almost untranslatable term "samovitoe slovo", coined by Xlebnikov and widely used in the Futurist publications.

[49] *Literaturnye manifesty,* p. 82.

[50] David Burljuk, `Galdjaščie Benoit i novoe russkoe nacional'noe iskusstvo` (Petersburg, 1913), pp. 12–13.

[51] Quoted in Roman Jakobson, *Novejšaja russkaja poèzija* (Prague, 1921), p. 9.

[52] Quoted from Roman Jakobson, *Novejšaja russkaja poèzija,* p. 7.

[53] *Ibid.,* p. 8.

What really matters is form: "If there is a new form, there must also exist a new content. . . . It is form that determines content." [54]

Primacy of form over content, this was the battle cry of early Russian Futurism. The verbal sign was conceived as "an independent entity organizing the material of feelings and thoughts" [55] rather than merely giving shape to them. "We decided", said one of the Futurist declarations, "to invest words with meanings, depending on their graphic and phonetic characteristics." [56] Attention was focussed on the outward form or sensory texture of the linguistic symbol rather than on its communicative value, on the sign rather than on its object. Indeed, a deliberate attempt was made to loosen the bond between the two, to emancipate the word, as Kručënyx put it, from its "traditional subservience to meaning".[57]

This revolt against meaning found its expression in the slogan of 'trans-sense language' (zaumnyj jazyk). The most extreme proponents of this notion were Kručënyx and Kamenskij. They tried to write verse composed solely of arbitrary combinations of sounds, and they advertised their accomplishments as vastly superior in expressiveness and vigor to Puškin's and Lermontov's 'effeminate' poetry.

If these rather crude experiments with nonsense syllables could be dismissed as Bohemian extravagance, V. Xlebnikov's poetic discoveries attest to a much higher degree of artistic maturity and linguistic virtuosity.

A "tireless path-finder of language",[58] Xlebnikov was too keenly aware of the organic relationship between sound and meaning to become the apostle of pure euphony. His verse, obscure and elliptic though it is, cannot, contrary to the widely held belief, be described as devoid of 'sense'. It is rather, to quote R. Jakobson's acute study of Xlebnikov,[59] poetry with a 'toned-down' semantics. The basic unit of Xlebnikov's bizarre idiom is not the individual sound, nor the syllable, but the morpheme; the latter, be it a root or an affix, is bound to have a certain, at least, a potential meaning. Xlebnikov's avowed, though obviously, unattainable goal, was to "find, without breaking out of the bewitched circle of the roots, the philosopher's stone of the mutual transformations of Slavic words, to fuse freely the Slavic

[54] Ibid.
[55] Vladimir Majakovskij, Polnoe sobranie sočinenij (Moscow, 1939–1947), I, 476
[56] Literaturnye manifesty, p. 79.
[57] A. Kručënyx, "Novye puti slova", Troe (Moscow, 1914).
[58] J. Tynjanov, "O Xlebnikove" (Velemir Xlebnikov, Poèmy, p. 26).
[59] Roman Jakobson, Novejšaja russkaja poèzija, p. 66.

words." [60] His favorite procedure was to break down the familiar words into their morphological components which he then reshuffled at will and reintegrated into new verbal units – poetic neologisms. One of Xlebnikov's poems, "Incantation by Laughter", is based on an astoundingly ingenious play with formants; it consists almost entirely of newly-coined derivatives from the root *smex* (Russian for 'laughter').[61]

The occasional use of poetic neologisms points up Xlebnikov's attitude to language. The words he invented were always certain to carry a number of connotations, however vague and embryonic, but they did not have, as a rule, any denotative value. As products of the poet's linguistic fancy, they clearly did not correspond or refer to any identifiable aspect of objective reality.

The slogan of the 'self-sufficient word' thus became a reality. The customary relation between the linguistic symbol and the referent was reversed. In 'practical' language the sign is obviously subordinated to the object to which it points. In Xlebnikov's 'trans-sense' verse the object appears, if at all, as a faint echo of the sign; it is overshadowed by the whimsical interplay of the word's potential meanings.

What is true of the referents of individual words also may be applied to the 'referent' of the whole work of poetry – the external world. This is how V. Majakovskij, in one of his articles, summed up the early Futurist notion of the relation between art and reality: "Art is not a copy of nature, but the determination to distort nature in accordance with its reflections in the individual consciousness." [62]

This principle of creative distortion which Futurist poetry shared with the cognate trends in visual arts, cubist and surrealist painting, operates not only on the verbal substratum of Futurist verse, but on the levels of imagery and plot as well. The tendency toward the "dynamic displacement of objects and their interpenetration" [63] asserts

---

[60]   Velemir Xlebnikov, *Sobranie proizvedenij*, II, 9.
[61]   "Zakljatie smexom", see *ibid.*, p. 35. An English translation of this poem is found in Kaun's *Soviet Poets and Poetry* (Berkeley and Los Angeles, 1943), p. 24.
[62]   Vladimir Majakovskij, *Polnoe sobranie sočinenij* (Moscow, 1939–1947), I, 268.
[63]   The above is a quotation from the article by V. Xardžiev, "Majakovskij i živopis", which appeared in an anniversary publication, *Majakovskij. Materialy i issledovanija* (Moscow, 1940). Xardžiev's study presents an impressive array of evidence as to the close affinity and cooperation between Futurist poetry and Cubist painting both in France and in Russia. This kinship was attested by the very name of that trend in Russian Futurism with which we are here primarily concerned. The Moscow Futurists led by Burljuk, Kručenyx, Xlebnikov and Majakovskij, called themselves 'Cubo-Futurists,' while the Petrograd faction, represented by Igor' Severjanin and Vadim Šeršenevič, adopted the name of 'Ego-Futurism'.

itself in the grotesque hyperboles of the early Majakovskij and in the 'incoherent sequence of events', the "dream-like logic" [64] of Xlebnikov's epic fragments, which make one think of Surrealism.

The far-reaching poetic innovations of the Futurists, as well as their persistent attempts at theorizing, were bound to have noticeable repercussions on the study of literature. This influence seems to have been at once beneficial and harmful.

The Futurist's shrill insistence on the complete autonomy of the poetic word was a wholesome, if extravagant, reaction against the disregard of form, still apparent in the textbooks of literary history, as well as against the far-fetched mystical interpretations of poetic imagery which had vitiated so much Symbolist criticism. The theory of the 'self-sufficient word' and its practical implementation highlighted the inadequacy of the purely thematic approach to verse. The activity of the Russian Futurists called attention to the inner dynamism of linguistic facts, since it demonstrated that the devices of poetic euphony, such as rime, alliteration, and assonance, can be employed for other than symbolic or sound-imitative purposes. In more general terms, it has brought to mind the apparently forgotten truth that the degree of correspondence with 'reality', be it the naturalist's world of senses or Ivanov's 'realiora', is not the only valid criterion for evaluating works of poetry.

If the preoccupation with the 'word as such' has encouraged the systematic study of poetic language, the glorification of literary change, of novelty, has tended to give prominence to problems of historical poetics.

The Symbolist theorist laid his principal stress on the oneness of artistic creation. He was engaged in a quest for the 'essence' of poetic art and was more likely than not to find this essence in the type of poetry which he and his contemporaries were writing. "All art", wrote Belyj, "is symbolic: that of the present, of the past and of the future." [65]

The Futurist, as a matter of principle, would reject such a sweeping and dogmatic generalization. In fact, he could be accused of the opposite fallacy. Viewing literary history as a series of successive revolts against prevailing canons, he was apt to overemphasize the differences between the various stages of literary evolution. Seeing the only legitimate touchstone in the degree of success with which a poet carries out the artistic program of his age, the Futurist spokesmen could not avoid

[64] N. Gumilëv, "Pis'ma o russkoj poèzii" (Petrograd, 1923), p. 205.
[65] Andrej Belyj, Simvolizm, p. 143.

the pitfalls of extreme critical relativism. Indeed, they went so far as
to deny that poetry of a past age could be an object of esthetic appreciation. The notorious call for "throwing Puškin, Dostoevskij and
Tolstoj from the steamer of modern times', obviously aimed at the
hated 'philistines', need not be taken too seriously. It is noteworthy,
however, that long after the early Futurist brawls had become history,
Majakovskij could write thus: "Every worker and peasant will understand Puškin exactly in the same way as we of the *Lef* [66] do: as the
finest, the most splendid, the greatest representative of his age. And
having understood him thus, they will stop reading him and hand him
over to the literary historians." [67]

It is hardly necessary to point out that Majakovskij's prophecy was
given the resounding lie by the ever-increasing interest the Russian
'workers and peasants' have exhibited in Puškin during the last two
decades. This striking error of judgment proves conclusively, if such
a proof were needed, that Majakovskij's methodological position could
be easily reduced to absurdity. It should be admitted, however, in all
fairness that this ultra-historicist approach was, up to a certain point, a
positive factor. The Futurist's concern with the uniqueness of each
literary school tended to bolster the tenet which had already been
championed by Brjusov and at times even by Belyj: notably, that the
artistic efficacy of a literary phenomenon must be judged first and
foremost according to the norms prevailing at the given period.

Another aspect of Futurist credo which pointed in the direction of
a systematic poetics was its belligerent, not to say crude empiricism.
The artistic Bohemians gathered under the Futurist banner had nothing
but scorn and mockery for the Symbolist talk about inspiration, about
'poetry as magic'. Art was brought down to earth and rudely stripped
of its halo. It was allowed, in fact it was encouraged to be alogical or
transrational, but not necessarily irrational or transcendental. Futurism
trampled upon the rules of cognitive language not for the sake of a
'higher' cognition, but in defence of the free, untrammelled verbal
play which presumably could dispense with metaphysical sanctions.
From a "guardian of mystery" [68] the poet became a craftsman. In his
much-quoted article, "How to Make Verses", Majakovskij wrote:
"Poetry is a kind of production ... a very difficult, very complicated

---

[66] An abbreviation of *Levyj Front* (Left Front), the name of the Russian Neo-
Futurist group founded in 1923.
[67] Vladimir Majakovskij, *Sobranie sočinenij*, V, 254.
[68] Valerij Brjusov, *Izbrannye stixotvorenija* (Moscow, 1943), p. 218.

one, to be sure, but still production."[69] Obviously, there was no reason why the modes of literary production could not be described and accounted for in intelligible terms. Poetic creation became a matter of technology rather than of theology.

The Futurist movement has undoubtedly dramatized the need for an adequate system of scientific poetics. Indeed, as will be shown in the next chapters, the movement was to become one of the main factors behind the emergence of Russian Formalism, which attempted to evolve such a system. But, by the same token, Futurism may be held responsible for some of the egregious fallacies and shortcomings of the new school of criticism. Much of the methodological onesidedness, philosophical immaturity, and psychological aridity of the early Formalist studies may by traced to the shrill exaggerations of the Futurist manifestoes and their obsessive concern with poetic technology. The slogan of the 'self-sufficient word' ran the danger of methodological isolationism, divorcing poetry from life, denying the relevance of psychological and social considerations. Kručënyx's assertion that 'form determines content' implied the notion of a literary evolution as a self-propelled and self-contained process.

The impact of the Futurist movement on the new criticism of the Formalist movement made itself felt in the critic's manner as well as method. Close association with the Futurist Bohemia was to impart to the writings of its critical fellow travelers the rare and refreshing quality of youthful vigor, of gay exuberance. But what was gained in boldness and vitality was lost in restraint and in a sense of responsibility. The cocksure impudence of the Futurist manifestoes found a scholarly counterpart in the excesses of early Formalist publications which deliberately overstated their theses in order to shock academic pundits.

The direct contribution of Russian Futurism to the theory of literature was of less consequence than the broader methodological implications of this movement. The Futurist artistic credo never developed into a full-blown esthetics. This was due both to the meagerness and to the light-weight quality of its theoretical output. Slogans shouted at the top of one's lungs could not serve as a substitute for a coherent system of intellectual concepts. Flamboyant declarations, often intended to baffle the audience rather than clarify the issues at stake, were productive of more heat than light.

Some of the points made in the collective statements were subse-

[69] Vladimir Majakovskij, *op. cit.*, V, 426.

quently elaborated in a more thoughful vein in the critical articles of
Majakovskij and Xlebnikov. Of the former's theoretical contributions,
the most pertinent is probably the article, "How to Make Verses",[70]
which contains invaluable observations on the role of rhythm in the
process of poetic creation. Xlebnikov's pronouncements on the nature
of poetic language and on the tendencies of modern poetry [71] deserve
undoubtedly more attention than they have thus far received. His
unusually keen feeling for the Russian language, coupled with passionate interest in problems of etymology and semantics, yielded several
insights of rare acuteness. Xlebnikov's philological intuition, however,
could not quite compensate for his lack of systematic linguistic training.
Some of his generalizations have a distinctly amateurish quality. Thus,
in his otherwise perceptive article, "Our Foundations", Xlebnikov
advanced the theory that words starting with the same consonant are
necessarily semantically interrelated.[72]

The Futurist movement failed to produce poet-scholars of Ivanov's
or Belyj's stature. Coming as they did from the plebeian intelligentsia
rather than from the leisure classes, the Xlebnikovs and Kručënyxs had
no opportunity to accumulate the literary and philosophical erudition
which was such a strong asset of the Symbolist theoreticians. These
buoyant outcasts of bourgeois society lacked both the intellectual
equipment and the frame of mind necessary for the exacting tasks
of scientific analysis. All they could do in the field of literary theory
was to postulate emphatically a new poetics.

To evolve a new poetics – to vindicate theoretically the Futurist
revolution in Russian verse – was the task which called for the efforts
of professional students of literature, conversant with, and sympathetic
to, the new poetry. Such a critical movement had indeed come into
being. Two parallel trends converged: if the poet needed the assistance
of the literary scholar, the latter sought in his alliance with the literary
avant-garde a way out of the impasse reached by the academic study
of literature.

[70]   *Ibid.*, pp. 381–428.
[71]   See particularly "O sovremennoj poèzii", "O stixax", "Naša osnova", *Sobranie
proizvedenij*, V, 222–243.
[72]   "Naša osnova", *ibid.*, p. 236.

III. THE EMERGENCE OF THE FORMALIST SCHOOL

1

By the beginning of the twentieth century an acute methodological crisis in various fields of scholarship had set in. The world view which had dominated the European intellectual scene for several decades was reexamined and found wanting. With the basic assumptions of positivist determinism shaken, drastic revision of the logical foundations of all the sciences became the order of the day.

The widespread reaction against positivism led to the resurgence of irrationalist trends. While Symbolism held sway in art, and Bergson's gospel of 'creative evolution' made headway in speculative philosophy, the Neo-Kantian theory of cognition insisted on the central role of empathy in the humanistic disciplines. Windelband, Rickert, Lask, and other representatives of the so-called Freiburg School in epistemology drew a sharp distinction between the procedures of the natural sciences and those of the humanities.[1] While the scientist, it was argued, seeks a causal explanation of the phenomena investigated, the humanist aims at 'comprehension', that is, intuitive reconstruction of the object of inquiry.

This change in the philosophical climate was bound to affect the study of literature. In Germany, the traditional stronghold of the cultural historical school, painstaking philological exegesis gave way either to broad philosophical syntheses of literary periods or to monumental spiritual biographies, combining 'Wahrheit' with 'Dichtung' – literary history with critical myth-making.[2] The formidable appara-

[1] See especially Wilhelm Windelband, *Präludien* (Tübingen, 1907); Heinrich Rickert, *Die Grenzen der naturwissenschaftlichen Begriffsbildung* (Tübingen & Leipzig, 1902).
[2] René Wellek, "The Revolt against Positivism in Recent European Literary Scholarship", *Twentieth Century English* (New York, 1946), pp. 67–89; Werner Mahrholz, *Literaturgeschichte und Literaturwissenschaft* (Berlin, 1923); Rudolf

tus of academic scholarship was ostentatiously discarded. The onus was put on the critic's capacity for recapturing the spirit of the creative personality or an entire literary epoch.

In Russia the Symbolist movement, while fostering interest in poetics,[3] had also given rise to the type of literary criticism which can be described as philosophical or metaphysical.[4] Critics preoccupied with religious and ethical problems, like Lev Šestov, creative writers with a metaphysical axe to grind, like Dmitrij Merežkovskij, and religious thinkers to whom literature was a battleground of ideas, like Nikolaj Berdjaev, probed perceptively the *Weltanschauung* of the great Russian novelists.[5] Some of their studies, illuminated by keen speculative minds and by genuine critical insights, rank with the most important achievements of Russian literary criticism. And yet these works suffer all too often from a purely external approach, from the critic's tendency to regard a literary production as a testing ground for his preconceptions, a philosophical parable.

This is especially true of Merežkovskij's celebrated work, *Tolstoj and Dostoevskij*,[6] where these two masters of the Russian novel are interpreted in terms of the eternal struggle between Christ and Antichrist, flesh and spirit. This antithesis − obviously the *idée maîtresse* of Merežkovskij's creative endeavor − lends undue schematicism to an otherwise deftly drawn parallel. Despite the wealth of penetrating observations, one feels at times that the study reveals more about the critic and his obtrusive dilemmas than about the writers under discussion.

Even Mixail Geršenzon, the most scholarly and text-minded of the Russian intuitionist critics, did not always succeed in avoiding the dangers of arbitrary speculation. In his much-quoted essay, "The Poet's Vision",[7] he pleaded for close textual analysis and extolled the virtues of 'slow reading'; but the theory of 'integral knowledge' (*celostnoe znanie*) which he advanced in the same article had

---

Unger, *Gesammelte Studien* (Berlin, 1929); Friedrich Gundolf, *Dichter und Helden* (Tübingen, 1907).

[3] See above, chapter II, pp. 36–41.

[4] As was indicated above, some of Andrej Belyj's critical studies represent a peculiar combination of both approaches.

[5] Cf. Lev Šestov, *Dostoevskij i Nicše* (Petersburg, 1909); Dmitrij Merežkovskij, *Tolstoj i Dostoevskij* (Petersburg, 1901–1902); Nikolaj Berdjaev, *Mirosozercanie Dostoevskogo* (Prague, 1923).

[6] See footnote 5.

[7] Mixail Geršenzon, "Videnie poèta", *Mysl' i slovo* (Moscow, 1918), II, 1, pp. 76–94.

distinct irrationalist undertones. A critic of great stature and one of the foremost Puškin scholars, Geršenzon laid himself open to the charge of strained and over-ingenious interpretation, in his speculations on 'Puškin's wisdom'.[8] B. Tomaševskij was justified in taking exception to Geršenzon's insistence on deducing from Puškin's work an integrated and esoteric philosophy of life. "One cannot paraphrase Puškin", cautioned Tomaševskij, "and still less can one draw a chain of logical inferences from a metaphorical paraphrase." [9]

This excessive reliance on the critic's 'sensibility' manifested itself on an appreciably lower level of philosophical acumen in the writings of one of the most representative critics of the time, Jurij Eichenwald. His *Silhouettes of Russian Writers* [10] tended to substitute pseudo-poetic verbosity for precision and loose impressionism for critical analysis.

Subjectivism had its heyday as criticism became, in Anatole France's phrase, "the adventure of a soul among the masterpieces".[11] Where the critic was a gifted and cultivated writer like France himself, such whimsical *causerie* was apt to be brilliant, if not always relevant. But in the hands of the mediocre essayists who followed in Eichenwald's footsteps, impressionism became more often than not simply an excuse for critical nonchalance and loose thinking.

If 'creative' criticism threw overboard scientific objectivity for the sake of 'appreciation', academic literary scholarship was guilty of the opposite fault. In his commendable but misguided devotion to science, the literary historian was all too eager to surrender his right to critical judgment, to sacrifice the hierarchy of values and his sense of perspective. Petty factualism, painstaking but sterile accumulations of disjointed bits of knowledge without any discernible effort towards a meaningful integration and interpretation – this was the prevailing procedure of Russian academic literary studies on the eve of the First World War.

The grand old men of nineteenth-century Russian literary scholarship – the Romanticists Buslaev and Miller, the positivists D. Tixonravov and A. Pypin, and last but certainly not least, Aleksandr Veselovskij – were no more. Their heirs were conscientious, often erudite, but on the whole unimaginative investigators. Most of them lacked the synthetic vision and intellectual courage of their masters and carefully

[8]   Mixail Geršenzon, *Mudrost' Puškina* (Moscow, 1919).
[9]   Boris Tomaševskij, *Puškin* (Leningrad, 1925), p. 106.
[10] Jurij Eichenwald (Ajxenval'd), *Siluèty russkix pisatelej* (Petersburg, 1908).
[11] Quoted by P. Souday in "Anatole France, critique littéraire", *Nouvelles Littéraires,* April 19, 1924.

avoided tackling fundamental problems of literary theory and methodology. 'A. Veselovskij", wrote one of their most brilliant and irreverent
students, "died long ago. His disciples have become grey, but they
still did not know what to do, what to write about." [12]

This mood of timidity and irresolution may have been responsible
to a large extent for that preoccupation with biographical trivia which
was so typical of Russian literary history in the first decades of this
century. Sterile 'biographism' which focussed attention on the minute
details of the poet's life rather than on the work of poetry and its
components was, as it were, the line of least intellectual resistance and
seemed to offer the safest escape both from the disturbingly broad
problem of the relation between literature and society and from the
exacting task of esthetic analysis.

Nowhere was this overriding concern with biography more apparent
than in the study of Puškin which by the turn of the century came close
to occupying a central place in Russian literary scholarship. A host of
zealous and hard-working researchers, grouped around the publication, *Puškin and His Contemporaries,*[13] tirelessly ransacked the
archives for relics of the great poet. N. O. Lerner and P. O. Ščëgolev
and their disciples reverently collected and commented upon every
scrap of documentary evidence however remotely related it may have
been to Puškin or to his family and friends. No piece of paper bearing
the master's signature, no biographical detail, however irrelevant to
Puškin's poetic achievement, was deemed unworthy of the closest
scrutiny.

Puškin's private life was dutifully explored in well-documented
studies. Respectable academicians busily recorded the poet's innu-
merable love affairs, drawing up "Puškin's Don Juan list".[14] Less exciting subjects, such as "the care of Puškin's children and property" [15]
or the vital question: "Did Puškin smoke?" [16] also received their share
of attention.

The more rewarding type of genetic approach to literature, the
sociological method, still had to prove its validity in critical practice.
Plexanov's pioneering efforts in the field of Marxian literary theory [17]

---

[12] Viktor Šklovskij, *O Majakovskom* (Moscow, 1940), p. 15.
[13] *Puškin i ego sovremenniki,* vols. 1–10 (Petersburg, 1903–1930).
[14] Cf. P. K. Gruber, *Don Žuanskij spisok Puškina* (Petrograd, 1923).
[15] Cf. *Puškin i ego sovremenniki,* IV (1910).
[16] Cf. Osip Brik, "T.n. formal'nyj metod", *Lef,* 1923, No. 1.
[17] Georgij Plexanov, *Za dvadcat' let* (Petersburg, 1905); *Literatura i kritika* (Moscow, 1922).

had not yet produced any worthy sequel. V. Friče's studies in the history of Western European literature,[18] which attempted to establish a direct correspondence between the prevailing mode of production and artistic creation, did little to validate the methodological assumptions of Marxian criticism. Nor was its prestige enhanced by the first collective pronouncement of its adepts, *Literary Disintegration*.[19] This publication, containing articles of Friče, Gor'kij, Kamenev, Lunačarskij, Steklov and others, was an impassioned indictment of all modernist literature, indiscriminately labelled as decadent and reactionary. At its best *Literary Disintegration* could be considered effective journalism, but, as a critical statement, it leaves a great deal to be desired. The publicist's vituperation, no matter how eloquent, was obviously an inadequate substitute for earnest sociological analysis.[20]

Before the 1917 Revolution few literary scholars of distinction espoused the Marxian conception of literature. Even fewer, like Professor P. Sakulin, managed to combine, if not actually integrate, the sociological method with a keen awareness of esthetic values.[21] Caught between the extremes of impressionism and pedantry, Russian literary study drifted aimlessly, painfully uncertain of its methods and of its province, and even of the very type of intellectual activity which it was supposed to represent. As B. Jarxo later complained, one wondered whether to class this hybrid discipline 'with lyric poetry or with science, with linguistics or with sociology.' [22] Veselovskij's description of literary history as a 'no man's land' still applied.[23]

2

While the bulk of literary scholars, engrossed in the hunt for minutiae lost sight of the aims of literary investigation, the more ambitious and method-conscious among Veselovskij's disciples tried bravely to find a way out of the prevailing chaos and confusion. They were becoming increasingly aware that, to quote a contemporary linguist, "if literary

[18] Vladimir Friče, *Očerki po istorii zapadno-evropejskoj literatury* (Moscow, 1908).
[19] *Literaturnyj raspad* (Petersburg, 1908–1909).
[20] It might be mentioned at this point that Plexanov, who himself was no admirer of Symbolism, sharply criticized *Literaturnyj raspad* as a crude application of the Marxian method (see Georgij Plexanov, *Sočinenija*, Moscow, 1923–1927, XIV, 188).
[21] P. N. Sakulin, *Novaja russkaja literatura* (Moscow, 1908).
[22] B. Jarxo, "Granicy naučnogo literaturovedenija", *Iskusstvo*, II (1925), p. 48.
[23] See above, chapter I, pp. 27–28.

history were to become a science, it had to find its hero".[24] This search for a 'hero', that is, for a distinct and integrated subject-matter in literary scholarship is apparent in the works of A. Evlaxov, V. Šišmarëv [25] and especially of V. Peretc.

Peretc, an eminent historian of Russian medieval literature, made a forthright attempt to distinguish between literary studies and cultural or intellectual history. Taking his cue from Veselovskij's latest pronouncements,[26] Peretc argued: "In the course of studying literary phenomena in their evolution, one must always bear in mind that in literary history the object of investigation is not *what* the authors are saying but *how* they are saying it. Thus, the aim of scientific literary history is an inquiry into the evolution of plots ... and of the style as embodying the spirit of the age and the poet's personality." [27]

This formula was undoubtedly a distinct improvement over perilously broad definitions of the Pypin School. It is quite obvious, however, that the hard and fast distinction between the 'how' and the 'what' was too mechanistic to provide an adequate solution. Peretc' notion of literary history was at once both too narrow and too inclusive. On the one hand he went unwittingly 'formalist' with regard to the method of inquiry by positing the 'how' as the only legitimate concern of literary scholarship. On the other hand he failed to delimit clearly the area of literary investigation, to ascertain the *specificum* of imaginative literature. As no fundamental difference was established between the work of poetry and, say, a legal document or a moral tract, it seemed natural to conclude that all documents of 'the written word' rightfully belonged in the province of the literary historian, provided that they were approached from the 'proper', that is, esthetic point of view.[28]

Peretc' methodological position was too strongly tainted with traditional eclecticism to satisfy the more exacting and inquisitive minds among the students. The new generation of literary historians who entered the Russian metropolitan universities on the eve of the First World War had no use for half-measures. Non-conformist and restless, intransigent, these young adepts of literary scholarship were markedly

---

[24] Roman Jakobson and Pëtr Bogatyrëv, *Slavjanskaja filologija v Rossii za gody vojny i revoljucii* (Opojaz, 1923).
[25] Cf. A. Evlaxov, *Vvedenie v filosofiju xudožestvennogo tvorčestva* (Warsaw, 1910–1912).
[26] See above, chapter I, pp. 27–28.
[27] Vladimir Peretc, *Lekcii po metodologii istorii russkoj literatury* (Kiev, 1914), pp. 344–345.
[28] *Ibid.*, p. 221.

distrustful of established procedures and single-mindedly intent on revitalizing Russian literary studies by giving them unity of purpose and subject-matter.[29] And to this essentially 'academic' task they brought such thoroughly unacademic virtues as "genuine revolutionary pathos ... merciless irony and determination to do away with all compromises".[30]

It should be recognized in all fairness that the fathers' proclivity for 'compromises', scoffed at by the irreverent sons, presented from the latters' point of view a distinct advantage. It is true that the eclecticism of the aging academicians took on not infrequently the form of sheer intellectual complacency. But in the best representatives of the older generation this eclecticism went hand in hand with genuine broad-mindedness, with tolerant hospitality to new ideas. The absence of a firmly established dogma gave rein to methodological heresies. The kindly tolerance of the teachers encouraged debate, in which independent and somewhat cocky young men felt free to criticize bluntly the views of their elders.

A case in point is the seminar on Puškin, founded in 1908 by S. A. Vengerov, a distinguished professor of Russian literature at Petersburg University. Vengerov's approach to literary history was essentially a traditional one – a mixture of moderate ideological criticism with academic biographism. This did not prevent his seminar from becoming eventually one of the chief nuclei of the incipient Formalist movement.[31]

Such a development was possible, because in this heterogeneous team, brought together by common devotion to the great poet, the teacher was willing and able to learn from his disciples and to adjust the curriculum of the seminar to what proved to be their overriding concern.

Vengerov told the story himself in a retrospective article published in 1916 in Puškinist.[32] "It was two or three years ago", wrote Vengerov

---

[29]   This very preoccupation with 'pure science', at a time when politics had become increasingly the overriding concern of the Russian student youth, could be regarded too, as an act of sui generis 'non-conformism'. This does not necessarily mean, however, that the charge of 'escapism,' so often levelled against the Russian Formalists, is totally justified (this problem will be dealt with in one of the subsequent sections of the present study).
[30]   Boris Ejxenbaum, Literatura (Leningrad, 1927), p. 120.
[31]   Some of the most vocal Formalist theoreticians such as Boris Ejxenbaum, Boris Tomaševskij, Jurij Tynjanov, received their basic training in literary research in Vengerov's seminar.
[32]   Puškinist (Petersburg, 1916).

"that I first noticed in my seminar a group of capable young men, applying themselves with astounding zeal to the study of style, rhythm, rime and epithets, to the classification of motifs, to the establishing of analogies between the devices of various poets, and to other problems of the outward shape of poetry." [33] At first, Vengerov admitted, he eyed the abstruse pursuits of his students with a certain degree of apprehension, but he was finally carried away by their enthusiasm.

The spontaneous preoccupation of the young Puškin scholars with 'the outward shape of poetry' was not an isolated instance. Nor was it, as P. Medvedev, the author of a comprehensive study of Russian Formalism, correctly pointed out,[34] a purely Russian phenomenon. In the West, too, formal considerations were increasingly receiving attention. The period immediately preceding the First World War saw in various European countries a rich crop of studies, sharply focussing attention on what A. Hildebrand had called "the architectonic structure of a work of art".[35]

One should be wary, however, of overemphasizing the impact of Western scholarship on the young Petersburg philologists. As will be shown later, the number of non-Russian studies which had noticeable repercussions on the 'Formalist School' was limited indeed.[36] Russian Formalism, not unlike Futurism, was essentially an indigenous movement.[37]

In the last chapter of this study an attempt will be made to outline briefly the basic 'convergences' between Slavic Formalism and similar developments in Western European thought. At this point it seems relevant to call attention to the essential differences in the starting points of these parallel movements.

In France the early symptom of the trend toward close criticism

---

[33]   *Ibid.,* p. IX.
[34]   Pavel Medvedev, *Formal'nyj metod v literaturovedenii* (Leningrad, 1928).
[35]   See Adolf Hildebrand, *Das Problem der Form in der bildenden Kunst* (Strassburg, 1893); English translation, *The Problem of Form in Painting and Sculpture* (New York and London, 1939), pp. 12–13.
[36]   Reference is made here mainly to such works as Th. Meyer's *Das Stilgesetz der Poesie* (Leipzig, 1901), and B. Christiansen's *Die Kunst,* which were on several occasions quoted by Viktor Šklovskij, Ju. Tynjanov and Viktor Žirmunskij (see below, chapters X, XI, p. 174, 178 and 200 respectively).
[37]   Medvedev deplores, in the study quoted above, the coterie habits and 'parochialism' of the Russian Formalist School (p. 60); he accuses its spokesmen of being unaware of the achievements of Western European 'Formalism'. While this accusation is only partly true, one can concur in Medvedev's assertion that 'there was apparently no direct genetic relationship between Russian Formalism and its Western counterparts.'

was the method of *'explication de textes'*, characterized by emphasis on matters of style and composition. This useful, though rather too standardized, procedure which at the beginning of the twentieth century gained wide acceptance in French universities and *lycées,* did not necessarily imply any novel conception of literature or literary studies. As Professor René Wellek has correctly pointed out,[38] the French *explications* were a device of literary pedagogy rather than a methodological principle. According to G. Lanson, one of the most distinguished practitioners of this method, it was simply an 'efficacious and necessary mental calisthenics', fostering the "habit of close reading and precise interpretation".[39]

In Germany the resurgence of intrinsic literary analysis had appreciably broader methodological and esthetic implications. This may have been partly owing to the fact that the principal stimulus for the reorientation of literary studies was provided here by an adjacent discipline – the study of the fine arts (*Kunstwissenschaft*). The chief pioneers of German Formalism were theoreticians of music such as Hanslick,[40] and historians of the visual arts, such as A. Hildebrand, W. Worringer and H. Wölfflin.[41]

Wölfflin's contribution is of particular consequence. In his celebrated work, *Kunstgeschichtliche Grundbegriffe,*[42] he advocated the overhauling of the traditional notions about art history by substituting the typology of artistic styles for the study of individual masters. Wöfflin went as far as to postulate 'a history of art without names', where the only 'heroes' would be the Gothic, the Renaissance, the Baroque and the like.

Wölfflin's studies deeply influenced the main exponent of the quasi-Formalist tendencies in German literary history, Oscar Walzel. He argued that literary evolution should be studied in close correlation with the history of art rather than with cultural history, and he advan-

---

[38]   See René Wellek, "The Revolt Against Positivism in Recent European Scholarship", *Twentieth Century English* (New York, 1946).
[39]   Gustave Lanson, "La méthode dans l'histoire littéraire", reprinted in *Études Françaises* (Paris, 1925), Vol. I.
[40]   In his study, *Vom Musikalisch-Schönen* (Leipzig, 1885), Hanslick maintained that music has no content apart from its medium. "The ideas", he declared, "which a composer expresses are mainly and primarily of a purely musical nature." (See English translation: Edward Hanslick, *The Beautiful in Music,* London and New York, 1941, p. 36.)
[41]   Adolf Hildebrand, *Das Problem der Form in der bildenden Kunst* (Strassburg, 1893); Wilhelm Worringer, *Formprobleme der Gotik* (Munich, 1911); H. Wölfflin, *Renaissance und Barock* (Munich, 1888).
[42]   Heinrich Wölfflin, *Kunstgeschichtliche Grundbegriffe* (Berlin, 1917).

ced the theory of "the mutual illumination of various arts".[43] Walzel's voluminous works in the theory and history of literature [44] were an interesting, though hardly a consistent, attempt to apply to literary studies stylistic categories derived from Wölfflin's *Kunstgeschichte*.

In Russia the situation was vastly different. Russian literary history had also lacked adequate methodological tools with which to attack in a systematic manner the problems of poetic form. Here, too, it seemed necessary to 'borrow' from a cognate discipline a viable set of concepts. But the Russian art criticism was not likely to be of any help. The pioneers of the new criticism had to turn elsewhere.

In their choice of allegiance they seemed to be guided by the premise on which Potebnja had already insisted, that imaginative literature is a *verbal* art. If Potebnja was right in maintaining that poetry was essentially a 'linguistic phenomenon',[45] the logical thing to do was obviously to look to the science of language for guidance.

It was fortunate indeed for the study of poetry in Russia that the linguists happened at this juncture to be as vitally interested in the 'mutual illumination' of the two disciplines as were the literary scholars. The problems of poetic language, the borderland between literary investigation and linguistics, became the common meeting ground of the form-conscious students of literature and young linguists who had compelling reasons of their own for venturing into this long-neglected field.

The 'hero' of Russian literary history was found: it was poetic speech — the medium of imaginative literature.

Russian linguistics, too, has felt the impact of the widespread recoil from positivism. In all humanistic disciplines preoccupation with genesis was being superseded by an emphasis on the purposes of human endeavor, and in linguistics it became increasingly clear that "language is a human activity directed in each case toward a definite goal".[46] The feeling was growing that linguistic facts should be studied not only in terms of their historical antecedents, but also in terms of the 'function' which they fulfill in contemporary speech patterns.

At Petersburg University the views of the 'neo-grammarian' school were sharply challenged by Jan Baudouin de Courtenay and his followers. While Lev Ščerba, one of Baudouin's most brilliant disciples,

---

[43]   Oscar Walzel, *Wechselseitige Erhellung der Künste* (Berlin, 1917).
[44]   Oscar Walzel, *Deutsche Romantik* (Leipzig, 1918); *Die künstlerische Form des Dichtwerkes; Gehalt und Gestalt im Kunstwerk des Dichters* (Berlin, 1923).
[45]   See above, chapter I, pp. 23–24.
[46]   *Russkaja Reč'*, collection of articles, ed. by Lev Ščerba (Petrograd, 1923), p. 9.

objected to onesided historicism and vindicated living speech as a *bona fide* object of linguistic inquiry, the master himself called attention to the multiple uses of language by drawing a distinction between formal and 'casual' speech.

Moscow University seemed for a while impervious to the 'functionalist' heresy. The 'neo-grammarian' orthodoxy was still firmly in the saddle. Under the expert guidance of Professor F. Fortunatov, the Moscow linguists had shown astounding ingenuity in morphological analysis, but they consistently shunned the questions of function and meaning as being outside the province of the grammarian.

The new generation, however, could not long remain immune to the scientific *Zeitgeist*. The more independently-minded among the younger Moscow linguists were growing dissatisfied with the 'formalistic' rigidity [47] and crude empiricism of Fortunatov's doctrine. They were eager to learn from their teachers how to dissect the form of grammatical categories and classify the paradigms of declension and conjugation. But not unlike the young Petersburg philologists, they were still more anxious to move beyond their masters – to attack new problems and experiment with new methods.

A potent factor in the espousal of the functional approach by the young Muscovites was the influence of the famous German philosopher Edmund Husserl. Husserl's epoch-making *Logische Untersuchungen* contributed greatly toward crystallizing the reaction against Fortunatov's school.[48]

Husserl's attitude to linguistic problems was that of a logician, more exactly, of a semasiologist. He saw language, to quote a Russian Husserlian, as "the central system of signs, the natural prototype of each expression invested with meaning",[49] and he probed into the logical function of the basic grammatical categories common to all languages. Reaching beyond the empirical data of comparative linguistics, Husserl introduced the concept of 'pure', universal grammar, of

---

[47] Because of its one-sided emphasis on grammatical form to the virtual exclusion of the problems of function (meaning), Fortunatov's school was often referred to as 'formalist'. It is imperative to bear in mind, that, apart from the name, this linguistic doctrine had little in common with Formalism in literary scholarship. Whatever its shortcomings, Formalist criticism certainly cannot be accused of eschewing the concept of function. (As will be shown later, the Formalist notion of poetry revolved around the functional distinction between poetic and practical language.)

[48] Edmund Husserl, *Logische Untersuchungen*, 2 vols. (Halle, 1913–21).

[49] Gustav Špet, "Predmet i zadači ètničeskoj psixologii", *Psixologičeskoe obozrenie*, 1917, I, 58.

"language as such".[50] The diehard Moscow professors tried to dismiss Husserl's ideas as so much antiscientific nonsense. But to a number of their unorthodox disciples, *Logische Untersuchungen* became virtually a Bible.

Husserl's abstruse theories would hardly have gained so many ardent followers among the Moscow students if it had not been for the efforts of his Russian disciple, Gustav Špet. Špet's provocative studies [51] and lectures familiarized the Moscow philologists with such 'metaphysical' notions as those of 'meaning' versus 'form' and of 'sign' versus 'referent' (object).

Armed with the heavy weapons of Husserlian phenomenology, the unorthodox Moscow linguists were able to press the fight against the genetic fallacy with greater vigor and consistency than was the case with their Petersburg counterparts. If Baudouin de Courtenay and his followers were not averse to describing linguistic phenomena in terms of their psychological genesis, the Husserlians were firmly committed to 'anti-psychologism'. In his acute study. "The Object and Aims of Ethnic Psychology",[52] Špet issued a timely warning against the tendency to confound linguistics and psychology, a tendency going back to such nineteenth-century scholars as Wundt, Steinthal, and Lazarus. Communication, insisted Špet, is a two-way street, a fact of social intercourse; "it represents a new area of inquiry, where explanations offered by individual psychology prove utterly inadequate". All forms of expression, including language, ought to be treated not as by-products or sensory symptoms of psychological processes, but as realities in their own right, as *sui generis* objects, which call for structural description.

In the light of these strictures, the main task of the student of language was to ascertain the objective, or, more exactly, 'intersubjective'[53] meaning of the utterance and of its components, to determine the specific purpose of various types of linguistic 'expression'.

It is not difficult to see how this methodological reorientation tied in with the growing interest in poetics. To move into a domain which

---

50 Edmund Husserl, *op. cit.*, II, 294–342.
51 Gustav Špet, "Predmet i zadači ètničeskoj psixologii", *Psixologičeskoe obozrenie*, 1917, I, 58; "Istorija kak predmet logiki", *Naučnye izvestija*, 1922, vol. II.
52 See footnote 49.
53 One of Husserl's key concepts. Apparently, Husserl was wary of the term 'objective' as it seemed to point toward a reality independent from the percipient subject. To Husserl, like to Kant, such a reality was not conceivable, let alone, discussable. Hence the preference for 'intersubjective', suggesting merely that the phenomenon in question is 'given' to, or exists for, a number of 'subjects.'

had been for many decades virtually 'off limits' to a self-respecting linguist, was not merely an act of defiance of traditional taboos. A distinct 'tactical' advantage could be gained from testing the validity of the new method in what was, from the standpoint of modern Russian linguistics, almost a virgin field. Just because poetic speech had been consistently ignored by the neo-grammarian orthodoxy, the functional heresy could assert itself here more easily, unhampered by the traditional canons and inhibitions which had cluttered up the study of cognitive language.

The main reason why poetic language seemed to hold such an attraction for the purpose-minded philologist was its peculiar nature. Here was a 'functional' type of speech *par excellence,* all the components of which were subordinated to the same constructive principle – a discourse 'organized' throughout in order to achieve the intended esthetic effect.

If this were true of poetry in general, it was doubly so of modern poetry. In Xlebnikov, Kručënyx, and the early Majakovskij the linguistic devices, to use the favorite Formalist expression, were 'laid bare'. The Futurists' 'trans-sense' experiments underscored the distinctive function of poetic language, differentiating it sharply from all types of communicative speech. It was much more than mere intellectual curiosity or temperamental affinity that prompted the innovating linguists to take a close look at the modern poet's laboratory.

Fascination with the discoveries of the literary vanguard and impatience with the obsolete procedures of academic scholarship – these were the chief symptoms of that intellectual ferment which in the second decade of this century crystallized into an organized movement. In 1915 a group of students of Moscow University founded the Moscow Linguistic Circle. A year later, in Petersburg, a few young philologists and literary historians banded together in the Society for the Study of Poetic Language, which was soon to become known as *Opojaz*.[54] Thus, Russian 'Formalism' was born.

3

The beginnings of Russian Formalism were anything but spectacular. The two centers of the movement – the Petersburg *Opojaz* and the Moscow Linguistic Circle – were at first simply small discussion groups, where young philologists exchanged ideas on fundamental problems

---

[54]   This abbreviation stands for "Obščestvo izučenija poètičeskogo jazyka".

of literary theory in an atmosphere free from the restrictions imposed by the official academic curricula.

Nearly all the participants of these gatherings have subsequently won distinction in either literary scholarship or linguistics. But in the years 1915–1916, when the Formalist School came into existence, its pioneers were still freshmen scholars: few of them were more than twenty years old. Inquisitive and uninhibited, they were eager to explore, by common effort, new ways in the study of language and of literature.

The Moscow Linguistic Circle was founded on the initiative of a group of capable and unorthodox students of Moscow University. Among its founders were Buslaev, the grandson of the noted literary historian and philologist, Pëtr Bogatyrëv, later an eminent authority on Slavic folklore, Roman Jakobson, who soon became one of the major figures in Russian Formalism, and G. O. Vinokur, subsequently a distinguished linguist.

The actual scope of the Circle's activity was broader than its name would imply. In the first two years problems of Russian dialectology and folklore held the center of the stage.[55] But eventually the chief emphasis shifted from gathering linguistic data to methodological discussions bearing on poetic as well as 'practical' speech.

The driving force behind these theoretical pursuits was the Circle's chairman, Roman Jakobson, who combined a vivid interest in Slavic folklore and ethnography with a keen speculative mind inquiring eagerly into the latest developments in Western-European theory of language and philosophy.

As the methodological orientation of the Moscow Linguistic Circle crystallized, the problems of poetic language achieved increasing prominence in the program. The report cited above stated that out of twenty papers which were read at the meetings of the Circle in the academic year 1918–1919, fifteen had to do with either the history or theory of literature. Among the items listed by Vinokur[56] are "On Poetic Epithets" and "On Verse Rhythm" by Osip Brik; "On Puškin's Iambic Pentameter" by Boris Tomaševskij; "The Problem of Literary Borrowings and Influences" by S. Bobrov, a collective study of Gogol's tale "The Nose" (Bogatyrëv, Brik, Buslaev, Jakobson, Vinokur), and last but certainly not least, "Xlebnikov's Poetic Language" by Roman Jakobson.

[55] See *Naučnye izvestija* (Moscow, 1922), Volume II: *Filosofija, literatura, iskusstvo.*
[56] *Ibid.*

This latter study was undoubtedly the most important contribution to poetics to come out of the Moscow Linguistic Circle. Jakobson's paper on Xlebnikov, which two years later appeared in a slightly enlarged form under the title of *Modern Russian Poetry*,[57] contained, apart from an incisive if somewhat sketchy analysis of Xlebnikov's poetic devices, a succinct statement of the early Formalist conception of poetry and literary studies.[58]

That this pronouncement was made in conjunction with a sympathetic inquiry into the idiom of a Futurist innovator was certainly no accident. It was rather an epitome of the literary 'modernism' of the young Moscow linguists who tended to model their notions of poetic art on the type of verse produced by their contemporaries.

It has already been indicated that the pioneers of Russian functional linguistics found the Futurist attempts at the 'liberation' of the poetic word a particularly rewarding field of study. One might add that in some cases this intellectual fascination was bolstered by strong personal ties. Jakobson was intimately acquainted with both Majakovskij and Xlebnikov [59] and was an habitué of the gatherings of the Moscow 'Cubo-Futurists'. Conversely, Majakovskij showed considerable interest in the work of the Moscow Linguistic Circle. His athletic figure was seen on more than one occasion at the meetings of the young linguists. He was present when Jakobson read his paper on Xlebnikov and listened intently to the speaker's abstruse argument in which he examined Russian Futurist verse in the light of concepts derived from E. Husserl and F. de Saussure.

Majakovskij's association with the Formalist movement was not confined to occasional appearances at the discussion evenings. Though no expert himself in matters of prosodic terminology, he felt keenly the need for a minute analysis of poetic form,[60] especially of verse

[57]   Roman Jakobson, *Novejšaja russkaja poèzija* (Prague, 1921).

[58]   See below, chapters IV and X, pp. 71 and 182–183 respectively.

[59]   Jakobson's friendship with Majakovskij is attested to by numerous affectionate references to 'Roma Jakobson' scattered throughout Majakovskij's writings. One might mention here a line in the famous poem "Tovarišč Nette" (Vladimir Majakovskij, *Sobranie sočinenij*, V, 160) and a passage in the "Travel Diary" (*op. cit.*, IX, 295). In the case of the hermit-like Xlebnikov the relationship was almost equally friendly. As early as 1914 Jakobson discussed with Xlebnikov the possibility of reforming the graphic aspect of traditional poetic language. In a letter quoted by V. Xardžiev (see *V. Majakovskij, Materialy i issledovanija*, Moscow, 1940, p. 386), the young linguist endorsed Xlebnikov's idea of using in verse mathematical symbols and 'syncretic graphic signs.'

[60]   "Each ... rime has to be counted", declared the *Lef* manifesto, edited and probably written by Majakovskij (see *Lef*, No. 1, 1923, p. 11).

rhythm, which he hailed as a primordial force in his article "How to Make Verses".[61] While urging his Formalist friends to pay more attention to the sociological implications of literature, the most eminent Russian Futurist did not hesitate to say that "the Formalist method is the key to the study of art".[62] It was this belief which prompted him to encourage, in 1919, the publication of Formalist studies [63] and to solicit, a few years later, the collaboration of their authors in the magazine *Lef* [64] which he then edited.

In Petersburg, too, the first steps of the Formalist movement were marked by a close alliance with the poetic avant-garde. Here, however, the acceptance of the Futurist credo was far from general.

The Society for the Study of Poetic Language or *Opojaz* was a somewhat more heterogeneous team than its Moscow counterpart. The latter represented the linguists' collective venture into poetics. The former was a 'coalition' of two distinct groups: the professional students of language of Baudouin de Courtenay's school, such as Lev Jakubinskij and E. D. Polivanov, and literary theoreticians like Viktor Šklovskij, Boris Ejxenbaum and S. I. Bernstein, who attempted to solve the basic problems of their discipline by making use of modern linguistics.

The members of the second group differed markedly in their literary preferences. Boris Ejxenbaum, who joined *Opojaz* shortly after it was formed and soon became one of its most articulate spokesmen, could hardly be regarded as a champion of Futurist poetics. A thoughtful and cultivated student of Western-European literature, combining an acute sense of contemporaneity with certain scholarly detachment, Ejxenbaum entered Russian literary criticism without any definite esthetic commitments. He was keenly aware of the crisis of Symbolist 'theurgy', but, in his recoil from it he was apparently more attracted by the neo-classicist lucidity of Gumilëv or Axmatova than by the 'trans-sense stammering' of Kručënyx and Xlebnikov.[65] Though scornful of eclectic compromises and quite intransigent in his methodological utterances, Ejxenbaum, in contradistinction to Šklovskij, was a reformer rather

---

[61]   "Kak delat' stixi" (Vladimir Majakovskij, *Sobranie sočinenij*, V, 381–428).
[62]   See above, footnote 60.
[63]   According to Šklovskij's testimony (see *O Majakovskom*, 1940), Majakovskij was instrumental in securing funds from A. V. Lunačarskij, then the People's Commissar of Education, for the publication of the *Opojaz* collection *Poètika. Sbornik po teorii poètičeskogo jazyka.*
[64]   *Lef* (the abbreviation stands for *Levyj Front,* or 'Left Front') was an organ of a literary group headed by Majakovskij, Tret'jakov and Čužak.
[65]   See Boris Ejxenbaum, *Anna Axmatova* (Petrograd, 1923), p. 19.

than a rebel, an unorthodox intellectual rather than a reckless Bohemian. He was apt to have more sympathy with the evolutionary course charted in Russian poetry by the Acmeists than with the revolutionary 'nihilism' of the Futurists.[66] It was indeed Acmeism, with its cult of craftsmanship, that helped Ejxenbaum to grasp the peculiar nature of poetic language and to realize that "verse is born from the need to concentrate attention on the word, to take a close look at it, to play with it".[67]

Fascinated with 'verbal play', Ejxenbaum soon abandoned the tradition of philosophical criticism to which he had paid his due in his first essays.[68] Together with the fellow members of *Opojaz* he embarked upon a detailed inquiry into literary technique.

Ejxenbaum was not the only one among the prominent Petersburg Formalists who kept aloof from the Futurist turmoil. But in the first years of *Opojaz* it was the fellow-travellers of the Futurist Bohemia who called the tune. I am referring primarily to Viktor Šklovskij, one of the founders of the 'Society' and its vocal chairman, and to the astute Formalist impressario Osip Brik.

Like Ejxenbaum, Šklovskij studied literary history at Petersburg University. But, if one is to believe his whimsical autobiography, *The Third Factory,*[69] academic philology had little to offer to this irreverent and restless student. "Nobody bothered here about the theory of prose and I was already working on it." [70] Brilliant, exuberant, versatile, oscillating between theorizing on literature and feuilleton writing, between philology and visual arts, this *enfant terrible* of Russian Formalism felt more at home amidst the noise of literary cafés than in the calm atmosphere of university classrooms.

The stimuli received *extra muros* were indeed of great consequence. A brief apprenticeship with a sculptor and close association with Futurist poets and painters apparently gave Šklovskij what most of his professors sadly lacked – awareness of literary form, and artistic construction. "With the aid of Futurism and sculpture one already could understand a great deal. It was then that I saw art as an independent

---

[66] *Ibid.*
[67] Boris Ejxenbaum, *Moj vremennik* (Leningrad, 1929), p. 40.
[68] Reference is made here to such essays as "Deržavin", "Karamzin", "Pis'ma Tjutčeva" (1916), which first appeared in the Acmeist review *Apollon*; later published in *Skovoz' literaturu* (Leningrad, 1924).
[69] Viktor Šklovskij, *Tret'ja fabrika* (Leningrad, 1926).
[70] *Ibid.*, p. 33.

system".[71] And it was then, one might add, that Šklovskij became 'eligible' for the role of Formalist chieftain.

Osip Brik, a staunch admirer and friend of Majakovskij and subsequently his close associate on the editorial staff of *Lef*, played a much more important part in the early stage of Russian Formalism than would be imagined from the scanty list of his publications.[72] According to the testimony of his colleagues, Brik talked more effectively and more copiously than he wrote. Discussing problems or poetics, in an intimate circle of friends, he would nonchalantly drop invaluable suggestions and coin terms which won wide currency. An almost pathological atrophy of personal ambition, a complete lack of what Šklovskij aptly called "the will to accomplishment" [73] prevented Brik in most cases from following through, from elaborating on his ideas. He was perfectly satisfied to hand over this task to his more prolific or more ambitious colleagues.

Though not a professional philologist, Brik was profoundly interested in, and thoroughly conversant with, the study of verse language. It was apparently his effort to attack the problems of poetic euphony in terms completely different from those of Symbolist poetics that gave the first impulse to the discussions on verse which led to the emergence of *Opojaz*.

This is how Brik's brilliant and attractive wife, Lili, described in an article "Reminiscences of Majakovskij",[74] the homely beginnings of *Opojaz:* "In connection with his hieroglyphs,[75] Osja launched into long philological conversations with Šklovskij. Kušner [76] joined them; Jakubinskij and Polivanov came, too. . . . Soon the philologists started to meet regularly at our place, to read papers and hold discussions. . . ."

The sophisticated hostess watched, with mildly amused surprise, the philologists' passionate interest in such technical aspects of verse analysis as the repetition of consonantal clusters, dealt with in Brik's notes. But she could and did share fully in that intoxication with modern poetic idiom which pervaded the early Formalist discussions, whether

[71] *Ibid.,* p. 51.
[72] Brik's 'Formalist' writings are confined to two brief studies, "Sound Repetitions" (*Sborniki po teorii poètičeskogo jazyka,* II, Petersburg, 1917) and "Rhythm and Syntax" (*Novyj Lef,* No. 3–6, 1927).
[73] Viktor Šklovskij, *Tret'ja fabrika,* p. 52.
[74] Lili Brik, "Iz vospominanij", *Almanax s Majakovskim* (Moscow, 1934), p. 79.
[75] Lili Brik is obviously referring here to her husband's notes on 'sound-repetitions' out of which grew his study under the same name.
[76] B. Kušner, a young Minsk-born linguist, was among the founders of the *Opojaz,* but did not play subsequently any conspicuous part in the movement.

they were held in Petersburg at Brik's or in Moscow at Jakobson's. "Verses were then", wrote Lili Brik, "our only passion. We gulped them down like drunkards. I knew all Volodja's [77] poems by heart, and Osja went completely wild over them." [78]

Even though many of the subjects discussed during the "evenings at the Briks" [79] would sound abstruse, if not dull, to a non-specialist, there was an air of intellectual excitement about these unique gatherings, combining the earnestness of the linguist's laboratory with the buoyant flippancy of a literary café. It was in this atmosphere of 'gay science', where a clever paradox counted for almost as much as a new concept, that the initial premises of Formalism were being hammered out.

---

[77] Diminutive of 'Vladimir' (naturally, V. Majakovskij).
[78] *Al'manax o Majakovskom*, p. 78.
[79] V. Šklovskij, *Tret'ja fabrika*, pp. 64–65.

IV. 'THE YEARS OF STRUGGLE AND POLEMICS'
(1916–1920)

1

Some retrospective accounts [1] may produce the impression that in the main Russian Formalism was the brain-child of Viktor Šklovskij. Now it would be incorrect as well as unfair not to admit that Šklovskij's was a very important role in organizing and making articulate the methodological ferment in the Russian literary studies. In the first years of *Opojaz* he made, by his articles and speeches, a stronger impact on the position and the strategy of the movement than any of its spokesmen, with the possible exception of Roman Jakobson. The fact of the matter is, however, that no individual theoretician, however dynamic or influential, could claim full credit – or assume full blame – for the Formalist methodology. It was a product of intellectual teamwork rarely paralleled in the history of literary scholarship, in which the keenest minds of *Opojaz* and of the Moscow Linguistic Circle played a conspicuous part.

The collective efforts of the Petrograd section of the Formalist movement were embodied in a series of articles put out by *Opojaz* in the years 1916–1919. The first such collection, featuring contributions of Jakubinskij, Kušner, Polivanov, and Šklovskij, appeared in 1916, under the title *Studies in the Theory of Poetic Language*.[2] A year later a second slightly enlarged issue of the *Studies* was published.[3] In 1919 the most important items from the two collections reappeared in *Poetics* which comprised also several new studies by Brik, Ejxenbaum and Šklovskij.[4]

---

[1] See especially Viktor Šklovskij, "Pamjatnik naučnoj ošibke", *Literaturnaja gazeta*, 27, I (1930).
[2] *Sborniki po teorii poètičeskogo jazyka*, I (Petersburg, 1916).
[3] *Sborniki po teorii poètičeskogo jazyka*, II (Petersburg, 1917).
[4] *Poètika. Sborniki po teorii poètičeskogo jazyka* (Petrograd, 1919).

The *Opojaz Studies in the Theory of Poetic Language,* expecially their 1919 version, along with Jakobson's *Modern Russian Poetry,* represent a comprehensive statement of the early Formalist position. Before we proceed to relate the subsequent developments in Russian Formalism, we ought to take a close look at the substance and the temper of these pronouncements.

An outstanding characteristic of the first Formalist publications was their belligerent attitude toward all the trends which had hitherto prevailed in Russian literary studies. The spokesmen of the new critical school attacked with equal vehemence the utilitarian approach of Pisarev's epigones, Symbolist metaphysics, and academic eclecticism. The latter approach reveived cavalier treatment at the hands of Roman Jakobson.[5] He described traditional literary history as a "loose conglomeration of home-bred disciplines", and compared its methods to those of the police "who, when ordered to arrest a certain person, would take along, to make sure, everybody and everything they happened to find in the culprit's apartment as well as all passers-by encountered in the street".[6] Likewise, "the literary historian took indiscriminately in his stride everything that came his way: mores, psychology, politics, philosophy".[7]

Ejxenbaum voiced his impatience with the 'naive psychological realism' at the base of the current preoccupation with the writer's life.[8] He took exception to the prevalent tendency to "regard literary 'statements' as a direct expression of the author's actual feelings".[9] And Brik ridiculed the biography-minded Puškin scholars as maniacs who worried themselves to death, trying to answer irrelevant questions.[10]

On the whole, however, the pioneers of Russian Formalism did not deem it necessary to spend too much time debunking the pundits of the 'obsolete' academic scholarship. "To fight them", Ejxenbaum declared disdainfully, "was hardly necessary." [11] The Formalist spokesmen were saving most of their ammunition for a more dangerous opponent, the Symbolists. In Ejxenbaum's words, "what brought together the initial group of the Formalists was the desire to liberate the poetic

5 Roman Jakobson, *Novejšaja russkaja poèzija.*
6 *Ibid.,* p. 11.
7 *Ibid.*
8 See above, chapter III, p. 54.
9 "Kak sdelana 'Šinel'' Gogolja", *Poètika* (Petrograd, 1919), p. 161.
10 Osip Brik, "T.n. formal'nyj metod", *Lef,* No. 1 (1923).
11 Boris Ejxenbaum, *Literatura,* p. 90.

word from the fetters of philosophical and religious tendencies, which had achieved considerable prominence in Symbolism." [12]

This choice of the main target was dictated by tactical considerations as well as by esthetic and methodological loyalties. For one thing, Symbolism was a more dangerous obstacle to the kind of reorientation of Russian literary studies postulated by the Formalists. In spite of the Acmeist defection and the Futurist revolt, such books as Belyj's *Symbolism* and Ivanov's *Furrows and Boundaries* [13] had still a stronger hold on Russian critical thought than the pedestrian monographs dutifully produced by the academicians.

An additional tactical reason for concentrating fire on the Symbolist position was its proximity. Belyj and Brjusov had worked diligently in the field of poetics and had all but monopolized the study of versification. In order to evolve a new conception of poetic language, it seemed imperative to challenge sharply the authority of the Symbolist theoreticians, and the validity of their premises. [14]

It is hardly necessary to say that this opposition to Symbolism was **not merely a matter of rivalry** or struggle for 'power'. The call for the liberation of the study of verse from 'religious and philosophical tendencies' was more than a polemical device. It reflected a genuine revulsion against metaphysics, 'the new pathos of scientific possitivism' [15] which was so characteristic of the early Formalist declarations. Bal'mont's flimsy impressionism and Ivanov's esoteric theurgy were categorically rejected. The structure of the new criticism was to be erected upon the solid foundation of 'the scientific study of facts'. [16]

This militant, not to say naive, empiricism [17] of the Formalist spokesmen was closely bound up with their Futurist orientation. Whether the theoretician's recoil from the transcendental was due to the impact of the new verse, or whether it was, on the contrary, one of the causes of his interest in modern poetry, seems immaterial here. Whichever the case might be, active involvement in the battles of a contemporary literary school gave added vigor to the Formalist offensive, while at the same time lending it a distinctly partisan coloring.

---

[12]   *Ibid.*, pp. 90–91.
[13]   See above, chapter II, pp. 36–37, 40.
[14]   Very characteristic in this respect is Jakobson's sharp blast at Brjusov's treatise, *Brief Course of Verse Study* (see Roman Jakobson, "Brjusovskaja stixologija i nauka o stixe", *Naučnye izvestija*, 1922).
[15]   Boris Ejxenbaum, *Literatura*, p. 120.
[16]   *Ibid.*
[17]   Ejxenbaum spoke, in the passage cited, of the need for "eschewing any and all philosophical pre-conceptions, psychological and esthetic interpretations".

It is enough to cast a superficial glance at the first publications of *Opojaz* and the Moscow Linguistic Circle to see how closely they parallel Xlebnikov's gospel of the 'self-valuable word'. The preoccupation with 'outward form' or phonetic texture of the verbal sign, which was so typical of the Futurist manifestoes, is attested to by the very titles of the *Opojaz* studies. Thus, L. Jakubinskij wrote on "The Sounds of Poetic Language" and on "The Accumulation of Identical Liquids in Practical and in Poetic Speech", Brik analyzed "Sound Repetitions", and Polivanov discussed "Sound-Gestures in the Japanese Language".[18]

Primacy of sound over meaning in certain types of speech was postulated explicitly by Šklovskij.[19] He cited examples of 'trans-sense language' occurring in fields so disparate as prose fiction and folklore, nursery rhymes and religious ritual. Šklovskij advanced the thesis that the tendency to use unintelligible or 'meaningless' words is a 'general speech phenomenon' corresponding to a deep-seated psychological need. The communicative function, he maintained, is only one of the possible uses of language. "People need words not only in order to express a thought or to designate an object. ... Words which are beyond sense are needed too." [20]

While Šklovskij's meanderings on 'poetry and trans-sense language' were a provocative, but rather inconclusive attempt at vindicating the Futurist experiments, Jakubinskij set out to demonstrate autonomy of sound in poetry in the cogent terms of functional linguistics. He started from the premise, obviously derived from Baudouin de Courtenay, that "linguistic phenomena ought to be classified, among other things, from the viewpoint of the purpose for which the speaker employs his linguistic material".[21] The next step of Jakubinskij's argument was to differentiate sharply between 'practical' language, "where the linguistic representations have no independent existence and serve only as means of communication",[22] and other types of speech where the sounds are valuable *per se*.[23]

'Practical' speech, maintained Jakubinskij, is esthetically neutral,

---

[18] Lev Jakubinskij, "O zvukax poètičeskogo jazyka" (1916), "Skloplenie odinakovyx plavnyx v praktičeskom i poètičeskom jazykax" (1917); Osip Brik, "Zvukovye povtory" (1917); E. D. Polivanov, "O zvukovyx žestax v japonskom jazyke".
[19] "O poèzii i zaumnom jazyke", *Poètika*, pp. 13–26.
[20] *Poètika*, p. 17.
[21] *Poètika*, p. 37.
[22] *Ibid.*
[23] The methodological significance of this distinction which is central to the Formalist theory of literature will be discussed in a subsequent section of this study.

amorphous. Hence the phenomenon of casual, 'sloppy' speech to which Baudouin de Courtenay called attention: in ordinary verbal intercourse a certain discrepancy between the intent and the acutal utterance is permissible, as long as the listener knows what the speaker is 'talking about'. Not so in poetic discourse: here the sounds are deliberately experienced; *"they enter the clear field of consciousness"*.[24]

According to Jakubinskij, the best proof of the 'perceptibility' (*oščutimost'*) of sound in verse is provided by the rhythmical organization of poetic speech. This thesis is amply substantiated in Brik's perceptive remarks on "sound repetitions".[25] The starting point of this pioneering study was an attempt to classify various types of alliteration occurring most frequently in the verse of Puškin and Lermontov. But the methodological importance of the article lies not so much in the ingenious typology of alliterative "figures",[26] as in the author's insistence upon the 'integral' character of poetic speech. Verbal orchestration in poetry, argued Brik, is not merely a matter of a few devices of 'harmony' which happen to strike the reader's ear. The entire phonetic texture of verse is involved here. Rime and alliteration are only the most tangible, the 'canonized' manifestations of 'basic euphonic laws', particular cases of 'sound-repetition' (*zvukovoj povtor*)[27] which constitutes the underlying principle of poetic language.

While the bulk of the *Opojaz* studies had to do with problems of poetic euphony or of general phonetics, two significant contributions to *Poètika* concerned themselves with the structure of prose fiction. One could safely say, however, that these 'exceptions' fully 'proved' the rule. In both cases the discussion of narrative techniques was curiously, though not always, artificially twisted to fit the *idée maîtresse* of the early *Opojaz* – its overriding concern with 'verbal instrumentation'.

[24]   The author's italics; *ibid.*, p. 30.
[25]   "Zvukovye povtory", *Poètika*, pp. 58–98.
[26]   One may observe, parenthetically, that in his explorations of poetic euphony Brik focuses not on assonance, which was the favorite theme of the Symbolist theoreticians, but on consonantal repetitions. Brik's proclivity for alliteration, as well as Šklovskij's preoccupation with the 'articulatory aspect', may be attributed in part to a Futurist bias. As was mentioned above, the Futurist poets scornfully rejected the traditional ideal of 'mellifluence' (*sladkozvučie*) in favor of difficult, unwieldy sound-combinations. Thus, Kručënyx composed his 'trans-sense' syllables like 'dyr, bul, ščur', while Majakovskij half-jokingly reminded his fellow-poets that there are still 'good letters left' in the Russian alphabet, such as 'er, ša, šča'.
[27]   The term 'zvukovoj povtor' received subsequently wide currency among the Russian students of verse — Formalist as well as non-Formalist.

In his suggestive, though obviously one-sided essay, "How Gogol"'s 'Overcoat' Is Made",[28] Ejxenbaum focuses attention on the narrative tone of the tale. The famous story is interpreted as a masterpiece of grotesque stylization, as a sample of expressive *skaz*,[29] making lavish use of word-plays, laying special emphasis on "articulation, mimicry and sound gestures".[30] The plot of the "Overcoat" is described entirely on a verbal level, as a resultant of the interplay between two stylistic layers – comic narration and sentimental rhetoric.

Likewise Šklovskij postulated, in his first venture into the theory of prose,[31] a close correlation between compositional and stylistic devices. He maintained that "techniques of plot-construction (*sjužetosloženie*) are similar to, and fundamentally identical with, the devices of verbal orchestration".[32] In line with this, an analogy is established between such seemingly disparate phenomena as architectonic 'tautology' – a recurrence of the same event in an epic song or a fairy tale [33] – and a verbal repetition. Alliteration in a poem by Puškin, 'tautological parallelism' in a folk ballad and the device of epic retardation or, to use Šklovskij's expression, "of the staircase-like structure",[34] are placed in the same category.

The laws of poetic euphony are projected here, as it were, into the sphere of narration; the plot is seen, to use Jakobson's term,[35] as a "realization" of the verbal device. The paramount importance of sound is emphasized, moreover, in general formulations which abound in Šklovskij's rambling essay. Thus, works of literature, including those of prose fiction, are described as a "warp woven out of sounds, articulatory movements and ideas".[36]

The Formalist notion of 'perceptibility of verbal construction' as the

---

[28] "Kak sdelana 'Šinel'' Gogolja", *Poètika*, pp. 151–165.

[29] 'Skaz', which soon became one of the key terms of Russian Formalist stylistics (see below, chapter XIII, p. 238), does not have any adequate counterpart in English nomenclature bearing on prose fiction. One could define this term tentatively as a narrative manner which focuses on the personal 'tone' of the fictional narrator.

[30] *Poètika*, p. 143.

[31] "Svjaz' priëmov sjužetosloženija s obščimi priëmami stilja", *Poètika*, pp. 113–150; later included in Šklovskij's book *O teorii prozy*.

[32] *Poètika*, p. 143.

[33] A typical example of architechtonic tautology, according to Šklovskij, is found in the old French *Song of Roland* where the motif of striking the stone recurs three times in the course of the poem.

[34] *Ibid.*, pp. 121–129. We shall return to the subject in chapter XIII of this study.

[35] Roman Jakobson, *Novejšaja russkaja poèzija*.

[36] *Poètika*, p. 153.

distinctive feature of poetic discourse made necessary a drastic overhauling of the prevalent theories about the nature of poetry. The
first casualty was Potebnja's popular teaching, positing imagery as the
specificum of poetic language. This theory seemed the more ominous,
since it was made wide use of by the Formalists' immediate predecessors and 'hostile neighbors', the Symbolist theoreticians.

The task of refuting Potebnjanism was eagerly undertaken by the
chief trouble-shooter of *Opojaz*, Viktor Šklovskij. In two articles, the
second of which is usually regarded as the manifesto of Russian Formalism – "Potebnja" and "Art as a Device" [37] – Šklovskij charged into
the schoolmaster's notion of the poetic image as a pedagogical device
explaining the unfamiliar in terms of the familiar. Actually, declared
Šklovskij, the direct opposite of this is true. The poetic use of the
image, as distinguished from the 'practical', lies in a "peculiar semantic
shift",[38] in the transfer of the object depicted to a different plane of
reality. The habitual is 'made strange'; it is presented as if it were
seen for the first time. The fundamental mission of poetic art is thus
accomplished: the poet's "braked, oblique speech" [39] restores to us the
fresh, child-like vision of the world.[40] As the "twisted, deliberately
impeded form" [41] interposes artificial obstacles between the perceiving
subject and the object perceived, the chain of habitual associations and
of automatic responses is broken: thus, we become able to *see* things
instead of merely *recognizing* them.[42]

The challenge to realistic esthetics was unmistakably clear. Not
representation of life in concrete images, but, on the contrary, creative
distortion of nature by means of a set of devices which the artist has
at his disposal – this was, according to Šklovskij, the real aim of art.

The device (*priëm*) conceived as a deliberate technique of 'making'
the work of poetry – of forming its material, language, and deforming
its subject-matter, 'reality' became the key term and the battle cry of
Formalism. "If literary history", categorically declared Jakobson,
"wants to become a science, it must recognize the artistic device as

[37] "Potebnja" (1916), "Iskusstvo kak priëm" (1917), *Poètika*, pp. 3–6; pp. 101–
114.
[38] *Poètika*, p. 112.
[39] *Ibid.*, p. 115.
[40] "Thus", wrote Šklovskij in a characteristic passage, "in order to restore to us
the perception of life, to make a stone stony, there exists that which we call art."
(*Poétika*, p. 105).
[41] *Ibid.*
[42] We shall revert to Šklovskij's theory of disautomatization in chapter X, pp. 176–
178.

its only concern." [43] All other components of the literary work, its 'ideo-logy', its emotional content, or the psychology of the characters were found secondary, if not totally irrelevant; they were airily dismissed as *post factum* "motivation" [44] of the devices employed, designed, pre-sumably, to make the 'literary product' more palatable, more appealing to the common sense of a Philistine reader.

Some of the more extreme Formalist statements went as far as to deny altogether the relevance of social and ideological considerations. "Art was always free of life", Šklovskij wrote petulantly, "and its color never reflected the color of the flag which waved over the fortress of the city." [45] And Jakobson did not hesitate to maintain that "to incrim-inate the poet with ideas and feelings ['expressed' in his work, V.E.] is just as absurd as the behavior of the medieval public which beat up the actor who played Judas".[46]

These were undoubtedly extravagant assertions which the young Formalist champions would have considerable trouble in substantiating. One need not, however, take Jakobson or Šklovskij at their word. Even though their actual views were at the time 'radical' enough, it is obvious that they did not quite mean what they said and were at least vaguely aware of having overstated the case.[47]

In his critical but remarkably fair appraisal of the Formalist School, Medvedev correctly pointed out that to treat its publications of 1916–1921 as academic studies would amount to ignoring history.[48] Indeed, in order to place the excesses of Russian Formalism in a proper histo-rical perspective, one would do well to take cognizance, with Medvedev, of the following passage from Ejxenbaum's stock-taking article, "Theory of the Formalist Method" (1925):

"During the years of struggle and polemics with such [ideological and eclectic, V.E.] traditions, the Formalists directed all their efforts

[43] Roman Jakobson, *Novejšaja russkaja poèzija*, p. 11.

[44] The term 'motivation of the device' (*motivirovka priëma*) which like the cor-relative notion of the 'laying bare of the device' (*obnaženie priëma*) was first introduced by Jakobson, will be discussed at greater length in a subsequent sec-tion of this study.

[45] Viktor Šklovskij, *Xod konja* (Moscow-Berlin, 1923), p. 39.

[46] Roman Jakobson, *op. cit.*, pp. 16–17.

[47] As I was told by Roman Jakobson, Šklovskij admitted in a private conversa-tion that in his flamboyant statement about the 'color of the flag' he had gone a bit too far. He claimed, however, that 'bending the stick over' was essentially good tactics. "There is no harm", he argued half-jokingly, "in overstating the case, since one never 'gets,' anyway, everything which one 'asks' for."

[48] Pavel Medvedev, *Formal'nyj metod v literaturovedenii* (Leningrad, 1928), pp. 91–92.

precisely toward demonstrating the paramount importance of constructive devices, while relegating everything else to the background.
. . . Many of the tenets laid down by the Formalists in the years of bitter
struggle with our opponents were not so much scientific principles as
slogans paradoxically sharpened for propaganda purposes." [49]

The shrill exaggerations of the early stage could be attributed, in
large degree, to the natural belligerence of a young school of criticism
bent on dissociating itself at any cost from its predecessors. One would
be equally justified in relating the half-deliberate overstatements of the
early Šklovskij and Jakobson to the Futurist tradition of shocking the
Philistines.

This, however, does not tell the whole story. The strident tone of the
Opojaz studies was not merely an echo of the Futurist brawls. It
reflected, not unlike the latter, the temper, or, more exactly, the timbre
of a generation. One had to talk loudly indeed to make oneself heard
in the marketplace of contending ideas during the years 1916–1921, the
turbulent and eventful years of War and Revolution.

2

From the strictly chronological point of view, Russian Formalism can
hardly be considered a product of the revolutionary era. As was shown
above, the Formalist School came into existence prior to the outbreak
of the 1917 Revolution. By the time the new critical movement had
gathered momentum, Russia was ablaze. The third and most significant
collective pronouncement of early Formalism, *Poètika* (1919), was
published in a grim Petrograd racked with Civil War. Both the shabby
appearance and the bellicose temper of these studies bear witness to
the impact of the conditions under which this *Opojaz* collection
originated.

To one who sees in Russian Formalism the epitome of "bourgeois
decadence",[50] any attempt to relate the Formalist tenets to the revolutionary ethos may appear futile if not preposterous. Was not the Formalist method first and foremost an asylum for the advocates of 'pure',
'apolitical' art? [51] Were not early Jakobson's single-minded preoccupation with the artistic device and Šklovskij's frantic efforts to 'free'

[49] Boris Ejxenbaum, *Literatura*, p. 132.
[50] See L. Plotkin, "Sovetskoe literaturovedenie za tridcat' let", *Izvestija Akademii
Nauk S.S.S.R., Otdel literatury i jazyka* (Moscow, 1947), II, 372.
[51] Cf. A. V. Lunačarskij, "Formalizm v nauke ob iskusstve", *Pečat' i revoljucija*,
1924, V, 23.

art from life typical attempts at an escape from the 'burning' issues of
the revolutionary era?

The question 'Formalism versus the Revolution' is not so simple as
it may seem on the surface. The charge of escapism, mercilessly abused
by the heavy-handed bureaucrats of 'social' criticism, ought to be handled with greater care. If we define this term as a withdrawal from
active involvement in contemporary political battles, the label could
scarcely be applied to such Formalist theoreticians as O. Brik or L.
Jakubinskij. The former worked tirelessly on the 'cultural front' of the
Revolution, first as a political commissar of the Moscow Academy of
Arts, then as a spokesman of the ultrarevolutionary Lef group.[52] Jakubinskij, though not quite so active as Brik, was in the first years of the
Revolution a regular member of the Bolshevik Party. As for Šklovskij,
presumably the main exponent of Formalist 'escapism', his attitude
towards revolutionary politics was more complex than some of his
extravagantly 'a-social' utterances would imply. In the Civil War period
he oscillated intermittently between the pose of an ironic spectator,
or passive victim, of the revolutionary upheaval and inconclusive
attempts at political action. This ambivalence found a characteristic
expression in the retrospective Sentimental Journey (1923);[53] "I think",
Šklovskij wistfully wrote, "that after all, I should have let the Revolution by-pass me. . . . When one falls like a stone, one should not think;
when one thinks, one should not fall. . . . I confused two incompatible
professions." [54]

That the Formalist's preoccupation with the 'how' of literature
rather than with the 'what' may have served in some cases as a refuge
from rigid ideological commitments or, more specifically, from unequivocally endorsing official ideology, is not to be denied. But the
Formalists hardly deserved the supercilious and misleading charges of
P. Kogan who dubbed them "poor, naive specialists, lacking any
contact whatsoever with their epoch".[55]

· The weakness of such diatribes lies in glibly equating a 'sense of
contemporaneity' with the 'proper' attitude to, or active interest in,
current political issues. It is highly doubtful whether the timeliness of

[52] In his book, O Majakovskom, Šklovskij calls Brik 'the doorman of the Revolution'.
[53] Viktor Šklovskij, Sentimental'noe putešestvie (Moscow-Berlin, 1923), p. 67.
[54] One might add at this point that Šklovskij's confessions need not be taken too
literally. The whimsical tone of his reminiscences, their all-pervading irony, lends
a tinge of ambiguity even to his seemingly 'straightforward' statements.
[55] Izvestija Vcika, Moscow, 1922, XVI. (See chapter VI of this study, pp. 99–100.)

an intellectual trend or of a scientific theory can be judged by means of narrowly ideological terms. A more relevant criterion might be provided by the manner in which the doctrine under discussion attacks the problems of its particular discipline.

Viewed from this vantage point, the Formalist School is apt to appear for better or worse as a legitimate, if somewhat eccentric, child of the revolutionary period, as part and parcel of its peculiar intellectual atmosphere.

The Revolution of 1917 did not confine itself to a thorough over-hauling of Russia's political and social structure; it also shook loose fixed patterns of behavior and accepted moral codes and philosophical systems. This cultural upheaval was not a mere by-product of political revolution; it was spurred and acclerated, rather than brought about, by the breakdown of the old regime. The tendency to revaluate all values, to re-examine drastically all traditional concepts and procedures transcended the boundaries of revolutionary Russia: during the after-math of the First World War, the determination to "eschew statics and bar the Absolute" [56] became well-nigh a universal phenomenon.

A noted physicist, Xvol'son, put it thus: "We live at a time of an unprecedented destruction of the old scientific structure. . . . Among the truths which are being demolished today are concepts which seemed self-evident and thus lay at the base of all reasoning. . . . A distinctive feature of this new science is the thoroughly paradoxical nature of many of its fundamental propositions; the latter are obviously at variance with what had come to be regarded as common sense." [57]

Xvol'son's formula of 'new science' is easily applicable to the 'new criticism' as exemplified by the early Formalist manifestoes. 'The destruction of the old scientific structure,' 'the paradoxical nature of fundamental propositions' – are not these apt descriptions of Jakobson's frontal attack on traditional literary history and of Šklovskij's lusty debunking of the 'self-evident truths' of Potebnjanism?

If the militant anti-traditionalism of the Formalists faithfully reflected, within the sphere of literary scholarship, the intellectual tenor of the time, the same is true of the other outstanding feature of the new critical movement – of its thoroughgoing empiricism.

The revolutionary iron age had no use for the 'Absolute', for other-worldly pursuits. Its mystique was earthly, its eschatology – materialist; its religion was an abiding, irrational faith in the potentialities of the

[56]   Roman Jakobson, "Futurizm", Iskusstvo, VII, 2 (1919).
[57]   Quoted in Roman Jakobson, op. cit.

human mind and the salutary effect of 'scientific' social engineering and technical progress. "Socialism means Soviet system plus electrification", declared the chief strategist and theoretician of the October Revolution, V. I. Lenin. Even though this was obviously a slogan deliberately simplified for propaganda purposes, its emphasis on technology was revealing.

A school of criticism scoffing at 'loose talk' about inspiration and verbal magic and proclaiming as its chief concern "the study of the laws of literary production" [58] was, from this standpoint, well attuned to the *Zeitgeist*. Some of the 'left-wing' Formalists did not hesitate to advertise their 'professional' approach to poetry as a distinct revolutionary virtue. Thus, Brik maintained that, owing to its emphasis on literary technique, *Opojaz* ought to be regarded as "the best educator of the young proletarian writers".[59]

Whatever one's judgment of this sincere but somewhat brash claim, it seems indubitable that the literary 'productionism' of *Opojaz* had at least as much in common with the industrial enthusiasm of the post-October period as with 'bourgeois professionalism' – another stock phrase of official Soviet criticism.[60]

The impact of historical circumstances made itself felt not only in the substance of the first Formalist utterances, but in the mode of presentation as well. The feverish atmosphere and the hardships of the Civil War period made impossible sustained research or large-scale publishing activity.[61] "Books were written hastily", testifies Šklovskij. "There was no time for earnest study. More was said than written." [62]

The hectic rhythm of the epoch called for aphoristic brevity and sloganlike shrillness. As should be clear from the samples quoted above,

---

[58] O. M. Brik, "T.n. formal'nyj metod", *Lef*, No. 1 (1923). It was no accident that this statement came from the pen of one to whom Formalism was primarily a theoretical rationale for Futurist poetry (cf. Majakovskij's dictum about poetry as a 'kind of production', see above, pp. 48–49).

[59] *Ibid.*

[60] The aim of the above remark is not to exonerate Russian Formalism in the eyes of the 'Marxist-Leninist' stalwarts — a thankless task if there ever was one — but to question the validity of hasty attempts to explain away Formalist criticism in pseudo-sociological terms.

[61] It is a testimony to the persistence and enthusiasm of Formalist researchers that they were able to carry on at all in the face of these formidable obstacles. "My colleague", wrote Šklovskij, "had to sacrifice some of his books to make a fire in the stove. The doctor who came to visit him on the day when his whole family was sick made all of them move into one tiny room. They warmed up a bit and somehow survived. It was in this room that Boris Ejxenbaum wrote his book, *The Young Tolstoj*." (See *Sentimental'noe putešestvie*, pp. 330–331.)

[62] *Ibid.*, p. 345.

the early Formalist writings, especially of Šklovskij, met both require-ments.

Some critics of the older generation deplored the 'loudness' of the Formalist polemics – their acrimony in attacking opponents and equal lack of restraint in self-advertising.[63] While these charges are not without foundation, it is essential to bear in mind that 'loudness' was by no means a monopoly of the *Opojaz* coterie; it was, in fact, an integral element of the Russian critical style during one of the most turbulent periods of Russian letters.

It would hardly be possible to find a more striking contrast to the dull uniformity of recent Soviet criticism than the gaudy variety of critical schools, the virtual inflation of literary manifestoes which char-acterized the period of the Civil War and the *NEP*. Futurists and Imaginists, Constructivists and the 'Smithy' group, the 'Proletkultists' and the 'On Guardists',[64] – to name only the most important organiza-tions – struggled fiercely for hegemony. Each of these groupings stridently advocated its program as *the* formula of proletarian art, the last word of the Marxist-Leninist esthetics, and contemptuously dis-missed rival claims as 'obsolete', 'reactionary' or 'mechanistic'.

The vehement debate on proletarian literature was not infrequently tainted with scholastic dogmatism: reverent quotations from the 'authorities' – Marx, Plexanov or Lenin – were used all too often as definitive arguments. The doctrinaire had a field-day as orthodox zealots postulated, in the midst of the revolutionary chaos, the creation of a 'monumental', full-blown proletarian culture. The *Proletkult* group headed by A. A. Bogdanov, expected to attain this goal by means of what might be called laboratory techniques, while the 'On Guardists' relied chiefly on the 'wise guidance' of the Communist Party.

It must be admitted, however, that this utopian bigotry was often sincere and spontaneous. The Party leaders were no believers in in-tellectual freedom. They kept a watchful eye on literature with the view of eliminating, by means of 'revolutionary censorship', all 'hostile' ideological manifestations. Moreover, they had thrown their full weight behind the 'only sound world-view' – the Leninist version of dialectical materialism – and had actively discouraged, if not yet forcibly sup-pressed, all rival philosophical systems or scientific theories. But

[63] E.g., A. G. Gornfel'd, "Formalisty i ix protivniki", *Literaturnye zapiski*, 1922, No. 3.
[64] See N. L. Brodskij and V. Rogačevskij, *Literaturnye manifesty* (Moscow, 1929).

within the limits of the officially approved methodology, there was still, in the early days, considerable latitude of interpretation: the fundamentals of Marxian literary theory were tossed back and forth in a spirited exchange between such pundits of early Soviet criticism as V. Friče, G. Lelevič, A. Lunačarskij, V. Pereverzev, V. Polonskij, L. Trockij, A. Voronskij.

As long as Marxian literary theory had not become a rigid dogma, a non-Marxian heresy such as Formalism still had a right to exist. Its chances of receiving a fair hearing were the better since it represented a novel and a scientific method of approach, and addressed itself to problems which were badly in need of elucidation.

Much of the current critical discussion centered around ideological problems. To the orthodox Soviet critic, art was a mode of cognition or a weapon in the class struggle; sometimes a combination of both. The natural corollary of these notions was the insistence on the 'primacy of content'.[65] Nevertheless, problems of literary form attracted considerable attention. The poet-innovators, whether of the Futurist, Imaginist or Constructivist persuasion, incessantly harped on the theme that revolutionary form is as essential a prerequisite of truly proletarian art as revolutionary content. These declarations were echoed by some *bona fide* Marxist theoreticians. A. Gastev, a spokesman of the *Proletkul't* group, maintained that "the notion of proletarian art implies an overwhelming revolution in the sphere of artistic devices".[66] At a time when the new was indiscriminately praised and the old excoriated, experiment in form seemed to be a historical necessity.

The formal preoccupations of the Civil War period focussed on poetry, which remained until 1922 the central literary genre. This time, the old Latin saying notwithstanding, the clatter of arms failed to drown out the singing of the Muses. The revival of Russian poetry which had set in at the end of the last century continued, under the impact of quite different factors, throughout the first five years of the Revolution. The frantic haste and the breath-taking pace of events discouraged the production of broad epic canvases. An acute shortage of paper stopped the novelist in his tracks.

The poet could for a while get along more easily without the printing presses than the prose writer, provided he was ready to follow Majakovskij's advice and 'go out into the street' to face his audience. Oral delivery, reciting poems on the floor of a metropolitan café or at a

---

[65] *Ibid.*
[66] *Ibid.*

workers' meeting, became for the creator the only means for disseminating his "products".[67] No wonder that many prominent poets availed themselves of this medium. What is perhaps more noteworthy is that the public hardly ever failed the artist, not even under the most trying conditions of blockade and near-starvation. In the literary cafés of besieged Petrograd or grim Moscow, the audience, underfed, restless and yet appreciative, listened eagerly to poems, descending upon the consumer without the normal 'cooling-off period'.

Strange as it may seem, it was not only the practitioner, roaring or chanting his poems, but also the theorist painstakingly explaining 'how verses are made', who managed to find keen and eager ears in those thoroughly unpredictable times. In his *Sentimental Journey* Šklovskij credited this popular appeal of poetics in the Civil War period to the sharpening of intellectual curiosity brought about by the Revolution. The frontiers of consciousness, he maintained, were pushed aside. People, snatched from the routine of a dull, uneventful existence, started looking around with wide open eyes. While everything was in flux, any venture, however extravagant of seemingly untimely, had some chance of success. "No matter what one would set out to do, open a prompters' school for a Red Fleet theater, or give a course in the theory of rhythm at a hospital, one was bound to find an audience. People were singularly receptive then." [68]

A not insignificant part in stimulating the interest in poetics was played by a few veteran students of verse who chose to collaborate with the new regime, e.g., V. Brjusov and A. Belyj. But the Formalist opposition to the chieftains of Russian Symbolism was steadily gaining ground. The experimental approach of *Opojaz* to the problems of versification suited better the empiricist frame of mind of the younger linguists and literary historians than Belyj's oscillation between metaphysics and prosody.

As for the older generation of Russian literary scholars, it was hardly a factor to be reckoned with. Šklovskij's and Jakobson's attacks on academic literary history elicited only a weak and half-hearted response on the part of its representatives.

The virtual lack of organized resistance paved the way for a rapid advance of the new critical movement. Five years after its emergence,

---

[67] A. Ležněv, the chief critic of the influential literary magazine, *Krasnaja nov'*, is quoted by Majakovskij as labelling the years 1917–1921 the 'oral period of Soviet literature' (see Vladimir Majakovskij, *Sobranie sočinenij*, IX, 230).
[68] Viktor Šklovskij, *Sentimental'noe putešestvie*, p. 59.

the Formalist School had not only attracted wide notice in the critical reviews, but also established powerful bases of operation in academic literary scholarship. One such position became the 'Division of Literary History' formed at the Petrograd State Institute of Art History, in 1920.[69]

The chairman of the newly-formed division was Viktor Žirmunskij, an erudite historian and theoretician of literature who could be described as one of the most influential sympathizers with the Formalist movement.[70] Besides Žirmunskij, the active participants in the new center of literary research were S. Baluxatyj, B. Engelhardt, B. Ejxenbaum, G. Gukovskij, V. Šklovskij, Ju. Tynjanov, B. Tomaševskij, and V. Vinogradov. Only a few of them belonged to the *Opojaz* old guard. The majority were newcomers to Formalist literary theory. Some, e.g., Tomaševskij or Tynjanov, accepted in the main the Formalist doctrine as evolved by Šklovskij and Jakobson and subsequently played a significant part in developing and modifying it. Others, such as the eminent young linguist Viktor Vinogradov, were soon to occupy distinctive positions on the periphery of the Formalist movement.

The organizational expansion of the Formalists had somewhat modified their status and their *modus operandi*. While *Opojaz,* strengthened by the accession of some brilliant neophytes, such as Tynjanov, remained the center of militant Formalism,[71] most of the Formalist pedagogical and publishing activity was carried on after 1921 by the Institute. It was there that Ejxenbaum, Šklovskij and Tynjanov discussed with a group of alert and hardworking young students problems of style and composition, verse structure and prose technique. And it was under the Institute's auspices that there would soon begin to appear a series, *Problems of Poetics,* containing some of the most important Formalist contributions to the history and theory of literature.

The 'sound and fury' of the early, formative years had somewhat subsided. Formalism was coming of age. The brilliant aphorisms, the

---

[69] N. I. Efimov, "Formalizm v russkom literaturovedenii", *Naučnye izvestija Smolenskogo Gosudarstvennogo Universiteta,* 1929, vol. 5, part III; Viktor Žirmunskij, "Formprobleme in der russischen Literaturwissenschaft", *Zeitschrift für slavische Philologie,* I (1925).
[70] Žirmunskij's position *vis-à-vis Opojaz* will be discussed in Chapter V, pp. 96–98.
[71] As for the Moscow Linguistic Circle, it did not play in the twenties any significant part in the Formalist movement. After Jakobson's departure from Moscow, in 1920, there was a noticeable slackening of the Circle's activities. A sharp split within the Circle between two philosophical orientations, the 'Marxist' and the 'Husserlian' led to further weakening and to eventual disintegration of the first Formalist nucleus.

"paradoxically sharpened slogans",[72] no longer sufficed. Manifestoes had to give way to critical studies. The initial tenets, stated succinctly and extravagantly, had to be tested on concrete material, vindicated and, if need be, modified in more substantial works bearing on various domains of theoretical and historical poetics.

[72] See above, p. 78.

V. TURBULENT GROWTH (1921–1926)

1

The maturing of the Formalist School was marked by an appreciable widening of its initial sphere of inquiry. The single-minded preoccupation with poetic euphony gave way to a more inclusive notion of literary form. The meaning, as well as the sound of the poetic idiom, was found worthy of critical scrutiny. The growing awareness of semantics gave rise to numerous studies focussing on questions of the style and composition, imagery and narrative techniques employed in literary works of art.

Problems of prose fiction loomed increasingly large in Formalist literary research. Viktor Šklovskij followed up his early essay, "The Relation Between Devices of Plot-Construction and General Stylistic Devices",[1] with a series of studies in the mechanism of the novel and short story. One ought to mention his papers "Tristram Shandy and the Theory of the Novel" and the "Unfolding of the Plot",[2] subsequently incorporated into the collection of essays *On the Theory of Prose*.[3]

While the *Opojaz* leader was thus laying the foundations of the Formalist theory of prose fiction,[4] independent researchers operating on the periphery of the Formalist movement, such as Viktor Vinogradov or M. Petrovskij, probed into the structure of Gogol"s tales [5] or Maupassant's short stories.[6]

---

[1] Viktor Šklovskij, "Svjaz' priëmov sjužetosloženija s obščimi priëmami stilja", *Poètika*, pp. 113–150 (later included in Šklovskij's book, *O teorii prozy*).
[2] Viktor Šklovskij, *Tristram Shandy Sterne'a i teorija romana* (Petrograd, 1921); *Razvertyvanie sjužeta* (Petrograd, 1921).
[3] Viktor Šklovskij, *O teorii prozy* (Moscow, 1929).
[4] See chapter XIII of this study, pp. 239–250.
[5] See Vinogradov, "Sjužet i kompozicija povesti Gogolja, 'Nos' ", *Načala*, 1921.
[6] M. Petrovskij, "Kompozicija novelly u Maupassanta", *Načala*, 1921; "Morfologija novelly", *Ars Poetica* (Moscow, 1927).

In spite of the marked interest in artistic prose, poetry remained the chief concern of many Formalist as well as quasi-Formalist literary scholars. However, within the realm of verse study a significant shift of emphasis was discernible. As the fascination with the Futurist's 'self-valuable word' wore thin, more attention was paid to the poet's lexical and phraseological apparatus. 'Poetic semantics' became a vital part of the Formalist theory of verse. In his often quoted "The Aims of Poetics" [7] Viktor Žirmunskij posited as one of the chief tasks of the literary theoretician the study of pervasive 'verbal themes' – words or word-combinations recurring in the poet's work.

These concepts stood Žirmunskij in good stead in his essay on Aleksandr Blok's imagery [8] – a thoughtful analysis of the interplay between various orders of metaphor in the verse of Russia's greatest Symbolist poet. In a similar fashion Vinogradov dissected the verbal repertory of another contemporary lyrist, Anna Axmatova. Axmatova's poetic style is discussed in Vinogradov's painstaking studies [9] in terms of peculiar 'semantic clusters' which keep reappearing in her sparse, intimate verse. The selection and the grouping of words, and their modification under the impact of the poem's total context seem to provide, in Vinogradov's opinion, the most valuable clue to Axmatova's narrowly circumscribed poetic world.

This modified view of poetic form, prevailing in the second period of Russian Formalism, found expression in numerous attempts at establishing close connection between sound and meaning in poetry. The Formalist theoreticians were too keenly aware of the organic unity of poetic language to be satisfied with a mere shuttling between prosodic and stylistic considerations. They tended to reject both the purely acoustic approach to versification, typical of the German *Schallanalyse*,[10] and the common tendency to classify poetic styles in terms of the poet's verbal repertory, without any reference to his prosody. "It was neces-

---

[7] Viktor Žirmunskij, "Zadači poètiki", *Načala,* 1921 (later included in Žirmunskij's book, *Voprosy teorii literatury,* Leningrad, 1928).
[8] Viktor Žirmunskij, "Poèzija Aleksandra Bloka", *Ob Aleksandre Bloke* (Petrograd, 1921) (later included in *Voprosy teorii literatury*).
[9] Viktor Vinogradov, *O poèzii Anny Axmatovoj (Stilističeskie nabroski)* (Leningrad, 1925). An extended version of this study appeared under the title "O simvolike Anny Axmatovoj", *Literaturnaja mysl'* (Leningrad, 1922).
[10] See the discussion of E. Sievers' school in the German study of verse, in B. Ejxenbaum's *Melodics of Verse* (*Melodika stixa,* Petrograd, 1922, pp. 12–13), and in Žirmunskij's article, "Melodika stixa", *Voprosy teorii literatury,* pp. 89–153.

sary", wrote Ejxenbaum in his article on "The Theory of the Formalist Method", "to focus on something that would be closely related to the sentence and yet would not lead us away from the verse as such, something that could be found in the borderland between phonetics and semantics. This something was the syntax."[11]

The emphasis on the inextricable relationship between rhythm and syntax and their interdependence became the leitmotif of the Formalist study of verse in the mid-twenties. Thus, Osip Brik attempted a classification of 'rhythmico-syntactical figures' recurrent in Russian poetry,[12] while V. Žirmunskij argued, in his study *Composition of Lyrical Verse*,[13] that the "stanza is a syntactical as well as a metrical unit". B. Ejxenbaum made an interesting attempt at devising a typology of Russian lyrical verse from the standpoint of phrase melody.[14]

A similar method of approach was used in other Formalist studies which were concerned specifically with the organization of phonic material in verse, that is, with metrics. Boris Tomaševskij expounded in his closely reasoned discussion, *Russian Versification*,[15] as well as in his analysis of iambic tetrameter,[16] the notion of a verse line as a series of intelligible word-units rather than a mere alternation of stressed and unstressed syllables. Of even greater methodological consequence was R. Jakobson's treatise, *On Czech Verse*,[17] demonstrating the relevance of semasiological criteria to the comparative analysis of metrical patterns.[18]

The change of emphasis in the domain of theoretical poetics was accompanied by increasingly frequent ventures into literary history. This development could be easily explained by the Formalist critic's natural desire to test the validity of his generalizations on concrete

[11] See Boris Ejxenbaum, *Literatura* (Leningrad, 1927).
[12] Reference is made here to Brik's paper on rhythmico-syntactical figures, read at an *Opojaz* meeting in 1920. This lecture served as a basis for a series of articles "Ritm i sintaksis", published in the *Lef* magazine, in 1927.
[13] Viktor Žirmunskij, *Kompozicija liričeskix stixotvorenij* (Petrograd, 1921).
[14] Boris Ejxenbaum, *Melodika stixa* (Petrograd, 1922).
[15] See Boris Tomaševskij, *Russkoe stixosloženie* (Petrograd, 1923). V. Žirmunskij hailed this work as the 'first scientific textbook of Russian prosody' (see "Formprobleme in der russischen Literaturwissenschaft", *Zeitschrift für slavische Philologie, I,* 1925).
[16] See Boris Tomaševskij, *O stixe* (Leningrad, 1929).
[17] Roman Jakobson, *O češskom stixe, preimuščestvenno v sopostavlenii s russkim* (Berlin-Prague, 1923).
[18] For a more detailed discussion of Tomaševskij's and Jakobson's views, see chapter XII of the present study, pp. 212–220.

literary material. That, however, does not tell the whole story. To quote Ejxenbaum, "the transition to literary history was not simply a matter of widening the initial field of investigation. It was closely related to the modification of our concept of form. It became clear that a work of art is never perceived in isolation, that its 'form is always seen against the background of other works." [19]

One of the antipathies of the early *Opojaz* had been the extreme historicism of the nineteenth-century literary studies. In their recoil from the 'genetic fallacy', the Formalists tended at first to take a purely descriptive view of literary art. Where the traditional literary historian inquired about the origin of the given phenomenon, the Formalist was interested solely in its composition. Where the former wondered how the 'literary fact' came about, the latter wanted to know what it was and what it consisted of. In order to answer these questions, it seemed necessary to extricate the phenomenon under consideration from the chain of historical antecedents and sequents, to break it down into its individual components and examine them carefully one by one.

"A work of literature", declared Šklovskij in 1921, "is the sum-total of all stylistic devices employed in it." [20] Quite apart from its blatant one-sidedness, Šklovskij's formula reveals a mechanistic fallacy, typical of early *Opojaz* thinking. The term 'sum-total' seems to imply the notion of literary form as a mere bundle, a loose aggregate of individual devices. Shortly afterwards this view was appreciably modified. Šklovskij's 'sum-total of devices' was supplanted by the concept of an esthetic 'system', where each device had a certain function to perform. The static approach to literary craft gave way to the notion of style as the principle of dynamic integration. "The unity of a literary work", wrote Tynjanov in 1924, "is not that of a close symmetrical whole, but . . . of a dynamic integration. . . . The form of the literary work must be described as dynamic." [21]

In less abstruse terms is meant that to identify and describe a given 'constructive device' was only part of the critic's job. His other, and perhaps more essential, duty was to "determine the specific function of the artistic device in each particular case".[22] This function, however, the Formalist would now insist, is not a constant. It is contingent on the esthetic whole, on the total context, and, thus, is bound to vary

[19]   Boris Ejxenbaum, *Literatura*, p. 113.
[20]   Viktor Šklovskij, *Rozanov* (Petersburg, 1921), p. 15.
[21]   Jurij Tynjanov, *Problema stixotvornogo jazyka* (Leningrad, 1924), p. 10.
[22]   Boris Ejxenbaum, *Literatura*, p. 114.

from one writer to another, from one literary school to another. What in one period may produce a comic effect, can in a different historical setting become an element of tragedy.[23] Thus, in order to differentiate between various uses of the 'device', in order to establish its role and relative value in a given esthetic system, whether an individual work of art, a poet's total heritage, or a whole literary movement, it became necessary to fall back upon the concept of literary evolution, to see the 'literary fact' in historical perspective. Ejxenbaum's diagnosis was essentially correct: it was the internal evolution of the Formalist theory of literature that created the necessity for branching out into literary history.

The years 1922–1926 saw a rich crop of Formalist and quasi-Formalist studies devoted to the history of Russian literature – unorthodox, bold and often penetrating revaluations of individual writers or literary schools.[24] One ought to mention here such works as Ju. Tynjanov's *Dostoevskij and Gogol'* (1921), "Archaists and Puškin" (1926), B. Tomaševskij's *Puškin* (1925), B. Ejxenbaum's *The Young Tolstoj* (1922) and *Lermontov* (1924), as well as his essays on "The Problems of Puškin's 'Poetics' " and "Nekrasov".[25] Of the near-Formalist contributions the most important were V. Vinogradov's explorations of Gogol' and the so-called 'natural school' in Russian prose fiction [26] and the scholarly analysis by V. Žirmunskij [27] of the Byronic impact on Puškin.

The noticeable preoccupation with the Golden Age of Russian Literature need not be interpreted as a retreat from the literary modernism which had been so typical of the early *Opojaz* studies. The concerted venture into the Puškin era went hand in hand with dissections of contemporary Russian literature. Vinogradovs and Ejxenbaum's studies of Anna Axmatova, as well as Šklovskij's widely-quoted essay on Roza-

---

[23] A good case in point was provided, according to the Formalist theoreticians, by the use made of the grotesque in Classicist and Romantic poetry respectively. As Tomaševskij correctly observed in his paper on Russian Formalism, published in *Revue des études slaves*, VIII (1928), the grotesque was used in the Classicist period exclusively as a comic device, while in the Romantic era it was often an element of tragedy.

[24] Some of the works mentioned below were first published in literary reviews, in the years 1921–1926, and did not appear in book form until the late twenties.

[25] See Ejxenbaum's collection of essays, *Skvoz' literaturu* (Leningrad, 1924).

[26] Viktor Vinogradov, *Gogol's i natural'naja škola* (Leningrad, 1925); *Ètjudy o stile Gogolja* (Leningrad, 1926).

[27] Viktor Žirmunskij, *Bajron i Puškin. Iz istorii romantičeskoj poèmy* (Leningrad, 1924).

nov,[28] testified to the Formalist critic's unabated interest in the modern literary idiom.

To Šklovskij or Ejxenbaum literary history was not a distinct field of inquiry, but a method of approach to literary problems. From this standpoint Anna Axmatova was as good a subject for 'historical' investigation as Lomonosov or Gogol'. What lay at the core of the incipient Formalist historicism was not so much an interest in the literary 'past', as a fascination with the historical process, the ebb and flow of succession and transformation, with 'the literary movement as such'.[29] The poet, or the literary grouping, was seen here as a factor rather than a fact, as an event-making power rather than an event – a lever, or a resultant of the forces operating in a given literary milieu. What mattered most to a Formalist literary historian was not the artist's creative personality – an inevitably unique, if not elusive entity – but his historical role, the place he occupied in the scheme of literary evolution. The poet's career appeared thus as an illustration of the general laws of literary mechanics. Historical research gave way increasingly to the theory of literary history. The Formalist critic's theoretical preoccupation reasserted itself again.

Some opponents of the Formalist School would have us believe that the historical studies produced by *Opojaz* were simply thinly disguised theorizing, deftly contrived empirical confirmations of preconceived general notions. One finds it difficult to agree with this opinion. We will try to demonstrate at a later stage of this study that the Formalist's interest in literary history was much more than a sham. It is undeniable, however, that critical practice here tended to overlap with theoretical considerations time and again. More often than not the examination of a literary school, a writer, or a single work of literature, would serve as a springboard for methodological generalizations, the import of which would be greater than that of the historical problem under consideration. "Our first assertions on the evolution of literature", wrote Ejxenbaum, "appeared in the form of casual remarks, made in conjunction with concrete material. A specific question would suddenly acquire the dimensions of a general problem." [30]

A good case in point is provided by Ju. Tynjanov's first contribution to Formalist literary research, a slight, but stimulating volume, *Dostoev-*

---

[28]   See footnote 20. V. V. Rozanov was a contemporary Russian critic, essayist, and philosopher.
[29]   See Boris Ejxenbaum, *Lermontov*, p. 8.
[30]   Boris Ejxenbaum, *Literatura*, p. 116.

skij and Gogol': Remarks on the Theory of Parody.[31] This acute study is ostensibly concerned with direct echoes from Gogol''s *Correspondence with Friends* in Dostoevskij's short novel, *Selo Stepančikovo* (The Friend of the Family). Tynjanov advanced the proposition that the orations of the novel's principal character, Foma Opiskin, were essentially a parody of key passages from Gogol''s highly controversial *Correspondence.* This novel thesis was bolstered by an impressive array of quotations. And yet it is not in the parallels between the two works, ingenious and convincing though they are, that the chief interest of Tynjanov's study lies. The center of density is shifted here to the flank. What matters most is the digressions, the 'casual remarks' on parody and stylization as catalysts of literary change.

Šklovskij's scheme of literary evolution, which ties in closely with Tynjanov's off-hand theorizing, was first expounded in the form of marginal notes apropos of a concrete literary analysis. In Šklovskij's study on Rozanov sweeping generalizations about the driving forces of literary change were interpolated into the discussion of Rozanov's stylistic devices, which constituted the ostensible subject of the book.[32]

This tendency to transcend the boundaries of the presumable topic is apparent also in Jakobson's discussion of Czech versification.[33] The actual scope of this pioneering work is appreciably broader than its rather awkward title would seem to indicate. Even though the bulk of Jakobson's study is actually concerned with problems of 'Czech prosody, primarily in juxtaposition with Russian', the historical significance of the treatise rests in its statement of the new 'phonemic' method of approach to comparative metrics.[34]

2

A natural concomitant of evolution is inevitably differentiation. This biological law seems to hold true in the history of ideas as well. The Russian Formalist School was no exception in this respect. Its growth meant not only broadening the field of investigation by attacking new problems. It also entailed reaching beyond the hard core of the

---

[31] In this case the broader methodological implications of the study are clearly indicated in its title.
[32] Šklovskij's and Tynjanov's ideas about literary evolution will be discussed in chapter XIV of this study, pp. 257–260.
[33] See footnote 18.
[34] See chapter XII of this study, pp. 218–220.

Opojaz stalwarts. In the process of transformation from a critical coterie into a full-fledged critical movement Russian Formalism attracted, and influenced, a number of literary researchers, differing appreciably as to their background and their methodological and esthetic allegiances. Thus, the way was paved for divergent interpretations of the basic Formalist tenets, for individual deviations from what could be regarded as 'orthodox' *Opojaz* doctrine. These heresies were bound to impair whatever homogeneity the Formalist School may have boasted at its earlier pioneering stage.

This is not to say that the first period of Formalism was altogether free from internal strife. Quite apart from individual divergences, indicated in the previous chapter, there was, from the very inception of the Formalist movement, a marked difference of emphasis between the Petrograd Society for the Study of Poetic Language *(Opojaz)*, and the Moscow Linguistic Circle. The main bone of contention was the problem of the mutual relationship between literary scholarship and linguistics. While both Formalist centers advocated close cooperation with the science of language, the linguistic orientation of the Moscow Formalists, as the very name of their association would imply, was especially pervasive and emphatic.

The *Opojaz* chieftains were primarily literary historians who turned to linguistics for a viable set of conceptual tools needed in grappling with problems of literary theory. The Muscovites, on the contrary, were predominantly students of language, who found in modern poetry a testing ground for their methodological assumptions. For Šklovskij and Ejxenbaum the study of language was a cognate field, more exactly – the most relevant of al auxiliary disciplines. For Jakobson or Bogatyrëv poetics was an integral part of linguistics.

This latter position found its most vigorous expression in the early works of Roman Jakobson, the chief spokesman of the Moscow Linguistic Circle in the period of 1915–1920. In his study of Xlebnikov,[35] Jakobson stated the case for a consistently linguistic approach to poetry in no uncertain terms. The hegemony of the science of language in the field of verse study, maintained Jakobson, was made necessary both by the methodological ineptness of traditional literary scholarship and by the very nature of poetic creativity. "Poetry", wrote Jakobson, "is simply language in its esthetic function." [36] The inevitable conclusion

[35]   Roman Jakobson, *Novejšaja russkaja poèzija,* p. 5.
[36]   *Ibid.,* p. 11.

was that the student of verse ought to take his cue from the science of language, more specifically, from that school in modern linguistics which made the 'function', or purpose, of speech-activity its primary concern.

To many pioneers and sympathizers of *Opojaz,* this smacked too much of 'linguistic imperialism'.[37] They did not deny the validity of Jakobson's assertion that "so far the study of poetic speech had lagged far behind linguistics".[38] They conceded the urgent need for a *rapprochement* with the modern science of language, but insisted on the fundamental autonomy of literary studies with regard to their aims and methods of inquiry.[39]

This thoroughly justifiable point of view was ostensibly weakened by some dubious reasoning. Žirmunskij was on safe ground, when, questioning Jakobson's formula, he pointed out that a literary work of art could not be reduced to its verbal substratum. But he was guilty of oversimplification when he blithely asserted that in some literary genres, such as the novel, the verbal material was esthetically "neutral".[40]

Likewise, Ejxenbaum revealed a certain methodological *naiveté* in his discussion of the relation between poetics and linguistics. Postulating a clear-cut distinction between the two fields, he argued thus: "Poetics is based on the teleological principle and therefore uses as its point of departure the concept of device. Linguistics, like all natural science, revolves around the category of causations, that is, the notion of the phenomenon as such." [41]

This passage appears to betray a lack of familiarity on Ejxenbaum's part with recent developments in the science of language. Bracketing linguistics with natural science could perhaps be justified in the late nineteenth century, when the linguist followed in the scientist's footsteps and concerned himself chiefly with the physiological (articulatory) and physical (acoustic) aspects of speech. But in the third decade of this century such a classification was apparently an anachronism. By then, through the efforts of such theoreticians of language as F.

---

[37] See Roman Jakobson, "Slavjanskaja filologija v Rossii za gody vojny i revoljucii", *Opojaz,* 1923.
[38] Roman Jakobson, *Novejšaja russkaja poèzija,* p. 5.
[39] Viktor Žirmunskij, "Zadači poètiki", *Načala,* 1921; Boris Ejxenbaum, *Melodika stixa.*
[40] Viktor Žirmunskij, *Voprosy teorii literatury,* p. 123.
[41] Boris Ejxenbaum, *Melodika stixa,* p. 14.

de Saussure or Baudouin de Courtenay, the 'teleological principle' was widely recognized as the cornerstone of modern linguistics.[42]

This fissure between the Moscow linguists and the Petrograd 'esthetes' was eventually superseded by a more fundamental cleavage which could be described as a rift between the 'extremists' and the 'moderates', the champions of 'pure' Formalism and their orthodox disciples on the one hand, and the independent 'fellow travellers' of the Formalist movement on the other.

An important part in this debate was played by Viktor Žirmunskij, the most distinguished among the quasi-Formalist moderates. In the early days of Formalism, as was just indicated, Žirmunskij had joined forces with Ejxenbaum to oppose the excessive claims of Jakobson.[43] With the focus of the discussion shifting from the question 'poetics versus linguistics' to "the limits of applicability of the Formalist method",[44] the alignment changed. This time Žirmunskij found himself at cross purposes with both Ejxenbaum and Jakobson, indeed, with all the leading spokesmen of the Formalist School.

An academician par excellence, Žirmunskij never felt at home in the Bohemian atmosphere which permeated the discussions and the publications of the early *Opojaz*. He looked askance at Šklovskij's Futurist antics and had little sympathy for either the extravagant brashness of the *Opojaz* manifestoes or for the Formalist's ostensible desire 'to go out into the street' and shock the cultivated Philistine into puzzled attention. "It is high time", he wrote in 1923,[45] that "scholarship say good-bye to the general public and ceases trying to make a hit with the so-called intelligent layman."

However, Žirmunskij's disagreement with *Opojaz* theoreticians was not confined to their *modus operandi*. It had to do with his interpretation of the Formalist approach to literature. A student of Western European romanticism, strongly influenced as he was by W. Dilthey's *Geistesgeschichtliche Schule*, Žirmunskij was less apt than the single-minded spokesmen of orthodox Formalism to disregard the role of

[42]   For a discussion of the question of 'linguistics versus natural science', see the excellent paper of E. Cassirer, "Structuralism in Modern Linguistics", *Word*, Vol. I, No. 2 (1945).

[43]   One may add at this point that some Petrograd Formalists, e.g., S. I. Bernstein, E. D. Polivanov and V. Vinogradov, were in fundamental agreement with Jakobson's position.

[44]   See Viktor Žirmunskij, "K voprosu o formal'nom metode", introduction to the Russian translation of Oscar Walzel's study *Problema formy v poèzii* (Petrograd, 1923), pp. 3–23 (this essay was later included in *Voprosy teorii literatury*).

[45]   Viktor Žirmunskij, *Voprosy teorii literatury*, p. 156.

'ethos' in literature, to minimize the import of the poet's world-view. Moreover, he was temperamentally too cautious and moderate a researcher to commit himself unequivocally to one methodology and thus bar the door to alternate solutions.

To Žirmunskij, Formalism meant not so much an over-all conception of literature and literary studies as preoccupation with a certain set of problems, notably "questions of poetic style in the broader sense of this word".[46] The fallacy of the *Opojaz* doctrine, maintained Žirmunskij, lay in confusing a sphere of scientific investigation with a method of inquiry, and furthermore, in elevating this method into an all-inclusive *Weltanschauung,* a sort of a critical panacea. "For some adherents of this new trend", he wrote pointedly, "the Formalist method becomes the only legitimate scientific theory, not merely a method, but a full-fledged world-view, which I would prefer to call formalistic rather than formal." [47]

Taking exception to the early dictum of Jakobson's about the device as the 'only concern of literary scholarship' [48] Žirmunskij pleaded for methodological pluralism. The formula 'art as a device', he asserted, is valid, inasmuch as it implies the need for studying "the work of literature as an esthetic system, determined by the unity of its esthetic intent, that is, as a system of devices".[49] This is, however, only one of the possible ways in which to approach literature. "The *Opojaz* formula 'art as a device' can exist side by side with equally legitimate formulas, for example, art as a product of spiritual activity, art as a social fact or factor, art as a moral, religious or cognitive phenomenon." [50]

Žirmunskij's objections to the dogmatic one-sidedness of the *Opojaz* doctrine were undoubtedly well taken. His warnings against playing down the links between literature and society and ignoring the presence of 'non-esthetic' elements in a literary work of art were hard critical common sense. And yet as a statement of methodology Žirmunskij's position somehow failed to hit the mark. To proclaim the permissibility of various methods of investigation without meaningfully correlating them and establishing the place of each method in a general scheme of literary research was scarcely a rewarding procedure. To posit the mere co-existence of esthetic and extra-esthetic elements in a work of literature without attempting to establish their relative

---

[46] *Ibid.*
[47] *Ibid.*
[48] See above, chapter IV, pp. 76–77.
[49] Viktor Žirmunskij, *Voprosy teorii literatury,* p. 158.
[50] *Ibid.*

hierarchy amounted to an evasion of the crucial problem of the structural properties of the literary work. In other words, Žirmunskij's 'appeal to reason' bore strongly the imprint of academic eclecticism.

In the eyes of the Formalist such a compromising attitude was not merely inadequate; it was also utterly reprehensible. In a spirited rejoinder to the critics of the Opojaz, Ejxenbaum spoke scornfully of Žirmunskij's "lack of intellectual passion",[51] and maintained with some heat that Žirmunskij had never been a 'real' Formalist.

Thus, after five years of close, though mildly critical association with the Formalist movement,[52] the independent sympathizer and the militant champion parted company. In an introduction to the Russian translation of Oscar Walzel's study, *The Problem of Form in Poetry*,[53] Žirmunskij dissociated himself explicitly from the official *Opojaz* doctrine. This, needless to add, did not dampen his interest in formal analysis – a concern which, as Žirmunskij himself had insisted, did not hinge on one's espousal of the whole Formalist *Weltanschauung*.

The growth of the Formalist School was bound to attract notice and provoke opposition on the part of rival critical groupings. Thus, while the 'finer points' of *Opojaz* doctrine were tossed about in internal debates, the very essence of the Formalist methodology was sharply challenged by a school enjoying hegemony in Soviet literary criticism – the 'Marxist-Leninists'.

[51] Boris Ejxenbaum, "Vokrug voprosa o formalistax", *Pečat' i revoljucija*, V (1924).
[52] Žirmunskij's critical support of *Opojaz* dated back to 1919, when in an article published in *Žizn' iskusstva*, he gave an essentially favorable, if somewhat ambiguous appraisal of the Formalist symposium *Poètika*.
[53] See footnote 44.

VI. MARXISM VERSUS FORMALISM

1

The Soviet Marxist literary theorists could ill afford to stand pat in the face of what one of them described as the "triumphant upsurge"[1] of the Formalist School in the years 1921–1925. The growing popularity of *Opojaz* among young Russian philologists and students of literature presented a serious challenge to the supremacy of 'historical materialism', proclaimed by the official Soviet critics as the only legitimate approach to literature and the only doctrine worthy of the revolutionary era.

It goes without saying that the Marxists' stiffening opposition to the Formalist movement was not solely a matter of a struggle for power in Russian literary scholarship. Many critical tenets of *Opojaz* were, or seemed to be, in flagrant contradiction with the Marxian interpretation of literature. The ultra-Formalist tendency to divorce art from social life was bound to provoke a vehement reaction on the part of critics bent, in the words of late G. Plexanov, on determining the 'sociological equivalent' of the literary phenomenon. Statements such as those of the early Jakobson and Šklovskij which denied the relevance of ideological considerations were obviously anathema to theorists who viewed literature as a weapon in the class struggle, as a potent means of 'organizing the social psyche'.[2] The aggressive and brash manner of the Formalist manifestoes gave additional offense to the Marxist critics and provided them with easy targets.

During the first years of the Revolution most Marxist-Leninist pundits chose to ignore or minimize the Formalist 'menace'. Whenever mentioned, the new critical school was airily dismissed as a minor intellectual fad or an innocuous pastime of dusty pedants. P. S. Kogan,

[1] See U. Foxt, "Problematika sovremennoj marksistskoj literatury", *Pečat' i revoljucija*, 1927, No. 2, p. 78.
[2] See V. Friče, *Sociologija iskusstva* (Moscow, 1929), p. 13.

a prolific Marxist literary historian, referred disdainfully to the *Opojaz* critics as "poor, naive experts (*specy*) [3] who are hopelessly out of touch with their epoch".[4] L'vov-Rogačevskij, some of whose critical writings represent a mixture of ill-digested 'dialectics' with glib impressionism, made an attempt at heavy-handed sarcasm. Hinting at the coterie-like character of the Formalist School, he spoke ironically about 'Vitja and Roma [5] of *Opojaz*' and tried to be flippant about Formalist successes: "during the last three years", he wrote, "the Formalists have certainly accomplished a great deal. They have become the talk of the town. There is nowadays hardly a town in Russia that does not harbor at least one *Opojaz* member." [6]

Eventually, however, it became clear that the Formalist challenge called for a more substantial rebuttal. By 1924–1925 a full-fledged Marxist offensive against *Opojaz* got under way: the methodological assumptions of the Formalist School were subjected to a sharp critical scrutiny.

The opening gun in this campaign was fired by no less a figure than Lev Trockij in his highly controversial book, *Literature and Revolution*.[7] It is indicative of the part played by *Opojaz* in the critical debates of the time that in a pronouncement on the crucial problems of Soviet literary life the brilliant Communist chieftain deemed it necessary to devote an entire chapter to the 'Formalist School in Poetry'.[8]

Trockij's attitude toward Formalism was sharply critical but not altogether hostile. He admitted grudgingly that "in spite of the superficiality and reactionary character of the Formalist theory of art, a certain part of the research work done by the Formalists is useful".[9] In another passage he wrote: "The methods of Formalism if confined within legitimate limits, may help to clarify the artistic and psychological peculiarities of literary form." [10]

---

[3]   The word *'spec'* is an abbreviation of 'specialist', used in the Soviet parlance to designate a technical expert: the word is used here in a derogatory sense: it connotes a narrow, purely technical approach to literature.
[4]   See *Izvestija Vcika*, XVI (1922).
[5]   'Vitja' and 'Roma' are Russian diminutives derived respectively from Viktor (Šklovskij) and Roman (Jakobson).
[6]   See *Novosti*, No. 6 (1922).
[7]   Lev Trockij, *Literatura i revoljucija* (Moscow, 1924). English translation: Leon Trotsky, *Literature and Revolution* (New York, International Publishers, 1925) (1st ed., 1923).
[8]   The above is obviously a misnomer: Formalism was a school in literary scholarship or, if one will, in poetics, rather than in poetry.
[9]   L. Trotsky, *Literature and Revolution*, p. 163.
[10]   *Ibid.*, p. 164.

The qualifying clause "if confined within legitimate limits" is of paramount importance here. Trockij's recognition of the validity of 'some' Formalist research was contingent upon his tendency to circumscribe narrowly the 'legitimate' area, and to underrate greatly the actual scope of Formalist inquiry. *Opojaz,* maintained Trockij, reduced the task of the literary historian to "an analysis, essentially descriptive and semi-statistical, of the etymology and syntax of poems, to the counting of recurrent vowels and consonants, of syllables and epithets".[11]

These unspectacular pursuits, argued Trockij, may be useful in their own right, but they obviously do not go beyond the preliminary stage of literary research. The trouble with the Formalists, he continued, is that they do not know their place: they fail to recognize the 'partial, scrappy, subsidiary and preparatory' character of their methods and insist on advertising their wares as a full-fledged theory of literature. These claims must be unequivocally rejected. Treated as an auxiliary device, Formalism is a legitimate, indeed, a rewarding critical procedure. Erected into a philosophy of art, a *Weltanschauung,* it becomes an utterly false and reactionary conception.[12]

It is this Formalist *Weltanschauung* that became the target of Trockij's acid pen. An expert polemist, he had a field-day, puncturing deliberately extravagant and juvenile passages from the early Formalist pronouncements. He seized eagerly upon extreme statements, denying the existence of ideas in poetry or its dependence on the social environment,[13] in order to demonstrate the 'arrogance and immaturity' of Formalist theorizing.

The core of Trockij's attack on Formalist esthetics is contained in his polemic with a stimulating but impertinent essay by Šklovskij purporting to demolish in five clipped aphorisms the sociological interpretation of literature.[14] Šklovskij's case for the complete independence

---

[11] Whatever one's opinion of Formalist theorizing, one must admit that Trockij's description of *Opojaz* research was grossly inexact. Even in the field of verse study alone, which represented only one sphere of Formalist inquiry, the *Opojaz* critics went far beyond the mechanical procedure of 'counting recurrent vowels and consonants'. One might also note that the terminology of the above passage, with its reference to the 'etymology and syntax of poems', falls short of the verbal precision typical of Trockij's writings. While Trockij was undoubtedly more keenly aware of esthetic considerations than Kogan, his nomenclature left a great deal to be desired whenever he approached the problems of poetic technique.

[12] *Literature and Revolution,* p. 164.

[13] See above, chapter IV, p. 77.

[14] See Viktor Šklovskij, *Xod konja* (Berlin, 1923).

of art revolved around the much discussed problem of migratory plots, i.e., narrative schemes recurring in prose fiction, both written and oral, of different countries and periods. If it were true, maintained Šklovskij, that literature is shaped by the environment in which it is produced, then literary themes would be tied to a definite national milieu. Actually, the opposite of this is true: 'the plots are homeless'.[15]

Trockij had little trouble punching holes in this tenuous reasoning. "It is not at all surprising", he rejoined, "that it is difficult to decide whether certain novels were made in Egypt, India, or Persia, because these countries have so much in common." [16] But this, he argued further, is only a part of the story: besides essential similarities in the social structure which may have given rise to similar literary manifestations the use of identical themes in various national literatures can at times be attributed to cultural intercourse, resulting in literary influences and borrowings.

Trockij's objections to the Formalist leader's hasty raid on sociological criticism were, on the whole, sagacious. His ideas on migratory plots combined neatly Andrew Lang's hypothesis about the 'self-generation', i.e., independent emergence of similar ethnic phenomena with Benfey's famous theory about the 'diffusion' of folktale motifs. This well-balanced argument went a long way toward explaining the recurrence of the same basic themes in the narrative fiction of different peoples or cultural areas. However, and it was here that Šklovskij seems to have scored an important hit, neither of these assumptions can account for the striking coincidences in the *treatment* of identical themes, in the similar arrangement of individual motifs, the temporal sequence of the incidents; in a word, in the plot structure. These amazing convergences seem to point in the direction of certain esthetic conventions, of immanent laws of narrative art, which obviously transcend national boundaries and cannot be reduced to sociological or ethnographical considerations.

It is worth noting that at one point Trockij came pretty close to saying just this. "The fact", he wrote, "that different people and different classes of the same people make use of the same themes merely shows how limited the human imagination is, and how man tries to maintain an economy of energy in every kind of creation, even in the artistic." [17] The vague psychological nomenclature, closely reminiscent

[15]   *Ibid.,* p. 39.
[16]   *Literature and Revolution,* p. 175.
[17]   *Ibid.*

of Spencer's law of 'mental hygiene',[18] need not blind one to the fact that Trockij focussed here on what is essentially an 'intrinsic' determinant: the nature of the human imagination and its impact on the creative process.

This awareness of the peculiar claims of artistic creativity distinguished Trockij markedly from the cruder practitioners of Marxist criticism. While the latter saw in literature a mirror of life, a medium for "registering social phenomena",[19] Trockij recognized that artistic creation was "a deflection, a transformation of reality in accordance with the *peculiar laws of art*." [20] "A work of art", he said elsewhere, in a veiled polemic with a more doctrinaire faction of Soviet Marxist criticism, "should, in the first place, be judged by its own law, that is, by the law of art." [21] Historical materialism *per se*, conceded Trockij, cannot yield any criteria for evaluating artistic phenomena: the Marxist's field of competence is not esthetic judgement but causal explanation. In this latter sphere, continued Trockij, a skilled dialectician has no equals. "Marxism alone can explain why and how a given tendency in art has originated in the given period of history." [22]

In Trockij's opinion, the fundamental weakness of Formalism lay in the fact that it made no attempt to raise, let alone to answer this crucial question. This significant omission was presumably no accident: it was rooted, according to Trockij, in the philosophical affiliations of *Opojaz* theoreticians.

Trockij refused to take at their face value B. Ejxenbaum's emphatic disavowals of "any and all philosophical preconceptions".[23] Behind 'purely empirical' and descriptive pursuits he detected, not without a certain justification, implicit philosophical premises which he labelled as an idealistic, or more specifically, a Kantian fallacy. The Formalist critics, insisted Trockij, were neo-Kantians, even if they did not know it. That is why they viewed all ideological constructs as independent and self-contained entities; that is why they tended to substitute a static description of the literary object for a dynamic notion of the literary process.

[18] See above, chapter I, p. 26, footnote 30.
[19] See V. Friče, *Očerki* (quoted by Il'ja Gruzdёv, *Utilitarnost' i samocel'*, Petrograd, 1923, p. 45).
[20] *Literature and Revolution*, p. 175.
[21] *Ibid.*, p. 178.
[22] *Ibid.*
[23] See above, chapter IV, footnote 17 (p. 72).

In the eyes of a Marxist-Leninist from 'idealism',[24] positing the primacy of the autonomy of the mental, it was but one step to faith in the supernatural, i.e., to religion. In his *Historical Materialism,* one of the basic texts of early Soviet Marxism, Nikolaj Buxarin maintained that "teleology leads straight into theology".[25] The Formalist School was presumably no exception to this 'law'. Was not the cult of the Word, inquired Trockij, the preoccupation with the verbal devices typical of *Opojaz,* a symptom of a *sui generis* religiosity? "The Formalists", concluded Trockij, "are followers of St. John. They believe that 'In the beginning was the Word.' But we believe that in the beginning was the deed. The word followed as its phonetic shadow." [26]

Trockij's assessment of the Formalist School strongly influenced other Marxist critics of the *Opojaz,* especially the more earnest and judicious among them. His reasoning contained in a nutshell all the main ingredients of what became in the mid-twenties the semi-official line on Formalism: the charges of methodological sterility and of philosophical heresy, coupled with a qualified praise of certain techniques of textual analysis devised by the Formalists.

This latter aspect of Trockij's position is closely parallelled in a statement of another prominent Communist leader who on several occasions was called upon to formulate Party policy on literature [27] – the versatile and erudite Buxarin.[28] Buxarin too saw considerable merit in some of the Formalist explorations of poetic craft. At the same time he went beyond Trockij in minimizing, not to say misrepresenting, the scope of Formalist concerns. If one were to believe Buxarin, all that the *Opojaz* researchers were trying to do was to draw up a list or compile a 'catalogue' of individual poetic devices. This "analytical job", declared Buxarin, "is wholly acceptable as the spadework, preliminary to future critical synthesis",[29] but as a substitute for such a synthesis it is sorely inadequate. "A catalogue is only a catalogue", he wrote. "It is a useful

---

[24]   The terms 'idealism', 'idealistic' have been used somewhat loosely by the Soviet Marxists. Any philosophy other than dialectical materialism is apt to be dubbed 'idealistic' in the Soviet Union (this label was recently attached to John Dewey's pragmatism).
[25]   Nikolaj Buxarin, *Historical Materialism* (New York, 1925), p. 25.
[26]   *Literature and Revolution,* p. 183.
[27]   Buxarin's discussion of the problems of poetics at the Congress of Soviet Writers in 1934 was one of the most intellectually rewarding and competent statements made at this heavily starred gathering.
[28]   N. Buxarin, "O formal'nom metode v iskusstve", *Krasnaja nov',* III (1925).
[29]   *Ibid.*

thing, all right, but please do not call this inventory genuine science." [30]

Trockij and Buxarin were quite broad-minded in their appraisal of the Formalist movement in comparison with the Marxist-Leninist stalwarts who took up cudgels against *Opojaz* in a symposium featured in the influential literary magazine, *Press and Revolution*. The general tenor of this concerted attack on Formalism was wholesale rejection. P. Kogan [31] invoked Trockij's authority, citing reverently his "brilliant analysis of the genesis of Formalism", but unlike the master, he did not seem to have any use whatsoever for *Opojaz* studies. A critic who prided himself on never having had "time for the study of literary form",[32] Kogan could hardly be expected to show any appreciation for the highly technical analyses of poetic language found in Jakobson, Ejxenbaum or Tynjanov. Preoccupation with literary craft was to him a pathological phenomenon, a symptom of distasteful "esthetic gourmandise".[33]

Similar was the attitude of another participant of the symposium, V. Poljanskij.[34] He had also apparently taken his cue from Trockij, for he sternly advised the Formalists to stick to their spadework and stay away from theorizing. And not unlike Kogan, Poljanskij was loath to give any credit to his battered opponents. He charged savagely into the Formalist spokesmen, accusing them of irrelevance, sterility, and even of ignorance.[35]

Somewhat more substantial than this inconclusive sniping was the article by A. Lunačarskij,[36] the first Soviet Commissar of Education, a prolific critic and publicist. Lunačarskij made an attempt to broaden the scope of the controversy. He saw in the debate on the Formalist School a good opportunity for a decisive showdown with what he described as an age-old Formalist fallacy, plaguing artistic creativity and art criticism in periods of spiritual decline.

The position from which Lunačarskij attacked 'Formalism in the study of art' was a curious combination of Marxist dialectics and

---

30   *Ibid.*
31   P. S. Kogan, "O formal'nom metode", *Pečať i revoljucija*, V (1924).
32   P. S. Kogan, *Literatura ètix let* (Leningrad, 1924).
33   *Pečať i revoljucija*, V (1924), p. 22.
34   V. Poljanskij, "Po povodu B. Ejxenbauma", *Pečať i revoljucija*, V (1924).
35   This latter charge was due to a terminological misunderstanding. Poljanskij apparently confused 'biographism' as a critical method with 'biography' as a literary genre and sternly took Ejxenbaum to task for referring to a 'biographical' approach to literature. Everybody knows, he exclaimed indignantly, that biography is a type of writing and not an 'approach' to it.
36   Lunačarskij, "Formalizm v iskusstvovedenii", *Pečať i revoljucija*, V (1924).

Tolstoyan philosophy of art. Together with some other Soviet Marxists who tended to view art as an affective rather than a cognitive mode of activity,[37] Lunačarskij stated his plea for ideological art in terms that closely resemble Tolstoj's 'infection theory'. "Real art", wrote Lunačarskij, "is always ideological. By 'ideological' I mean one stemming from an intense experience which drives the artist ... toward spiritual expansion, toward rule over souls." [38]

Proclaiming emotional intensity and spontaneity to be ultimate tests of greatness in art, Lunačarskij scornfully rejected the Formalist preoccupation with the device, with the '*coûp de théatre*' as a sign of intellectual and moral aridity. He spoke with genuine indignation about Ejxenbaum's 'soulless' analysis of Gogol''s famous story, "The Overcoat",[39] accusing the Formalist critic of transforming a heart-rending tale into a mere stylistic exercise. To these sterile mental acrobatics, Lunačarskij proudly opposed such indubitable achievements of Marxist criticism, as Pereverzev's 'masterful' monograph on Gogol'.[40]

However, to establish the inadequacy of the Formalist School on literary or methodological grounds was obviously not enough. In order to demolish Formalism completely, it seemed necessary to 'expose' it, as well as refute it, that is, to prove that in addition to being an erroneous critical doctrine, it was also a 'reactionary' social phenomenon. Lunačarskij did not shy away from this assignment. His diatribe represents the first explicit attempt to explain away Formalism in 'sociological' terms.

Formalist criticism, maintained Lunačarskij in what has since become a stock argument, is a form of escapism, a product of the decadent and spiritually sterile ruling class. "The only type of art", he wrote, "which the modern bourgeoisie can enjoy and understand is nonobjective and purely formal art. ... In order to meet this need the petty bourgeois intelligentsia has brought forth a brigade of Formalist artists as well as an auxiliary corps of formalistically oriented students of art." [41]

---

[37] See an interesting discussion of Buxarin's and Lelevič's definitions of art in a book by Vjačeslav Polonskij, *Na literaturnye temy* (Leningrad, 1927).

[38] *Pečat' i revoljucija*, V (1924), p. 25.

[39] Reference to Ejxenbaum's essay "How Gogol's 'Overcoat' was Made", which appeared in the 1919 *Opojaz* collection. See above, chapter IV, p. 75.

[40] It is worth noting that Pereverzev's study *Tvorčestvo Gogolja*, cited by Lunačarskij as a model of Marxist analysis, was to be bitterly denounced six years later, and it has been treated ever since by official Soviet critics as an epitome of 'crude sociologism' in the study of literature.

[41] *Pečat' i revoljucija*, p. 25.

One may wonder, continued Lunačarskij, how such a decadent movement could come into fruition in revolutionary Russia. This apparent contradiction according to Lunačarskij is easily explained: Russian Formalism was simply a cultural survival, one of the relics of old Russia amidst the revolutionary upheaval. "Before October, Formalism was a vegetable in season. Today it is a stubborn relic of the *status quo,* the last refuge of the unreconstructed intelligentsia, looking furtively toward bourgeois Europe." [42]

The above diagnosis is open to attack on several counts. For one thing, one can hardly help but feel that Lunačarskij greatly overestimated the esthetic sophistication of the 'bourgeoisie': actually, the average representative of the European 'ruling class' had no more use for non-objective art than the Bolshevik Commissar. For another thing, Lunačarskij's description of *Opojaz* as merely a relic of the old regime does not exactly square with the iconoclastic attitude of the Formalists toward all authorities, old as well as new, nor with the fact that some of the pioneers of *Opojaz* were active members of the Communist Party.

Whatever the validity of Lunačarskij's sociological analysis, coming from an influential politician and government educator, it was a significant and an ominous statement. The implication that Formalism was a foreign body in the organism of Soviet society was a dire warning, foreshadowing the eventual amputation of the 'alien' limb. It was the same kind of reasoning that six years later, in an atmosphere of growing intellectual conformity, was invoked to justify the outright liquidation of the Formalist heresy.[43]

But in 1924 such drastic measures were not resorted to. Literary controversy was still a two-way street. A dissident, condemned and 'exposed' by critical officialdom, still had a right to ask for the floor for a purpose other than that of 'frankly' admitting his errors. He still had a chance, albeit a limited one, to make himself heard amidst the deafening barrage of official dialectics: he still could talk back. Thus, one finds in the *Press and Revolution* symposium, alongside the virulent attacks on *Opojaz,* an article by Ejxenbaum which is a spirited rejoinder to the opponents of Formalism, as well as to its half-hearted allies.[44]

Brushing aside the smug sallies of Kogan and L'vov-Rogačevskij as

[42] *Ibid.*
[43] See below, chapter VII, pp. 137–138.
[44] Boris Ejxenbaum, "Vokrug voprosa o formalistax", *Pečať i revoljucija,* V (1924).

irrelevant,[45] Ejxenbaum paused for a while before Trockij's strictures in which he saw correctly the first earnest appraisal of Formalism by a prominent Marxist. While he acknowledged with ostensible satisfaction Trockij's grudging praise of a "certain part of formalist research",[46] Ejxenbaum was, naturally, not prepared to accept the humble, subsidiary role assigned to him and his colleagues in *Literature and Revolution*. There is much more to the Formalist study of literature, declared Ejxenbaum, than gathering raw materials, accumulating statistical data on verse, rhythm, or style. The real objective of *Opojaz* was not to record the individual components of poetic art, but to ascertain its laws. Had Trockij been more consistent, continued Ejxenbaum, his tongue apparently in his cheek, he would have lent his active support to this undertaking. Had he not recognized, in the course of his polemic with Šklovskij, that literary creation was 'a transformation of reality, in accordance with the peculiar laws of art"? If so, the Formalist spokesman argued, it is incumbent upon the literary theoretician to elucidate the nature of these laws. This, claimed Ejxenbaum, is precisely the job which the Formalists propose to undertake and which all other critical schools, including the Marxist, persist in shirking.

However, it was not the significance or the scope of the Formalist pursuits which were primarily at issue in Ejxenbaum's polemic with Trockij. The central problem here was the question of mutual relationship between Formalism and Marxism. Trockij erred, Ejxenbaum argued, in asserting that "Formalism wages a relentless war against Marxism". Actually, he declared, Formalism and Marxism are not so much polar as incommensurate concepts: the former is a school within an individual humanistic discipline, namely literary scholarship; the latter, a philosophy of history. To put it in operational terms, Marxism sociology inquires into the mechanism of social change, while Formalist study of literature deals specifically with the evolution of literary forms and traditions.

Theoretically, continued Ejxenbaum, one would expect that common interest in the problem of evolution would provide a meeting ground

---

[45]   Since Ejxenbaum's article was, technically speaking, a starting point for the *Pečat' i revoljucija* symposium, it could deal only with those criticisms of *Opojaz* which had preceded this discussion.

[46]   According to Ejxenbaum, the admission by a powerful Communist leader that "a certain part of Formalist research is very useful" proved to be a substantial boost for the dissident movement: Trockij's statement "has strengthened the socio-pedagogical position of the Formalist School" (*Pečat' i revoljucija*, p. 9).

between the two schools; actually, this is hardly the case. As long as the Marxist discusses the socio-economic process, he talks evolution. Whenever he shifts his attention to literature or other 'ideological' phenomena,[47] he starts talking genesis. Instead of seeking the variables operating within a given field of culture, the historical materialist focuses on external causes – the so-called underlying factors, economic, social or socio-psychological. This, insisted Ejxenbaum, is methodologically an inadmissible procedure. No cultural phenomenon can be reduced to, or derived from, social facts of a different order (*rjad*). To account for literature in terms of sociology or economics means to deny the autonomy and inner dynamism of literature – in other words to renounce evolution for the sake of genesis.[48]

Apart from certain perilously neat formulations, which were apparently Ejxenbaum's own, the above argument reflected quite accurately the official *Opojaz* position on Marxism. The orthodox Formalist's attitude in the mid-twenties was distinctly non-Marxist, if not actively anti-Marxist. What Ejxenbaum's contribution to the symposium actually boiled down to was this: 'dialectical materialism' may be a very fruitful concept in the field of sociology, but because of its extrinsic frame of reference, it has little to offer literary scholarship.

A similar viewpoint was expressed two years later by Viktor Šklovskij, who suggested that the question of applying the Marxist doctrine to literature was a matter of critical expediency rather than of methodological principle. "We are not Marxists", he wrote, with his characteristic nonchalance, "but, if we ever happen to be in need of this utensil . . . we will not eat with our hands out of sheer spite." [49]

This airy remark, like Ejxenbaum's more earnest strictures, reminds one of the dictum attributed to the famous French astronomer Laplace: "God is a hypothesis for which I have not yet had any use." To Šklovskij and Ejxenbaum of 1924–26, still sanguine about the potentialities of 'pure' Formalism, Marxism was a hypothesis with which one could easily dispense.

---

[47]   It is essential to bear in mind that in Marxist terminology the word 'ideological' has asquired a very broad meaning. The so-called ideological superstructure which, according to historical materialism, is conditioned by the 'economic base' of society, encompasses all the forms of 'social consciousness', such as art, science, philosophy, religion, law, and morals.

[48]   The opposition between the 'evolutionary' and 'genetic' approach to literature was to play a vital part in the Formalist theory of literary history.

[49]   Viktor Šklovskij, *Tret'ja fabrika* (Leningrad, 1926).

2

With the orthodox Marxists rejecting Formalism more or less emphatically, and the 'pure and simple' Formalists proclaiming lack of interest in Marxism, the chasm between the two doctrines seemed well-nigh unbridgeable. However, on the periphery of both movements a number of literary theoreticians were at work trying painstakingly to find a common ground, to reconcile somehow the Formalist emphasis on the artistic 'device' with Marxist dialectics. In these laboriously prepared concoctions the ratio between the two basic ingredients – the Formalist and the 'sociological' – varied depending on the individual critic's major emphasis. The attempts at synthesis ranged from a predominantly intrinsic approach to literature made 'respectable' by a protective cover of Marxist terminology, to a 'sociologism' tempered by awareness of esthetic considerations.

On the 'right wing'[50] of this synthetic spectrum one finds a young critic and literary theorist, A. Zeitlin. His article on "The Marxists and the Formalist Method", published in the *Lef* magazine in 1923,[51] was an able statement of a methodological position combining Marxist long-range objectives with a near-Formalist short-range program.

Zeitlin disapproved of 'hasty monistic raids' on literature by sociologists who were apparently impatient with literary values. Such ventures, he maintained, could result only in pseudo-sociological impressionism. He did not hesitate to take to task the authoritative but heavy-handed Marxist theoretician of literature V. Friče for reducing literary scholarship to a mere subdivision of social history. Quoting Friče's assertion that "literary works . . . translate socio-economic life into the language of peculiar symbolic signs",[52] Zeitlin deplored the fact that Friče had never attempted to inquire into the specific nature of these signs.

The same crudely monistic fallacy, argued Zeitlin, which was so apparent in Friče vitiated much recent Marxist critcism; a good example of this was provided by V. Pereverzev's study of Gogol'. In this monograph all the characteristics of Gogol''s literary art were deduced from the fact that he was a small landowner.

To be sure, continued Zeitlin, literary scholarship must take cognizance of social factors. The culmination of the critic's analytical efforts is a larger view, an act of synthesis, placing the phenomenon under

---

[50] See U. Foxt, "Problematika sovremennoj marksistskoj literatury", *Pečat' i revoljucija*, No. 2 (1927).

[51] A. Zeitlin (Cejtlin), "Marksisty i formal'nyj metod", *Lef*, III (1923).

[52] V. Friče, *Očerki* (quoted by A. Zeitlin).

consideration within a recognizable social context. However, at the present stage of Russian literary studies such a synthesis is not yet feasible. "There is no point", wrote Zeitlin, "in discussing the sociological implications of literary facts, as long as the facts themselves are not established." "Before one sets out to interpret an object of analysis", he continued, echoing what has by the time become a standard Formalist argument,[53] "one ought to delimit its area, to find out what it is. . . . Interpretation must be preceded by description." [54]

Hence the importance and the timeliness of the Formalist contribution. The *Opojaz* criticism, focussing on the close analysis of the text, on systematic description of literary facts, was breaking ground for a truly scientific study of Russian literature. The Formalists, declared Zeitlin, were the "engineer batallions of the army of Russian literary historians".[55]

Zeitlin's argument was virtually duplicated by M. Levidov, in his spirited contribution to a 1925 symposium called *Proletariat and Literature*.[56] Levidov's conclusion was rather unorthodox: "Only the joint efforts of the Formalist and the sociologist can produce a Marxist literary scholarship worthy of the name." [57]

Plainly, what Zeitlin and Levidov were arguing for was an interpretation of Marxian criticism flexible enough to accommodate some Formalist insights and techniques. A more ambitious effort was made by Boris Arvatov, a spokesman of the *Lef* (Left Front) group. His 'formalist-sociological method' was scarcely a compromise formula. Instead of seeking to bring together two widely divergent schools by reducing their respective claims, Arvatov advanced a new super-theory – a curious blend of militant Formalism and crude Marxism – and proudly advertised it as the last word of Marxist dialectics.

Apparently, this synthetic product was designed to serve as a rationale for the *Lef* – an offshoot, but hardly a replica, of the pre-revolutionary Futurist movement. Russian Futurism had come a long way since the carefree days of Bohemian brawls in literary cafés and of preoccupation with 'trans-sense language'. After 1917 it had grown in-

---

[53] In a representative Formalist study of the Russian byliny (A. P. Skaftymov, *Poètika i genezis bylin*, Saratov, 1924) one finds the following assertion: "Genetic study must be preceded by a static, descriptive one."
[54] "Marksisty i formal'nyj metod", p. 125.
[55] *Ibid.*, p. 131.
[56] Mixail Levidov, "Samoubijstvo literatury", *Proletariat i literatura* (Leningrad, 1925), pp. 160–169.
[57] *Ibid.*, p. 167.

creasingly ideologically and socially minded, intent on matching revolutionary form with an equally revolutionary content, and on active
participation in 'socialist construction'. In the neo-Futurist esthetics of
the *Lef,* passionate concern with the word, with formal experiment,
was wedded to the pragmatic slogan of the 'social command'.[58]

This dual emphasis was clearly reflected in Arvatov's position. He
was at one with *Opojaz* in insisting on the paramount importance of
craftsmanship. He warned against the tendency of many orthodox
Marxists to ignore or underestimate the role of fiction and convention
in imaginative literature. Not unlike Ejxenbaum and Šklovskij, Arvatov
saw in the work of literature neither a direct reflection of social reality
nor the creator's self-expression, but something artificially 'made' or
invented, a *sui generis* object (*vešč'*), produced by deliberately applying technical skill to a certain physical medium. In rejecting both
the 'naively realistic' and the 'psychologistic' view of art, Arvatov was
quite ready to echo the early Formalist slogan: "Art is a device."

However, in Arvatov's hands this proposition acquired a peculiarly
utilitarian twist. The *Lef* theorist managed to disengage the concept of
'device' from the correlative notion of the intended artistic effect. The
'formalist-sociological theory' discarded esthetic criteria as genteel and
obsolete. The "fetishism of esthetic devices, esthetic materials and
esthetic tools" [59] was contemptuously rejected. The ultra-Futurist debunking of the artist with a capital A, reinforced by 'ultra-leftist' insistence on the direct propaganda value of poetry, resulted in a purely
instrumentalist esthetics. Arvatov went so far as to deny any essential
difference between artistic creativity and other types of production.
Art became just another branch of 'industry'. Indeed, by confusing
two different meanings of the word 'art' (*iskusstvo*), Arvatov finally
identified artistic creation with skill, technical proficiency. "Art", he
declared, "should be regarded simply as the most efficacious organization in any field of human activity." [60]

In Arvatov's pragmatic theory of art 'social practice' was both the
ultimate touchstone and the causal determinant. Arvatov commended

[58] It might be worth noting that this key term of Soviet criticism originated with
the *Lef* group, which was often accused of revolutionary Bohemianism. The
slogan was subsequently appropriated by the critical hacks of the *On Guard* faction and thus became associated with the political regimentation of literature. To
the *Lef* spokesmen, however, 'social command' connoted not so much direct Party
controls over writers, as the spontaneous response of the poet to the social needs
of his epoch or of his class.
[59] Boris Arvatov, *Iskusstvo i proizvodstvo* (Moscow, 1926), pp. 98–99.
[60] *Ibid.*, p. 97.

the Formalists for having focussed attention on 'literary production', but took them to task for their failure to relate the process of 'making' poetry to the economic foundation of society. The "formalist-sociologists", he boasted, knew better than this. They were fully aware that the "material and form of a work of art are conditioned by the prevalent methods of its production and consumption",[61] and that the latter, in turn, are determined by the type of economy prevailing at the given period.

This mental shortcut from art to economics was made possible to a large degree by Arvatov's militant anti-psychologism – an attitude he shared with early Futurist and Formalist spokesmen. With such factors as the creator's personality or the psychology of his milieu dismissed as irrelevant, it seemed possible, indeed mandatory, to discuss the problem 'art and society' in purely technological, impersonal terms. Sociological analysis of the literary process was reduced to establishing a direct relation between two series of artifacts – the literary and the industrial, or more exactly, between two sets of techniques used respectively in producing these objects.

Thus, the emergence of rime in Western European poetry was, to Arvatov, an inevitable concomitant of the market economy, "a manifestation of bourgeois poetic labor, of individual consumption of verse and specialized poetic production",[62] attendant upon the breakdown of the feudal system. By the same token the rise of the novel as a distinct literary genre was related in Arvatov's scheme to the growth of the industrial bourgeoisie.

The 'formalist-sociological' theory of Arvatov's held little attraction for either Formalists or sociologists. The former took exception to Arvatov's crudely utilitarian view of art, the latter dissociated themselves emphatically from his "technological aberration".[63] Il'ja Gruzdëv, an able disciple of Šklovskij and Tynjanov and one of the leading spokesmen of the *Serapion Brotherhood*,[64] argued persuasively against Arvatov's tendency to equate 'art' with 'craft' and insisted on the autonomy of esthetic criteria. In an earlier essay Gruzdëv had stated his position as follows: "The essence of art lies in the organization of

---

[61] Boris Arvatov, "O formal'no-sociologičeskom metòde", *Pečat' i revoljucija,* III (1927), p. 64.
[62] *Ibid.,* p. 57.
[63] See U. Foxt, "Problematika sovremennoj marksistskoj literatury", *Pečat' i revoljucija,* II (1927), p. 86.
[64] See below, chapter VIII, pp. 150–153.

the material, irrespective of whether or not the object constructed out of this material serves any immediate practical purpose." [65]

A few years later U. Foxt, a Marxist critic with a strong bent toward social psychology, castigated Arvatov's theory as a sterile mixture of Formalism and Futurism in an article in which he drew up a balance sheet of the critical debates of the mid-twenties.[66] While rejecting categorically Arvatov's extravagances, Foxt likewise had little use for more modest synthetic schemes. A strong believer in 'sociological monism', he felt that the Marxist student of literature had little to learn from a school so thoroughly alien to the spirit of dialectics as *Opojaz*.

If Foxt was at one with Lunačarskij and Kogan in assuming the basic incompatibility of Formalism and Marxism, he was less sanguine, or complacent, than were most orthodox stalwarts about the results heretofore achieved by Marxist criticism. He felt keenly that a purely extraneous approach to literature was inadequate. He realized that the Formalist challenge could be met not by dodging the question of the specific characteristics of literary art raised by *Opojaz*, but by coming to grips with this crucial problem. "Marxist literary scholarship", Foxt wrote candidly, "cannot as yet meet the Formalists on their own grounds; it lacks a well worked out system of literary concepts; it does not yet have its own poetics." [67]

It was this desire to carry the attack to the 'enemy', by evolving within a broader sociological framework a typology of poetic forms and devices, that provided the impetus behind the most extended and scholarly critique of *Opojaz* ever undertaken by a Marxist – the study of *The Formalist Method in Literary Scholarship* by P. N. Medvedev.[68]

The very subtitle of this earnest book, "A Critical Introduction to Sociological Poetics" indicates a constructive approach to the problem. Like Foxt, Medvedev was aware that there was little point in trying to "establish the correspondence between certain poetic styles and certain economic styles",[69] without elucidating first the concept of 'poetic style' and cognate literary categories.

[65] See Il'ja Gruzdëv, *Utilitarnost' i samocel'* (Petrograd, 1923) (quoted from *Sovremennaja kritika*, Leningrad, 1925, p. 248).
[66] See footnote 63.
[67] *Ibid.,* p. 91.
[68] Pavel Medvedev, *Formal'nyj metod v literaturovedenii* (Leningrad, 1928)
[69] The above is an excerpt from V. Friče's formula of sociological poetics (cf. "Problemy sociologičeskoj poètiki", *Vestnik Kommunističeskoj Akademii*, XVII, 1926, p. 169; quoted by P. Medvedev in *Formal'nyj metod. . . .*).

Whether Medvedev was successful in this undertaking is quite another matter. He started from the correct premise that literature is a social phenomenon *sui generis,* but he failed to achieve a workable balance between the two components of this definition. He could not resolve, apparently, the seeming conflict between the interest in the 'social' aspect of literature – its relatedness to other fields of human activity – and the equally legitimate concern with the unique features of literary art. Medvedev's attempt at a 'sociological poetics' seems to have been inhibited by his fear of lapsing into the 'immanent' fallacy of his opponents. Often, while trying to define such basic terms of poetics as rhythm, style and genre, he would suddenly 'pull out' only to fall back on the initial proposition about the "thoroughly social nature of . . . all poetic structures", a formulation so broad as to be almost meaningless.

But whatever the shortcomings of Medvedev's positive program, he did accomplish an important negative task: he made a strong case for the necessity of going beyond the a-social poetics of pure Formalism and the a-literary sociologism of crude Marxists.

The precarious slogan of 'sociological poetics', suggested by Foxt and cautiously probed by Medvedev, marked a watershed between two fundamentally different undercurrents in Marxist-Leninist criticism.

Soviet Marxist literary theorizing of the twenties was not a monolithic body of thought. At the time when a *bona fide* methodological discussion was still possible, the Marxian approach to literature proved susceptible of widely divergent interpretations. This differentiation – while, in one sense, a proof that the official doctrine had not yet hardened into a rigid dogma – was closely bound up with the inclusive character of Marxist dialectics. As a general theory of social evolution, historical materialism did not solve, nor could it be expected to solve, the specific problems of individual humanistic disciplines. While it assumed the ultimate causal dependence of 'ideological' phenomena, such as art, science, philosophy, religion, on the economic process, the Marxist doctrine in its original form has neither precluded nor specifically encouraged inquiry into the forces operating within the particular field of culture. The problems which had to do with the meaning of the ideological construct in terms of the given realm of 'ideology' remained unanswered by Marxism, though not necessarily unanswerable within its framework. To borrow an apt metaphor from A. Kazin,[70] dialectical

---

[70]   See Alfred Kazin, *On Native Grounds* (New York, 1942), p. 413.

materialism became a vast filing-cabinet the particular compartments of which were still waiting to be filled with appropriate studies. The state of the 'compartments', reserved for the study of literature, hinged largely on the Marxist critic's resourcefulness and acumen, on the degree of flexibility and common sense he was prone to exhibit in applying the Marxian tenets to his particular discipline.

Thus, as long as it was possible to disagree openly on fundamentals, the heated controversy as to what represented the truly Marxist conception of literature raged unabated. The points of difference were many. But of particular methodological significance was the debate revolving around the problem of 'sociological poetics'. The discussion of this controversial concept pointed up what Jakobson correctly described as the basic ambiguity of Marxist literary theorizing, oscillating uneasily between a purely genetic and a quasi-structural approach to literature.[71]

The 'geneticists' were quite content with probing the social derivation of the literary work, with translating, to use Friče's terminology, the 'literary signs' back into the language of sociology and economics. The structure-minded Marxists sought to combine a sociological synthesis of literary facts and literary evolution with an intrinsic analysis. They felt with Zeitlin that in order to be able to explain a phenomenon one ought first to find out what it was.

To more rigid exponents of Marxism-Leninism, this latter question seemed irrelevant, if not illicit. Where causality was seen as the only legitimate frame of reference, the problems of the nature and function of literary creation were overshadowed, if not submerged, by the overriding concern with its origins, the 'underlying' social forces. Thus, V. Pereverzev, a critic more interested in textual analysis than most of his colleagues but unduly narrow in his methodological pronouncements, maintained that the 'teleological value of a device' cannot be understood without a genetic explanation. One cannot answer the question

---

[71] In an article, published in 1929 (cf. "Über die heutigen Voraussetzungen der russischen Slavistik", *Slavische Rundschau*, I, 1929), R. Jakobson showed how the controversy between geneticism and structuralism, rending twentieth-century European sholarship, found its way into Slavic studies, presumably guided by Marxist-Leninist methodology. In the Soviet Union as well as in Western Europe, Jakobson observed correctly, one could discern in the 1920's two distinct trends: "the structuralist one, inquiring into the immanent laws of the system ... and analyzing the components of this system from the standpoint of their functions ... and the genetic method which sought to explain the phenomena of the same order in terms of another series." (p. 64).

'what for' without answering the question 'why'.[72] Percov put it even more drastically: "I cannot visualize a Marxist raising the question of 'how this work of literature is constructed?' without this question being immediately superseded by another question: Why is this work of literature constructed in this way and not another?" [73] Having thus completely dissolved the 'what' and the 'how' of critical analysis in the 'why,' Percov went on to reject the very concept of "Marxist poetics" as a contradiction in terms, as an "oxymoron".[74]

The debate on Formalism had dramatized a split in the official camp, more essential than many terminological and pseudo-philosophical squabbles which often held the center of the stage. Most Marxist theoreticians were fairly unanimous in rejecting the *Opojaz* doctrine, but their arguments, as shown above, differed substantially. By focussing sharply on the specific aims and methods of literary scholarship, the Formalists had induced their Marxian opponents to get off the high horse of dialectical generalizations and take a stand on concrete problems connected with literary studies. In the process of doing so the Soviet Marxist critics voiced widely divergent views on the limits and capabilities of the genetic method of approach to the study of literature.

If the Formalist challenge compelled the Marxists to clarify their methodological position and, in part, to recognize the limitations of their doctrine, the reverse of this is also true. The showdown with Marxism had a visible impact upon the subsequent evolution of the Formalist movement. This influence would have been more fertile had the attack been conducted along more constructive lines. The Marxist criticisms of *Opojaz* were for the most part too crude and indiscriminately hostile (Kogan, Poljanskij, Lunačarskij), or else too mechanistic (Arvatov), to yield, or suggest, any positive solutions. But the very vigor of the assault and the persistence of the charges of esthetic isolationism had dramatized the need for a re-examination of the initial *Opojaz* position on the vital issue of 'literature versus society'.

---

[72] F. Pereverzev, *Tvorčestvo Gogolja* (Leningrad, 1926), p. 10.
[73] V. Percov, "K voprosu ob edinoj marksistskoj nauke o literature", *Literaturnaja gazeta,* April 14, 1930.
[74] *Ibid.*

VII. CRISIS AND ROUT (1926–1930)

1

The charge of denying the impact of society upon literature, leveled against the Formalists by their Marxist opponents, was only partly justified. Šklovskij's often quoted dictum, "Art was always free of life" [1] need not be taken too literally. As indicated above,[2] this was a deliberately exaggerated claim aimed to increase the 'bargaining power' of *Opojaz* and to shock the critical Philistines.

Even in the early stage of *Opojaz* its spokesmen were at least vaguely aware that literature is not produced in a vacuum. In their more sober moments they would not deny the relevance of social considerations. Some of their flamboyant rhetoric notwithstanding, the Formalist theoreticians were far from certain that art is nothing but a device. They felt, however, that it is the 'device' which ought to be the prime concern of literary scholarship as a distinct intellectual discipline. Formalist a-sociologism was a matter of methodological expediency rather than of esthetic principle, a proposition about the critic's main sphere of interest rather than about the nature of literary art.[3]

It is in these pragmatic terms that Šklovskij described his technological approach to literature in the introduction to his collection of essays, *On The Theory of Prose*.[4] After having acknowledged in passing the influence of social conditions on language, both ordinary and poetic, he went on to say: "In my theoretical work I have been concerned

---

[1]   Viktor Šklovskij, *Xod konja* (Berlin-Moscow, 1923), p. 39.
[2]   See above, chapter IV, footnote 47 (p. 77).
[3]   It was a sign of the philosophical immaturity of the Formalist School that most of its spokesmen failed to distinguish clearly between these two types of propositions and glided almost imperceptibly from the postulate that, for the purposes of literary scholarship, 'art ought to be regarded as a device' to the ontological statement that art *is* a device.
[4]   Viktor Šklovskij, *O teorii prozy* (Moscow, 1925).

with the internal laws of literature. To use an industrial metaphor, I am not interested in the condition of the world cotton market or in the policies of the trusts, but solely in the count of yarn and the weaving techniques."[5]

To proclaim one's lack of interest in the 'world cotton market' of 'the policies of the trusts' was undoubtedly a more justifiable procedure than to deny flatly the existence or relevance of these factors. But exclusive preoccupation with 'weaving techniques', whether a matter of philosophical belief or critical tactics, was in the long run an untenable position, as it implied narrowing down arbitrarily the scope of literary research. Isolating one particular aspect of the investigated object in order to bring all the mental resources of a critical movement to bear on a largely neglected set of problems, may have been up to a certain point a legitimate, indeed a rewarding, methodological device.[6] But it was too artificial a procedure to withstand sustained scrutiny. The purely intrinsic view of literature failed conspicuously to do justice to the close interdependence of various domains of culture; it seemed to ignore, in Trockij's words, "the psychological unity of the social man who creates and who consumes what has been created".[7]

Thus, as time went by, the Formalist spokesmen were bound to move beyond their initial position, the more so since its limitations were revealed by current developments in the fields of criticism and of creative writing. The 'official' literary theorists scorned the 'methodological sterility' of the *Opojaz* doctrine. More friendly critics such as Majakovskij, while praising warmly the *Opojaz* contribution to poetics, urged their Formalist friends to pay more heed to social considerations.[8] More important still, the tremendous impact of the revolutionary upheaval upon the tempo, tenor and modes of literary production provided the Formalists with an incontrovertible proof that art is *not* free from life.

One of the first symptoms of the Formalist's growing tendency toward 'sociologism' is found in Šklovskij's autobiography, *The Third Factory* (1926).[9] This book – a peculiar blend of literary theorizing and soul-

[5] *Ibid.*, p. 6.
[6] Some of the more fair-minded among the Marxist opponents of Formalism were willing to admit that much (*cf.* E. Mustangova, "Put' naibol'šego soprotivlenija", *Zvezda*, No. 3, 1928).
[7] *Cf.* Leon Trotsky, *Literature and Revolution* (New York, 1925), p. 171.
[8] "Every flea-rime has to be counted", wrote Majakovskij with his characteristically coarse bluntness, "but stop counting fleas in a vacuum" (*Lef*, No. 1, 1923, p. 11).
[9] Viktor Šklovskij, *Tret'ja fabrika* (Moscow, 1926).

searching – was indicative of an acute spiritual and methodological crisis. In Šklovskij's deliberately disjointed meanderings there stood revealed a bewildered and bewildering mind, oscillating uneasily between a frantic effort to get in step with the 'pressure of the times' and an equally sincere desire to preserve its creative and critical integrity.

On the methodological plane *The Third Factory* was clearly an attempt to reach beyond 'pure' Formalism toward a position more inclusive and more congruent with the 'social demands' of the time. Writing in a somewhat confessional vein, Šklovskij pleaded guilty of having ignored the 'extra-esthetic series' (*rjad*). This, he admitted, was a grave error: "changes in art can and do occur on account of extra-esthetic factors, whether because a given language was influenced by another language or because a new social demand has arisen." [10]

The phrasing was rather slipshod (apparently, Šklovskij could be pungent only when he was extravagant). But the general intent of the passage quoted was clear enough: there is no unbridgeable chasm, indeed, no fixed boundary, between literature and 'life,' between the esthetic and the non-esthetic.

This thesis – obviously a far cry from the ivory-tower estheticism of which the Formalists were so often accused – was designed to perform a double function. On the one hand, it provided an excuse for recourse to certain 'non-literary' criteria in critical analysis. On the other, like most of Šklovskij's critical generalizations, the new formula was to serve as a rationale for the trends in current literary practice with which Šklovskij chose to associate himself.

The post-Civil War period was marked by a vigorous growth of documentary literature. Even though narrative fiction, after a temporary eclipse, had begun to come into its own, the time for large epic panoramas was still far ahead. The hectic pace of events favored brevity. A turbulent actuality, which often made invention seem pale and superfluous, encouraged 'straight reporting'. With the newspaper becoming a powerful channel of literary communication, as well as a medium of political propaganda, semi-journalistic genres, such as reportage and the feuilleton or feuilleton-like short story, achieved increasing prominence.

In keeping with their utilitarian esthetics,[11] the *Lef* theorists welcomed enthusiastically this development and hailed 'factography'

---

[10]   *Ibid.*, p. 96.
[11]   See above, chapter VI, pp. 111–113.

(*literatura fakta*) as a perfect example of the integration of literature with life. Šklovskij, always ready to applaud a radical deviation from literary tradition, joined his neo-Futurist friends in praising these 'half-finished literary products' as a new departure in Russian prose.

One may wonder how Šklovskij managed to reconcile his enthusiasm for reportage with a literary theory which saw the chief aim of art in the creative deformation of reality. The fact of the matter is that Šklovskij's theorizing was often more ingenious than consistent. There are periods in the history of literature, he argued, when age-old esthetic formulae lose their effectiveness, when traditional art forms such as the novel seem to have exhausted their potentialities. At such moments literature, threatened with paralysis, must reach beyond itself in order to recover its vitality: it must "invade non-literature",[12] by drawing into its orbit 'raw materials of life', by making use of 'extra-esthetic' designs. Where narrative fiction wears out, it is often the "unadorned fact that is perceived esthetically".[13]

It would be an oversimplification to see in this reasoning merely a *tour de force*, a piece of special pleading. Up to a certain point Šklovskij's apology for factography is made methodologically plausible by the ultra-relativistic position of the Formalist School. Even though the Formalists focussed sharply on the specific properties of literature, they took pains to avoid defining this differentia as an absolute, immutable essence. In his closely reasoned article on "The Literary Fact",[14] Tynjanov warned against static, *a priori* definitions of literary phenomena and insisted that, while at any given moment a clear distinction can be made between what is and what is not literature, "the notion of literature changes all the time".[15] The boundary between literature and life is fluid – it shifts from period to period. "Literature", Tynjanov said, "never mirrors life, but it often overlaps with it." [16]

Tynjanov illustrated his thesis about 'overlapping' and cross-fertilization of literature and 'mores' (*byt*) by citing a number of relevant examples from the Russian literary past. Sometimes, he observed, a literary phenomenon may become a marginal 'fact of life'. The eighteenth-century Russian ode had degenerated into the so-called *šinel'-nye stixi* – versified petitions addressed to high officials and written in

12   *Tret'ja fabrika*, p. 99.
13   Viktor Šklovskij, *Gamburgskij ščët* (Moscow, 1928), p. 19.
14   *Cf.* Jurij Tynjanov, *Arxaisty i novatory* (Leningrad, 1929).
15   *Ibid.*, p. 9.
16   Jurij Tynjanov, *Arxaisty i novatory*, p. 15.

a pseudo-elevated and archaic style. Conversely, a document, an account of an authentic event, may at a certain point be raised to the status of literature. That is what happened during the period of Russian sentimentalism to such 'sub-literary' genres as memoirs and diaries. Even letter-writing felt the impact of literary norms: Karamzin, the leading historian and prose-writer of the time, set out to compose a manual of epistolary style.[17]

Clearly, the moral to be drawn from these shrewd observations was that in his inquiry into literary dynamics the historian of literature could ill afford to ignore the 'contiguous' facts of social life.

Šklovskij, more given to slogan-like formulae, and, in spite of his truculence, more responsive to the *Zeitgeist* than was Tynjanov, hastened to translate this proposition into ultra-Marxian terms. Under his hands the impact of social environment on the literary process became largely a matter of the writer's 'class allegiance'.

Šklovskij's emerging 'socio-formalist' approach, pitting esthetic conventions against class ideology, was tested in his study *Materials and Style in Lev Tolstoj's War and Peace* (1928).[18] Tolstoj's epic is analyzed here in terms of the tension between 'class' and 'genre'.

To Šklovskij *War and Peace* is a resultant of a clash between the novel as an art form – inherited and revitalized by Tolstoj – and the 'social command' which he undertook to fulfill in his panorama of Russia in 1812. *War and Peace,* argued Šklovskij, is not an accurate historical novel, but 'the canonization of a legend.' In order to counteract, he continued, the ideological offensive of the radical plebeian intelligentsia (*raznočincy*) and to bolster the badly shaken morale of the landowning class, Tolstoj had undertaken the apotheosis of the Russian nobility and the part it had played in the '*Fatherland War*' of 1812. He minimized the Russian defeats and magnified the victories, he sugarcoated or ignored the bitter historical truths, such as the apathy of the peasant masses in the face of the invasion and their sullen, if not openly rebellious, attitude toward the landowners.

At some point, however, Šklovskij asserted, the novelist's 'pragmatic orientation' (*celevaja ustanovka*),[19] crisscrossed with the "line of genre – of certain literary traditions, narrative techniques, habits, etc.". If Tolstoj's class bias compelled him to distort or color historical truth,

---

[17]   *Ibid.*
[18]   Viktor Šklovskij, *Material i stil' v romane L'va Tolstogo Vojna i mir* (Moscow, 1928).
[19]   One of the favorite terms of *Lef* criticism.

this deformation was in turn deformed and modified by the exigencies of the medium which Tolstoj chose to employ.[20]

The way in which Šklovskij, by-passing the cumbersome problem of the creative personality, proceeded to establish a direct relation between class and genre is a testimony to his resourcefulness as well as to the makeshift quality of his constructions. Tolstoj, argued Šklovskij, set out to write his apology for early nineteenth-century Russia in the form of a fairly traditional novel. However, his desire to give a comprehensive and allegedly authentic picture of Russian society in 1812 led Tolstoj to push aside the limits of the genre by introducing various historical and quasi-historical materials. The compositional ties of the novel were loosened up, as a giant, panoramic chronicle with a constantly shifting focus was substituted for a more closely-knit type of novel, centering around individual destiny.

The same desire to create an illusion of authenticity, closely related to the novel's polemical intent, resulted in a wealth of ultra-realistic detail in the portrayal of historic figures. It so happened, however, that the emphasis on the homely was an outstanding trait of the radical prose fiction of the time – the novel of social protest, given to debunking traditional values by means of a 'deglamorizing' (*snižajuščaja*) psychological vivisection. Thus, in the mind of many contemporary readers, *War and Peace* became associated precisely with the type of writing the influence of which it sought to challenge.[21]

Under the impact of this false analogy, argued Šklovskij, the general tenor of the novel was largely misjudged. It was interpreted by most contemporaries, even the astute critic Straxov, as a liberal satire rather than a conservative apologia.[22] The 'genre' had asserted its autonomy. The 'device' had backfired. The style and mode of characterization 'demanded' by the writer's ideological purpose, through the medium of autonomous literary associations had turned against this design and given rise to an interpretation which was the direct opposite of that intended by Tolstoj.

Apart from some interesting if not always convincing confrontations, and a number of incisive remarks on narrative techniques employed

[20] *Material i stil'* ... (Moscow, 1928), p. 237.
[21] *Ibid.*
[22] One may note that the above interpretation did not represent Straxov's definitive assessment of *War and Peace*. In a passage quoted by Ernest J. Simmons (*Leo Tolstoy*, Boston, Mass., 1946, p. 274), Straxov speaks of Tolstoj's epic as "a complete picture of Russia of that time", indeed a "complete picture of human life" rather than merely a satirical portrayal of Russian society in 1812.

in *War and Peace,* Šklovskij's discussion of the epic strikes one as
farfetched and unduly streamlined: it leaves out more than it includes.
The above explanation, for instance, of what D. S. Mirsky calls 'the
homely effects . . . of realism' [23] in *War and Peace,* if not altogether
false, is singularly narrow. One could plausibly argue that this attention
to the trivial is to be attributed not so much to Tolstoj's polemic with
historians of the 1812 campaign as to his struggle against traditional
conception of history – to his determination to strip the 'hero' of romantic glamor and bring him down to human, homely proportions.
One could also add that the playing up of the physical detail, for
instance, the famous upper lip of Princess Bolkonskij was a typical
Tolstoyan mode of characterization, indicative of that passionate interest in the human body which was insisted upon by critics so different
as D. S. Merežkovskij and Stefan Zweig.[24]

In analyzing the novel's underlying philosophy, Šklovskij is also
guilty of oversimplification. While his emphasis on the patriotic apologetics and conservative 'archaism' of *War and Peace* comes closer to the
truth than the numerous attempts to interpret the novel in terms of
liberal populism or anti-patriotic debunking, Šklovskij's formula fails
signally to do justice to the complexity of Tolstoj's attitude toward the
world he portrayed. Perhaps it is this complexity and the determination
of all too many critics to ignore it that is responsible in a large degree
for the widely divergent readings of *War and Peace.* Some of Tolstoj's
contemporaries may have been 'misguided' by formal analogies with
the Russian radical novel of social protest. But this could hardly be
the case with the modern American writer, James T. Farrell. And yet
he, too, in a recent essay,[25] spoke of *War and Peace* as an incisive
critique of Russian feudal nobility.

Šklovskij's study of *War and Peace* of 1928 brought into focus the
limitations of his new critical method. The dynamic interaction between
'class' and 'genre' was potentially a more relevant frame of reference
than the one-way causal dependence of literature upon society. Unfortunately, the crucial concept of tension was, as it were, taken too
literally. It was projected from the object of analysis into its method.
The sociological and formal categorieš were mechanically superimposed
on each other rather than integrated, which produces often the im-

---

[23]   D. S. Mirsky, *Contemporary Russian Literature* (New York, 1926), p. 12.
[24]   *Cf.* D. S. Merežkovskij, *Tolstoj i Dostoevskij* (Petersburg, 1914); Stefan Zweig,
Drei Dichter ihres Lebens (Leipzig, 1918).
[25]   *Cf.* James T. Farrell, *Literature and Morality* (New York, 1947).

pression of a critical tug-of-war. Šklovskij got caught between militant Formalism and a somewhat ill-digested Marxism. Thus, in an article written in 1930,[26] he could refer to *War and Peace* as an "abortive attempt at a nobleman's *agitka*" [27] – a term reserved in Soviet parlance for a piece of crude political propaganda posing as literature and thus singularly inappropriate in this context. On the other hand, he could still advance a thesis which in spite of its Marxian verbiage represented a *sui generis* Formalist determinism: "the mode of existence of the literary *genre* determines in the last analysis the writer's consciousness".[28] Oscillation between two rigid and thus essentially incompatible monistic schemes was scarcely a substitute for a workable synthesis.

2

Šklovskij was not the only *Opojaz* leader who essayed a synthesis of the Formalist and the sociological approach. Another, more cautious attempt at a methodological compromise was made by B. Ejxenbaum in his article, "Literature and Literary Mores" (1927).[29] Ejxenbaum shared Šklovskij's and Tynjanov's increasing dissatisfaction with the purely intrinsic approach to literature. At the same time he was wary of the official brand of sociologism. He eschewed both the study of the writer's class ideology and the tendency to deduce literary forms from the socio-economic structure. "To seek out", he wrote, "the prime causes of literary forms and literary evolution is sheer metaphysics." [30]

Intent on sticking as closely as possible to the literary facts, Ejxenbaum had little use for social 'determinants' of literature so remote as the 'productive forces'. He proposed to focus instead on a more pertinent social area – one whose relation to imaginative writing could actually be established rather than baldly postulated. According to Ejxenbaum, it was the 'literary mores' (*literaturnyj byt*) that provide the most natural bridge between literary studies and sociology.

The term 'literary mores' which played a crucial part in Ejxenbaum's writings during the late twenties designated a cluster of problems

[26] *Cf.* Viktor Šklovskij, "Pamjatnik naučnoj ošibke", *Literaturnaja gazeta,* 27, I (1930).
[27] The word 'abortive', which suggests, apparently, that *War and Peace* 'ultimately' became something else, or more, than a mere '*agitka*', can hardly save this unfortunate formulation.
[28] *Material i stil'*, p. 199.
[29] Boris Ejxenbaum, "Literatura i literaturnyj byt", *Na literaturnom postu,* 1927, later published in B. Ejxenbaum, *Moj vremennik* (Leningrad, 1929).
[30] *Moj vremennik,* p. 54.

bearing on the writer's social status, such as the relations between the literary artist and his public, the conditions of his work, the scope and mechanism of the literary market. Here, insisted Ejxenbaum, was a proper field of inquiry for a literary critic willing to take account of socio-economic considerations, insofar as the apply to the literary scene. To give an example, he continued, Puškin's iambic tetrameter bears no relation whatsoever to the mode of production prevailing at the time, but Puškin's shift to prose and to journalism can be intelligibly traced to the growing professionalization of Russian letters, the emergence of great literary reviews, etc.[31]

Ejxenbaum's new position was a curious attempt at an 'immanent' sociology. Instead of literary scholarship becoming a subdivision of social history, as was the case with some Marxist theoreticians, sociology was injected here into literature, translated, as it were, into literary terms. Literature was considered not so much as an integral part of the social fabric, a resultant of external social forces, but as a social institution, an economic system in its own right. The writer appeared not as a member of a certain social class in the Marxian sense of this term, whether gentry, bourgeoisie or proletariat, but first and foremost as a representative of the literary profession. Where a Pereverzev was concerned with the artist's social provenience and its impact upon his work, Ejxenbaum was concerned with his condition *qua* writer. Where the former was apt to wonder whether the ideology embodied in the given work of literature was that of the small landowner or of the merchant class, Ejxenbaum would want to know if the author were producing for an anonymous market or for a limited number of connoisseurs, if he were an aristocratic dilletante or a professional, depending on writing for his livelihood.

An interesting aspect of Ejxenbaum's article on 'literary mores' was the way in which he tried to validate his emphasis on the conditions of writing. The case for his new 'working hypothesis' was only partly stated in methodological terms. The basic inadequacy of the initial Formalist premises and the proximity of literary economics were not the only factors invoked in order to justify this departure from Formalism 'pure and simple'. It was presumably also the change in the literary situation that made it imperative for the literary scholar to focus sharply on the profession of letters.

To use Toynbee's terminology, Ejxenbaum's new conception was a critic's response to a contemporary literary challenge. If Šklovskij's new

[31] *Ibid.,* p. 56.

emphasis on 'extra-esthetic factors' was bound up with his attempt at a theoretical justification of neo-Futurism, Ejxenbaum's theory of 'literary mores' was frankly an effort to erect into a law of literary sociology the predicament of the Russian writer in the late twenties.

Ejxenbaum stated this motivation in no uncertain terms. Early Formalism, he asserted, was born at a time when literary controversy centered around the type of art to be created, the type of poetic language to be used. Today, he continued, it is the problem of literary mores that holds the center of the stage. The question 'how to write?' is overshadowed by another query: 'how to be a writer?'.[32]

Some of the implications of this remark are spelled out in a surprisingly candid essay of Ejxenbaum's, written in 1929.[33] "A writer", he said pointedly, "cuts today a rather grotesque figure. He is by definition inferior to the average reader, since the latter, as a professional citizen, is assumed to have a consistent, stable and clear-cut ideology. As for our reviewers – critics we do not have any more, since no differences of opinion are permissible – they are certain to be infinitely superior to, and more important than, the writer in the same way in which the judge is always superior to, and more important than, the defendant." [34]

Ejxenbaum's intransigent remarks pointed up the fact that his preoccupation with literary mores was more than a purely academic matter. In the grim context of the growing political regimentation of literature the question 'how to be a writer' acquired an almost tragic poignancy.

Ejxenbaum's venture into sociology elicited a favorable response among most of his associates and disciples. Šklovskij seized eagerly upon his friend's formula and hailed the theory of 'literary mores' as a solid contribution to a truly scientific study of the literary process, indeed, as the most legitimate type of sociological inquiry into literature. The "professional sociologists", he snapped, are apparently too busy writing popular syllabuses to address themselves to their 'proper' job – that of studying the literary market.[35]

---

[32] *Moj vremennik,* p. 51.
[33] The essay appeared in *Moj vremennik* (Leningrad, 1929), a one-man magazine, mixing freely criticism, reminiscences, creative writing and journalism. The non-conformist tenor of this topical soliloquy was more than a Soviet censor in 1929 could tolerate. Ejxenbaum's unique 'periodical' had to be discontinued.
[34] *Ibid.,* p. 49.
[35] "V zaščitu sociologičeskogo metoda", *Novyj Lef,* 1927, No. 4 (later published in Šklovskij's *Gamburgskij ščët,* Moscow, 1928).

Ejxenbaum's and Šklovskij's ideas about literary economics provided the impetus behind a full-length study of the commercial aspect of the Puškin era, undertaken by three young Formalist researchers, T. Gric, V. Trenin and N. Nikitin. Their book, *Literature and Commerce* (1927),[36] discussed in minute and often tedious detail the *modus operandi* of the Smirdin publishing house which, during the first half of the nineteenth century, well-nigh dominated the Russian literary market. The impact of this business enterprise on the tempo and distribution of Russian literary productions and on the writers' financial situation was illustrated by an impressive array of facts and figures, sometimes quite revealing, but thrown together without any discernible attempt at integration.

The 'professional sociologists', that is, the orthodox Marxists, challenged by Šklovskij, were not impressed. In an article published in a symposium on *Literature and Marxism*,[37] A. Zeitlin, who by this time had managed to live down his inital pro-Formalist bias, attacked *Literature and Commerce* as chaotic, sloppy, and irrelevant. "In this book", he wrote bitingly, "one can find commerce, but one would look in vain for literature." "Sociology of Puškin's style", he charged, "is supplanted here by an inept sociology of the printing presses on which his works were published." [38]

Another participant in the symposium, S. Breitburg, was less caustic but equally critical of the "shift in Formalism".[39] He claimed that Ejxenbaum's theory of 'literary mores' was simply watered-down Formalism. The concessions to the causalist viewpoint were half-hearted and essentially 'tactical', as the critic justified the use of some 'relevant' extra-literary categories by invoking the historical circumstances, the literary situation and the like. Even though, continued Breitburg, the new version of the Formalist method avoids some of the most glaring fallacies of the early *Opojaz*, it spells methodological regression rather than progress. "A shift away from monism, even idealistic monism, to pluralism means moving one step away from a truly scientific approach to literature." [40]

These criticisms seem unduly harsh and high-handed. One gets the impression that Zeitlin and Breitburg resented the intrusion of non-Marxists into what they considered an exclusive domain of 'dialectical

[36]   T. Gric, N. Nikitin, V. Trenin, *Slovesnost' i kommercija* (Moscow, 1927).
[37]   *Literatura i marksizm*, Vol. I (Moscow, 1929).
[38]   *Ibid.*, pp. 167, 169.
[39]   S. Breitburg, "Sdvig v formalizme", *Literatura i marksizm*, I.
[40]   *Ibid.*, p. 45.

materialism' and did not bother to examine more closely the hypotheses of the 'amateur sociologists'. As a good many Occidental literary theorists would readily acknowledge,[41] the problems of the literary profession, of the writer's social status, constitute an entirely legitimate area of inquiry, indeed, an area promising an appreciably higher degree of verifiability than, let us say, the attempts to explain the composition of *The Dead Souls* from the mode of living of the small landowner. The Soviet Marxist critics were scarcely justified in their disdain for the Formalists' dabbling in sociology. Whatever one may think of pedestrian studies in 'literature and commerce', their cognitive value was greater than that of the 'sociological' label-mongering and mental shortcuts from economics to poetics which vitiated so much of Marxist-Leninist critical practice.

And yet Breitburg's strictures were not wholly without foundation. As a solution to the problem of 'literature versus society' Ejxenbaum's concept of 'literary mores' was clearly inadequate. The attempt to reduce the interaction between the writer and his social environment to the mechanism of the literary market was indicative of an unduly narrow empiricism, which evaded broader problems and tended increasingly to bog down in pure 'research'. The very fact that a work such as *Literature and Commerce,* a collection of largely undigested data, could be heralded by some Formalist spokesmen as a new departure in the study of literature was in itself a significant and somewhat disquieting symptom.

The efforts of Šklovskij, Ejxenbaum and their disciples to do away with esthetic separatism were *per se* a heartening phenomenon. Unfortunately, what was gained in breadth of view was lost in sharpness of focus, in clarity of theoretical formulations. The 'shift in Formalism' meant not so much a moving towards a more inclusive and flexible critical scheme as a piecemeal, haphazard retreat from an obviously untenable position.

This impression of drift is reinforced by the theoretical passages from the first volume of Ejxenbaum's broadly conceived monograph, *Lev Tolstoj* (1928). This work, regarded by many authorities as one of the most solid contributions to the study of Tolstoj, differed markedly in its method and scope from Ejxenbaum's earlier historical studies, written in the period of militant Formalism. In such works as *The Young Tolstoj* (1923) or *Lermontov* (1924), biographical material was virtually

[41] *Cf.* René Wellek and Austin Warren, *Theory of Literature* (New York, 1949), pp. 93–97.

excluded. In the first volume of *Lev Tolstoj*, dated 1928, Ejxenbaum partly reverted to the traditional pattern of a critical monograph, where the writer's work is discussed against the background of, and in close conjunction with, his life.

It is true, as Ejxenbaum himself was quick to point out, that his concern with Tolstoj's biography was a far cry from that favorite target of *Opojaz* critics – preoccupation with biographical detail for its own sake. The writer's life interested Ejxenbaum only to the extent that it was related to his literary career. The focus of attention here was Tolstoj's 'literary behavior' – the role he played in the literary life of his times, his relations with his fellow writers, his attitudes toward contemporary literary groupings.

Thus, one finds in Ejxenbaum's new study of Tolstoj, along with revealing observations on the literary influences which shaped his style and world-view, a vivid portrayal of Tolstoj's conflicts with the plebeian radicals grouped around the magazine *Contemporary,* as well as with the more genteel liberal intellectuals of the Turgenev variety. Tolstoj's retreat into the splendid isolation of Jasnaja Poljana was interpreted as a challenge to the editorial offices and publishing houses of literary Petersburg, as a symbol of supreme aloofness from the social forces which shaped the *belles lettres* of his day. Tolstoj's famous residence, where, far away from the hustle and bustle of the metropolitan literary market, he wrote his masterpieces and conducted his educational experiments, was in itself, according to Ejxenbaum, "a peculiar form of literary mores and of literary production".[42]

This socio-biographical departure from the pure Formalist canon was complicated by what might be called an ideological deviation. Tolstoj's quarrels with his confrères, such as Černyševskij or Turgenev, were not merely a matter of personal incompatibility or of literary rivalry. They were often precipitated by ideological disagreement. Thus, in analyzing Tolstoj's 'literary behavior', Ejxenbaum felt compelled to take account of his pattern of thought to a much larger extent than was the case with the more consistently Formalist study, *The Young Tolstoj*. Not only Tolstoj's general attitudes – his anti-intellectualism, his instinctive revulsion from modern civilization, but also his positons on such specific issues as the emancipation of the peasants came in for extended treatment.

One would be ill advised to deplore this attention to ideology. No account of Tolstoj's heritage would be reasonably complete which

[42] Boris Ejxenbaum, *Lev Tolstoj,* I, 392.

would ignore these problems. But, while one may only rejoice in this broadening of Ejxenbaum's critical vision, the reasoning behind the inclusion of the 'non-esthetic materials' fails to carry conviction.

Apparently Ejxenbaum was concerned lest his pluralism be interpreted as methodological inconsistency, if not 'capitulation'. There is nothing wrong, he argued somewhat defensively, with modifying one's initial position. Evolution of a doctrine is a natural and wholesome development, a proof of resilience and growth rather than an admission of weakness. Scientific theory is not an immutable dogma; it is a working hypothesis which can and should change under the impact of 'new materials', brought into the orbit of critical investigation. The literary historian, continued Ejxenbaum, should address himself first and foremost to the new, the unknown or the little known, he should seek out problems neglected by his predecessors. Such an area of investigation is provided today by 'literary mores' – the conditions of writing.[43]

Ejxenbaum was certainly on safe ground when he invoked the flexibility of scientific hypotheses, when he insisted on the right, indeed the duty, of the theorist to modify his position under the impact of new relevant evidence. But from a literary scholar so keenly aware of method one could expect something more searching and rewarding than a set of 'tactical' deviations from a too rigid scheme, motivated alternately by the exigencies of the moment [44] or by the challenging novelty of the materials.

3

The makeshift quality of Formalist thinking in the years 1927–29, the growing uncertainty of aims and methods, testified to a distinct crisis in Russian Formalism, which by this time was harassed by outside pressures and plagued by an internal sense of inadequacy. The cocky self-assurance of the early days gave way to Ejxenbaum's defensiveness and to the malaise pervading Šklovskij's Third Factory.[45]

[43] Ibid., p. 6.
[44] It is an undubitable fact that the major emphasis of literary scholarship at any given moment is affected to a large extent by the prevailing 'literary situation'. However, one should not mistake what might be partial explanation of the emergence of a certain methodology for a proof of its validity.
[45] One of the most striking symptoms of this spiritual crisis is Šklovskij's painful uncertainty as to the historical role played by Opojaz. Did the Formalists open a new era in Russian critical thought or did they merely close an old one? "Were we meant to be the seed or the stalk?" he inquired anxiously in The Third Factory (Tret'ja fabrika, p. 80).

The adversaries of *Opojaz* eagerly seized upon these portents to an-
nounce the intellectual bankruptcy of Formalism.[46] One wonders whether
what was happening to the Formalist movement in the late twenties could
not be more properly described as a temporary methodological impasse.

Pure Formalism was re-examined and found wanting. The original
working hypothesis had outlived its usefulness. The one-sided emphasis
of the orthodox *Opojaz* doctrine had become an obstacle to the further
growth of the Formalist movement.

This is not to say that the *Opojaz* theory of literature had to be
discarded *in toto*. As we shall try to demonstrate below, some of the
Formalist tenets contained, even though in an exaggerated and immature form, seminal methodological insights. But in order to preserve
this healthy core, it was necessary to overhaul the basic Formalist
assumptions, to reject the spurious and the obsolete, and restate the
essentially sound.

Such a thoroughgoing critical revision, however, could not be arrived
at by means of makeshift constructions, reducing the relation between
the artist and society to the sociology of literary production. What was
needed was a critical scheme, salvaging the central literary emphasis
of early Formalism and yet capable of relating imaginative literature
to other domains of culture; a scheme flexible enough to do justice to
the multiple facets of a literary work, and sufficiently integrated to
reflect the basic unity of the esthetic structure. What was called for
was a theory of poetry, paying due attention to the sensory texture of
the poetic idiom – the main concern of the early *Opojaz* – and at the
same time drawing all the necessary conclusions from the invaluable
work done in the second period of Formalism in correlating sound
with meaning.

This was, obviously, a very difficult undertaking, requiring the best
efforts of the best critical minds. It presupposed a higher degree of
methodological sophistication, a keener understanding of the dialectical tension between literature and society, a more thorough familiarity
with such 'contiguous' fields as logic, epistemology and theory of language than either Ejxenbaum or Šklovskij could boast.

To say this is not to minimize the achievement of these eminently
able men. Ejxenbaum was a first-rate critic and a distinguished literary
scholar, a man of rare erudition and sensibility, deeply steeped in Russian and Western European literature. But, in spite of his abiding

[46]   See especially G. Gorbačëv, "My ešče ne načinali drat'sja", *Zvezda*, 1930,
No. 5.

interest in theoretical problems, Ejxenbaum was not a methodologist *par excellence*. He was capable of acute insights, as long as he dealt with purely literary matters, be it problems of verse rhythm [47] or of narrative fiction.[48] But he was often singularly unconvincing, not to say inane, whenever he attacked methodological problems outside the pale of imaginative literature, such as the status of linguistics, or the question of "philosophical pre-conceptions".[49]

As for Šklovskij, he was still less fitted for the task of solidifying or deepening the Formalist doctrine. This versatile trouble-shooter of Formalism lacked the background, the temperament and the intellectual discipline required for this arduous task. His equipment was too lightweight, his terminology too loose, his acquaintance with linguistics and philosophy too casual. In literature Šklovskij's reading was wide but spotty. Erudition was never his *forte*. Most of his critical successes were due to brilliant 'hunches' rather than to factual knowledge. G. Gukovskij, one of his ablest disciples who in the late twenties parted ways with *Opojaz,* put it very aptly:

'The effectiveness of Šklovskij's writings did not lie in the factual material; he always worked by intuition, he was apt to misstate some details, to construct his theories above and beyond historical data. But nobody could cavil at Šklovskij either for his factual errors or the paucity of concrete material. Both defects were outweighed by the consistency and freshness of his views on art. In his hasty and brilliant formulas he embodied the yearnings of Russian scholarly and literary thought of the Futurist era with a clarity and pungency hardly paralleled by any of his contemporaries." [50]

This admirably fair appraisal of Šklovskij's historical role, contained in a sharply critical review of one of his late studies,[51] applied to the early period of *Opojaz*. In the era of 'struggle and polemics', when the new movement was trying to establish itself amidst the noise of the literary market-place, aptness of formulation and shrillness of voice were of paramount importance. At a later stage, however, when the catchy slogans had to be restated in more balanced and logically rigorous

---

[47]   See especially Boris Ejxenbaum, *Melodika stixa* (Petrograd, 1922); also *Lermontov* (Leningrad, 1924); *Anna Axmatova* (Petrograd, 1923).
[48]   Boris Ejxenbaum, "Kak sdelana '*Šinel'* ' Gogolja", *Poètika* (Petrograd, 1919); "O. Henri i teorija novelly", *Literatura* (Leningrad, 1927).
[49]   See above, chapters IV, V, p. 72 and 95 respectively.
[50]   G. Gukovskij, "Viktor Šklovskij kak literaturnyj istorik", *Zvezda*, 1930, No. 1.
[51]   Reference is made here to Šklovskij's study of Matvej Komarov, a minor literary figure of eighteenth-century Russian literature.

terms, 'hunches' proved to be an inadequate substitute for a sustained scholarly effort. Šklovskij's liabilities – his nonchalance in using concepts, his liberties with factual material – became a major handicap.

If Ejxenbaum and Šklovskij lacked some assets necessary for a constructive restatement of the original Formalist premises, there were among the leading spokesmen of *Opojaz* two men who, under more favorable historical circumstances, could have perhaps been more successful in this undertaking. I refer to Tynjanov and Jakobson.

The former, endowed with a critical intelligence no less supple or sensitive than Ejxenbaum's, but more rigorous and acute, combined a keen sense of literary values with a firm grasp of methodological problems. The latter, a theorist of language as well as an astute student of poetry, was at the time playing a conspicuous part in the process of overhauling the conceptual framework of modern linguistics.[52]

Significantly, it was Jakobson and Tynjanov who were responsible for the only serious, if belated, attempt to find a way out of the impasse reached by the Formalist movement and to prevent it from bogging down in extreme empiricism. In 1928 there appeared in the magazine *Novyj Lef* a compact statement on the relation between literary scholarship and contiguous disciplines, signed jointly by Jakobson and Tynjanov.[53] In a set of mathematically terse propositions the signatories repudiated doctrinaire Formalism, which abstracted the esthetic 'series' from other domains of culture, as well as mechanical causalism, which denied the inner dynamism and the specificity of each individual realm. "Literary history", they declared, "is closely bound up with other historic 'series.' Each of the series is characterized by peculiar structural laws. Without an inquiry into these laws, it is impossible to establish the connection between the literary 'series' and other sets of cultural phenomena. To study the system of systems, while ignoring the internal laws of each individual system, is a grave methodological error." [54]

The Jakobson-Tynjanov theses indicated, or foreshadowed, a position which could provide a much more solid theoretical basis for Russian neo-Formalism than the efforts of Ejxenbaum or Šklovskij. The notion of the literary process as a 'system' where every component has a certain 'constructive function' to perform came close to the fertile concept of esthetic structure, which was to play a crucial part in the

---

[52]   See below, chapter IV, pp. 159–160.
[53]   J. Tynjanov and R. Jakobson, "Voprosy izučenija jazyka i literatury", *Novyj Lef*, 1928, pp. 26–37.
[54]   *Ibid.*

Czech version of Formalist doctrine.[55] The view of the social fabric as a 'system of systems' substituted the postulate of *correlating* various self-evolving series for the insistence on *reducing* the 'secondary' sets of data to the 'primary' ones. The student of culture was thus confronted with the twin task: (a) that of ascertaining what makes each of the individual systems 'tick', i.e., inquiring into their immanent laws; (b) of determining the 'transcendent' organizing principle, or the nature of the cross-connection between these systems. These were, as Tynjanov and Jakobson clearly implied, two distinct, if closely interdependent, levels of analysis, either of which the literary scholar could ignore only at his own peril.

In spite of its cogency, the attempt to revise Russian Formalism in quasi-structuralist terms did little to prevent the gradual decline of the Formalist movement. The schematic theses of the Tynjanov-Jakobson declaration were never elaborated.[56] What was potentially a harbinger of Russian structuralism turned out to be a short-lived episode.

The spirited effort to overcome the philosophical immaturity of *Opojaz* had come too late. The time for experimenting with non-Marxian concepts was long past. Soviet criticism was being whipped into uniformity.

The end of the twenties was the turning point in the history of Soviet letters. As the First Five-Year Plan got under way, Russian literature and criticism were turned into a handmaiden of 'Socialist Construction'. The doctrinaire literary faction, so-called RAPP (Russian Association of Proletarian Writers) was empowered by the Party to streamline Soviet criticism. All 'unorthodox' interpretations of the Marxist approach to literature, whether Voronskij's 'objectivism', or Pereverzev's 'crude sociologism', were ruthlessly suppressed.

Where Marxian 'deviations' were thus excommunicated, a non-Marxian heresy could not survive. The Formalists found themselves under a savage attack. The only alternative left to them was to become silent or to acknowledge 'frankly' their errors.

Paradoxically, it was the most aggressive and, presumably, the most intransigent of the Formalist spokesmen who chose the latter course of action. Šklovskij was the first to disavow publicly the *Opojaz* doctrine.

---

[55] For a more extended discussion of this concept see below, chapters IX and XI, pp. 159–161 and 198–200 respectively.
[56] One ought to add, perhaps, "in the context of *Russian* critical debate", as the so-called Czech Structuralism (see chapter IX) could be regarded as the further development of methodological suggestions, contained in the Jakobson-Tynjanov theses.

To one who had followed closely Šklovskij's career, this should not have come as a complete surprise. This *enfant terrible* of Formalism had started losing his nerve rather early. In 1922, threatened with arrest for earlier political 'sins', he fled abroad. But homesickness proved eventually stronger than opposition to the Soviet regime. In a bizarre book *Zoo or Letters Not About Love* (1923),[57] written on the eve of his return to Russia, Šklovskij had symbolically 'surrendered' to the powers that be. "My youth is gone", he had written wistfully, "and so is my self-assurance. I raise my hand and surrender." [58] Now, in the face of a fierce onslaught, Šklovskij, to quote a hostile critic, Gorbačëv, "simply repeated the device he had once used in the *Zoo* – and recanted again." [59]

The 'recantation' referred to by Gorbačëv was the article published by Šklovskij in January, 1930, in the *Literary Gazette* and bearing the characteristic title, "A Monument to a Scientific Error".[60] Some of it was sound and probably genuine self-criticism,[61] but the general tenor of the statement and its conclusions seem to have the earmarks of an externally induced capitulation.

Casting a melancholy retrospective glance at the evolution of the Formalist School, Šklovskij conceded some of the charges leveled against *Opojaz,* even while he tried to restate them in somewhat milder terms. By ignoring the class warfare waged in the domain of literature, Šklovskij admitted sadly, Formalism has indeed committed a grave error, as this attitude tended to bring about the "neutralization of certain sectors of the front".[62] Likewise, the Formalist tendency to separate the literary process from the underlying social forces was an erroneous procedure even though it may have served for a while a useful purpose.[63]

Yes, continued Šklovskij, as a temporary expedient the abstracting of the literary 'series' was, perhaps, a legitimate procedure. "Where we erred", he wrote, "was not in introducing this working separation (*raboče otdelenie*) but in trying to perpetuate it." [64]

[57] Viktor Šklovskij, *Zoo ili pis'ma ne o ljubvi* (Berlin, 1923).
[58] *Ibid.*
[59] Cf. G. Gorbačëv, "My ešče na načinali drat'sja", *Zvezda,* 1930, No. 5.
[60] Viktor Šklovskij, "Pamjatnik naučnoj ošibke", *Literaturnaja gazeta,* 27, 1 (1930).
[61] In view of the loose use of this term in the official Soviet parlance it may be necessary to add that the word 'self-criticism' is used here in its normal sense.
[62] Cf. *Literaturnaja gazeta.*
[63] *Ibid.*
[64] *Ibid.*

This is not to say, Šklovskij went on, that the Formalists had not budged from their initial position. He acknowledged gratefully Tynjanov's part in substituting the dynamic conception of literary process for what had been presumably a static view of the literary form and in drawing attention to the fact that the same literary device may in different historical contexts perform different functions. Needless to add, Šklovskij did not fail to mention his own attempt to improve upon the original Formalist position. "I did not want", he declared, "to stand as a monument to my own error." Hence his shift from morphological description of literary devices to historical studies with a strong sociological emphasis, such as *Materials and Style in War and Peace.*

However, according to Šklovskij, none of these efforts could rescue what was fundamentally an untenable position. "As far as I am concerned", he solemnly announced, "Formalism is a thing of the past. All that has remained from the Formalist is terminology, which today is generally accepted, and a number of technological observations." [65]

Gone were the days when Šklovskij referred airily to Marxism as a gadget which some day might come in handy, when he wrote that "dialectical materialism is a very fine thing for a sociologist, but it is no substitute for a knowledge of mathematics or astronomy".[66] Now he was quite ready to swear by the name of the master and to recognize Marxist dialectics as the *alpha* and *omega* of literary scholarship. "Sociological dilettantism", he wrote in the concluding passage, "simply will not do. It is necessary to undertake a thorough study of the Marxist method in its entirety." [67]

The implications of this statement were unmistakably clear. But for the official and semi-official zealots, clamoring for the pound of Formalist flesh, Šklovskij's qualified self-repudiation was not abject enough.

The first to attack Šklovskij's confession was a certain M. Gel'fand. His article, published in *Press and Revolution,*[68] was a piece of vituperation so savage that Lunačarskij's diatribes against Formalist decadence seem by comparison academic and mild.

Gel'fand charged into the Formalist leader with the rhetorical vehemence of a prosecutor exposing a dangerous and crafty criminal. He branded Šklovskij's declaration as a vicious manoeuver, aimed to deceive and morally demobilize Soviet public opinion. Any attempt

[65] *Ibid.*
[66] Viktor Šklovskij, *Tret'ja fabrika.*
[67] *Literaturnaja gazeta,* 27, I (1930).
[68] M. Gel'fand, "Deklaracija carja Midasa ili čto slučilos' s Viktorom Šklovskim?", *Pečať i revoljucija,* II (1930).

at a compromise with Formalism, warned Gel'fand, any symptom of leniency toward this still unreconstructed enemy is treason to Marxism.

To Gel'fand, Šklovskij's self-criticism was simply apologetics in disguise. "Neutralization of certain sectors of the front!", he cried indignantly. "What a misleadingly euphemistic name for vicious ideological sabotage, carried out at the behest of the bourgeoisie!" [69]

Gel'fand self-righteous rage apparently dimmed his reasoning capacities. His tirades culminated in the following logical monstrosity: "Formalist philosophy ... is utterly false, because it is completely reactionary, and it is reactionary because it is utterly false." [70]

Where name-calling was substituted for discussion, the only possible conclusion was a blood-curdling call for the 'intellectual' lynching of the enemy or, as Gel'fand elegantly put it, "the absolute neutralization of the neutralizers by an ideological firing squad".[71]

G. Gorbačëv was almost equally vehement.[72] He announced gleefully the 'disintegration' of the Formalist School, citing the 'defection of some of its ablest disciples', notably, G. Gukovskij and the novelist V. Kaverin. "The Formalist School", he wrote, "is going to pieces. Its more promising members will have to undergo a thorough re-education in the tough elementary school of Marxism. ... They will have to go to an ideological Canossa. ... As for us, instead of following the Pope's example and mocking at the repentant enemy, we ought to send him to forced labor under good surveillance." [73]

It is indeed ironical that shortly afterwards both Gel'fand and Gorbačëv were to be branded as 'deviationists'. The sword of the literary inquistion which these two self-styled prosecutors of Formalism so lustily brandished fell on them, too.

Šklovskij made a feeble attempt at a rebuttal.[74] It was essentially a tactical retreat, covered by an impressive array of quotations from 'authorities' such as Labriola, Marx, Engels, Plexanov and Mehring (Šklovskij was learning the Marxist-Leninist etiquette pretty fast!). While effecting this manoeuver, he succeeded in making some valid methodological points. Thus, taking exception to Gel'fand's sociological 'explanation' of Formalism, he correctly observed: "At any rate, the

---

[69]   *Ibid.,* p. 11.
[70]   *Ibid.*
[71]   *Ibid.,* p. 12.
[72]   G. Gorbačëv, "My eščë ne načinali drat'sja", *Zvezda,* 1930, No. 5.
[73]   *Ibid.,* p. 125.
[74]   Viktor Šklovskij, "Suxoplavcy ili uravnenie s odnim neizvestnym", *Literaturnaja gazeta,* 13, III (1930).

genesis of the Formalist movement does not in itself prejudge its social function." Elsewhere he mildly dissociated himself from crude economic determinism, as he called attention to the interaction between the 'base' and the 'superstructure': "Once brought into existence, literature can in turn exert a certain influence on economic relations."[75] But the validity of the orthodox Marxist scheme was not questioned any more. The primacy of the economic factor was taken for granted. The formula 'in the last analysis', criticized by the *Opojaz* spokesmen as 'metaphysics' as late as 1927, was now invoked by the repentant Formalist: "In the last analysis, it is the economic process which determines and reorganizes the literary series and the literary system." [76]

With the fiery champion of *Opojaz* declaring Formalism to be a thing of the past, the remaining Formalist spokesmen had no other choice but to acquiesce in their own extinction. Whatever their reaction to Šklovskij's statement, they were in no position to dissociate themselves publicly from it.

Šklovskij may have been too rash in burying Russian Formalism as a body of critical thought. But, as an organized movement, as a distinct school in Russian literary scholarship, Formalism had, to all intents and purposes, become history.

75   *Ibid.*
76   *Ibid.*

VIII. REPERCUSSIONS

1

The extinction of the Formalist School did not result in the disappearance from the literary scene of its chief spokesmen. However, the latter were apparently compelled to forego literary theorizing, from now on an exclusive domain of 'Marxism-Leninism', and turn toward safer modes of expression. Thus, Tynjanov virtually relinquished literary scholarship to devote himself to historical fiction – a genre at which he had first tried his hand in the mid-twenties.[1] Šklovskij, having publicly disavowed his contribution to *Opojaz,* had to fall back on other fields for his versatile activities, documentary films, scripts, memoirs, reportage.[2] Ejxenbaum and Tomaševskij since 1930 have also steered clear of methodological problems and confined themselves to text exegesis, contributing critical introductions and explanatory notes to the new academic editions of Puškin, Lermontov, Gogol', Dostoevskij and other classics.[3]

Similar was the situation of the quasi-Formalists. Vinogradov managed to publish in the early thirties one work of a theoretical nature [4] but he, too, as a literary scholar has subsequently concentrated on concrete studies, dealing with the style and language of the great

---

[1] Reference is made here to the fictionized biography of Küchelbecker, a minor poet of the Puškin era (Jurij Tynjanov, *Kjuxlja,* Leningrad, 1925). Tynjanov's subsequent contributions to historical fiction included: *Smert' Vazir-Muxtara* (Leningrad, 1927); *Puškin* (Leningrad, 1936), as well as a number of historical tales (*Podporučik Kiže, Voskovaja persona,* etc.).
[2] Viktor Šklovskij, *O Majakovskom* (Moscow, 1940); *Vstreči* (Moscow, 1944).
[3] The fact that, in spite of their 'objectionable' past, Tomaševskij and Ejxenbaum were on several occasions called upon to edit the texts of the Russian classics was a reluctant tribute to the soundness of their scholarship and their adeptness at textual analysis.
[4] Viktor Vinogradov, *O xudožestvennoj proze* (Leningrad, 1930).

Russian poets, especially of Puškin.[5] Žirmunskij abandoned literary theory to go into historical research in the field of Germanic languages and literatures and, more recently, in Oriental folklore.[6]

This careful shunning of theoretical problems did not save the former members and sympathizers of *Opojaz* from eventually incurring the wrath of officialdom. In the course of a vehement campaign launched in 1947 against the dean of the Russian 'comparatists' Aleksandr Veselovskij,[7] Žirmunskij, Tomaševskij and Ejxenbaum were taken to task for perpetuating Veselovskij's 'bourgeois cosmopolitanism', i.e., drawing parallels between Russian and Occidental literature.

The scholars attacked promptly acknowledged their guilt. Žirmunskij, having written in 1940 an appreciative critical introduction to the new edition of Veselovskij's *Historical Poetics*,[8] had a great deal to answer for, and he was particularly emphatic in his recantation. He went as far as to link Veselovskij's 'cosmopolitanism' to the sinister designs of the 'American imperialists', and he profusely thanked "the Party for having pointed out the right path for correcting our mistakes".[9]

As for Ejxenbaum, his association with the 'reactionary' school of Veselovskij was not the only offense of which he was accused during the cultural purge set off by A. Ždanov's now famous 1946 speech on the literary magazines *Leningrad* and Star (*Zvezda*). It seems that Ejxenbaum was severely censured for his favorable reaction to the recent poems of Anna Axmatova, one of Russia's foremost lyrical poets, who had reemerged from her long silence only to be stigmatized by Ždanov as a 'half-nun, half-harlot'. At a meeting of the Leningrad Institute of Literature held under the auspices of the Soviet Academy of Science, Ejxenbaum pleaded guilty to 'political naiveté': he did not realize, presumably, that Axmatova's verse, especially her melancholy poem about a black cat, which was singled out for attack by Ždanov, had 'tragic overtones'. And these – the aging scholar admitted ruefully – cannot be countenanced at a time when Soviet society has to cope with the threat of Anglo-American imperialism. . . .[10]

[5]   Viktor Vinogradov, *Jazyk Puškina* (Moscow-Leningrad, 1935); *Stil' Puškina* (Moscow, 1941).
[6]   Viktor Žirmunskij, *Uzbekskij narodnyj geroičeskij epos* (Moscow, 1947).
[7]   See above, chapter I, pp. 26–31.
[8]   See Aleksandr Veselovskij, *Istoričeskaja poètika* (Leningrad, 1940).
[9]   See G. Struve, "The Soviets Purge Literary Scholarship", *The New Leader*, New York, April 2, 1949.
[10] *Izvestija Akademii Nauk, Otdelenie literatury i jazyka*, Vol. V, No. 6 (Moscow, 1946), p. 518.

Nor was this the end of Ejxenbaum's ordeal. In September 1949 *Zvezda* carried a long and scurrilous article by one Papkovskij on "The Formalism and Eclecticism of Professor Ejxenbaum". It is, perhaps, no accident that for a number of years Ejxenbaum's name was conspicuously absent from Soviet publications.

As brutal harassment of the intellectuals gave way to the somewhat more permissive climate of the first post-Stalin decade, the erstwhile Formalists and Formalist sympathizers were afforded more latitude. The change in the atmosphere affected appreciably the writings of Viktor Šklovskij. His 1953 collection of essays dealing with the prose of the 19th Century Russian masters [11] is an appallingly pedestrian and timid rehash of official clichés bolstered time and again by quotations from the alleged forerunners of 'Socialist Realism' – Belinskij, Černyševskij and Dobroljubov. By comparison Šklovskij's book on Dostoevskij published in 1957 [12] – though often farfetched and occasionally irritating – seems a partial comeback. The best insights of this remarkably spotty volume, especially the provocative discussion of the *Doppelgänger* theme in Dostoevskij, have something of the freshness and vigor of Šklovskij's early writings. More recently, Šklovskij returned to the theory of narrative fiction in a wide-ranging, bulky volume, *Artistic Prose, Reflections and Analyses* (1959).[13] Mixing as it does history and theory of prose with snatches of memoirs and tortured, self-conscious polemic, shuttling between sound structural observations and safe platitudes, this rambling book is testimony both to a life-long dedication to literature and to the strains and stresses of what Soviet critics like to call, euphemistically, a 'complex path' (*složnyj put'*).

For Boris Ejxenbaum the late fifties were a period of intensive scholarly activity, brought to an abrupt halt by his death in 1959. The following year saw the appearance of the third volume of Ejxenbaum's invaluable study of Tolstoj.[14] Another posthumous publication of Ejxenbaum's [15] comprised short studies on Lermontov written over the period of 1941–1959, fragments of a larger monograph which was to present Lermontov within the framework of the intellectual and social cross-currents of his time. Ejxenbaum's literary erudition and

---

[11]   *Zametki o proze russkix klassikov* (Moscow, 1953).
[12]   *Za i protiv. Zametki o Dostoevskom* (Moscow, 1957).
[13]   *Xudožestvennaja proza. Razmyšlenija i razbory* (Moscow, 1959).
[14]   *Lev Tolstoj. Semidesjatye gody* (Leningrad, 1960).
[15]   *Stat'i o Lermontove* (Moscow-Leningrad, 1961).

his richly textured sense of history are very much in evidence here, though at times one may be inclined to cavil at some heavily ideological interpretations of the late Lermontov, perhaps, an inevitable tribute to the *Zeitgeist,* or else, as Jakobson surmises in his eloquent obituary of Ejxenbaum,[16] a grimly suggestive code. (Jakobson detects in Ejxenbaum's account of the oppressive 1830's thinly veiled hints at the recently experienced ordeal.)

Shortly before his death Ejxenbaum demonstrated once more his characteristic intransigence. In answering a questionnaire prepared by the Steering Committee of the International Congress of Slavists in Moscow (1958) he indicated in no uncertain terms his impatience with such queries as "how did the shift from Romanticism to Realism occur in the Slavic countries". The question, he said, was asked not in a scholarly but in a schoolmasterish vein. "Only authors of textbooks", he continued, "know for sure how to locate in Puškin, Gogol or Mickiewicz a shift from Romanticism to Realism." Ejxenbaum concluded by calling for a drastic reëxamination of these much abused terms and for a renewed emphasis on the "distinctive characteristics of art and artistic creation".[17]

Boris Tomaševskij's last years, like Ejxenbaum's, were marked by a sustained scholarly effort. Here, too, an untimely death prevented the completion of a *magnum opus.* In 1956 Tomaševskij published the first volume of a broadly conceived study of Puškin which promised to offer the most comprehensive and rigorous analysis of the great poet yet undertaken. The second volume, brought out posthumously in 1961, comprises a small portion of the unfinished monograph along with articles of varying nature and weight.[18] Another miscellany, *Verse and Language* (1959),[19] harks back to Tomaševskij's path-breaking studies in versificaticion published in the 1920's.

Theoretical considerations have bulked large in the recent writings of Viktor Vinogradov. In the course of the last five years Vinogradov has published three books concerned with literary theory – *On the Language of Imaginative Literature* (1959), *The Problem of Authorship and a Theory of Styles* (1961), and *Stylistics. Theory of Poetic*

---

[16] *International Journal of Slavic Linguistics and Poetics,* VI (The Hague, 1963), pp. 160–167.
[17] *Ibid.,* p. 166.
[18] *Puškin,* vol. I: *1813–1824* (Moscow-Leningrad, 1956); vol. II: *1824–1837* (Moscow-Leningrad, 1961).
[19] *Stix i jazyk. Filologičeskie očerki* (Moscow-Leningrad, 1959).

Language. Poetics (1963).[20] (Incidentally, the 1959 volume contains a critical but not altogether hostile account of the Formalist-Structuralist tradition.) While one can not help but marvel at Vinogradov's industry and energy, at the scope of his reading and awareness, one is likely to miss in his current output the incisiveness and originality of his earlier analyses of Avvakum, Gogol or Axmatova. At least one reader finds the recent methodological pronouncements of Vinogradov all too often weighed down by ponderous nomenclature and occasionally vitiated by a marked proclivity for an elaborate statement of the obvious.

2

Even though Formalist doctrine had been officially excommunicated and its spokesmen temporarily forced into silence or, worse still, self-abnegation, one would be wrong to infer that Soviet literary studies were completely cleansed of Formalism. Fifteen years of *Opojaz* research in the field of historical and theoretical poetics could not be read out of existence by a bureaucratic fiat. Formalist literary theory had a stronger impact on many Soviet Marxist critics and literary investigators than they would care to admit, indeed, than they knew. Šklovskij was not far off the mark when he boasted in 1926: "even while our theories are being attacked, our terminology is generally accepted and . . . our 'fallacies' find their way somehow into the textbooks of literary history." [21]

Indeed, some of the terms of Formalist poetics, especially those which had to do with versification, received wide currency in Soviet critical literature. A good case in point are the writings of L. Timofeev, regarded as one of the foremost Soviet authorities on prosody. Timofeev criticized the Formalist approach to versification harshly and often unfairly. And yet in his nomenclature and methodological postulates he seems at times to take his cues from the late *Opojaz*. He speaks about "sound-repetitions" [22] and "inter-verbal pauses", a concept closely akin to the Formalist notion of "word-limits",[23] and, as if echoing

---

[20]   *O jazyke xudožestvennoj literatury* (Moscow, 1959); *Problema avtorstva i teorija stilej* (Moscow, 1961); *Stilistika. Teorija poètičeskogo jazyka. Poètika* (Moscow, 1963).
[21]   Viktor Šklovskij, *Tret'ja fabrika* (Moscow, 1926), p. 88.
[22]   As indicated above (see chapter IV of this study), the concept of 'sound-repetitions' was introduced by O. Brik in his paper, published in *Poètika*.
[23]   A term coined by Valerij Brjusov, but popularized subsequently by the Formalist theoreticians of verse, especially Brik, Tomaševskij and Jakobson.

Tynjanov's and Jakobson's dissection of poetic language, he postulates a structural analysis of verse.[24]

Similar is the case of Ivan Vinogradov, the author of the collection of theoretical essays, *The Struggle for Style* (1937).[25] This ultra-orthodox literary theorist, who could hardly be accused of pro-Formalist leanings,[26] felt constrained in his discussion of verse rhythm to quote repeatedly such *Opojaz* stalwarts as Brik, Jakobson and Tynjanov.[27] Apparently, in his attempt to evolve a coherent system of Marxist poetics, Vinogradov could not afford to ignore the Formalist contribution, the more so since, as he admitted himself, he derived but little solace from the pundits of his own camp. In spite of his respect for V. Friče, one of the pioneers of Marxist criticism in Russia, Vinogradov was admittedly unimpressed with Friče's attempts to 'explain' free verse by references to the rhythms of the capitalist city.[28]

Another instance of Formalist influence was cited ten years earlier by the noted Soviet critic, V. Polonskij, in his polemic with G. Lelevič, one of the chief spokesmen for the doctrinaire *On Guard* faction.[29] Polonskij pointed out with visible glee that this Marxist-Leninist zealot had drawn lavishly on Ejxenbaum's 1923 study of Anna Axmatova.[30] The significance of this rather unexpected borrowing is underlined by the fact, also mentioned by Polonskij, that Lelevič tended toward glib impressionism whenever left to his own devices in the field of formal analysis. When, in discussing another contemporary poet, Doronin, Lelevič chose to discard the *Opojaz*-like 'fastidiousness' and 'technical detail', he had recourse to dubious metaphors about 'sprightly streamlets of verse' and the like.[31] Just because this crudely ideological critic lacked conceptual tools of his own, adequate for the analysis of form, he was apt to go over to the Formalist 'enemy' in those rare moments when he felt like being 'fastidious' about problems of poetic style.

The above examples, cited at random, seem to indicate that no Marxist student of literature who addressed himself to the problems of

[24] Cf. L. Timofeev, *Teorija literatury* (Moscow, 1945); resp. pp. 179–187, pp. 210–211, p. 191.
[25] Ivan Vinogradov, *Bor'ba za stil'* (Leningrad, 1937).
[26] See his indictment of Formalism in literary scholarship and imaginative literature (*Bor'ba za stil'*, pp. 387–448).
[27] *Ibid.*, p. 124, *et al.*
[28] Vinogradov is referring here to Friče's study on modern European literature published in 1919 (V. M. Friče, *Novejšaja evropejskaja literatura*, Vol. I, 1919).
[29] V. Polonskij, *Na literaturnye temy* (Leningrad, 1927), p. 115.
[30] Boris Ejxenbaum, *Anna Axmatova* (Petrograd, 1923).
[31] V. Polonskij, *Na literaturnye temy*, p. 94.

poetic language could fail to take note of the pioneering work done by the Formalists in this field, no matter how critical he may have been of *Opojaz Weltanschauung*. N. Buxarin came close to admitting this, in his level-headed speech on "Problems of Poetry and Poetics", delivered at the Congress of the Soviet Writers in Moscow in 1934.[32] Buxarin insisted on a clear distinction between the "extreme Formalism which tears art out of its social context" and thus dooms literary studies to sterility, and "formal analysis which is highly useful and now, when one of our chief tasks is to master the technique (*ovladet' texnikoj*), is absolutely indispensable". In this respect, added Buxarin, "we may learn something even from the Formalists who dealt systematically with these problems, while Marxist literary scholars blithely ignored them".

Buxarin's judicious critique of *Opojaz* was scarcely typical of the official pronouncements about Formalism in the 'thirties. The tone was now set by self-appointed zealots of the Gel'fand and Gorbačëv variety or by party bureaucrats lacking Buxarin's breadth and literary erudition. Rational polemics gave way to intellectual pogroms.

Even though the Formalist movement never exhibited any visible symptoms of resurgence since the 1930 punitive expedition, 'Formalism' became on two subsequent occasions a target of vehement campaigns emanating from the highest official quarters. The first such offensive was launched in January 1936, when *Pravda* published a scathing denunciation of the 'formalists and esthetes'. This new attack had little to do with either criticism or literature. This time the vestiges of the Formalist heresy were discovered in music, more specifically in a recent opera by D. Šostakovič, *Lady Macbeth of the Mcensk District*.

The *Pravda* article which, as A. A. Ždanov authoritatively stated in 1948,[33] "expressed the Central Committee's view of the opera", rapped the composer for a "crudely naturalistic" treatment of a rather "objectionable" theme,[34] and for replacing the "clear melodic pattern"

---

[32] N. Buxarin, "Poèzija, poètika i zadači poètičeskogo tvorčestva v S.S.S.R." (cf. Stenographic Report of the Congress of the Soviet Writers in Moscow, 1934; p. 227); English translation in *Problems of Soviet Literature*, H. G. Scott ed. (New York, n.d.), pp. 185–258.
[33] I am referring to the speech delivered by A. A. Ždanov on behalf of the Central Committee of the All-Union Communist Party at the conference on Soviet music, held in January 1948 (quoted from A. Werth, *Musical Uproar in Moscow*, London, 1949, p. 48).
[34] The theme of Šostakovič's *Lady Macbeth of the Mcensk District* and of N. Leskov's story on which the opera is based was adultery and murder, committed by a sensuous and crafty woman.

of Čajkovskij and Rimskij-Korsakov with "musical chaos". "This crude, primitive and vulgar music", the official publicist continued, "can only appeal to esthetes and formalists who have lost all healthy tastes." [35]

This bracketing together of Formalism and of what is often considered its opposite, 'crude naturalism', may strike one as a piece of far-fetched rhetoric. But the *Pravda* writer was patently uninterested in critical distinctions. The only distinction that mattered here was that between the 'healthy' dogma of Socialist Realism and any 'unhealthy' esthetic heresies. 'Formalism', which even to Lunačarskij had smacked of 'decadence', seemed to be a convenient stigma for all deviations from the path, whether 'rightist' or 'leftist'.

The 1936 campaign against Formalism, precipitated by the Šostakovič case, was soon extended to other domains of Soviet culture. The famous director Meyerhold, the boldest innovator of the Russian stage, apparently had to pay a heavy price for his 'ultra-Leftist experiments', while in literary criticism Bolshevik vigilance was mobilized once more against the defeated and yet insidious enemy. But Formalist-baiting of 1936–37 has been vastly outstripped both in scope and in vehemence by the more recent campaign against 'bourgeois Formalism'.

Ever since A. Ždanov's 1946 blast at the independent Leningrad writers and critics,[36] the term 'Formalism' has been used so widely and indiscriminately that is has become increasingly difficult to disentangle its precise meaning, to locate its referent. In the course of the cultural purges of the late 40's the Formalist label was pinned on offenders so dissimilar as (1) literary historians who engaged in comparative research (Žirmunskij, Tomaševskij, Šišmarëv and others), (2) 'decadent', 'esthetizing' poets – wheter Axmatova or Pasternak, Bagrickij or Antokol'skij, (3) the foremost Soviet composers – Šostakovič, Prokof'ev, Xačaturjan, accused of "Formalist distortions and anti-democratic tendencies",[37] (4) painters and architects who had strayed from the path of Soviet neo-academicism, misnamed Socialist Realism.

Nor does this tell the whole story. If one is to believe the Soviet publicist of the Zhdanov era, the Formalist heresy is not confined to arts or art criticism; it has wormed its way into the natural sciences as well. The author of a vehement blast at 'bourgeois trends in Soviet physics'

[35] Quoted in A. Werth, *Musical Uproar in Moscow*, p. 49.
[36] See A. A. Ždanov, "On the Errors of the Soviet Literary Journals *Zvezda* and *Leningrad*", English translation: Andrei A. Ždanov, *Essays on Literature, Philosophy, and Music* (New York, 1950).
[37] A. Werth, *Musical Uproar in Moscow*, p. 29.

published in *Zvezda* in 1949 [38] declared: "A ruthless struggle against reactionary Formalism is being waged in all domains of our culture, science, and art. Physics is no exception." Indeed, the vaunted Bolshevik vigilance did not fail to bring to light reactionary infiltration into scientific research. Soviet nuclear physics was found to be infected by the Formalist bacilli under the guise of widespread adherence to the theories of Niels Bohr.

As one takes cognizance of these strictures, one wonders whether 'Formalism', like other 'isms' of Soviet journalism, e.g., 'Cosmopolitanism', 'Trotskyism', 'Menshevism', has not degenerated here into a mere term of censure or, as Hayakawa would put it, "a meaningless noise registering disapproval".[39]

The above examples are sufficient proof that what is branded 'Formalist' in the Soviet press bears at times only the remotest relation to real Formalism. And yet, while the manipulation of the label has often been reckless, the choice of the bogeyman was not wholly accidental.

The substitution of emotionally loaded epithets for clearly defined concepts makes it very difficult to determine the real issues at stake. But to the degree that it is possible to cut through the smokescreen of official jargon, it is safe to assume that the official Soviet campaign against Formalism was aimed at two, closely interrelated trends: (a) any experimentation with the medium of art, labeled conveniently 'pseudo-innovation', and (b) insistence on creative freedom, misrepresented as advocacy of pure art.

To be sure, neither tendency could be considered the exclusive property of the Formalists. Yet both had found vigorous expression in critical pronouncements emanating from the Formalist movement or stimulated by it.

3

As indicated above,[40] the Formalist movement had ever since its inception made common cause with the artistic *avant-garde*. In their early writings, Šklovskij and Jakobson sought to elevate the Futurist experiments into general laws of poetics. Other Formalist spokesmen were less partisan. Ejxenbaum and Tynjanov, on the whole, tended to steer clear of special pleading. But this relative detachment should not be

---

[38]   *Zvezda,* I (1949).
[39]   S. I. Hayakawa, *Language in Action* (New York, 1946).
[40]   See chapters III and IV, pp. 65–69 and pp. 72–73 respectively.

mistaken for aloofness from the contemporary literary scene. Ejxenbaum saw the task of the student of literature *qua* critic [41] as that of helping the writer "decipher the will of history", "discover rather than invent the form that must be" [created].[42]

What was the form which 'history' demanded of the Russian writer in the early twenties? To this question the Formalists as a group had no positive answer. They were at one, however, in postulating an acute crisis in Russian imaginative writing, expecially in prose fiction, and in calling for a radically new departure. Šklovskij debunked lustily the tedious social panorama of M. Gor'kij, *The Life of Klim Samgin*. The old-fashioned Russian problem-novel, he insisted, with its slow-moving introspection, is hopelessly out of step with the tempo of the revolutionary era.[43] In an essay written in 1924 Tynjanov argued thus: "The novel finds itself in an impasse; what is needed today is a sense of a new genre, i.e., a sense of decisive novelty in literature. Anything less than that is merely a half-measure." [44]

The way out of the impasse was seen now in factography (*literatura fakta*), or rather, in half-fictional, half-documentary genres,[45] then in the intricate plot patterns, the color and pace of the Western *roman d'aventures*.[46]

Clearly, in the Formalist responses to contemporary literature, the diagnosis mattered more than the prescription, the will to change was more crucial – and more widely shared – than the commitment to a particular set of innovations. Whatever the nature or direction of the literary 'upheaval' championed at the moment, the emphasis of Formalist criticism was invariably on a bold and uninhibited search for novelty; its watchword – 'inventiveness' (*izobretatel'stvo*).[47]

If the Formalist's insistence on 'decisive novelty' encouraged the quest for unorthodox and 'difficult' modes of expression, his emphasis

---

[41] Boris Ejxenbaum, "Nužna kritika", *Žizn' iskusstva*, IV (1924).

[42] The expressions 'will of history', 'form that must be' (*dolženstvujuščaja forma*) are indicative of that peculiar determinism which characterized the Formalist view of literary history. We shall revert to the matter in chapter XIV of this study, p. . . .

[43] Viktor Šklovskij, *Gamburgskij ščët* (Moscow, 1928).

[44] Jurij Tynjanov, "Literaturnoe segodnja", *Russkij sovremennik*, I (1924), p. 292.

[45] Good examples of this trend are Šklovskij's own experiments in the field of creative writing, e.g., *Sentimental Journey, Zoo or Letters Not About Love*, or *Third Factory*, which mix freely *belles lettres* motifs with elements of essay, memoir, diary, and letters.

[46] Lev Lunc, "Na zapad!", *Beseda*, Sept.–October, 1923; Viktor Šklovskij, *Gamburgskij ščët*, p. 84.

[47] N. Stepanov, "V zaščitu izobretatel'stva", *Zvezda*, VI (1929), p. 189.

on the uniqueness of literary art provided the theoretical basis for a vigorous, if short-lived, campaign against the political regimentation of literature.

Some of the more memorable statements came from the Formalist leaders themselves. In his survey of contemporary Russian prose, Tynjanov exposed the futility of bureaucratic 'social commands' with his usual pungency: "Russian literature has been given many assignments, but all to no avail. Tell the Russian writer to sail for India and he will discover America." [48]

In his irreverent collection of essays, *The Knight's Move* (1923),[49] Šklovskij sounded a similar warning: "Comrades in revolution, comrades in war, leave art free, not for its own sake, but because we must not regulate the unknown." "The greatest misfortune of Russian art", he continued, "is that it is not allowed to develop organically like the heart-beat within man's breast, but is being regulated like the movement of trains." [50]

In *The Third Factory* (1926) Šklovskij's attitude was clearly more ambivalent. Apparently, his intransigence had been sapped by the growing external pressures, as well as by inner uncertainty as to the 'timeliness' of the values he championed. The result was anguished, self-contradictory meanderings about the limits of creative freedom and occasional attempts to justify 'unfreedom' in terms of historical necessity.

The gnawing doubts, which marked here the beginning of the end of militant Formalism, are conspicuously absent from the fiery challenge to social utilitarianism delivered a few years earlier by one of Šklovskij's most brilliant disciples, Lev Lunc. His often-quoted credo [51] became the manifesto of the literary grouping, known as 'The Serapion Brotherhood'.[52]

It is no accident that this belligerent statement – the most forthright plea for creative freedom to be found in the annals of Soviet literature – was to issue from a literary faction which felt the impact of For-

---

[48] *Russkij sovremennik*, I (1924), p. 306.
[49] Viktor Šklovskij, *Xod konja*.
[50] *Ibid.*, p. 17.
[51] Lev Lunc, "Počemu my Serapionovy brat'ja", *Literaturnye zapiski*, III (1922).
[52] The Serapion Brotherhood was a literary grouping founded in Petrograd in 1921. The bulk of its members were young prose writers who later achieved considerable renown, such as K. Fedin, V. Ivanov, V. Kaverin, N. Nikitin, M. Slonimskij, M. Zoščenko. The name of the group was borrowed, significantly, from Hoffmann.

malist theorizing more strongly than any other group of Russian writers. The two chief spokesmen of the 'Serapions', Lev Lunc and Il'ja Gruzdëv, served their apprenticeship in literary seminars conducted by Šklovskij and Tynjanov. One of the ablest and most representative among the Serapion prose writers, Venjamin Kaverin, tried his hand at literary research under the auspices of *Opojaz*.[53] Last but not least, Šklovskij was an active and, according to a recent testimony,[54] influential member of the 'Brotherhood'. No wonder that Lunc's argument often parallels the pronouncements of the Formalist chieftains.

The starting point of Lunc's manifesto was a spirited plug for diversity in art: "We have adopted the name of the 'Serapion Brothers'', because we do not want uniformity in art. Each of us has a drum of his own. . . . We will have none of utilitarianism. We do not write for propaganda. . . . Art is real, like life itself, and like life itself, it has no ulterior goal or meaning; it exists because it cannot help existing." [55]

"We have gathered together", Lunc continued, "in the days of the revolution, in days of powerful political tension. Whoever is not with us, is against us – we have been told from the right and the left. With whom then are you, Serapion Brothers? With the Communists or against the Communists? With the revolution or against the revolution? We are with the hermit Serapion." [56]

Lunc apparently felt that his words could be easily construed as a profession of the artist's supreme aloofness from politics and he hastened to add: "That means – with nobody? Intellectual esthetes? Without ideology, without convictions? No. Each of us has his own ideology, each paints his hut in his own color. We all together, however, we

---

[53]   I am referring to Kaverin's monograph on Brambeus-Senkovskij, a controversial literary figure of the Puškin era (cf. *Baron Brambeus*, Leningrad, 1929).

[54]   "Among the older colleagues who took part in the discussions of the Serapions' literary workshop", reminisced one of the former Serapions, K. Fedin, in a vivid account of the early twenties (K. Fedin, *Gor'kij sredi nas*, Moscow, 1943), "there were Ol'ga Forš, Marietta Šaginjan, K. Čukovskij. And last but not least there was Viktor Šklovskij who spoke of himself as a Serapion and was indeed the eleventh or, perhaps, the first of the Serapions, owing to passion which he brought into our life, and to cogency of questions which he injected into our debates" (p. 115).

[55]   Ju. Tynjanov expressed essentially the same idea, when he wrote in his study *Problema stixotvornogo jazyka* (1923): "I do not deny the existence of the links between literature and life. I merely doubt whether the problem is posed correctly. Can we talk about 'life vs. art,' when art too, is life? Do we need to prove the social usefulness of art, if we do not bother to demonstrate the usefulness of life?" (p. 123).

[56]   *Literaturnye zapiski*, p. 31

the Brotherhood, demand but one thing: that the voice not ring false. . . . That we may believe in the work, whatever color it may have." [57]

The above passage is conveniently ignored by the 'Leninist-Stalinist' zealots who, like the late A. A. Ždanov, fulminate against the "rotten apoliticism" of the "Serapion Brothers".[58] Actually, it is not necessary to agree with Lunc in order to see that his position was not identical with the late nineteenth-century doctrine of 'pure art'. Lunc did not claim that art was above politics: he merely insisted that it ought not to be subordinated to narrowly political consideration, measured by party yardsticks. What the spokesman of the 'Serapions' was trying to say, overstating his case time and again with characteristic juvenile flamboyance, was simply this: the writer should be judged by his literary accomplishment rather than by his political allegiance – by the sincerity and integrity of his artistic vision rather than by the 'timeliness' of his subject-matter or the orthodoxy of his 'message'.

It is true that the phrase 'art has no ulterior goal or meaning' comes dangerously close to the 'art for art's sake' theory. But let us not jump to conclusions. Lunc did not deny that genuine art could serve socially useful purposes. He only maintained that a literary work does not have to justify its existence by immediate social usefulness, that art transcends the social uses it is being put to.

In his informative and sympathetic paper on "The Serapion Brothers",[59] W. Edgerton called attention to some 'logical holes' in Lunc' reasoning. Indeed, there is hardly any doubt that the problem of the artist versus society is susceptible of a more constructive formulation than Lunc's brash aphorisms seem to imply.

The manifesto of the 'Serapions' was essentially a negative response to a negative challenge, notably, to the threat of ideological uniformity – a battle-cry rather than a positive statement of principles. Now declarations of war seldom solve complex problems; at best they dramatize the issue at stake.

It may be added that the grouping for which Lunc tried to provide the rationale was hardly capable of producing an integrated literary program. This heterogeneous fraternity, in which M. Zoščenko, a satirist working in the native tradition of Gogol', Leskov and Remizov, rubbed shoulders with the extreme 'Westernizer' Lunc, the enthusiastic disciple

---

[57] *Ibid.*
[58] See footnote 36.
[59] W. Edgerton, "The Serapion Brothers. An Early Soviet Controversy", *American Slavic and East European Review*, February, 1949, pp. 47–64.

of A. Dumas and R. L. Stevenson, in which the 'old-fashioned lyrical realism of Fedin' [60] lived side by side with Kaverin's Hoffmann-like grotesque, was a defensive alliance rather than a literary school. What brought together these defiant and gifted writers was not a common faith, political or artistic, but a common determination to wage an uphill fight against authoritarian pressures, a common insistence on the survival of literature as an autonomous activity.

In challenging the growing trend toward bureaucratic controls over literature, Lunc spoke for many independent writers and critics far beyond the purview of the 'Serapion Brotherhood' or of the Formalist school. But his truculent non-conformism was undoubtedly an organic part of the Formalist 'ethos' in the early twenties. It was this spirit, above all, irreverent and restless, that Ždanov and his henchmen were trying to exorcize, when they were flaying busily the dead horse of 'Formalism.' . . .

[60]   See Lev Lunc, "Počemu my Serapionovy brat'ja".

IX. FORMALISM REDEFINED

1

If in the Soviet Union Formalism was stopped in its tracks and thus never given a chance to overcome its weaknesses, some of the Formalist tenets found refuge in a neigboring country, not yet committed to the 'Marxist-Leninist' dogma. In the mid-twenties Czechoslovakia became a vigorous center of linguistic and literary study. This intellectual ferment was noticeably spurred by stimuli received from Moscow and Leningrad.

One who was especially instrumental in familiarizing the Czech philologists with the methods and achievements of Russian Formalism was the erstwhile chairman of the Moscow Linguistic Circle, who after 1920 lived in Prague. Thanks to Jakobson the categories of the Formalist theory of poetry were brought to bear on some crucial and highly controversial problems of Czech prosody.

In his study *On Czech Verse* [1] (1923) Jakobson threw a monkey wrench into a debate on the rhythmical pattern of Czech poetry which at the time was raging among native Prague poets and literary scholars. The so-called *přízvučníci*,[2] led by the eminent metrist, J. Král, insisted that the only metrical system true to the spirit of the Czech language was accentual verse. The opposite school of thought, the *iločasovci*,[3] argued with equal conviction for quantity as the only 'natural' basis of Czech versification.

The young Russian linguist approached the problem in somewhat different terms. Taking sharp exception to the arguments of the venerable Král, he asserted that from the linguistic standpoint the proponents

---

[1] Roman Jakobson, *O češskom stixe preimuščestvenno v sopostavlenii s russkim* (Berlin, 1923).
[2] A word derived from *přízvuk,* Czech for 'accent'.
[3] *Iločas* is Czech for 'quantity'.

of quantitative metrics had a much stronger case. The prosodic elements, he argued, which in the given language are most likely to provide a 'basis of rhythm', are usually those 'phonemically relevant', that is, which serve to differentiate word-meanings. In Russian, where quantitative differences are a subsidiary factor and accent is free, it is the stress which has acquired phonemic value. In Czech, where the accent always falls on the first syllable, quantity rather than stress serves to differentiate meanings.

Then, inquired Jakobson, how does one account for the fact that during several periods in the history of Czech poetry the prevalent metrical system was accentual? The crux of the matter is, he continued, that versification cannot be deduced mechanically from the sound-pattern of everyday speech. References to the 'spirit' of the given language, to the 'natural' basis of prosody, cannot quite solve the problem, since poetry always presupposes artifice – a set of rigorous esthetic conventions superimposed upon the verbal material.[4]

Jakobson's challenge to the authority of Král may have scandalized some traditionalists. But his analytical ground-breaking was highly appreciated by Czech scholars, groping for new ideas, new approaches to language.

One of them was Vilém Mathesius, a leading Czech authority on the English language. A disciple of Sweet and Jespersen, Mathesius became in the early twenties acutely dissatisfied with the excessive historicism of nineteenth-century linguistics. What was needed, he felt, was a 'horizontal rather than vertical' view of language. As he was to admit later,[5] his methodological reorientation was accelerated by the close contact with a group of younger colleagues, especially with Jakobson.

In an article written in 1936 Mathesius gratefully acknowledged the valuable assistance he received at this juncture from Jakobson. "This versatile and unusually astute young Russian", wrote Mathesius, "brought with him from Moscow a vivid interest in precisely those linguistic problems which fascinated me most and was of great help to me by providing a living proof that elsewhere, too, these problems were at the center of scholarly debate." [6]

---

[4] We shall revert to the problems raised by Jakobson's treatise in chapter XII of this study, pp. 219–220.
[5] Vilém Mathesius, "Deset let pražského linguistického kroužku", *Slovo a slovesnost*, II (1936).
[6] *Ibid.*, p. 138.

Out of these informal methodological discussions grew an organization which soon became a vital force in European linguistics and literary scholarship, the Prague Linguistic Circle.

The first meeting of the Circle was held on October 6, 1926. Mathesius, the oldest in the group, presided. Among other participants were Roman Jakobson and three young Czech linguists: B. Havránek, Jan Rypka, and B. Trnka.[7] Shortly afterwards the Circle expanded beyond the initial core. The founding fathers were joined by Pĕtr Bogatyrĕv, mentioned in the earlier part of this story,[8] Dmitrij Čiževskij, who combined literary criticism with the history of ideas, Jan Mukařovský, a linguistically oriented literary theorist and esthetician, N. S. Trubetzkoy, the eminent Slavic philologist, and René Wellek, an authority on English and comparative literature.[9] Boris Tomaševskij is known to have participated in several meetings of the Circle.

As can be gleaned from this incomplete list, Russian scholars of Formalist and near-Formalist persuasion [10] played a conspicuous part in the activities of the Prague Linguistic Circle. In an article commemorating the tenth anniversary of the Circle,[11] Mathesius spoke of the 'working symbiosis' between Czech and Russian philologists. "Our meeting of minds with the Russians", wrote Mathesius, "was both stimulating and fortifying; it is only fair that I tell them today how much we appreciate their contribution." "However", continued Mathesius, "we were more than disciples. In our collaboration we have achieved a high degree of intellectual cross-fertilization, which is a

---

[7] *Ibid.*

[8] See above, chapter III, p. 64.

[9] At present Chairman of the Comparative Literature Department at Yale University and co-author (with Austin Warren) of *Theory of Literature,* a work often quoted in these pages.

[10] Trubetzkoy could not be described as a full-fledged Formalist: he was never affiliated either with *Opojaz* or with the Moscow Linguistic Circle and did most of his work in comparative or general linguistics — fields to which Formalist concepts were not directly applicable. But in his highly rewarding ventures into literary history, such as his study of a fifteenth-century Russian literary monument or his lectures on Russian literature at Vienna University, Trubetzkoy came fairly close to the Formalist position. "You will be probably glad to hear", he wrote to Jakobson in a letter of January 18, 1926, "that in my course of early Russian literature I am using the Formalist method to a very large degree." In another letter to Jakobson he praised the Formalists for having grasped "the meaning and internal logic of literary evolution" (N. S. Trubetzkoy, *Principes de Phonologie,* Paris, 1949, pp. xxiii, xxv).

[11] Vilém Mathesius, "Deset let pražského linguistického kroužku", *Slovo a slovesnost,* II (1936).

prerequisite for the success of any collective scholarly undertaking." [12]

Mathesius was correct in describing as a 'working symbiosis' this teamwork which Trubetzkoy hailed in the same issue of *Slovo a slovesnost* as a "collective effort of researchers bound by a unity of methodological objective and inspired by the same guiding principle". Indeed the 'meeting of minds' between the Russians and Czechs was a two-way street, a matter of dynamic interaction rather than of mechanical imitation. If the Czech members of the Circle, from Mathesius down, were 'stimulated and fortified' by their Russian colleagues, the latter stood to gain a great deal from the direct contact with Occidental scholarship afforded by the intellectual atmosphere of Prague. For most of the Russian Formalists such a contact became well-nigh unattainable in view of the growing cultural isolation of the Soviet Union.

Another initial advantage of the Prague Linguistic Circle over its Moscow and Petrograd predecessors had to do with the substantial progress made in the theory of language and semiotics during the decade which elapsed between 1915–16 and 1926.

The points of departure of the Prague group and of the Russian Formalist School were very similar indeed. The methodological position of both movements was characterized by a functional rather than genetic or, in Mathesius' words, 'a horizontal rather than vertical' approach to language. Moreover, in both cases the functional view of language provided a common ground for linguists and linguistically oriented students of literature.

In the programmatic statement published in 1935 in *Slovo a slovesnost*,[13] the organ of the Prague Linguistic Circle, the signatories – B. Havránek, R. Jakobson, V. Mathesius, J. Mukařovský, B. Trnka – postulated an inextricable tie between the science of language and the study of poetry. The relation between the 'esthetic function in language' and other uses of speech was referred to as one of the most challenging problems of modern linguistics. Hence the importance of poetic speech. "Only poetry", declared the manifesto, "enables us to experience the act of speech in its totality and reveals to us language not as a ready-made static system but as creative energy." [14]

One may add that the alliance of linguistics and poetics postulated and practiced by the Slavic Formalists proved beneficial to both parties. On the one hand, the students of literature among the Prague

---

[12] *Ibid.*, p. 145.
[13] *Slovo a slovesnost*, I (1935), 5.
[14] *Ibid.*

group, like their Russian counterparts, leaned heavily upon linguistic categories in their analyses of prosody and style. On the other, some of the more incisive 'Formalist' studies in verse yielded insights and formulations which were of crucial importance to general linguistics. Thus, the notion of the phoneme, which marked a new departure in the study of speech-sounds, was first stated or rather hinted at in a treatise on comparative metrics. Jakobson's treatise *On Czech Verse* introduced the distinction between 'significant' and 'non-significant' prosodic elements. This, as was recently pointed out,[15] amounted to anticipating by nearly a decade a concept which lay at the core of Trubetzkoy's and Jakobson's own pioneering studies in phonemics.[16]

If the close cooperation of linguistics and poetics remained a primary article of faith of Slavic Formalism in its Czech phase, the original formulation of the problem of the interrelationship between these two disciplines was restated. The slogan of the Moscow Linguistic Circle, "poetry is language in its esthetic function",[17] was significantly amended.

The Czech position was hardly a vindication of the struggle against the 'linguistic imperialism' of the Muscovites waged by Žirmunskij and Ejxenbaum.[18] The spokesmen of the Prague Linguistic Circle revised the early Jakobson formula for reasons other than those advanced by the Petrograd literary historians. The equating of poetry with 'language in its esthetic function' was now found wanting, not because, as Žirmunskij had argued rather inanely, in some works of literature language could be esthetically neutral, but because literature transcends language. It became clear that some strata of literary works, e.g. narrative structures, can be rendered into non-verbal systems of signs, such as film.

During the 'heroic' period of Russian Formalism the science of signs was virtually non-existent. Ferdinand de Saussure was practically isolated in postulating a new discipline, 'semasiology'.[19] But by 1930, under the impact of the studies of Ernst Cassirer and of the logical positivists,[20] this new discipline was well under way. The theory of

---

[15] See N. S. Trubetzkoy, *Principes de Phonologie* (Paris, 1949), pp. 5–6.
[16] See especially Roman Jakobson, *Remarques sur l'évolution phonologique du russe* (= *Travaux du Cercle Linguistique de Prague*, II, 5), and N. S. Trubetzkoy, *Grundzüge der Phonologie* (Prague, 1939).
[17] Roman Jakobson, *Novejšaja russkaja poèzija* (Prague, 1921), p. 11.
[18] See above, chapter V, pp. 94–96.
[19] Ferdinand de Saussure, *Cours de linguistique générale* (Lausanne, 1916).
[20] Cf. especially Ernst Cassirer, *Philosophie der symbolischen Formen* (Berlin, 1923–1931).

language was being fitted into the larger framework of a philosophy of symbolic forms which considered language as the central, but not the only possible system of symbols.

The literary theorists of the Prague Linguistic Circle took account of these developments. The conceptual framework of Slavic 'Formalism' had expanded: to Mukařovský and now to Jakobson poetics was an integral part of semiotics rather than a branch of linguistics. "Everything in the work of art,' wrote Mukařovský, 'and in its relation to the outside world . . . can be discussed in terms of sign and meaning; in this sense, esthetics can be regarded as a part of modern science of signs, semasiology." [21]

If the Prague Formalists managed to avoid the methodological error of reducing a literary work to its verbal substratum, they also eschewed another fallacy of the early *Opojaz,* the tendency to equate literature with 'literariness'.[22] In his introduction to the Czech translation of Šklovskij's *O teorii prozy* (On the Theory of Prose),[23] Mukařovský praised the acuteness of the autor's best insights but deplored the deliberate exclusion of so-called extra-literary factors. Šklovskij's single-minded preoccupation with "weaving techniques",[24] asserted Mukařovský, narrows unduly the area of literary investigation.

Esthetic isolationism was discarded, and the province of literary scholarship was extended to encompass the work of literature in its totality. This meant that ideological or emotional content was a legitimate object of critical analysis, provided that it is examined as a component of an esthetic structure. Pure Formalism gave way to Structuralism, revolving around the notion of a dynamically integrated whole, which was referred to either as a 'structure' or as a 'system'.[25]

This key concept was also a pivotal point of the theory of language propounded by the Prague Linguistic Circle. Structuralism was the

---

[21] Jan Mukařovský, "Strukturalismus v estetice a ve vědě o literatuře", *Kapitoly z české poetiky* (Prague, 1946), I, 25.
[22] For a more extended treatment of the matter see below, chapter XI, pp. 198–200.
[23] Jan Mukařovský, "K českému překladu Šklovského *Teorie prozy*", *Čin*, VI (1934), pp. 123–130.
[24] See above, chapter VII, p. 119.
[25] The term 'structure' in English may be somewhat ambiguous as it is often used to denote 'composition', e.g., 'structure of the novel', that is, a part of the work of literature rather than the entire work, the 'organized whole' (*Gestalt*). In a self-explanatory context the word 'system' may be less confusing. Incidentally, as will be mentioned below (see chapter XI), the use of the word 'system' as an equivalent of 'Gestalt' occurs already in some of the later writings of Tynjanov.

battle cry of the spokesmen of the Circle at the international linguists' congresses held in the late twenties and in the thirties. It was Jakobson and Trubetzkoy who, along with like-minded Western-European linguists, such as Bally, Bröndal, and Sechehaye, led a successful fight for the proposition that language is not an aggregate of isolated facts, but a system, "a coherent whole in which all parts interact upon each other".[26]

However, it would be erroneous to conclude that the 'Structuralist' approach to literature was merely a matter of borrowing a key term from a contiguous discipline. As Mukařovský pointed out, the notion of 'structure' received equally wide currency in the modern psychology of perception, indeed in many other branches of contemporary scholarship. To quote a recent paper of Ernst Cassirer, 'structuralism' in linguistics was an "expression of a general tendency of thought that in these last decades has become more or less prominent in almost all fields of scientific research".[27]

The anchoring of literary research in a concept with such a wide range of applicability indicated the Prague Circle's tendency toward a broader framework than the one sought by the Russian Formalists. The problem of the relation between science and philosophy was reexamined. The instinctive distrust of 'philosophical preconceptions'[28] which characterized the early *Opojaz* was abandoned. "Trends in scholarship", Mukařovský wrote pointedly, "which pretend to be completely unconcerned with philosophy simply surrender any conscious control over their underlying assumptions."[29] "Structuralism", he continued, "is neither a *Weltanschauung*, antedating and transcending empirical data, nor is it merely a method, that is, a set of research techniques applicable to only one field of inquiry; it is a noetic principle which today asserts itself in various disciplines – in psychology, linguistics, literary scholarship, theory and history of art, sociology, biology, etc."[30]

The Structuralist position precluded methodological separatism not only in the definition of the literary object, but in the conception of the literary process as well. The notion of social evolution as a

---

[26] The above is a quotation from Ernst A. Cassirer, "Structuralism in Modern Linguistics", *Word,* Vol. I, No. II (1945), pp. 99–120.

[27] *Ibid.,* p. 120.

[28] See above, chapter IV, footnote 17 (p. 72).

[29] Jan Mukařovský, *Kapitoly z české poetiky* (Prague, 1941), I, 14–15.

[30] *Ibid.,* p. 16.

'system of systems', which Jakobson and Tynjanov had expounded in 1928,[31] was now vindicated and amplified. The poet's achievement was seen as the result of an interplay between style, milieu, and personality. The relation between art and society was construed as a dialectical tension.

This approach to literature found its fullest expression in a collection of studies, *The Core and the Mystery of Mácha's Work,* published in 1938.[32] Čiževskij, Jakobson, Havránek, Mukařovský, Wellek and others subjected to a close scrutiny the heritage of Mácha, Czechoslovakia's greatest Romantic poet. Compared to the *Opojaz* studies, this provocative publication testified to a keener awareness of social considerations and a more intense interest in the 'ethos' of literature.

The introduction to the symposium took notice of the change in the esthetic climate which had occurred between the early twenties and the mid-thirties: "Again, as so many times before, art is requested to perform its fundamental duty – that of anticipating man's attitude toward reality." [33]

The editor of *The Core and the Mystery of Mácha's Work* was careful to point out that this rediscovery of the social significance of art was not, or ought not to be, repudiation of the form-consciousness so typical of modern art. "Art can fulfill this task successfully," he continued, "only in its own terms, i.e., making the fullest use of all the components of its medium." [34]

The central problem of the Mácha symposium was described as that of the "relationship between the semantic aspect of Mácha's work and the artistic devices employed in it".[35] This emphasis is amply evidenced by most of the individual contributions. Mukařovský's study, "The Genesis of Meaning in Mácha's Poetry," [36] focussed on the 'semantic dynamics of the context', on the poet's use of ambiguity and irony, on the oscillations between the habitual and the figurative word-meanings and like problems. Čiževskij dealt with "Mácha's World-View", analyzing it carefully into elements of such diverse philosophical systems as neo-Platonism, medieval mysticism, Hegelian dialectics and Romantic *Naturphilosophie*. However, Čiževskij was too context-

[31]   See above, chapter VII, pp. 134–135.
[32]   Jan Mukařovský *et al., Torso a tajemství Máchova díla* (Prague, 1938).
[33]   *Ibid.,* p. 8.
[34]   *Ibid.,* p. 9.
[35]   *Ibid.,* p. 10.
[36]   *Ibid.,* pp. 13–110.

minded a critic to be satisfied with a mere identification of the extra-literary sources of Mácha's *Weltanschauung* and translating his poetic vision into the language of philosophy. A true Structuralist, he insisted on examining the use to which these heterogeneous ideas were put in Mácha's poetry. The most interesting result of this inquiry was an analogy between philosophical antitheses inherent in the conceptual framework of Mácha's work and the antithetic character of his imagery.

If Čiževskij worked his way from the 'semantic aspect' of poetry to the 'artistic device', Jakobson proceeded in the opposite direction. His paper "Toward the Description of Mácha's Verse" was an extremely ingenious attempt to demonstrate a correlation between the meters used by Mácha and his perception of the world.

In his essay on "Poetic Language" Mukařovský called attention to the methodological significance of Jakobson's argument. Jakobson showed in his study, maintained Mukařovský, that "Mácha's perception of space was different in the poems written in an iambic meter, the canonic pattern of Czech accentual verse, from what it was in his trochaic verse. In Mácha's iambic space appears as a one-way continuum, produced by a regressive motion from the observer toward the background; in his trochees it acquires a restless multilinear quality." [37] "Now the rhythm", continued Mukařovský, "is essentially a linguistic phenomenon, as it is contingent upon the organization of the phonic stratum. The perception of space, on the other hand, has to do with thematology. Thus, the above analysis is another proof that linguistic analysis can be applied to the various layers of a work of poetry." "The use of the linguistic apparatus", the Czech theorist added, "constitutes here a general methodological orientation – the emphasis on the medium – rather than a delimitation of the area of inquiry." [38]

The studies of Čiževskij, Jakobson, and Mukařovský, bearing on various aspects of literary theory and the history of literature, had a profound impact upon a number of younger linguists and literary scholars. The most capable among them were apparently Mikuláš Bakoš, Josef Hrabák and A. V. Isačenko. [39]

[37] Jan Mukařovský, "O jazyce básnickém", *Kapitoly z české poetiky*, I, 79–142.
[38] For one who is not thoroughly familiar with Czech prosody, the import of Jakobson's observation may not be immediately obvious.
[39] See especially Mikuláš Bakoš, *Vývin slovenského verša* (Turč. Sv. Martin, 1939); also a very useful selection from Russian Formalism, edited by Bakoš, *Teória literatúry* (Trnava, 1941); Josef Hrabák, *Staropolský verš ve srovnání se staročeským* (Prague, 1937); *Smilova škola (Rozbor básnické struktury)* (Prague, 1941); A. V. Isačenko, *Slovenski verz* (Ljubljana, 1939).

After 1945, Structuralism found itself on the defensive, its influence appreciably weakened. This was partly owing to the fact that such active members of the Prague Linguistic Circle as Jakobson and Čiževskij had left Czechoslovakia shortly before 1939 and have remained abroad. But the predicament of the Prague Structuralists, like that of the Russian Formalists in 1929–30, transcended personalities. The intellectual atmosphere prevailing in post-war Czechoslovakia was hardly propitious for a trend which, while not anti-Marxian, was a far cry from the official brand of Marxist methodology. As was indicated above, 'Formalism' became in 1946 the chief whipping boy of Soviet literary officialdom. With Prague taking its cue from Moscow the Czech counterpart of *Opojaz* was placed in what has been an increasingly precarious position. Jan Mukařovský, the only prominent Structuralist to remain in Czechoslovakia, renounced his initial stand and put his considerable ratiocinative powers at the service of the official creed.

2

Czechoslovakia was not the only Slavic country where the impact of Russian Formalism made itself felt. The Formalist influence can also be detected in Polish literary scholarship, which during the period between the two wars was becoming increasingly aware of the inadequacy of its methodological premises.

The situation in Polish literary studies in the 1920's was somewhat similar to that prevailing in Russia on the eve of the Formalist movement. Free-lance criticism fluctuated between impressionistic 'appreciation,' mostly a hangover from the *fin-de-siècle*, and a purely ideological approach to literature. Academic literary history was still largely under the sway of the method misleadingly labelled 'philological' and more appropriately described as cultural historical [40] – a method which paralleled in many respects the Pypin-Skabičevskij school.[41] The chief difference between the two trends lay, perhaps, in their ideological tenor. If the formula for the Skabičevskij type of criticism was roughly

---

[40]   The above usage of the term 'philological' was probably an offshoot of the notion of 'philology' prevailing in nineteenth-century German scholarship. According to this interpretation, all manifestations of national culture embedded in language are within the philologist's jurisdiction.

[41]   See above, chapter I, p. 22.

Kulturgeschichte plus liberalism, in the Polish version, the latter in-gredient was supplanted by patriotic didacticism.[42]

One of the most distinguished representatives of the 'philological' school in Polish literary studies defined the "history of literature as the history of the verbal embodiment of national ideals in their gradual evolution".[43] From this it was only natural to conclude that 'the literary historian must concern himself with all the works in which the national ideals find strong expression.' [44]

The tendency to confuse the history of literature with the history of ideas often went hand in hand with the same sort of 'biographism' which had loomed so large in Russian literary scholarship at the turn of the century. In Poland this preoccupation with biography had not infrequently an apologetic or hagiographic tinge. The historian's interest in the poet's actual experiences as an alleged clue to his crea-tions was often compounded here with an almost religious reverence for the relics of the spiritual leaders of an embattled nation. In volu-minous and learned monographs about Poland's great Romantics – Mickiewicz, Słowacki and Krasiński, 'life' was often accorded as much or more space than 'work'; love affairs rated as high as love poems.

By the third decade of this century the validity of the traditional methods was being challenged from various quarters. Polish literary scholarship could not remain immune to the trend toward intrinsic analysis which was gaining ground simultaneously in Western Europe and in the Slavic countries. It became increasingly clear that the student of literature ought to address himself to "the content of the literary text as a distinct sphere of human reality".[45] There appeared a number of gifted literary researchers who attacked in systematic fashion the problems of style and composition: Stanisław Adamczewski, Wacław Borowy, Juljan Krzyżanowski, Leon Piwiński, Wiktor Weintraub, Kon-stanty Wojciechowski, K. W. Zawodziński.

The rationale for the structural approach to literary art was provided in a closely reasoned treatise by Manfred Kridl, *The Introduction to*

[42] In Poland as in Russia, imaginative literature often served as a potent weapon in the struggle against Tsarist autocracy. But the nineteenth-century Polish poet's challenge to authority was mostly a matter of national resistance rather than social protest.

[43] Ignacy Chrzanowski, *Literatura i Naród* (Lwów, 1936), p. 149 (quoted from Manfred Kridl, *Wstęp do badań nad dziełem literackiem*, Wilno, 1936, p. 28).

[44] *Ibid.*

[45] Juljusz Kleiner, *Studja z zakresu literatury i filozofji* (quoted by Manfred Kridl, *op. cit.*, p. 29).

the Study of the Work of Literature (1936).[46] Professor Kridl, hitherto an eminent repesentative of the cultural-historical school, now took exception to its eclecticism and sought to delimit the area and define more rigorously the subject of literary studies.

"To blur the boundaries between individual disciplines", Kridl insisted, following Kant, "amounts not to enriching but to distorting them." [47] He also cited with approval Jakobson's sarcastic dig [48] at the indiscriminate inclusiveness of traditional literary history.

Jakobson was not the only theorist of Russian Formalism whose name appears in Kridl's erudite study. In discussing the basic problems of literary theory, such as the difference between poetic and practical language, or the relation between literature and empirical reality, Kridl quoted repeatedly the studies of Jakobson, Šklovskij and Žirmunskij. Kridl's affinity with these critics was clearly attested to by his tribute to the 'fruitful insights' of the Russian Formalists. The Polish scholar described the Formalist School as a "fresh, dynamic movement ... which could boast of a number of gifted researchers in the field of literary theory and criticism, possessed not only of an original approach to literary problems, but of a thorough knowledge of European literature as well." [49] Even if they often overstated their case, continued Kridl, these exaggerations seem in retrospect justified by the vistas which their pioneering work had opened before the study of literature.

While taking a sympathetic view of Formalist 'excesses', Kridl apparently did his best to avoid them. On the whole, his position was more closely akin to the Czech Structuralist version of Slavic Formalism than to its mere extreme, Russian brand. Kridl himself described his view of literature as 'ergocentric' or 'integral'. The first term implied the determination to place in the center of critical analysis literary creation rather than the 'underlying factors'. The adjective 'integral' pointed to a scheme of criticism which would do justice to all aspects of literature, the 'esthetic' as well as the 'extra-esthetic', but would examine both within the context of the literary work.[50]

Kridl's emphasis on the poetic use of language, his interest in verbal

---

[46] See footnote 43.
[47] Manfred Kridl, *Wstęp do badań nad dziełem literackiem.*
[48] Roman Jakobson, *Novejšaja russkaja poèzija* (Prague, 1921), p. 11.
[49] *Wstęp do badań ...*, p. 69.
[50] "The philosophy of the author", asserted Kridl, "is not irrelevant to critical analysis, but it should be examined in its literary function, i.e., in its impact on characterization, plot, etc." (*ibid.*, p. 76).

devices, made him more linguistics-conscious than was the case with those of his confrères to whom the study of literature was but a branch of cultural history. But the Polish 'Formalist' was less inclined than his Russian or Czech counterparts to state his plea for the autonomy of literary scholarship in purely linguistic or semasiological terms. Kridl's conceptions of literary art seemed to owe almost as much to Western esthetics and philosophy – to Croce, Dessoir, Husserl, and Kant, as it did to Slavic Formalist poetics.

It may be noted parenthetically that Husserl's phenomenology which in Russia had exerted some influence on Formalist thinking through the agency of Gustav Špet [51] provided in Poland the conceptual frame for a significant attempt at an 'ontology' of literary creation. In his abstruse but rewarding work, *Das literarische Kunstwerk*,[52] Roman Ingarden, a professor of Lwów University, sought to apply the Husserlian categories to one of the most difficult problems of literary theory – that of the mode of existence of literary work.[53] As will be mentioned later, some of Ingarden's ideas, especially his remarks on the 'pseudostatements' found in imaginative literature come very close to Formalist-Structuralist formulations. But there is no reason to ascribe these points of contact to the actual impact of Formalism on the Polish-German philosopher.

Kridl's work had a considerable effect on the younger generation of Polish literary scholars. Not unnaturally the 'integral' method gained a number of adherents among the students of Wilno University, where Professor Kridl taught Polish and comparative literature. Kridl's seminar in poetics and in the methodology of literary studies became in the mid-thirties an important center of research in the structure of literary works of art.[54]

Another such center was the Polish Literary Circle at Warsaw University (Koło Polonistów Studentów Uniwersytetu Józefa Piłsudskiego). The most capable members of the Circle were Kazimierz Budzyk, Dawid Hopensztand, Franciszek Siedlecki, Stefan Żółkiewski. At the time when the Circle was founded, all of them were graduate students in Warsaw University.

---

[51] See above, chapter III, p. 62.
[52] Roman Ingarden, *Das literarische Kunstwerk* (Halle, 1931).
[53] A brief but informative statement of Ingarden's position is found in *Theory of Literature* by René Wellek and Austin Warren, p. 152.
[54] One of the studies which emanated from Kridl's study group was J. Putrament's structural analysis of the short story of Bolesław Prus, the master of Polish realism (Jerzy Putrament, *Struktura nowel Prusa*, Wilno, 1936).

The methodological leanings of the Warsaw group found clear expression in an ambitious translation project which aimed at rendering into Polish the most significant studies in the theory of literature and critical methodology published recently in Western European countries and in Russia.

In this series Russian Formalist and near-Formalist writings were accorded preferential treatment. The first foreign item selected for translation by the Warsaw Literary Circle was Žirmunskij's paper quoted above, "The Aims of Poetics".[55] The second issue of the *Archive of Translations,* devoted to problems of stylistics, included two studies by Viktor Vinogradov.[56] The subsequent issue was to represent a selection from Russian Formalist writings featuring Ejxenbaum, Jakobson, Šklovskij, Tomaševskij, Tynjanov, and Žirmunskij.[57] This publication, one may add, has never materialized, as the outbreak of the Second World War disrupted the activities of the Circle.

The original studies which emanated from the Warsaw group also bore a strong imprint of Formalist influence. Franciszek Siedlecki, a brilliant student of verse, was greatly indebted to *Opojaz.* His *Studies in Polish Metrics* [58] were an apt restatement of the Formalist theory of poetry as evolved by Brik, Jakobson, and Tomaševskij, as well as an imaginative application of these tenets to the problems of Polish prosody. In defining meter and rhythm and in pleading eloquently for the 'freedom of Polish verse' [59] Siedlecki made extensive use of Šklovskij's concepts of 'disautomatization' and 'perceptibility' (*oščutimost'*).[60]

In discussing the controversial problems of 'free' and regular verse, Siedlecki ranged himself with the standard-bearers of *Opojaz* rather than with its moderate sympathizers. He tilted his lance with an esthetically-minded but somewhat eclectic student of metrics, K. W. Zawodziński,[61] who played in Polish criticism a role comparable to that of Žirmunskij in Russia. In the course of these polemics, Siedlecki questioned the authenticity of Zawodziński's 'Formalism' in terms very

[55] Viktor Žirmunskij, *Wstęp do poetyki* (Warszawa, 1934) (= *Archiwum tłumaczeń,* I).
[56] *Z zagadnień stylistiki.* Leo Spitzer, Karl Vossler, Viktor Vinogradov (Warszawa, 1937) (= *Archiwum Tłumaczeń,* II).
[57] *Rosyjska szkoła formalna 1914–1934* (Warszawa, 1939) (announced and ready for publication on the eve of the War).
[58] Franciszek Siedlecki, *Studja z metryki polskiej* (Wilno, 1937).
[59] Franciszek Siedlecki, "O swobodę wiersza polskiego", *Skamander,* vol. II (1938), No. XIII–XIV.
[60] See chapters X and XII of this study, pp. 176–178 and 214–215 respectively.
[61] Cf. Karol W. Zawodziński, *Zarys wersyfikacji polskiej,* Vol. I (Wilno, 1936).

similar to those used by the orthodox Russian Formalists with reference to Žirmunskij.[62] Zawodziński, Siedlecki wrote disapprovingly, is a „Formalist only in the sense of being vitally interested in the formal elements of the work of poetry. But this is something vastly different from the real Formalism – of Šklovskij and Jakobson."[63]

Siedlecki's sympathy with the pure, unadulterated brand of Russian Formalism stemmed from the young critic's fondness for sharply focussed theoretical formulations, rather than from esthetic purism. Toward the latter the Warsaw Formalists were no more inclined than the Prague Structuralists. Their preoccupation with poetic language was matched by a keen awareness of social considerations. Shortly before his premature death, in a letter to Jakobson written from German-occupied Warsaw, Siedlecki hinted at the need for a creative synthesis of Formalism and Marxism. Hopensztand, in an interesting paper on the style of a modern Polish novel, sought to combine elaborate semantic analysis with categories drawn from the sociology of language.[64]

The war brought to an abrupt halt the activity of this dynamic group and soon made a noticeable breach in its ranks. Its most promising members, Siedlecki and Hopensztand, perished in Nazi-occupied territory. The bulk of the survivors have thrown in their lot with the official school of criticism. The articulate Stefan Żółkiewski seems to be one of the leading literary theorists of Communist Poland. In his strenuous campaign for 'Socialist Realism' Żółkiewski has been moving away increasingly from the critical and methodological position of the Formalist-Structuralist movement.

The recent evidence seems to indicate that in Poland, as in Czechoslovakia, Formalism, to use Lunačarskij's expression, is no longer a 'vegetable in season'. Its promising growth has been stunted by the same trend which two decades ago brought about, or precipitated, the disintegration of *Opojaz*. Apparently Slavic Formalism has run its course. But if the Formalist movement has disappeared from the scene, the sizeable and provocative body of critical writing which emanated from it is still with us. The Formalist heritage calls for a summing up, an assessment. That is what the subsequent chapters will attempt to provide.

[62] See above, Chapter V, p. 98.
[63] *Skamander*, II (1938), 100.
[64] Dawid Hopensztand, "Mowa pozornie zależna w kontekście *Czarnych skrzydeł* Kadena-Bandrowskiego", *Prace ofiarowane Kazimierzowi Wóycickiemu* (Wilno, 1937).

PART II

DOCTRINE

X. BASIC CONCEPTS

1

Russian Formalism has been often represented as merely a refurbished version of the late nineteenth-century 'art for art's sake' doctrine. This notion is largely misleading. For one thing, the Russian Formalists were not primarily concerned with the essence or purpose of art. Avowed champions of 'neo-positivism', they sought to steer clear of "philosophical pre-conceptions"[1] as to the nature of artistic creation; they had little use for speculations about Beauty and the Absolute. Formalist esthetics was descriptive rather than metaphysical.

"Our method", wrote B. Ejxenbaum in one of his early studies, "is usually referred to as 'Formalist'. I would prefer to call it morphological, to differentiate it from other approaches such as psychological, sociological and the like, where the object of inquiry is not the work itself, but that which, in the scholar's opinion, is reflected in the work."[2]

'Morphological' was not the only term which the Formalist spokesmen[3] have used in describing their methodological position. In a polemic with the orthodox Marxists[4] Ejxenbaum once declared: "We are not 'Formalists,' but if you will, *specifiers (specifikatory)*."[5]

'Morphological method', 'specifiers' – these were indeed apposite concepts which highlighted two crucial and closely interrelated tenets of Russian Formalism – (a) its emphasis on the 'literary work' and its constituent parts, and (b) its insistence of the autonomy of literary scholarship.

The driving force behind Formalist theorizing was the desire to bring

[1] See above, chapter IV, footnote 17 (p. 72).
[2] Boris Ejxenbaum, *Molodoj Tolstoj* (Petrograd, 1922), p. 8.
[3] See also Viktor Šklovskij, *Literatura i kinematograf* (Berlin, 1923), p. 50.
[4] See above, chapter VI, pp. 107–109.
[5] Boris Ejxenbaum, "Vokrug voprosa o formalistax", *Pečat' i revoljucija*, No. 5, p. 3.

to an end the methodological confusion prevailing in traditional literary studies and systematize literary scholarship as a distinct and integrated field of intellectual endeavor. It is high time, argued the Formalists, that the study of literature, so long an intellectual no-man's land,[6] delimit its area and define unequivocally its subject of inquiry.[7]

This was exactly what the Formalists set out to do. They started from the premise – which today is widely accepted – that the literary scholar ought to address himself to the actual works of imaginative literature rather than, to quote Sir Sydney Lee, to the 'external circumstances in which literature is produced.'[8] Literature, argued M. Kridl, ought to be in itself the subject of literary scholarship and not a means to some extraneous studies.[9]

But to the militant Formalist 'specifier' this was not specific enough. In order to disengage the study of literature from obtrusive contiguous disciplines, e.g., psychology, sociology, and cultural history, it seemed necessary to narrow down the definition still further. "The subject of literary scholarship", wrote Jakobson, "is not literature in its totality, but literariness (*literaturnost'*), i.e., that which makes of a given work a work of literature." [10] "The literary scholar *qua* literary scholar", added Ejxenbaum, "ought to be concerned solely with the inquiry into the distinguishing features of the literary materials." [11]

This, in turn, begged the most important single question of literary theory: what are the distinguishing features of imaginative literature? What is the nature and the locus of 'literariness'? The bulk of Formalist theoretical pronouncements deal directly or indirectly with this problem.

In their attempts to answer those crucial queries the Formalists sought to steer clear of traditional answers and pat solutions. In line with their deep-seated distrust of psychology, they were impervious to all theories locating the differentia in the poet rather than in the poem, invoking a 'faculty of mind' conducive to poetic creation. The Formalist theoreticians would brush aside impatiently all talk about 'intuition', 'imagination', 'genius', and the like. The locus of the peculiarly

---

[6]   Roman Jakobson, *Novejšaja russkaja poèzija,* p. 11.
[7]   "Like other *bona fide* disciplines", wrote Kridl, "literary scholarship must have its own subject of investigation, its own method and its own aim", *Wstęp do badań nad dziełem literackiem* (Wilno, 1936).
[8]   Quoted by R. Wellek and A. Warren, *Theory of Literature,* p. 139.
[9]   M. Kridl, *op. cit.,* p. 30.
[10]   Roman Jakobson, *Novejšaja russkaja poèzija,* p. 11.
[11]   Boris Ejxenbaum, *Literatura* (Leningrad, 1927), p. 121.

literary was to be sought not in the author's or reader's psyche, but in the work itself.

But if the Formalists rejected the tendency to account for imaginative literature in terms of underlying psychological processes, they were equally averse to seeking the clue to 'literariness' in the mode or level of experience embodied in the literary work. They were not impressed with the familiar thesis that poetry deals in emotions, while 'prose' works with concepts. Relativists, keenly aware of the protean character of the 'literary fact', they knew better than to regard certain motifs as more poetic than others. In his essay "What is Poetry?", Jakobson rejected the notion of intrinsically poetic themes as dogmatic and obsolete. The almost unlimited variety of subjects, he argued, which has in modern times proved capable of poetic treatment, gives the lie to all such restrictive schemes: "today anything can serve as a material for a poem." [12]

The relativistic view of literary phenomena, the insistence on literary change, which, in Tynjanov's words, renders meaningless 'static definitions of literature",[13] made the Russian Formalists more wary than is usually the case with esthetic criticism of drawing rigid distinctions between poetic fiction and actuality. "The boundaries between literature and life are fluid",[14] wrote Tynjanov. It was this awareness, combined with a sympathetic interest in documentary literature, e.g., reportage, autobiography, and diary,[15] which prevented the Formalist theoreticians from emphasizing fictionality as one of the principal earmarks of imaginative writing.[16]

Clearly, the difference between literature and non-literature was to be sought not in the subject-matter, i.e., the sphere of reality dealt with by the writer, but in the mode of presentation. But in tackling this latter problem, the Formalists found themselves confronted with a time-honored notion, dating back to Aristotle and upheld in modern times by critics so dissimilar as Samuel Taylor Coleridge, Cecil Day

---

[12] Roman Jakobson, "Co je poesie?", *Volné směry,* quoted from M. Bakoš, *Teória literatúry* (Trnava, 1941), p. 170.

[13] Jurij Tynjanov, "O literaturnoj èvoljucii", *Arxaisty i novatory* (Leningrad, 1929), p. 9.

[14] *Ibid.*

[15] See above, chapter VII, pp. 120–122.

[16] The Polish 'Formalist' theoreticians seem to have given more weight to this criterion than either the Russians or the Czechs. Thus, M. Kridl argued in his *Introduction to the Study of the Literary Work of Art,* that "the verbal apparatus exists in the work of literature not solely for the sake of 'beauty', but so that a new fictitious reality may emerge from it".

Lewis, George Plexanov, and Herbert Read. I am referring to the theory which proclaims the use of images as the outstanding characteristic of imaginative literature, or of 'poetry' in the broader, Aristotelian sense of the word. The Formalist and near-Formalist critics subjected this doctrine to a searching criticism.

Gustav Špet, an astute esthetician who exerted considerable influence on some Formalist spokesmen,[17] deplored the glib talk about the 'vividness' of the poetic image. Ascribing to a poetic image pictorial quality, argued Špet, implied a misjudgment of the real nature of poetic discourse. "An image not on canvas", wrote Špet, "is merely an image, a figure of speech; poetic images are metaphors, tropes, inward forms. Psychologists did poetics a great disservice, when they interpreted inward form as primarily a visual image." . . . "A visual image", continued Špet, "hinders poetic perception. . . . To strain oneself toward the visual perception of Puškin's 'monument built not with human hands' (*nerukotvornyj*) or of his 'flaming word', indeed, of any image, any symbol, the forms of which are not visual, but fictitious, is to strain oneself toward the misunderstanding and misperception of poetic speech." [18]

In his study of "The Aims of Poetics" Žirmunskij took a similar position. Quoting the recent German literary theoretician, Th. Meyer, Žirmunskij cautioned against attaching too much weight to the sensory qualities of poetic imagery.[19] The visual images evoked by poetry are vague and subjective, as they hinge to a large degree on the individual reader's sensibility and his often purely idiosyncratic associations.[20] In vividness, continued Žirmunskij, that is, in intensity of sensory effects, poetry is obviously inferior to painting. But it has at its disposal the "whole nexus of formal-logical relations inherent in the language and incapable of expression in any other branch of art".[21]

---

[17] See above, chapter III, p. 62.

[18] Gustav Špet, *Èstetičeskie fragmenty* (Petrograd, 1922), pp. 28–29.

[19] One is reminded of a pertinent statement by I. A. Richards: "Too much importance has always been attached to the sensory quality of images. What gives an image efficacy is less its vividness as an image than its character as a mental event peculiarly connected with sensation." (I. A. Richards, *Principles of Literary Criticism*, London, 1948, 119).

[20] R. Ingarden put it in very similar terms. In his study *Das literarische Kunstwerk*, he maintained that the visual images evoked by imaginative literature are merely subjective supplements to the 'given' verbal structures, words, and sentences contained in the literary text.

[21] Viktor Žirmunskij, "Zadači poètiki", *Voprosy teorii literatury* (Leningrad, 1928), pp. 26–27.

Žirmunskij's concluding statement is indicative of the Formalists' preoccupation with language: "The material of poetry is neither images nor emotions, but words. . . . Poetry is verbal art." [22]

By making a clear-cut distinction between literature and the visual arts Žirmunskij rather appropriately shifted the debate from the problem of pictorial representation to that of poetic 'diction'. However, this frame of reference did not in itself preclude a preoccupation with the image. Indeed, many champions of the 'imagery' doctrine, from Aristotle down to J. L. Lowes, interpreted the 'image', as Špet felt it ought to be interpreted, as a *verbal* phenomenon. They saw in the use of the trope, especially of the metaphor, the chief point of difference between poetic and prosaic speech.

The Formalists were not convinced. In fact, as was already indicated,[23] the starting point of Šklovskij's programmatic essay, "Art as a Device", was a spirited attack on the imagery doctrine.

To proclaim the use of images, argued Šklovskij, as the distinctive feature of literary art is to posit a frame of reference at once too broad and too narrow. Poetic diction and imagery, he continued, are not coextensive notions. On the one hand, the area of figurative speech is much broader than that of poetry, as 'tropes' appear on various levels of language, for instance in picturesque colloquialisms or in the rhetorical figures of oratory. On the other hand, as Jakobson has pointed out,[24] a work of poetry can sometimes dispense with 'images' in the usual sense without losing any of its suggestiveness. According to Jakobson, a good exemple of this is provided by Puškin's famous lyric, "I Loved You Once", which achieves the intended effect – that of wistful resignation, half-concealing a still smouldering passion – without having recourse to any figures of speech. The efficacy of this lyrical masterpiece rests solely on a successful manipulation of grammatical oppositions and of phrase melody.[25] Obviously, insisted the Formalists, there is such a thing as a non-figurative poem, as well as a non-poetic image.

"The poet", wrote Šklovskij, "does not create images; he finds them [in ordinary language – V.E.] or recollects them." [26] Consequently, it is

---

[22]   *Ibid.*, p. 28.
[23]   See above, chapter IV, p. 76.
[24]   See Jakobson's introduction to Puškin's *Selected Works in Czech* (*Vybrané spisy A. S. Puškina*, Vol. I, Prague, 1936).
[25]   We shall revert to Jakobson's thesis in chapter XIII of this study, p. 232.
[26]   Viktor Šklovskij, "Iskusstvo kak priëm", *Poètika*, 1919, p. 102.

not in the mere presence of imagery, but in the use to which it is being put that one should seek the differentia of poetry.

This was the crucial and most valuable phase of the Formalist argument. Šklovskij and Jakobson were fundamentally on safe ground when they protested against equating poetic language with imagery, even if in the heat of polemics they went a bit too far in questioning the strategic importance of the metaphor.[27] But they undoubtedly scored their heaviest hits in postulating a clear-cut functional distinction between the poetic and the prosaic image.

Šklovskij argued persuasively against the rationalistic notion of the poetic image as an explanatory device, a mental shortcut. "The theory", he wrote, "that the 'image' is always simpler than the notion for which it is substituted is totally erroneous." If this were true, asked Šklovskij, how could we account for Tjutčev's famous simile – his likening of clouds to 'deaf-mute demons' *(demony gluxonemye)*? [28]

Herbert Spencer's law of 'economizing mental energy', insisted the *Opojaz* manifesto, so popular with dilettante estheticians, is not applicable to imaginative literature. If in informative 'prose', a metaphor aims to bring the subject closer to the audience or drive a point home, in 'poetry' it serves as a means of intensifying the intended esthetic effect. Rather than translating the unfamiliar into the terms of the familiar, the poetic image 'makes strange' the habitual by presenting it in a novel light, by placing it in an unexpected context.[29]

Šklovskij's theory of 'making strange' the object depicted switched the emphasis from the poetic use of the image to the function of poetic art. The trope was seen here merely as one of the devices at the poet's disposal, exemplifying the general tendency of poetry, indeed of all art. The transfer of the object to the 'sphere of new perception",[30] that is, a *sui generis* 'semantic shift' effected by the trope, was proclaimed as the principal aim, the *raison d'être* of poetry.

"People living at the seashore", wrote Šklovskij, "grow so accustomed to the murmur of the waves that they never hear it. By the same token, we scarcely ever hear the words which we utter. . . . We look at

---

[27] As will be shown below (chapter XIII), the late Formalist writings exhibited the tendency to restore to the metaphor some of its traditional status.

[28] Viktor Šklovskij, "Iskusstvo kak priëm", p. 101.

[29] This phase of Šklovskij's argument seems to have a counterpart in H. Konrad's who draws a distinction between the 'linguistic' and the 'esthetic' metaphor and describes the aim of the latter as 'bathing it in a new atmosphere' (see Wellek and Warren, *Theory of Literature*, p. 201).

[30] "Iskusstvo kak priëm", p. 112.

each other, but we do not see each other anymore. Our perception of the world has withered away, what has remained is mere recognition." [31]

It is this inexorable pull of routine, of habit, that the artist is called upon to counteract. By tearing the object out of its habitual context, by bringing together disparate notions, the poet gives a *coup de grâce* to the verbal cliché and to the stock responses attendant upon it and forces us into heightened awareness of things and their sensory texture. The act of creative deformation restores sharpness to our perception, giving 'density' to the world around us. "Density *(faktura)* is the principal characteristic of this peculiar world of deliberately constructed objects, the totality of which we call art." [32]

As if in order to prove that 'the device of making it strange' *(priëm ostranenija)* was not merely a slogan of the literary avant-garde, but an omnipresent principle of imaginative literature, Šklovskij drew his most telling exemples from the master of the 'realistic' novel, Lev Tolstoj. [33]

Tolstoj's works, Šklovskij observed astutely, abound in passages where the author 'refuses to recognize' the familiar objects and describes them as if they were seen for the first time. Thus, while describing in *War and Peace* an opera performance, he refers to the setting as 'pieces of painted cardboard' and in the scene of the mass in *The Resurrection* uses the prosaic expression 'small pieces of bread' to designate the host. The same technique is employed on a broader scale in Tolstoj's short story "Xolstomer", a first-person narrative, where the narrator is a horse. The social customs and institutions, exemplified by the horse's owner and his friends, are presented here from the vantage point of a perfect outsider, an animal, surprised and dismayed by the inconsistency and hypocrisy of humans. [34]

That in the above examples 'making it strange' became a vehicle of social criticism, of the typical Tolstoyan debunking of civilization on behalf of 'nature', is incidental to Šklovskij's argument. He is not concerned here with the ideological implications of the device. What he is interested in is Tolstoj's challenge to the cliché – the elimination of the

---

[31] Viktor Šklovskij, *Literatura i kinematograf* (Berlin, 1923), p. 11.

[32] Viktor Šklovskij, *Xod konja* (Moscow-Berlin, 1923).

[33] As the quotation marks may imply, the Formalists did not take too seriously Tolstoj's realism nor for that matter realism in general. They were justifiedly critical of the current usage of the term. As Jakobson pointed out, literature which advertises itself as 'truer to life' than its less 'realistic' counterparts, is actually but another mode of illusion.

[34] Viktor Šklovskij, "Iskusstvo kak priëm"; "Paralleli u Tolstogo", *Xod konja*.

'big words', the technical claptrap invoked usually in discussing the stage performance, the mass, or the institution of private property, for the sake of a basic, 'naive' vocabulary.

At first glance it may seem strange that a champion of esthetic sophistication should derive aid and comfort from Tolstoyan 'simplicity'. Actually, no contradiction was involved here. 'Making is strange' did not necessarily entail substituting the elaborate for the simple; it could mean just as well the reverse – the use of the profane or earthy term instead of the learned or genteel one, provided that the latter represented in the given case the accepted usage. What mattered was not the direction of the 'semantic shift', but the very fact that such a shift had occurred, that a deviation from the norm had been made. It was this deviation, insisted Šklovskij, this 'quality of divergence' [35] that lay at the core of esthetic perception.

The transfer of meaning inherent in the metaphor, is according to Šklovskij, only one of the means of achieving this esthetic effect, only one of the ways of constructing a 'perceptible' and 'dense' universe. Another crucial aspect of the 'deliberately impeded form' (zatrudnënnaja forma) is rhythm – a set of contrivances superimposed upon ordinary speech. Verse writing, maintained Šklovskij, is verbal tight-rope walking, a "dance of the articulatory organs".[36] The poet's 'twisted', oblique mode of discourse hinders communication and forces the reader to come to grips with the world in a more strenuous and, thus, more rewarding fashion.

In discussing Šklovskij's dichotomy of 'automatization' versus 'perceptibility', Medvedev, one of Šklovskij's Marxist opponents, accused the Formalist spokesman of straying from the path of objective analysis and bogging down in "the psycho-physiological conditions of esthetic perception".[37] Disregarding the completely misapplied adjective 'physiological'. Medvedev's charge seems unwarranted. Works of literature are knowable objects, accessible only through individual experience. Consequently, the mechanism of the esthetic response is a legitimate concern of an 'objectivist' art theoretician, provided that the emphasis

[35]   The above expression was borrowed from a German esthetician, B. Christiansen, whose work Philosophie der Kunst (Hanau, 1909) was one of the few Western European studies quoted approvingly by the Opojaz theorists. As will be shown below (cf. chapters XI, XIV, XV) Christiansen's Differenzqualität became one of the key terms of Formalist esthetics.

[36]   Viktor Šklovskij, O teorii prozy (Moscow, 1929), p. 25.

[37]   Pavel Medvedev, Formal'nyj metod v literaturovedenii (Leningrad, 1928), p. 52.

is placed not on the individual reader's idiosyncratic associations, but on the qualities inherent in the work of art and capable of eliciting certain 'intersubjective' responses.

But if the charge of psychological 'deviation' was scarcely justified, it may plausibly be argued that, in spite of his descriptive point of departure, Šklovskij came to define poetry not in terms of what it is, but in terms of what it is for.[38] The Formalist theory turned out to be a new 'defence of poesie' rather than a definition of 'literariness'. Furthermore, it may be noted, without detracting from the validity of Šklovskij's formulations, that his notion of art as a rediscovery of the world had more in common with traditional or popular views than the Formalist critic would have cared to admit.[39] As Wellek and Warren pointed out, the criterion of 'strangeness' was anything but novel. Aristotle had known that a perfect poetic 'diction' cannot dispense with 'unusual words'.[40] More recently, Romantic esthetics proclaimed, with Coleridge and Wordsworth, "the sense of novelty and freshness' as one of the earmarks of true poetry.[41] Likewise, to the surrealists, art is fundamentally "a renascence of wonder", "an act of renewal".[42] This latter analogy is especially worth emphasizing. In an essay written in 1926,[43] Jean Cocteau, one of the leading poets and critics of French Surrealism, described the mission of poetry in terms practically identical with Šklovskij's.

"Suddenly", wrote Cocteau, "as if in a flash, we *see* the dog, the coach, the house for the first time. Shortly afterwards habit erases again

---

[38] The above discrimination is borrowed from T. S. Eliot (cf. *The Use of Poetry and the Use of Criticism,* Cambridge, 1933, p. 111).

[39] The therapeutic value of art as the last line of defense against the routine and shallow pragmatism of everyday life was recently reaffirmed by two Western critics so dissimilar as Max Eastman and T. S. Eliot. Eastman describes the function of art as 'arousing and heightening consciousness' (Max Eastman, *Art and the Life of Action,* London, 1935, p. 81). T. S. Eliot's concluding statement in his book *The Use of Poetry and the Use of Criticism* is equally reminiscent of Šklovskij's credo: "Poetry", wrote Eliot, "may help to break the conventional modes of perception and valuation ... and make people see the world afresh, or some new part of it. It may make us from time to time a little more aware of the deeper, unnamed feelings which form the substratum of our being, to which we rarely penetrate; for our lives are mostly a constant evasion of ourselves and an evasion of the visible and sensible world." (p. 149).

[40] Quoted from S. H. Butcher's English translation of Aristotle's *Poetics* (cf. *Criticism,* ed. by Mark Shorer, Josephine Miles, Gordon McKenzie, New York, 1948, p. 212).

[41] Samuel Taylor Coleridge, "Occasion of the Lyrical Ballads", *Criticism,* p. 253.

[42] Herbert Read, "Surrealism and the Romantic Principle", *op. cit.,* 116.

[43] Jean Cocteau, "Le Secret Professionel", *Le Rappel à l'Ordre* (Paris, 1926).

this potent image. We pet the dog, we call the coach, we live in a house; we do not see them anymore."

"Such", continued Cocteau, "is the role of poetry. It takes off the veil, in the full sense of the word.[44] It reveals ... the amazing things which surround us and which our senses usually register mechanically. Get hold of a commonplace, clean it, rub it, illuminate it in such a fashion that it will astound us all with its youth and freshness, with its primordial vigor, and you shall have done the job of the poet. *Tout le reste est littérature.*" [45]

The striking similarity between the two pronouncements is not to be ascribed to Šklovskij's influence on Cocteau. There is no reason to suppose that Cocteau was familiar at all with the writings of the *Opojaz* theoretician. Nor is this virtual identity of formulation merely a matter of convergence of views between two essayists who wrote about poetry lovingly and imaginatively. It is certainly no accident that a statement which sounds at times like a French rendition of the *Opojaz* manifesto was made by one who, like Šklovskij, carried the torch for the literary avant-garde.

It is essential to keep in mind that Šklovskij's improvised philosophy of art was as much of a paean for the Russian Futurist movement as it was a contribution to the theory of literature. It was this unequivocal esthetic commitment – more pronounced in Šklovskij than in other Formalist spokesmen – which accounts for the tenor of the spirited essay: the rather unexpected preoccupation with the uses of poetry and the therapeutic value of creative deformation. Each school of poetry, no matter how unconcerned it professes to be with 'life', feels compelled, in its bid for an audience, to claim for itself and for poetic art a singularly effective mode of dealing with reality.

2

Šklovskij's able apologia for poetry had a considerable influence on subsequent Formalist theorizing. His key terms, e.g., 'making it strange', 'automatization', 'perceptibility', received wide curency in the writings

---

[44] One wonders whether the above phrase is a direct echo from a passage in *Anna Karenina* in which the painter Mixajlov describes the creative art as "taking the veils off" the actual, i.e. reaching beyond the surface of things into their very essence.

[45] *Le Rappel à l'Ordre*, pp. 215–216.

of the Russian Formalists. But, on the whole, Šklovskij's argument was more typical of Formalism as a rationale for poetic experimentation than as a systematic methodology of literary scholarship. The formalists' attempt to solve the fundamental problems of literary theory in close alliance with modern linguistics and semiotics found its most succinct expression in the studies of Roman Jakobson.

"The function of poetry", wrote Jakobson in 1933,[46] "is to point out that the sign is not identical with its referent. Why do we need this reminder?" "Because", continued Jakobson, "along with the awareness of the identity of the sign and the referent (A is A_1), we need the consciousness of the inadequacy of this identity (A is not A_1); this antinomy is essential, since without it the connection between the sign and the object becomes automatized and the perception of reality withers away." [47]

Jakobson's tersely abstract definition of the poetic quality ('básnickost') paralleled in many respects Šklovskij's eulogy of the creative act. Both critics credited poetry with enhancing our mental health by counteracting the pernicious tendency toward the 'automatization' of our responses. But Jakobson's emphasis is somewhat different from Šklovskij's. To Jakobson, the immediate critical problem is not the interaction between the perceiving subject and the object perceived, but the relationship between the 'sign' and the 'referent'; not the reader's attitude toward reality, but the poet's attitude toward language.

It is in the way in which the poet uses his medium that Jakobson, along with the bulk of the Formalist theoreticians, saw the situs of 'literariness'. In other words, the task of locating the differentia of imaginative literature became fundamentally a matter of delimiting 'poetic speech' from other modes of discourse.

Already the first Formalist manifestoes discriminated between poetic language and 'practical' or informative language.[48] The latter was declared to be esthetically neutral, amorphous, while poetry was described as a discourse organized throughout for esthetic effect. In communicative language, it was argued, no attention is paid to the sound or texture of the verbal 'sign'. In ordinary speech and even more so in scientific discourse, the word is a transparent counter, a mere tag. In imaginative writing, especially in verse, deliberate use is made of

[46] Roman Jakobson, "Co je poesie?", *Volné směry*, XXX (1933–34), pp. 229–239.
[47] Quoted from Mikuláš Bakoš (ed.), *Teória literatúry* (Trnava, 1941), p. 180.
[48] See above, chapter IV, pp. 73–74.

speech-sounds. Verbal play, characteristic of poetic language, 'lays bare' the phonic texture of the word.[49]

The earlier Formalist writings tended to confuse the issue by equating the dichotomy of poetic vs. 'practical' language with the semanticist's distinction between the cognitive and emotive uses of speech.[50] In what was obviously a concession to the popular affective theory of poetry, the *Opojaz* critics spoke of poetic language as an expressive or an alogical mode of communication. In his essay "On Poetry and Trans-Sense Language", Šklovskij bracketed together interjections, emotionally loaded archaisms and euphonic devices such as alliteration.[51] Jakubinskij quoted approvingly the theory about the potential expressiveness of phonemes advanced by Maurice Grammont, who tried to analyze the sound-patterns of French verse from the standpoint of the emotional coloring of individual vowels and consonants.[52]

But this 'emotionalist' deviation was soon discarded. In the course of their struggle against Symbolist esthetics, the Formalists became increasingly wary of the mystical 'correspondences' between sounds and the ineffable emotions which their 'verbal magic' was said to evoke. "It is as erroneous", declared Jakobson, "to equate poetic speech with emotive speech as it would be to reduce poetic euphony to onomatopeia." [53] The poet can and does occasionally make use of the resources of expressive language, but in doing so he furthers his own aims.[54]

What are the 'aims' of poetic speech, as distinguished from those of affective utterance? Jakobson stated the matter with the utmost clarity. He conceded that poetry is more akin to the emotive than to the cognitive mode of discourse. In the former, he admitted, the "relation

---

[49]   It is worth noting that this typically Formalist phrase is a free translation of a passage from James' *Psychology,* dealing with the impact of verbal repetition on the perception of individual words. The passage was quoted by Jakubinskij in his essay on "The Sounds of Poetic Language" (*Poètika,* 1919). The original text reads as follows: "it [the repeated word] is reduced, by this new way of attending to it, to its sensational nudity" (William James, *Psychology,* New York, 1928, p. 315). The Russian translation of James' work, Jakubinskij's direct source of reference, actually anticipates the Formalist terminology: "having thus looked at the word from a new viewpoint, we have laid bare (*obnažili*) its purely phonetic aspect".

[50]   See R. Ogden and I. A. Richards, *The Meaning of Meaning* (New York, 1936).

[51]   Viktor Šklovskij, "O poèzii i zaumnom jazyke", *Poètika* (Petrograd, 1919), pp. 13–26.

[52]   Lev Jakubinskij, "O zvukax poètičeskogo jazyka", *Poètika.*

[53]   Roman Jakobson, *O češskom stixe . . .* , p. 66.

[54]   *Ibid.*

between sound and meaning is more organic, more intimate" than in cognitive language: the attempt to convey emotions by means of "appropriate" sound combinations necessitates closer attention to the phonic texture of the word. Here, however, insisted Jakobson, the similarity ceases. In emotive speech the "apporpriate" sound-cluster is valued not for what it is, but for what it conveys: euphony is a handmaiden of communication, as "the emotion dictates its laws to the verbal mass". Not so in poetry, where "the communicative function, inherent in both 'practical' and emotive language, is reduced to a minimum". "Poetry, which is simply an *utterance oriented toward the mode of expression* (*vyskazyvanie s ustanovkoj na vyraženie*), is governed by immanent laws." [55]

Such was Jakobson's position in his provocative, if extremist, study of Russian Futurist poetry. Fifteen years later he restated the same ideas in more measured terms:

"The distinctive feature of poetry lies in the fact that a word is perceived as a word and not merely a proxy for the denoted object or an outburst of an emotion, that words and their arrangement, their meaning, their outward and inward form acquire weight and value of their own." [56]

Another Formalist theoretician, B. Tomaševskij, seems to have taken his cue from Jakobson. In Tomaševskij's *Theory of Literature*,[57] the most comprehensive exposition of Formalist methodology, poetic language was defined as "one of the linguistic systems where the communicative function is relegated to the background and where verbal structures acquire autonomous value". And Efimov, the author of a study of Russian Formalism, summed up the Formalist conception of poetry in the following phrase: "verbal activity, characterized by the maximum perceptibility of the modes of expression".[58]

'Emphasis on the medium', 'perceptibility of the modes of expression' – these were the crucial formulations, which sharply juxtaposed the language of imaginative literature with other types of discourse. The dichotomy of cognitive vs. affective was supplanted here by the distinction between the referential language of informative prose and the sign-oriented language of poetry, geared to the 'actualization' of

---

[55] Roman Jakobson, *Novejšaja russkaja poèzija*, p. 10.
[56] Cf. "Co je poesie?", Mikuláš Bakoš, ed., *Teória literatúry*, p. 180.
[57] Boris Tomaševskij, *Teorija literatury* (Moscow-Leningrad, 1925), p. 8.
[58] N. I. Efimov, "Formalizm v russkom literaturovedenii", *Naučnye izvestija Smolenskogo Gosudarstvennogo Universiteta*, vol. 5 (1929), part III, p. 70.

the linguistic symbol. All the techniques at the poet's disposal – rhythm, euphony and, last but not least, the startling word-combinations known as 'images' – were seen as converging upon the word in order to throw into relief its complex texture, its 'density'. In poetry, the Formalists insisted, the word is more than a verbal shadow of the object; it is an object in its own right.[59]

It has been argued that this doctrine was essentially a reflection of Futurist poetics with its slogans of 'liberation of phonic energy' and the 'self-valuable word'. This is an oversimplification. It cannot be denied that the early Formalist notion of poetic language was strongly affected by Russian Futurism. Jakobson cited Xlebnikov's 'trans-sense' experiments in support of his thesis that "poetic speech ... tends toward its ultimate limit – the phonetic, or more exactly, the euphonic word",[60] i.e. sheer sound. Šklovskij savored the 'dance of articulatory organs' and spoke of verse-making as "filling the distances between rimes with free phonic spots".[61]

This preference for the type of poetry where 'semantics was toned down' and sound 'laid bare' was not entirely attributable to the Futurist impact. For the new school of criticism the emphasis on poetic euphony was the most effective way of dramatizing the issue – of 'laying bare' the differentia of imaginative literature. Because of its highly formalized structure verse seemed to be a better case in point than prose fiction; and an experimental poem, based on untrammelled verbal play, a better touchstone than a more 'conventional' brand of poetry.

But whatever the motives behind the early Formalist utterances, the Formalist critic's fascination with the 'self-valuable word' was a short-lived affair. As was indicated above,[62] the emphasis of Formalist research soon shifted from phonetics toward semantics or more exactly, toward the interrelations between sound and meaning. This increasing awareness of semantics was not merely a matter of widening the scope of inquiry. What was involved here was a broader and more mature notion of the verbal sign that the one which was typical of the early period.

The Futurist could talk glibly about liberating the word from its meaning because he tended to reduce the verbal sign to its sensory

---

[59] "But the word is not a shadow", wrote Šklovskij, in a polemic with Trockij. "The word is a thing." (Viktor Šklovskij, *O teorii prozy*, Moscow, 1929, p. 51).
[60] Roman Jakobson, *Novejšaja russkaja poèzija*, p. 68.
[61] Viktor Šklovskij, *Xod konja* (Berlin-Moscow, 1923), p. 29.
[62] See above, chapter V, pp. 87–89.

texture – or what is perhaps the same thing – because he confused the meaning of the word with its referent.

Edmund Husserl, a philosopher who had a considerable impact on some of the Formalist theoreticians, made a fruitful distinction when he differentiated between the 'object' (*Gegenstand*), the non-verbal phenomenon denoted by the word, and the 'meaning' (*Bedeutung*), i.e., the way in which the 'object' is presented. In other words, to Husserl the meaning is not an element of extra-linguistic reality, but a part and parcel of the verbal sign. But if this is the case, the Futurist watchword becomes an absurdity or at least a misnomer.

Indeed, as the Formalist spokesmen could not help but recognize, no poetry, however non-objective, can dispense with meaning. Even in the most experimental poem of, say, Edith Sitwell or Ezra Pound, even in the most bewildering passage from *Finnegans Wake,* replete as it is with quasi-words, coined *ad hoc* from familiar morphemes, the meaning is always present somehow, even if in an 'approximate', potential form. The impact of the context, as well as analogies with cognate 'real' words, endow these bizarre products of the poet's linguistic fancy with a certain semantic aura.

Clearly what was really at issue was not emancipation from meaning, but autonomy *vis-à-vis* the referent. This latter tendency is especially pronounced in the case of a poetic neologism, which has no denotative value, as it does not point to any recognizable element of extra-linguistic reality. But this is obivously an extreme poetic situation. More often than not, we have to do in poetry not with what might be called 'pseudo-reference' (Yvor Winters' term),[63] but with 'ambiguity' in the Empsonian sense of the word.[64] The oscillation between several semantic planes, typical of the poetic context, loosens up the bond between the sign and the object. The denotative precision arrived at by 'practical' language gives way to connotative density and wealth of associations.

In other words the hallmark of poetry as a unique mode of discourse lies not in the absence of meaning but in the multiplicity of meanings. This was indeed the view expressed in mature Formalist statements. "The aim of poetry", wrote Ejxenbaum, "is to make perceptible the texture of the word in *all* its aspects." [65] But this meant clearly that the

[63]   Cf. Yvor Winters, "The Experimental School in American Poetry", *Criticism* (ed. by Mark Schorer, pp. 288–309).
[64]   Cf. William Empson, *Seven Types of Ambiguity* (London, 1930).
[65]   Boris Ejxenbaum, *Lermontov* (Leningrad, 1924), p. 35.

'inward form' of the word – i.e., the semantic nexus inherent in it, is no less essential to the esthetic effect than the sheer sound. The 'actualization' of the verbal sign achieved by poetry was recognized as a complex transaction involving the semantic and morphological, as well as the phonetic, levels of language.

3

From insisting on the complex unity of the verbal sign there was but one step to postulating the indivisibility of that peculiar system of signs which is the work of literature. If in the individual word 'meaning' could not be divorced from sound, it seemed equeally futile to separate the cumulative meaning of the literary work, its 'content', from the artistic embodiment commonly known as 'form'.

The Russian Formalists had little patience with the traditional dichotomy of 'form versus content', which, as Wellek and Warren put it, "cuts a work of art into two halves: a crude content and a superimposed, purely external form".[66] Boris Engelhardt, a thoughtful philosophical sympathizer of Russian Formalism who tried to restate the tenets of *Opojaz* in categories of Neo-Kantian esthetics, speaks of the Formalist determination to do away with the dualism of the 'object expressed' and the 'means of expression'.[67]

The case for the inextricable unity of the 'how' and the 'what' of literature was stated by Žirmunskij in terms of plain critical common sense.[68] He took issue with the naive, uncritical notion of form as mere clothing for the poet's ideas or a bowl into which a ready-made content is 'poured'. In imaginative literature content – emotional or cognitive – appears only through the medium of form and thus cannot be profitably discussed, indeed conceived of, apart from its artistic embodiment. "Love, sorrow, tragic inner strife", wrote Žirmunskij, "a philosophical idea, etc., do not exist in poetry *per se* but only in their concrete form." Žirmunskij warned correctly against the tendency of crudely extrinsic criticism to tear the emotions or ideas embodied in the work of poetry out of their literary context and discuss them then in psychological or sociological terms.

[66]   René Wellek and Austin Warren, *Theory of Literature* (New York, 1949), p. 140.
[67]   Boris Engelhardt, *Formal'nyj metod v istorii literatury* (Leningrad, 1927), p. 13.
[68]   Viktor Žirmunskij, "Zadači poètiki", *Voprosy teorii literatury* (Leningrad, 1928).

"In literary art, the elements of so-called content", Žirmunskij continued, "have no independent existence and are not exempt from the general laws of esthetic structure; [69] they serve as a poetic 'theme', an artistic 'motif' or image, and in this capacity participate in the esthetic effect to which the work of literature is geared." [70]

Šklovskij charged into the fallacy of 'separable content" in his characteristic brisk and flippant manner. He poked fun at critics who treat form as a 'necessary evil', a guise for the 'real thing', and who brush form impatiently aside in order to grasp the 'content' of the work of art. "People who try to 'solve' paintings as if they were crossword puzzles want to take the form off the painting in order to see it better."[71]

An Occidental 'contextualist' critic could have no quarrel with the above strictures. But he might grow somewhat restive with Šklovskij's definition of art as 'pure form' or with his declaration in a self-congratulatory passage: "The most amazing thing about . . . the Formalist method is that is does not negate the ideological content of art, but considers the so-called content as one of the aspects of form." [72] One wonders what the Formalist spokesman was actually trying to say: was he denying the relevance or the separability of 'content?' Was he implying that all that matters in art is form, or was he simply saying that everything in the work of art is necessarily *formed,* i.e. organized for an esthetic purpose?

It seems that we are confronted here with a double confusion – both philosophical and semantic. Šklovskij's position on content versus form is vitiated by a lack of clarity as to the relative importance of the esthetic criteria, as well as by an inconsistent usage of the word 'form'. The Russian Formalist leader seemed to fluctuate between two differing interpretations of the term: he could not quite make up his mind as to whether he meant by 'form' a quality inherent in an esthetic whole or an esthetic whole endowed with a certain quality.

Whenever the former seems to be the case, the tendency to equate art with form smacks of sterile 'purism', which Šklovskij rejected in one

---

[69] A similar position was taken by Manfred Kridl. "The so-called ideology", he wrote, "has no independent existence in a work of literature; it does not exist in it in the same way as outside of it, in 'life,' in philosophy or journalism. Thus, it must be examined in its specific, let us say, literary shape, in its literary function." (Manfred Kridl, *Wstęp do badań nad dziełem literackiem,* Wilno, 1936, p. 159).

[70] Viktor Žirmunskij, *Voprosy teorii literatury,* pp. 20–22.

[71] Viktor Šklovskij, *Literatura i kinematograf,* p. 7.

[72] Id., *Sentimental'noe putešestvie* (Moscow-Berlin, 1923), p. 129.

of his studies as "mechanistic and obsolete".[73] Where the key term
'form' is used in a more inclusive sense, the above objections clearly
become invalid; indeed, one can readily agree with Žirmunskij that
"if by 'formal', we mean 'esthetic', all the facts of content become in
art formal phenomena".[74] One may question, however, as M. Kridl has
done,[75] the practicability of treating 'form' as a generic term for artistic
creation — an interpretation so broad as to become well-nigh useless,
if not misleading. Where 'formal' is used interchangeably with 'esthetic', one would be well advised to discard the concept of 'form', which
commonly implies a part rather than a whole, and talk of 'structure'
instead.

The Russian Formalists were apparently not unaware of the pitfalls
of traditional terminology. They were never too happy about the notion
of form, nor, for that matter, about the 'Formalist' label, pinned on
the movement apparently by its bystanders rather than its followers.
It has already been indicated that in defining their methodological
position the Formalists were only too eager to have recourse to some
such concepts as 'morphological method', 'specifiers', and the like. In
discussing the structure of the 'literary fact' and the mechanism of the
literary process, they tended increasingly to substitute for the static
dichotomy 'form versus content' a dynamic pair of notions, 'materials'
and 'device' (priëm).

From the Formalist standpoint the latter set of terms presented
several methodological advantages. The organic unity of a work of
literature was salvaged, as the notion of coexistence in the esthetic object of two simultaneous and seemingly detachable components gave
way to that of two successive phases in the literary process — the pre-
esthetic and the esthetic. In Formalist parlance, the 'materials' represented the raw stuff of literature which acquires esthetic efficacy [76] and
thus becomes eligible for participation in the literary work of art only
through the agency of the 'device', or, more exactly, a set of devices
peculiar to imaginative literature.

It may be noted that in the early Formalist writings, one encounters

---

[73]   Id., *Literatura i kinematograf*, p. 3.
[74]   Viktor Žirmunskij, *Voprosy teorii literatury*, p. 77.
[75]   Manfred Kridl, *Wstęp do badań nad dziełem literackiem*, p. 151.
[76]   In their recent work *Theory of Literature*, which has many points of contact
with the Formalist-Structuralist position, Wellek and Warren adopt a similar
terminology: "It would be better to rechristen the esthetically indifferent elements
'materials', while the manner in which they acquire esthetic efficacy may be
styled 'structure' " (*Theory of Literature*, p. 141).

a *sui generis* terminological compromise, notably the dichotomy of 'form versus materials'. The more objectionable of the two traditional concepts – 'content' – was dropped, while the other was reinterpreted as a formative principle of dynamic integration and control rather than merely an outer shell or external embellishment. This was a notion closely akin to Aristotle's *eidos,* which in the words of a modern philosopher of language, Anton Marty,[77] connotes the "inward shaping power applied to raw matter".

Now, what was the nature or locus of the 'materials'? Do they constitute the subject matter of the work, i.e., the sphere of reality embodied in literature, or its medium, language? On this score there was apparently no complete unanimity among the Formalist and near-Formalist spokesmen. To Engelhardt, who as a philosopher was more concerned with ontology than linguistics, 'materials' meant the extraesthetic residue of the poetic 'communication', the 'controlling' segment of actuality. Šklovskij paid his due to both rival interpretations; consitency or terminological neatness was not his *forte.* "The outside world", he wrote in his booklet on *Literature and the Film,*[78] "is for the painter not the content, but merely material for his painting." The same applies, he continued, to the psychoideological components of literature usually classified under the heading 'content'. Ideas and emotions, "expressed in a work of literature, as well as events depicted in it", are treated here as "building materials" for the job of artistic construction, phenomena of the same order as words or word-combinations.[79]

In the same collection of essays we find the following passage: "At any rate, it seems obvious to me that for a writer words are not a necessary evil, or merely a means of saying something, but the very material of the work. Literature is made up of words and is governed by the laws which govern language." [80]

This latter interpretation seems to have prevailed in other Formalist writings. Žirmunskij as well as Jakobson – to name two otherwise dissimilar representatives of Russian Formalism – equated the 'materials' of literature with its verbal texture. The poet, it was argued, works in language in the same way in which the musician deals in tones and the painter in colors.

[77] Anton Marty, *Psyche und Sprachstruktur, Nachgelassene Schriften* (Bern, 1940), p. 13.
[78] Viktor Šklovskij, *Literatura i kinematograf,* p. 5.
[79] *Ibid.,* p. 16.
[80] *Ibid.,* p. 15.

This immanent view was more congruent with the Formalist insistence on the self-contained character of the literary work. The conception of the creative process as a tension between ordinary speech and the artistic devices which shape or deform it corroborated the Formalist tenet that literature is essentially a linguistic or semiotic phenomenon – an 'unfolding of the verbal material', in the early Formalist lingo, 'a system of signs', in the Czech Structuralist parlance. Once again the poet's job was defined as manipulation of language rather than as representation of reality. The actual was relegated to the role of the cumulative referent of the literary work, an empirical series contiguous with literature, but enjoying a different ontological status.

If the above notion of 'materials' was another testimony to the linguistic or semasiological orientation of Formalism, the correlative term 'device' was still more crucial. It ought to be obvious by now that 'device' was the watchword of Russian Formalism. 'Art as a Device,' 'the device of 'making it strange' ' (*priëm ostranenija*), 'a device laid bare' (*obnaženie priëma*), 'the literary work is the sum-total of devices employed in it' – in all these crucial formulations '*priëm*' appears as a key term – the basic unit of poetic form, the agency of 'literariness'.

The very choice of the term was significant. Many a form-conscious critic speaks about 'means of expression'. To the Russian Formalists this would have smacked of psychologism, of the "naive realistic formula that poetry lays bare the poet's soul".[81] Like Veselovskij, to whose 'historical poetics' they were in many ways indebted,[82] the Formalist theoreticians were intent on side-stepping the vexing issue of the creative personality. Literary technology seemed to them a much firmer ground than the psychology of creation. Hence the tendency to treat literature as a suprapersonal, if not impersonal, phenomenon, as a deliberate application of techniques to 'materials' rather than as self-expression, as a convention rather than as a confession.

"The literary work of art", wrote Ejxenbaum in a characteristic passage, "is always something made, shaped, invented – not only artful, but artificial in the good sense of the word." [83] And Šklovskij offered the following apology for the tortuous quality of his critical essays in *The Knight's Move:* "There are many reasons for the oddity of the

---

[81]   Boris Tomaševskij, *Puškin* (Moscow, 1925), p. 57.
[82]   See above, chapter I, pp. 28–31.
[83]   Boris Ejxenbaum, "Kak sdelana '*Šinel'* ' Gogolja", *Poètika* (Petrograd, 1919), p. 161.
[84]   Viktor Šklovskij, *Xod konja*, p. 9.

knight's move, but the principal reason is the conventionality of art. I write about the conventions in art." [84]

'The conventionality of art' — this was the pervasive theme not only of Šklovskij's writings, but of Russian Formalist criticism in general. And appropriately so. If imaginative literature was a system of signs, organized so as to be 'perceptible', it was necessary to establish for each period or type of literature the organizing principle, the esthetic *modus operandi* — the set of conventions superimposed on the materials. Indeed, when faced with a new literary object the Formalist critic would want to know not why or by whom it was created, but 'how it was made'.[85] He would not start by inquiring into the social pressures or psychic drives which had shaped the work, but into the esthetic norms which inhered in the given type of literature and imposed themselves upon the author, irrespective of his social allegiances or his artistic temperament.

[85] See, for instance, Boris Ejxenbaum, "Kak sdelana *'Šinel''* Gogolja" (How *'The Overcoat'* was Made), and Viktor Šklovskij, "Kak sdelan *Don Quixote*" (How *Don Quixote* was Made), *O teorii prozy* (Moscow, 1929).

XI. LITERATURE AND 'LIFE' – FORMALIST AND STRUCTURALIST VIEW

1

The passionate concern with craftsmanship, the habit of taking a work apart to see what 'makes it tick', applied with an irreverent lack of discrimination to celebrated masterpieces and third-rate productions alike, brought upon the Formalists charges of esthetic epicurism and 'soullessness'.[1] One of the accusers, the old fashioned 'realistic' novelist Veresaev, irritated by Ejxenbaum's treatment of Gogol''s "The Overcoat" and of Tolstoj's inner strife, gave rein to his imagination to picture the Formalists as "probably, toothless old pedants, incapable of any emotions".[2]

While Veresaev's psychological whistling in the dark need not be taken seriosly, it cannot be denied that the Russian Formalists laid themselves wide open to attack. Some of them, particularly Šklovskij, liked to strike the pose of the connoisseur and discuss, say, the respective merits of contemporary Russian writers in the hard-boiled technical lingo of a prize fight expert, appraising the 'form' of contending champions.[3]

More important still, some of the *Opojaz* statements seemed to imply that the work of literature was nothing but artifice, nothing but the set of devices employed in it.

This narrowness of focus found expreession not only in methodological generalizations, but in the choice of illustrative material as well. The Formalists were quick to accord preferential treatment to cases where the conventional nature of literary art was, to use the *Opojaz* term, 'laid bare'; they consistently played up those literary works the

---

[1] See above, chapter VI, pp. 105, 106.
[2] V. Veresaev, "O komplimentax Ruzvel'ta i o knižnoj pyli", *Zvezda,* 1928.
[3] Viktor Šklovskij, *Gamburgskij sčët* (Moscow, 1928).

only content of which was form. In their assessments of contemporary Russian literature they praised 'naked' verbal play in verse and encouraged techniques of indirection in prose fiction, e.g. parody, stylization, whimsical toying with the plot. The same tendency is discernible in the early Formalist ventures into the history of literature. It was certainly no accident that Ejxenbaum chose as the topic of his first 'Formalist' essay Gogol's famous short story "The Overcoat", a masterpiece of grotesque stylization.[4] It was still more significant that Šklovskij, who incidentally prided himself on having 'brought Sterne to Russia', in his *Theory of Prose* used *Tristram Shandy* as a touchstone of the novelist's art.

What endeared Sterne to Šklovskij was obviously his adeptness at parody and his mockery of conventional narrative schemes. The Formalist critic discovered an analogy between Sterne's 'poetics' and that of Futurist verse: the difference, Šklovskij argued, between *Tristram Shandy* and a conventional novel is equivalent to the difference between a traditional poem which employs alliteration and a Futurist poem. Sterne's grotesquely long and irrelevant digressions, continued Šklovskij, such devices as placing the preface in the middle of the book or the playful 'omission' of several chapters, are eloquent testimony to his keen awareness of literary form and its essential conventionality. "It is this taking cognizance of form through violating it that constitutes the content of the novel." [5]

Now this is precisely the aspect of Sterne's art which disturbs those critics or readers who expect a novelist to tell a coherent and absorbing story rather than 'lay bare a device'. For these detractors of Sterne Šklovskij has nothing but scorn: "One often hears an assertion that *Tristram Shandy* is not a novel. For people who hold this view only opera is real music; symphony to them is mere disorder." "Actually", declared Šklovskij, "the reverse of this is true. *Tristram Shandy* is the most typical novel in world literature." [6]

This was indeed a strong statement. That *Tristram Shandy* is a much greater novel than many a 'good story' can readily be granted. One can also agree with Šklovskij that toying with the medium is not only a recurrent theme in world literature, but also a procedure essential to its efficacy and growth. Awareness of form as form is indispensable to

---

[4] See above, chapter IV, p. 75.
[5] Viktor Šklovskij, *O teorii prozy* (Moscow, 1929), p. 180.
[6] *Ibid.*, p. 204.

esthetic perception. 'Laying bare the device' throws into focus the tension between 'form' and 'materials' and thus performs with regard to literary craft a service similar to that performed by the poet's verbal play *vis-à-vis* the 'sign'. Moreover, as Tynjanov shrewdly observed,[7] parody is often a lever of literary change; by poking fun at a specific set of conventions which tend to degenerate into stale clichés the artist paves the way for a new, more 'perceptible' set of conventions – a new style.

And yet the adjective 'typical' in Šklovskij's eulogy of *Tristram Shandy* is characteristically misapplied. The use of this term betrayed the Formalist's 'modern' bias in favor of non-objective art, his tendency to mistake the extreme for the representative, the 'pure' for the 'superior'. Obviously, the differentia of literature, its concern with its medium, was more conspicuous where the device, instead of serving as a catalyst to blend heterogeneous elements into unity, was made to recoil upon itself. But did this make Xlebnikov necessarily more 'literary' than Puškin, or Sterne more 'typical' than Henry James, indeed, than the large majority of novelists?

Even in their orthodox period the Russian Formalists were not quite impervious to this argument. They would admit not infrequently that a 'naked' device was in literature the exception rather than the rule. They would grant that more often than not a literary technique, be it a 'self-valuable' sound pattern, a 'semantic shift' or a plot structure, is disguised or justified by non-artistic considerations, such as verisimilitude, psychological plausibility, and the like. In most works of literature, it was conceded, the device is 'motivated' rather than 'laid bare'.

'Motivation of the device' (*motivirovka priëma*) – this was another key concept of Formalist criticism. With regard to the study of prose fiction, where the concept was most frequently used, 'motivation' meant, in Šklovskij's words, an "explanation of a plot-structure in terms of actual mores".[8] With reference to the entire field of imaginative literature the above expression denoted a justification of an artistic convention in terms of 'life'.

At first, in their single-minded devotion to the 'device', the Formalists held 'motivation' in low esteem. It was dubbed a secondary phenomenon, a necessary evil – apparently a concession to the unsophisticated reader who cannot fully appreciate the all-important play with

[7] Cf. Jurij Tynjanov, *Gogol' i Dostoevskij. K teorii parodii* (Petrograd, 1921).
[8] Viktor Šklovskij, *Literatura i kinematograf* (Berlin, 1923), p. 50.

the medium and thus has to be lured to the literary work under false pretenses. But the competent critic should know better than that; he need not take at its face value what is merely a *post-factum* justification of, if not a pretext for, something else.

Having thus stated the problem, the Formalists set out briskly to explain away the 'ethos' of various works of literature. In his study of Xlebnikov Jakobson interpreted the 'urbanism' of the Futurist poets, their cult of machine civilization, as an ideological justification of the revolution in poetic vocabulary, a Futurist's expedient for introducing new and unorthodox word-combinations. "A number of poetic devices", wrote Jakobson, "found their application in urbanism." [9]

In the same study a spirited attempt was made to construe the Romantic conception of the creative personality – the titanic soul rent by inner contradictions – as primarily a psychological motivation of the fragmentary, disjointed quality of the Byronic poetic tale.[10]

Psychological considerations were not taken too literally even in the analysis of intensely personal lyrical verses. In his provocative study of Anna Axmatova, Ejxenbaum advanced an interesting thesis: the apparent dualism of Axmatova's lyrical 'I', the *poetic alter ego,* now a "sinner in the sway of stormy passions, now a destitute nun",[11] is interpreted in a striking phrase as a 'personified oxymoron'. Axmatova's favorite figure of speech, says Ejxenbaum, was projected onto the plane of psychological drama; a stylistic paradox became a mental split. "The lyrical theme", he wrote, "of which Axmatova is the center unfolds by means of antitheses and paradoxes; it eludes psychological formulation; it is 'made strange' by the incongruency of her states of mind." [12]

A similar procedure was brought to bear on some masterpieces of

---

[9] Roman Jakobson, *Novejšaja russkaja poèzija* (Prague, 1921), p. 16.

[10] While it is difficult to accept Jakobson's explanation *in toto,* this was more than a far-fetched projection of Futurist Bohemianism into the Puškin era. To corroborate his interpretation of Romanticism Jakobson quoted a pertinent excerpt from an appraisal of Byron's role by a contemporary of Puškin. This is how the author of an article, published in 1829 in the Russian literary review *Syn otečestva,* described the Byronic innovations: "Comprehending fully the needs of his contemporaries, he [Byron] created a new language in order to express new forms. Systematic, detailed description, all the preliminaries of exposition ... were rejected by Byron. He introduced the fashion of starting the narration from the middle or from the end, with an apparent lack of concern for integrating the parts. His poems are made of fragments." (Quoted in Roman Jakobson, *Novejšaja russkaja poèzija,* p. 13.)

[11] Boris Ejxenbaum, *Anna Axmatova* (Petrograd, 1923), p. 114.

[12] *Ibid.,* p. 130.

Russian prose. In his ultra-Formalist study of the young Tolstoj, Ejxenbaum incurred the everlasting ire of Veresaev [13] by suggesting that Tolstoj's passion for minute psychological analysis, for ruthless introspection and discursiveness, was fundamentally a matter of his struggle for a new narrative manner, his challenge to the clichés of romantic literature.

The psychology of the characters was not treated any more seriously than that of the author. In his essay "How Don Quixote was Made",[14] Šklovskij spoke disdainfully of the critics who seemed to be puzzled by the fact that Cervantes' sorrowful knight now acted as a madman, then delivered erudite and coherent orations on literary and philosophical topics. A literary character, he argued, cannot be expected to be consistent or credible. Apparently Cervantes wanted to interject into his narrative some critical comments, in line with his general tendency to focus on the problems of literary craft. Cervantes' form-consciousness, observed Šklovskij, is pointed up by the scenes in the 'literary tavern', where the audience passes judicious judgements on the quality of the stories told. The scholarly aspect of Don Quixote, however little it may square with his vagaries, was needed simply to make the critical interpolations possible. In art, Šklovskij insisted, everything – the hero's fate, character, the setting of the action, attitudes and ideas – can be made to serve as a "motivation of the articice".[15]

Such reinterpretations – and there are others – were often astute and invariably ingenious, yet the cavalier treatment accorded the 'ethos' of literature was both far-fetched and mechanistic. As was to be expected, the scheme proved fully applicable only to what might be called extreme literary situations. It fitted perfectly *Tristram Shandy,* the most non-objective and form-conscious of the famous novels; it would be almost equally applicable to Byron's *Don Juan,* where the story was admittedly a sham, a mere pretext for the firework-like display of 'conversational facility', or to Puškin's whimsical poem *Domik v Kolomne,* which Šklovskij aptly described as "a work almost entirely devoted to the description of the device employed in it".[16] But the pooh-poohing of 'motivations' in a literary work with a significant ethos was indefensible. Šklovkij's discussion of *Don Quixote* is a good case in point. The Formalist spokesman was well advised in emphasizing Cervantes' form-

---

[13] See above, footnote 2.
[14] Viktor Šklovskij, "Kak sdelan *Don Quixote*", *O teorii prozy.*
[15] Viktor Šklovskij, *Xod konja* (Moscow-Berlin, 1923), p. 125.
[16] Viktor Šklovskij, *Literatura i kinematograf,* pp. 16–17.

consciousness, a quality overlooked by many critics. But his treatment of Don Quixote's characterization clearly revealed the limitations of his method. By explaining away the contradictions between Don Quixote's 'madness' and 'wisdom' as a mere technical expedient, Šklovskij seems to have missed the crucial philosophical dilemma implicit in the novel. I have in mind the problem of the fundamental ambiguity of the terms 'madness' and 'wisdom', in other words, the problem of reality versus illusion.[17]

If *Don Quixote,* a novel making lavish use of the devices of parody and irony, does not lend itself too well to ultra-Formalist operations, one shudders at the thought of applying Šklovskij's scheme to, say, *The Divine Comedy.* Could any one seriously maintain that Dante's theology was merely a 'motivation' of a heterogeneous plot, an ideological pretext for the fictional exploration of various planes of existence?

The early Formalist notion of *motivirovka* was empirically faulty, because it left out more than it included. It was also methodologically untenable by the Formalists' own standards. This concept which tended to explain away a component of literary endeavor implied the existence in a full-fledged work of art of a 'foreign body' – an extrinsic, if not superfluous, element. This in turn tended to weaken the Formalist tenet about the organic unity of the literary work of art, and to revive the mechanistic dichotomy of form versus content which the Formalists worked so hard to demolish. The fallacy of the 'disengageable form' was found almost as objectionable as its reverse – that of the 'detachable content'.[18] As early as 1923 Šklovskij himself conceded that the esthete's insistence on the primacy of 'form' was as mechanistic as the utilitarian's call for the hegemony of 'content'.[19]

2

The fallacy underlying the early Formalist position was of a dual nature – epistomological as well as esthetic. The narrowly empiricist tenor of *Opojaz* theorizing found expression in an excessive concern with the immediately 'given' – the linguistic stratum as the only tangible element of literature, the sound as the only palpable component of poetic

---

[17] See a provocative discussion of the problem in Lionel Trilling's *The Liberal Imagination* (New York, 1950).
[18] I am saying "*almost* as bad", since a device can exist in art without a 'motivation', while 'content' without 'form' is unthinkable.
[19] Viktor Šklovskij, *Literatura i kinematograf,* p. 3.

language. The 'unfolding of the verbal material' *(razvertyvanie sloves-nogo materiala)*, to use Šklovskij's favorite term, was the 'datum'. The poet's world-view was the inference. The emotions and ideas embedded in literature seemed to be a sphere of reckless speculation, something which more often than not did not reside in the work itself, but was being read into it by critics grinding their ideological axes. This scepticism was undoubtedly bolstered by many known instances of arbitrary or oversimplified interpretations of literature.

Of still greater importance was the frame of mind produced by that passionate search for the differentia of literature which was the starting point of Formalist theorizing. The concern with the idiosyncratic, the purely literary, gave rise to the tendency to equate literature with literariness, to reduce art to its distinguishing feature.

As was shown above, the Russian Formalists realized eventually the inadequacy of this reduction. The later studies of Šklovskij and Ejxenbaum in literary history treated with full earnestness, and a great length, such 'motivations' as Tolstoj's 'class-determined' view of the 1812 campaign or his 'archaist' philosophy of life.[20] In general terms, the Formalists felt compelled to admit that there are periods in the history of literature, when ideological or social considerations loom rather large and thus ought to be taken seriously by the critic.

But this was still a far cry from the sorely needed reexamination of the Formalist position. It was left to the critical supporters of Russian Formalism in Czechoslovakia and Poland – the Prague Structuralists and the Polish adepts of the 'integral method'[21] – to reopen the problem of 'literariness' and to place it in a proper perspective.

In his 1933 essay Jakobson stated the new methodological orientation succintly when he postulated "the autonomy of the esthetic function rather than the separatism of art".[22] Autonomy but not separatism – this was the crux of the matter. This meant that art was a distinct mode of human endeavor, not wholly explicable in terms of other spheres of experience, yet closely related to them. It implied the notion of 'literariness' as neither the only pertinent aspect of literature, nor merely one of its components, but a strategic property informing and permeating the entire work, the principle of dynamic integration, or, to use a key term of modern psychology, a *Gestaltqualität*. Conse-

---

[20] See above, chapter VII, pp. 122–124, 130.
[21] Cf. Manfred Kridl, *Wstęp do badań nad dziełem literackiem*.
[22] Roman Jakobson, "Co je poesie?", *Volné směry*, XXX (1933–34), quoted from Mikuláš Bakoš, *Teória literatúry* (Trnava, 1941).

quently, 'ethos' appeared not as a pseudo-realistic camouflage for the 'real thing,' but as a *bona fide* element of the esthetic structure and, as such, a legitimate object of literary study, provided that it is examined from the standpoint of its 'literariness', i.e., within the context of the literary work. And finally the work itself was defined not as a cluster of devices, but as a complex, multi-dimensional structure, integrated by the unity of esthetic purpose.[23]

As can be seen from the previous discussions,[24] the basic aspects of this doctrine were contained in a nutshell in the most mature and logically rigorous statements of Russian Formalism. The Prague concept of esthetic structure as a dynamic 'system of signs' was clearly anticipated by Tynjanov's notion of 'system'. In his acute essay "On Literary Evolution" (1927), he defines the system as a complex whole, characterized by interrelatedness and dynamic tension between individual components and held together by the underlying unity of the esthetic function. "The constructive function of each component of the system", wrote Tynjanov, "lies in its relatedness to other components and, *eo ipso,* to the entire system." [25]

If Tynjanov ultimately construed the work of literature as a *Gestalt,* it was only natural that 'literariness' be interpreted as a *Gestaltqualität.* Indeed, the Structuralist view of the 'esthetic function' was foreshadowed by the fruitful concept of *dominanta,* i.e., the dominant quality, developed by Ejxenbaum and Tynjanov and borrowed apparently from the German esthetician Christiansen. "A system", wrote Tynjanov, "does not mean coexistence of components on the basis of equality; it presupposes the preeminence of one group of elements and the resulting deformation of other elements." [26]

It is the 'preeminent component or group of components', or the *dominanta,* which insures the unity of the work of literature as well as its 'perceptibility', i.e., the fact that is recognized as a literary phenomenon. In other words, the 'dominant quality' of literature is also its distinguishing feature, the core of its 'literariness'.

It is typical of that thoroughgoing relativism which characterized

[23] See especially Roman Jakobson, "Randbemerkungen zur Prosa des Dichters Pasternak", *Slavische Rundschau,* Nr. 7 (1935). One may add that Roman Ingarden was much more specific in discussing the 'polyphonic unity' of the literary work (see *Das literarische Kunstwerk,* Halle, 1931) than official Formalist or Structuralist theoreticians have ever managed to be.
[24] See above, chapter VII, pp. 134-135.
[25] Jurij Tynjanov, *Arxaisty i novatory* (Leningrad, 1929), p. 33.
[26] *Ibid.,* p. 41.

Formalist thinking both in its early and its maturer phases, that Tynjanov was much less specific as to the nature of the *dominanta* than he
was as to its status. The set of characteristics by virtue of which the
work of literature is 'perceived' or identified as such was said to vary
from one period to another. Literary evolution brings about shifts in
the hierarchy of literary genres as well as in the relationship between
literature and other contiguous cultural spheres, e.g., science, philosophy, politics. Thus, the dominant quality of imaginative literature or
of a literary species is subject to change. What remains constant is the
very feeling of divergence from non-literature. We are thrown back on
Christiansen's *Differenzqualität,* invoked by Šklovskij in 1919 in his
manifesto, "Art as a Device".[27] But this time the conceptual framework
was essentially structuralist.

If one is justified in saying that Russian Formalism at its best was or
tended to be Structuralism, it would be equally correct to argue that
in many crucial areas the Prague Linguistic Circle merely amplified
the Formalist insights. That is why, with all necessary qualifications,
Czech Structuralism as well as the Polish 'integral' method can be considered a part of our story. The Western Slavic 'Formalists' discarded
some of the Russian tenets which seemed obsolete or extravagant; they
restated many other assumptions. But they salvaged the healthy core
of the *Opojaz* message: the notion of the 'perceptibility' of the verbal
sign, of the emphasis on the medium, as the differentia of poetic language; the insistence on the basic conventionality of literary art, and
the concomitant opposition to literal readings of imaginative literature.
This latter warning, one may add, one of the most valuable aspects of
Formalist methodology, stood only to gain in cogency and persuasive
power for being stated in more judicious terms. Significant differences
of emphasis and phrasing serve only to underline the basic unity of
theme. While a 'pure' Formalist brashly denied the existence of ideas
and feelings in a work of poetry,[28] or declared dogmatically that "it is
impossible to draw any conclusions from a work of literature",[29] the
Structuralist would emphasize the inevitable ambiguity of the poetic
statement, poised precariously between various semantic planes, and
would warn against expecting from the poet an unequivocal, easily
paraphrasable message.

---

[27] See above, chapter X, p. 178.
[28] Roman Jakobson, *Novejšaja russkaja poèzija,* pp. 16–17.
[29] Viktor Šklovskij, *Literatura i kinematograf,* p. 16.

In a perceptive introduction to the selected works of Puškin in Czech,[30] Jakobson took issue with the numerous attempts to make Puškin's poetry yield an integrated philosophy. He pointed to the elusive quality of 'Puškin's wisdom,' the 'multiplicity of the points of view' in his verses, which made it possible for each generation, each milieu, and each school of thought to read its own set of values into the works of Puškin.[31] A good example of this, argued Jakobson, is the image of Evgenij Onegin [32]: Russian critics have been sharply divergent in their interpretations of Onegin's personality. Some saw in Onegin a debonaire hedonist; others, a glum non-conformist. "Each image of Puškin", remarked Jakobson, "is so elastically ambiguous that it could be easily fitted into most diverse contexts."

The perennial problem of *Dichtung und Wahrheit,* the relation between poetry and reality, was handled in similar fashion. The orthodox Formalist position was a vehement, if understandable reaction against academic 'biographism'. In his early collection of essays, *Skvoz' literaturu,* Ejxenbaum sought to disengage poetry from the poet. Art, he declared, is a self-contained, 'continuous' process which does not bear any causal relation to 'life,' 'temperament,' or 'psychology'.[33]

The Structuralist critic would qualify this statement by adding the adjective 'direct' to the words 'causal relation'. Rather than deny the bond between the work and 'experience', he would emphasize the oblique, tenuous character of this connection.

For a succinct formulation of the problem we will have to turn again to Jakobson's essay "What is Poetry".[34] Every verbal phenomenon, wrote Jakobson, stylizes and modifies in a certain degree the event described. This stylization may hinge on the effect intended, on the audience, preventive censorship, or the repertory of available formulas. Under the impact of all these factors an actual experience depicted in a poem may virtually turn into its opposite.

Jakobson's test-case is the work of the Czech Romantic Jan Mácha. This intensely personal, almost confessional poetry appears to the Formalist critic as a bewildering interplay between fact and fiction; Jakobson called attention to the stark contrast between the devotional reverence of Mácha's love poem and cynically coarse references to its heroine

30   *Vybrané spisy A. S. Puškina,* ed. by A. Bém and R. Jakobson (Prague, 1936).
31   *Op. cit.,* I, 265.
32   *Op. cit.,* II, 257–263.
33   Boris Ejxenbaum, *Skvoz' literaturu* (Leningrad, 1924), pp. 256–257.
34   Roman Jakobson, "Co je poesie?".

in the poet's diary.[35] "Which version of the experience is true?", asks Jakobson, "Both and neither." [36]

But if the fact of life, filtered through the prism of convention, may sometimes be deformed beyond recognition, conversely it is the conventional nature of poetry which makes it possible for the poem to come dangerously close to the actual when we least expect it. We should not believe a poet, warned Jakobson, when he assures us that 'this time' he will offer us unadulterated truth; nor should we take him any more literally when he insists that his tale is pure invention.[37] Since we do not expect the poet *qua* poet to tell 'nothing but the truth', since, as Ejxenbaum put it, "in poetry the face of the author is a mask",[38] the inner censorship usually attendant upon confessions may be considerably relaxed in literature. Thus, to return to the Jakobson essay, the great Slovak lyrical poet, Janko Král, could in his verse be more candid about the passionate love he felt for his mother, apparently the real *Leitmotif* of his life, than he would have been in a non-poetic statement. He had a right to assume that this exhibitionistic display of the Oedipus complex would be mistaken by the reader for a mere 'mask', a pretense of infantilism.

But the complexity of the problem does not end here. As Tomaševskij pointed out, the relationship between poetic fiction and psychological reality is not a one-way causal dependence. Poetry mythologizes the poet's life in accordance with the conventions prevalent at the time, the idealized image of the Poet typical of the given literary school. An 'autobiographical' poem relates often not what has occurred but what should have occurred.[39] Thus, out of a discordant welter of fact and of indispensable accessories there emerges a literary biography-myth.[40] But this myth may become a fact of life in its own right. Literary mystification may be projected back into actuality, the 'mask' may obtrude upon the 'man' as an ideal to be lived up to, a pattern of behavior to be emulated. Byronism as a way of life is obviously a good

---

[35] A similar discrepancy, noted Jakobson, is found in Puškin, who in a letter to a friend referred to the 'angelic' heroine of the famous lyric "Ja pomnju čudnoe mgnovenie" (I Remember a Wonderful Moment), A. P. Kern, as 'Babylonian whore'. Characteristically, the letter and the poem were written about the same time.

[36] Quoted from Mikuláš Bakoš, ed., *Teoria literatúry*, p. 175.

[37] *Ibid.*, p. 172.

[38] Boris Ejxenbaum, *Anna Axmatova*, p. 132.

[39] Boris Tomaševskij, *Puškin* (Moscow, 1925), p. 6.

[40] *Ibid.*

case in point.[41] But the Formalist critic knows of some more recent examples. In his revealing article on Majakovskij's death, Jakobson refers to Majakovskij's poetry as a turbulent lyrical drama – a scenario to be acted out in 'real life.' [42]

Clearly, insisted the Formalists, there is no point-to-point correspondence between imaginative literature and personality. The notion of the 'naive psychological realists' that art is an oracular outpouring, a spontaneous eruption of emotions, was sharply challenged in terms which would have pleased T. S. Eliot.[43] The work of literature, argued M. Kridl, transcends individual psychology. In the process of artistic objectification the work of literature becomes separated from its creator and acquires a life of its own.[44] Roman Ingarden insisted that the psychological experience which gives rise to a work of art ceases to exist *qua* experience the moment this work comes into being.[45]

Where most of the Russian Formalists invoked the impact of suprapersonal techniques on the inchoate individual experience, Mukařovský stated the problem in his favorite terms – those of semiotics. "Like language, art", he argued, "is a system of signs, invested with intersubjective meaning." Because of its semiotic value (*znákova pováha*), the work of art does not correspond completely either to the frame of mind from which it sprang or to the one which it induces. Whatever alleged expression of the author's experience we find in a work of art is simply an element of meaning integrated into an artistic structure. Sometimes the creator anticipates life, sometimes we have to do with pure invention – a situation utilized artistically, but never actually experienced.[46] "The poetic I", observed Mukařovský in another passage, "is not identical with any empirical personality, not even with that of the author. It is the pivotal point in the composition of the poem." [47]

What all this meant to a literary historian was aptly summarized by Tomaševskij, an eminently sane scholar who managed to steer clear

[41]   See the paper by Dmitry Čiževskij "K Máchovu světovému názoru", in the collection *Torso a tajemství Máchova díla* (Prague, 1938).

[42]   Roman Jakobson, "O pokolenii, rastrativšem svoix poètov", *Smert' Vladimira Majakovskogo* (Berlin, 1931), 7–45.

[43]   In his essay "Tradition and the Individual Talent", T. S. Eliot writes: "Poetry is not a turning loose of emotion, but an escape from emotions; it is not the expression of personality, but an escape from personality" (T. S. Eliot, *Selected Essays*, New York, 1932, p. 10).

[44]   Manfred Kridl, *Wstęp do badań nad dziełem literackiem* (Wilno, 1936), p. 102.

[45]   Roman Ingarden, *Das literarische Kunstwerk* (Halle, 1931).

[46]   Jan Mukařovský, *Kapitoly z české poetiky* (Prague, 1941), I, 19.

[47]   *Ibid.*, p. 21.

both of Bohemian extravagance and of academic eclecticism. "Lyrical poetry is not worthless material for biographical investigation. It is simply unreliable material." [48] Lyrical testimony is not evidence *per se;* it becomes such only when it is corroborated by other, auxiliary testimonies.

What is true of individual self-expression is equally applicable to the 'reflections of society' in literature. The same factors which made a lyrical poem an unreliable psychological document militate against considering a work of fiction as a piece of sociological or anthropological evidence.

This point was cogently argued in the Formalist studies of folklore.[49] Šklovskij and Bogatyrëv took issue with the 'ethnographism' of A. Veselovskij and his school. Folktales, they maintained, are never a direct reflection of actual mores. Bogatyrëv pointed out that the folktale plot is the more effective the greater the distance between the situation utilized in the story and the audience. In order to qualify as a subject for popular fiction, the motif has to be either exotic, i.e, drawn from a remote culture, or archaic – a matter of 'ancient history'.[50] Acting on this assumption, Šklovskij warned against taking too literally the Greek popular fiction which deals with the rape of brides; it would be a risky procedure, he remarked, to draw from these tales a conclusion that rapes of brides were at the time an everyday occurrence. Oral tradition, wrote Šklovskij, does not reflect contemporary customs; it brings to mind customs which have become obsolete. Passing over to written literature, Šklovskij discovered a similar law in Maupassant's short story, where "a custom can become a literary theme, only when it is no longer customary".[51]

An interesting critique of the purely 'realistic' approach to folklore is found in A. Skaftymov's provocative, if somewhat turgid, study *The Poetics and Genesis of Byliny.*[52] Skaftymov offered a new, 'intrinsic' solution to one of the controversial problems of Russian folklore study

---

[48]   Boris Tomaševskij, *Puškin* (Moscow, 1925), p. 69.

[49]   It may be noted at this point that, Sokolov's statement notwithstanding (Jurij Sokolov, *Russian Folklore,* New York, 1949), the Formalist School made a substantial contribution to folklore study. In fact, two of the least 'vulnerable" Formalist studies, Skaftymov's *Poètika i genezis bylin* (Poetics and Genesis of *Byliny*) and Propp's *Morfologija skazki* (Morphology of the Fairy Tale), have to do with oral tradition.

[50]   See Pëtr Bogatyrëv and Roman Jakobson, *Slavjanskaja filologija v Rossii za gody vojny i revoljucii* (Berlin, 1923).

[51]   Viktor Šklovskij, *O teorii prozy* (Moscow, 1929), p. 31.

[52]   A. Skaftymov, *Poètika i genezis bylin* (Saratov, 1924).

– that of the treatment accorded in the *byliny* to Prince Vladimir, the King Arthur of the Russian oral epic tradition.

Many a student of Russian folklore wondered why in the *byliny* this able and, according to the popular legend, kindly ruler is invariably overshadowed by the 'hero' *(bogatyr')*, more often than not a member of Vladimir's retinue. The chieftain's part, it had been noted, is usually unspectacular and at times rather unattractive. Vladimir of the *byliny* is not immune to such foibles as confusion and fear in the face of a formidable enemy, nor is he above unfairness and treachery with regard to the *bogatyr'*, who always proves more than a match for the foe.

Some Russian folklorists have seen in this portrayal of the Prince a reflection of an anti-authoritarian attitude on the part of the court's democratic 'retainers'.[53] To Skaftymov, Vladimir's role in the oral epic is a matter of composition rather than of ideology. A *bylina*, he argued, is a streamlined apotheosis of the man of war, a closely knit narrative centering around the dramatic conflict between the hero and his enemy. All other protagonists, including the central figure in the Russian 'feudal' hierarchy, Prince Vladimir, provide merely a 'resonant background'.[54] Now according to the law of artistic perspective, the foreground must loom larger in the story than the background. Moreover, since everything in the *bylina* is geared to the ultimate glorification of the hero, all secondary characters, including the Prince, can be expected to behave in a manner which is most likely to enhance the final effect. Thus, in an emergency the Prince would tend to fall victim to general panic only to throw the hero's courage into still sharper focus. Until the showdown comes, Vladimir would be apt to be incredulous, indeed slighting, with regard to the knight, only to make his ultimate triumph still more resounding.

The methodological moral to be derived from the above analysis is obvious enough: there is no point in seeking an extrinsic explanation for a character's behavior, or for that matter, any element of the plot, if the latter can be accounted for in terms of the internal exigencies of the esthetic structure. In other words, it is hazardous to draw sociological or psychological conclusions from the work of literature before examining closely its structural properties: what may seem on the surface to be a manifestation of reality may at closer range turn out to be an

[53] Cf. Roman Jakobson and Mark Szeftel, "The Vseslav Epos", *Russian Epic Studies,* ed. by Roman Jakobson and Ernest J. Simmons (Philadelphia, 1949), p. 74.
[54] A. Skaftymov, *Poètika i genezis bylin,* p. 95.

esthetic formula, superimposed on this reality. Since whatever segment of life finds expression in art is always deflected by the 'convention', the first task of the literary critic is to determine the angle of this deflection. As Skaftymov put it, structural description must precede genetic study.[55]

The fundamental Formalist tenet was thus reaffirmed. 'The autonomy of the esthetic function' was successfully demonstrated with regard to various types of imaginative writing and various levels of literary creation. The Formalist-Structuralist theory of literature had worked its way from the autonomy of the individual poetic word *vis-à-vis* its object to the autonomy of the literary work of art with regard to reality – both subjective (the creator) and objective (the social environment).

This case for the specificity of literary art was the more convincing, the keener and more explicit was the critic's awareness of the multiple links between literature and society.

A good example of this can be found in Jakobson's observations on the prose of B. Pasternak,[56] one of modern Russia's foremost lyrical poets. In this stimulating, if somewhat too compact, essay Jakobson sought to deduce the thematology of Pasternak from the structural properties of his poetics.[57] He noted Pasternak's penchant for the figures of contiguity – metonymy and synecdoche, a tendency to substitute the 'action' for the 'actor' and the 'setting' for the 'action', to 'resolve the image of the hero into . . . a series of objectified states of mind or of surrounding objects'.[58] This pattern of imagery is used by Jakobson as a clue to the deeply passive quality of Pasternak's poetic world.[59]

This brilliantly executed critical *tour de force* had a twofold implication. It was testimony to the organic interrelations between various strata of the literary work. It was also presumably a proof that style is as good a point of departure for integral critical analysis as any.

Indeed, if poetry, to borrow a phrase from a modern German esthetician, H. Konrad, is "the world transformed into language",[60] the verbal device is the poet's most potent means of grappling with reality. In literary art ideological battles are often acted out on the plane of the op-

---

[55] *Ibid.*, p. 127.
[56] Roman Jakobson, "Randbemerkungen zur Prosa des Dichters Pasternak", *Slavische Rundschau*, VII (1935), 357–374.
[57] *Ibid.*, p. 369.
[58] *Ibid.*
[59] *Ibid.*, p. 369–371.
[60] See René Wellek and Austin Warren, *Theory of Literature* (New York, 1949), p. 341.

position between metaphor and metonymy, or meter and free verse.

The more vehement critics of Russian Formalism seem to have failed to realize this. When Veresaev indignantly denounces Ejxenbaum's treatment of the young Tolstoj's moral crisis as a pedant's attempt to turn a great novelist into an arid craftsman, weighing cold-bloodedly the respective merits of alternate turns of phrase, one cannot help but feel that the defender of Tolstoj misses the point. To a creative writer who comes to terms with the world through the agency of style, the choice of the 'device' is no trivial matter. Indeed, in spite of its one-sidedness, Ejxenbaum's incisive and well documented description of Tolstoj's struggle against the clichés of Romantic prose conveys better the drama of Tolstoj's moral crisis than many a platitudinous ideological critique of Tolstoj; even while denouncing art, Tolstoj was an artist, not a theologian. As Harry Levin recently pointed out, technicalities help us more than generalities.[61]

At the same time it must be said that in his early works Ejxenbaum could only indirectly hint at the philosophical or psychological implications of the writer's artistic method. In 1935 Jakobson could be much more explicit about this, for by that time he was ready to postulate for the 'motivation' the same autonomy which Russian Formalists claimed for the device. It would be equally erroneous, he argued, to deduce Pasternak's passive attitude toward the world from his preference for metonymy as it would be to deduce this attitude, like some of the poet's crude Marxist critics, from the apolitical disposition of the poet's milieu.[62]

"The desire", continued Jakobson, "to establish a correlation between various spheres of reality is perfectly legitimate. So are the attempts to deduce from the facts of one sphere the corresponding facts of another sphere, as long as this procedure is understood to be merely a method of projecting a multidimensional reality onto a single plane. It would be, however, an error to confuse the projection with reality and to ignore the peculiar structure as well as the internal dynamism (Selbstbewegung) of the individual planes. Among the actual possibilities of an artistic trend a given environment or individual can

---

[61] Harry Levin, "Notes on Convention", Perspectives of Criticism (Cambridge, Mass., 1950), p. 80.
[62] Wellek and Warren seem to take a similar position. "A procedure leading from style to problems of 'content'," says Theory of Literature, "must not, of course, be misunderstood to mean a process ascribing priority, either logical or chronological, to any of these elements. Ideally, we should be able to start at any given point and should arrive at the same results" (Theory of Literature, p. 186).

choose the one which suits best the social, ideological, psychological, or other needs involved; conversely, a set of artistic forms brought forth by the inner laws of their development, seeks out an adequate milieu or creative personality for its realization." – "One should not", Jakobson added significantly, "construe this correspondence between levels as an idyllic harmony. It is necessary to keep in mind that between various levels of reality there may occur dialectical tensions." [63]

This conception of the literary process as a dialectical tension between esthetic form, creative personality, and social milieu was a view worthy of the complexity and richness of imaginative literature. It was also a critical position which seemed to offer a hope of solving one of the most vexing problems of literary theory – that of poetic truth.

It was shown above how insistent were the Formalist warnings against treating literature as evidence, as a reliable source of information about life. Jakobson postulated the orientation toward the sign rather than toward the referent as the differentia of poetry. Kridl saw the aims of imaginative literature in the construction of a new, fictitious reality.[64] R. Ingarden added a new dimension to this argument – that of logic: he argued cogently that a sentence found in a work of literature, as distinguished from an informative utterance, does not purport to be 'true' or, in Ingarden's own words, does not lay claim to trtuhfulness (*Wahrheitsanspruch*).[65]

This was a point well taken. And yet, as Ingarden would undoubtedly admit, great works of literature, though not 'truthful' in the literal sense of the word, may be conducive to truth, as they often yield crucial insights into the human predicament. In the process of manipulating the medium or of constructing a fictitious world the creative writer may indirectly reveal more about reality than many a scholar bent on the search for 'truth'. Clearly Proust's novels tell us more about the human psyche than a run-of-the-mill textbook of psychology. And Dostoevskij's "Legend of the Grand Inquisitor" stated the tragic dilemma of freedom versus authority with pungency scarcely paralleled by any social treatise.

Slavic Structuralists never addressed themselves explicitly to this indirect truth-function of imaginative literature. But some of their formulations seem to shed significant light on the mechanism whereby literature can be relevant without being 'truthful'. One may cite the

---

[63]   *Slavische Rundschau*, VII (1935), pp. 372–373.
[64]   See above, chapter X, footnote 16 (p. 173).
[65]   Roman Ingarden, *Das literarische Kunstwerk* (Halle, 1931), p. 167, a.o.

thesis that literature does not reflect reality but overlaps with it, as well as the fruitful notion of the dynamic interaction of art with its creator and his environment. The literary work, said Mukařovský, is a "sign which may indicate the characteristics and the state of society, but it is not an automatic by-product of its structure".[66] Literature signifies in a sense all the factors with which it comes into contact, e.g., the author, his milieu, his audience, without ever becoming a proxy for any one of them.

It is possible to go one step farther. The cognitive value of literature does not rest on the fact that the writer can unearth more relevant data than the scientist, nor is it wholly attributable to the artist's capacity for making the universal concrete or the abstract tangible. As Lionel Trilling recently put it, literature is the "human activity that takes fullest possible account of variousness, possibility, complexity and difficulty".[67] Now could not this unique command of the ambiguity of human experience, this adeptness at conveying the 'formidable density' of the world's body (John Crowe Ransom), be construed as a counterpart of that density of the medium, which, according to the Formalists, is typical of poetry? Could not the complex and often bewildering vision of reality, i.e. of the 'referent' of the literary work, be traced to the semantic shifts occurring on the level of the 'sign'?

Jakobson came very close to drawing this conclusion in his discussion of Puškin's *Weltanschauung*.[68] The bulk of the Russian Formalists were too busy disengaging art from life to admit that poetry could be as potent on the cognitive or affective levels as it was on the sensory. In one of his attacks on the unwarranted claims of the emotionalist theory, Šklovskij wrote: "Fundamentally art is trans-emotional. 'Blood' in poetry is not bloody . . . it is a component of a sound-pattern (e.g. rime), or of an image." [69]

Like all too many of Šklovskij's hasty generalizations, this was a half-truth. Undoubtedly, the word 'blood' has a different impact upon us when used in a poem than when heard in 'real life'. And, as Šklovskij shrewdly observed, one of the points of difference may be due to the formal structure of verse; the 'artificiality' of the rime produces what I. A. Richards called a 'frame effect' [70] – the sense of distance from

[66] Jan Mukařovský, *Kapitoly z české poetiky*, I, p. 19.

[67] Lionel Trilling, *The Liberal Imagination* (New York, 1950).

[68] *Vybrané spisy A. S. Puškina*, I (Prague, 1936), 259–267.

[69] Viktor Šklovskij, *O teorii prozy*, p. 192.

[70] I. A. Richards, *Principles of Literary Criticism*, 2nd ed. (London, 1948), p. 145.

reality. But this is not to say that 'blood' in literature is wholly 'blood-less'. The ordinary word, transferred into poetry, is not cleansed of its emotional coloring or the multiple associations which have clustered around it in the course of its history. As the formalist theoreticians themselves indicated, verse 'actualizes' the verbal sign in all its properties. The distinguishing characteristic of poetic language lies not in the fact that it is 'trans-emotional', but in that its emotional load, along with its acoustic texture and grammatical form, becomes an object of esthetic contemplation rather than a catalyst of fear, hatred, or enthusiasm; something to be 'perceived' and 'experienced', as part of a symbolic structure rather than acted upon. As Wellek and Warren have pointed out, "emotions represented in literature are ... feelings of emotions, the perceptions of emotions".[71]

This raises the problem of the esthetic response. I. A. Richards notwithstanding, we tend to believe that the emotions aroused by art are different not only in degree but also in kind from those experienced in life. A tragic climax – say, the death of Hamlet on a Broadway stage – affects us in a way ostensibly different from a car accident witnessed on the street of our native town. The quality of detachment inherent in the former response obviously has to do with the awareness, always present in 'the back of our mind', that the drama unfolding before our eyes is not real, that the catastrophe is a part of a make-believe world. At the same time no successful response to a dramatic denouement can dispense with a degree of emotional involvement if not actual identification.

Literary art is at once fictional and reality-like, idiosyncratic and relevant. Both sets of qualities are crucial; either can be ignored by the critic only at his own peril. Obviously it is the specificity which makes the esthetic response what it is. But it is the relatedness of literature to other human activities that insures the potency of this response, indeed, makes the response possible at all.

One may add that these two aspects of esthetic experience are not only compatible but interdependent. Just because art is not primarily a call for action or a source of information, but a disinterested contemplation of the medium, 'purposiveness without purpose' (Kant), can it bring within its orbit so many, often discordant, elements and become involved with so many interests and endeavors.

Extrinsic criticism which, as Šklovskij aptly put it, brushes aside the form in order to grasp the 'content', was too preoccupied with the 'rele-

[71] René Wellek and Austin Warren, *Theory of Literature*, p. 28.

vance' of literature to pay attention to its uniqueness. Pure Formalism
– a justified if extravagant reaction against the genetic fallacy – tended
toward the other extreme. Structuralism, the final result of Formalist
theorizing, points the way toward a conception of literature that would
do full justice to both the uniqueness and the relevance of literary art.

XII. VERSE STRUCTURE: SOUND AND MEANING

1

In the preceding chapters an attempt was made to outline the conceptual framework of Formalist criticism. Obviously, our next step must be an examination of the way in which the above methodological assumptions were applied to specific problems of theoretical and historical poetics.

The domain in which the Formalist concepts were used to greatest advantage was undoubtedly the theory of versification. Whether because poetic language was the 'first love' of the *Opojaz* theorists [1] or because the Formalists who addressed themselves primarily to problems of versification, for example Jakobson, Tomaševskij and Tynjanov, graduated to Structuralism at a rather early stage, it is in this sphere that Formalism made its most impressive contribution.

The Formalist approach to versification was shaped by two basic tenets: (a) an insistence on the organic unity of poetic language, and (b) the notion of the *dominanta*, that is, the dominant or organizing property. Verse, claimed the Formalists, is not merely a matter of external embellishments such as meter, rime, or alliteration, superimposed upon ordinary speech.[2] It is an integrated type of discourse, qualitatively different from prose, with a distinctive hierarchy of elements and internal laws of its own – 'speech organized in its entire phonic texture.' [3]

Now the 'constructive factor' in verse [4] – the element which modifies and deforms all other components and thus exerts an impact upon the semantic and morphological as well as the phonetic levels of poetic

---

[1] See above, chapters III–IV, pp. 63–69 and 73–74 respectively.
[2] Boris Tomaševskij, "La nouvelle école d'histoire littéraire en Russie", *Revue des études slaves*, VIII (1928).
[3] Boris Tomaševskij, *O stixe* (Leningrad, 1929), p. 8.
[4] Jurij Tynjanov, *Problema stixotvornogo jazyka* (Leningrad, 1924).

language – is the rhythmical pattern. Rhythm, defined rather broadly [5] as a "regular alternation in time of comparable phenomena",[6] was found to be both the distinguishing feature and the organizing principle of the language of poetry.

That rhythm or the tendency toward rhythm may also be encountered in informative prose the Formalists did not deny. But in line with their functional approach they saw the differentia of verse not in the mere presence of an element – in this case , a regular or semi-regular ordering of the sound-pattern – but in its status. In 'practical' language, it was argued, in ordinary speech or in scientific discourse, rhythm is a secondary phenomenon – a physiological expedient or a by-product of syntax; in poetry it is a primary and 'self-valuable' quality. "Verse", observed Tomaševskij, "has at its disposal extra-syntactical means of breaking the phonic flow into recognizable units." [7] "In poetry", wrote Tynjanov, "the meaning of words is modified by the sound, in prose sound is modified by meannig." [8]

More important still, in prosaic discourse – except for rhythmical or poetic prose, which is clearly a borderline case – so-called isochronism, that is, a tendency toward equal time intervals between 'rhythmical signals', is the exception rather than the rule. As Tomaševskij demonstrates in his analysis of Puškin's *Pikovaja dama* (The Queen of Spades),[9] a prose passage can exhibit a fairly regular stress distribution. But this regularity, insisted Tomaševskij, is an accidental rather than a structural quality, something which we may discover at closer inspection, but which we have no reason to expect. Conversely, the rhythm of a poem hinges not so much on the actual distribution of the rhythmical accents as on our anticipation of their recurrence at certain intervals. To Jakobson, as well as to Wellek and Warren, "the time of verse language is the time of expectation".[10]

The notion of rhythm as a *Gestaltqualität,* as a property which informs and pervades all levels of verse language, saved the Formalists

---

[5] It may be noted that while the following is a very flexible definition, it precludes the use of the term 'rhythm' with reference to spatial arts (Brik was especially explicit on this score). The Formalists insisted on periodicity, i.e., recurrence of 'comparable phenomena' *in time* as the inalienable characteristic of rhythm.

[6] Boris Tomaševskij, *O stixe,* p. 257.

[7] *Ibid.,* p. 312.

[8] Jurij Tynjanov, *Arxaisty i novatory* (Leningrad, 1929), p. 409.

[9] Boris Tomaševskij, "Ritm prozy", *O stixe.*

[10] René Wellek and Austin Warren, *Theory of Literature* (New York, 1949), p. 171.

from the fallacy of traditional metrists – that of equating rhythm with meter. The Formalists were fully aware that verse can dispense with meter, but not with rhythm. "Speech can sound like verse", wrote Tomaševskij, "without exhibiting any metrical pattern".[11] It was indicated above [12] that to an *Opojaz* theorist rime was simply a particular case of 'sound repetition' *(zvukovoj povtor),* a case, one may add, especially conspicuous, because of the strategic location of the rime. By the same token, meter was construed as merely a particular case of rhythm, or, more exactly, as the most tangible proof of its existence. The metrical scheme was reduced to the status of an auxiliary device, signalizing the 'organized' character of verse language by breaking the rhythmical flow into 'equivalent intonational segments'.[13]

This argument recalls the distinction made by Andrej Belyj between the ideal metrical pattern and the actual rhythm of verse.[14] Even though little love was lost between Belyj and the *Opojaz* spokesmen, the Formalist studies in verse structure had many points of contact with the pioneering work done by the Symbolist theoretician. Tomaševskij, Tynjanov and Brik shared Belyj's interest in rhythmical variations, as well as his preoccupation with the way in which the same metrical norm is realized by different poets or schools of poetry. Like Belyj, they saw divergences from the canon, occurring as they do even in the most 'regular' verse, as part and parcel of rhythm – a factor not only unavoidable in view of the 'resistance of the verbal material', but crucial to the esthetic effect.

While the Symbolists and Formalists were at one in postulating the indispensability of metrical irregularities, they differed in the criteria invoked. Where Belyj pleaded for rhythmical 'variety', the Formalists tended to fall back on Šklovskij's doctrine of 'disautomatization'.

The brilliant Polish Formalist, Franciszek Siedlecki, declared: the tight organization typical of verse tears the sound-stratum of language out of the amorphous inertia which is its lot in ordinary speech.[15] But the artificially imposed isochronism, continued Siedlecki, could in turn lead to automatization, if it were not for occasional deviations from the norm – for the "moments of frustrated anticipation" (Jakobson's term). A rhythmical variation, for example, an absence of stress accent

---

11   Boris Tomaševskij, *O stixe,* p. 9.
12   See chapter IV, p. 74.
13   Boris Tomaševskij, *O stixe,* p. 11.
14   See above, chapter II, pp. 37–38.
15   See Franciszek Siedlecki, "O swobodę wiersza polskiego", *Skamander,* III (1938), 104.

in what is metrically a 'strong' position, generates a tension between ordinary language and the esthetic norm, and thus underscores the dynamic and artful character of verse rhythm.

It is clear from Siedlecki's argument that the Formalists favored the irregular 'free' verse. But in spite of a distinct critical bias, they managed to avoid the dogmatism of Belyj's position. To Belyj, as indicated above, rhythm was a triumph over meter, or, in his own words, "a symmetry in deviations from meter". The Formalist students of verse found this definition too narrow and too negative.

Actually Formalist studies in versification yield two notions of verse rhythm – a broad and a narrow one. The former, which may be called the Formalist's maximum definition of rhythm, encompassed "the totality of actually perceptible phonic phenomena",[16] that is, the sumtotal of the esthetically organized elements of sound in the poem. This obviously included both the 'quantitative', or 'relational' factors [17] usually discussed under the heading of metrics, such as stress, pitch and length, and the 'qualitative' or 'inherent' ones – alliteration or vowel harmony.

This catholic conception of rhythm was clearly a corollary of the Formalist emphasis on the organic unity of poetic speech. The scope of rhythmical analysis was appreciably widened in order to bring within the compass of verse study all the strata of poetic language directly or indirectly affected by the organizing power of the rhythmical *dominanta*.

In Formalist studies on problems of prosody rhythm was discussed in somewhat more specific terms. "Rhythmics", said Tomaševskij, "deals with the phonic phenomena produced in the course of realizing the metrical norms in actual poetic speech." [18] But, in contradistinction to Belyj's view, this actual fulfillment of meter was seen not merely as a set of violations of the canon, but as the canon plus these violations, as a 'contrapuntal' tension between the norm and ordinary language.[19]

If the Formalists were less 'militant' than was Belyj in their treatment of metrical verse, they were a good deal more radical in their conceptual framework. Not only did they push far beyond the limits of tradi-

---

[16] Boris Tomaševskij, *O stixe*, p. 11.
[17] René Wellek and Austin Warren, *Theory of Literature*, p. 160.
[18] Boris Tomaševskij, *O stixe*, p. 260.
[19] The above formulation is borrowed from a brief but very helpful account of the Formalist approach to prosody by Wellek and Warren (*Theory of Literature*, p. 173).

tional verse study in focussing on such problems as verbal orchestration and phrase melody. Moreover, in their rhythmical analyses of Russian poetry, they questioned the usefulness of the key concept of Graeco-Roman prosody, that of 'foot'. Such terms as 'amphibrach', 'trochee', or 'iamb', argued the Formalists, are of little value to the student of Russian poetry, since they imply a more regular alternation of accented and unaccented syllabes and a more precise quantitative relationship between 'strong' and 'weak' elements than can be observed in Russian verse, even in its 'classical' stage. "The notion of foot' ", wrote Tomaševskij, "is the weakest aspect of the old metrics." [20] To Jakobson and Tomaševskij, the basic unit of verse rhythm is not an 'imaginary' foot, but the verse line, seen as a distinct 'rhythmico-syntactical' or 'intonational' segment.[21]

This view of verse structure found clear expression in Tomaševskij's scholarly analysis of Puškin's iambic pentameter.[22] To Belyj a line of a poem written in this meter was a series of five bisyllabic feet, known as iambics, with occasional 'missing accents'. Tomaševskij would prefer to speak of a sequence of ten syllables, marked by an iambic 'rhythmical impulse', that is, a tendency for the stress to fall on the even syllables. This underlying 'impulse', the Formalist theoretician would add, is persistent enough to make the deviations from the norm, the 'moments of frustrated anticipation', perceptible and thus esthetically significant.

In recording painstakingly the sound-pattern of a poem the Formalist metrists were not content with listing the number of syllables and the stress distribution within the verse line. They were equally concerned with the position of the stress accent with regard to word-units. The 'word-boundaries' *(slovorazdely),* it was argued, are an important factor in our perception of the poem.

Like Fëdor Korš, one of the pioneers of comparative metrics in Russia, the Formalists refused to treat the verse line as merely a series of sounds, a succession of strong and weak syllables. In his study *On Czech Verse* Jakobson tried to illustrate the impact of the shifting limits of words by juxtaposing the following four lines from Puškin's poem "Utoplennik" (The Drowned Man):

---

[20] Boris Tomaševskij, *O stixe,* p. 138.
[21] The former term was used by Žirmunskij in his valuable *Introduction to Metrics (Vvedenie v Metriku, Teorija stixa,* Leningrad, 1925), the latter, by Tomaševskij.
[22] Boris Tomaševskij, "Pjatistopnyj jamb Puškina", *O stixe,* pp. 138–253.

'A ne tó ‖ pokoločú
Pritaščíli ‖ mertvecá
Nevidímkoju ‖ luná,
Utoráplivaet ‖ šág.'

From the purely acoustic point of view, asserted Jakobson, the structure of the above lines is identical. The number of syllables in all is seven, the 'rhythmical impulse' trochaic, with only two actual strong beats, the first and fifth syllable being 'weak'. And yet, insisted Jakobson, the fact that in each of the four lines the interverbal pause is differently located, though not perceptible acoustically, is something which rhythmical analysis cannot afford to disregard.[23]

As Jakobson pointed out elsewhere, there are cases where the position of the accent *vis-à-vis* the word is of direct relevance to prosody, inasmuch as it affects the actual stress distribution in a verse line. This may occur in passages exhibiting rhythmical variations. The outcome of the tension between the metrical norm and the verbal material often hinges on the location of the word-limit. Sometimes rhythm may triumph over usage. A monosyllabic word which in ordinary speech never carries a stress, being subordinated logically to the following or preceding word, may under the impact of rhythmical inertia acquire a full-blown accent. More generally, a normally unaccented syllable can realize the rhythmical signal, or, conversely a normally accented syllable can lose the stress, unless such a process entails a shift of accent within a word-unit Should the latter be the case, the rhythmical impulse is bound to be blocked. The prosodic structure of the Russian language does not permit of an 'internal shift of accent' *(pereakcentirovka),* since in Russian such poetic license would be prone to change the meaning of the given word.[24]

This pointed up the interaction between the sound of the poem and its meaning, between prosody and semantics. Indeed, after a brief period of fascination with pure euphony, the Formalists became keenly aware of this mutual relationship. Ejxenbaum, Jakobson and Tynjanov argued persuasively against the purely acoustic approach to verse, as championed by Sievers and Saran in Germany and by Verrier in France.[25] They took strong exception to Sievers' dictum that a theoretician

[23] Roman Jakobson, *O češskom stixe* (Berlin, 1923).
[24] *Ibid.*
[25] Cf. Boris Ejxenbaum, *Melodika stixa* (Petrograd, 1922); Roman Jakobson, *O češskom stixe* (Berlin, 1923); Jurij Tynjanov, *Problema stixotvornogo jazyka* (Leningrad, 1924).

of verse ought to adopt the attitude of a foreigner who listens to a poem without understanding the language in which it was written.[26] Such an attitude, asserted the Formalists, was neither desirable nor psychologically possible. The sound-structure of a language, as Jakobson and Mukařovský made amply clear, is perceived first and foremost as a system of 'phonemic' oppositions, serving to differentiate word-meanings, or, to use L. Bloomfield's terminology,[27] as a set of 'significant' phonetic distinctions. This hierarchy of phonic values, added Jakobson, embedded as it is in the collective 'linguistic consciousness' of the given speech community, is apt to condition to a large extent the response of Sievers' 'foreigner'. When hearing an unintelligible utterance, we cannot help but 'transphonologize' it in terms of our own linguistic habits. Listening to a poem written in a foreign language, we tend half-consciously to break down the alien sequence of sounds into what we take to be lexical and phraseological units.[28]

The above reasoning pointed in the direction of the so-called phonemic prosody. As could be expected, the Formalists were eager to bring the study of verse closer to linguistics. Thus, they wholeheartedly endorsed Verrier's definition of prosody as a "discipline studying the speech-sounds from the standpoint of those properties which play a significant part in the versification of the given language".[29] But if the Formalists were at one with Verrier in emphasizing the importance of linguistic considerations for metrics, they disagreed with the French scholar as to the type of language study which was most pertinent to the theory of verse. Rejecting Verrier's thesis that 'metrics is concerned solely with the sound, not with the meaning,'[30] the Formalists sought guidance from modern functional linguistics. Prosody, they argued, must be 'oriented' not toward phonetics, that is, the physical and physiological description of speech-sounds, but toward phonemics, which examines the speech-sounds *sub specie* of their linguistic function, that is, their capacity for differentiating word-meanings.[31]

This emphasis on phonemics proved very fruitful. A clearcut distinction between 'significant' and 'non-significant' phonetic differences makes it possible to ascertain the hierarchy of prosodic elements in

---

[26]   E. Sievers, *Deutsche Verslehre*, § 1, as quoted by Jakobson in *O češskom stixe*.

[27]   L. Bloomfield, *Language* (New York, 1933).

[28]   Roman Jakobson, *O češskom stixe*.

[29]   *Ibid.*, p. 45.

[30]   *Ibid.*

[31]   *Ibid.*

each language and thus provides a workable basis for a typology of metrical patterns.

A good example of utilizing the phonemic approach for the purposes of comparative metrics is found in Jakobson's study *On Czech Verse*. In general, Jakobson argued, language has at its disposal three means of realizing 'rhythmical signals' (Verrier's *temps marqués*), three potential 'bases of rhythm' – the stress or 'dynamic accent', the pitch or 'musical accent', and quantity. Actually, each individual language, at a given period of its evolution, favors one of the above elements as the organizing principle of its versification.

Now this choice, continued Jakobson, is always influenced, if not wholly determined, by the relative phonemic status of the three prosodic factors. Other things being equal, the relational element of sound, which in the given language is most likely to become the basis of rhythm, is the one which has the greatest phonemic relevance. It is no accident that in the course of its development Russian verse has veered increasingly toward the accentual pattern. In Russian, where the meaning of the word often hinges on the position of the stress,[32] the 'dynamic accent' is the only phonemic element of prosody, quantity being here simply a by-product of the stress. By the same token, it is only natural that length should be the organizing principle of versification in Greek, where quantitative differences are 'significant', or that the prosody of Serbo-Croatian, the only modern Slavic language with a 'phonemic' pitch, should revolve around the 'musical accent'.

Jakobson was too keenly aware of the essentially artificial character of poetic language to let his case rest there. He realized that the hierarchy of prosodic elements inherent in a language is not the only determinant of the metrical system. Since poetry is "organized violence committed on ordinary speech",[33] the choice of a prescribed rhythmical scheme is influenced at any given moment by such extra-linguistic factors as "the poetic tradition, the authority of the classics and foreign literary influences operative at the time".

However, as N. Trubetzkoy pointed out in a friendly critique of Jakobson's study,[34] "one should not forget that the patience of language is not unlimited. In each language there are elements which must be utilized by prosody if the latter is to be vital." Poetic form must take

[32]   Thus, a substitution in the word *muka* of a stressed 'u' for an unstressed 'u' can turn 'flour' into 'suffering'.
[33]   Roman Jakobson, *O češskom stixe*, p. 16.
[34]   Cf. *Slavia*, II (1923–1924).

account of the basic properties of the linguistic pattern either by making use of them, that is, choosing the 'significant' phonic value as the basis of rhythm, or by not violating them.

This brings us back to the problem of the limits of metrical license, and more specifically to the Jakobson-Tomaševskij thesis about the impossibility of shifting the accent in Russian within a word. In the first line of *The Aeneid,* "Arma virumque cano", the dactylic rhythmical impulse shifts the stress arbitrarily from the first to the second syllable of "cano". In Russian, as Jakobson and Tomaševskij have shown, this type of 'organized violence' could not occur, for the same reason that Serbo-Croatian prosody balks at a shift of a 'musical accent' within a word-unit. Apparently, suggested the Formalist theoreticians, some phonic values loom too large in our linguistic consciousness to be disregarded or tampered with by the poet.

2

The Formalist's insistence on word-boundaries as a rhythmical factor and his attempts at phonemic prosody testified to that abiding interest in meaning which characterized the later phase of *Opojaz* verse study.[35] This awareness of the interdependence between the phonetic and semantic aspects of poetic language was operative on several levels of critical analysis. From the phoneme, the smallest unit of sound capable of differentiating meanings, and the word, the smallest independent unit of meaning, the Formalist theory of verse moved upward toward the higher unit, the sentence. Problems of poetic syntax appeared as a natural link between purely metrical analysis and the study of poetic semantics.

The first to focus sharply on the poetic use of sentence structures was Osip Brik, who ever since the inception of the Formalist movement had been preoccupied with 'sound-repetitions' – phonic configurations discernible in verse apart from its prosodic scheme. In his first paper on "Sound-Repetitions",[36] Brik attempted a classification of alliterative figures in early nineteenth-century Russian poetry, according to such criteria as the number of repeated consonants or consonantal clusters, the order of their recurrence and the position of the constituent sounds *vis-à-vis* the rhythmical units. Characteristically, Brik's next contribution dealt not with 'verbal orchestration,' the favorite topic of the early

---

[35]   See above, chapter V, pp. 88–89.
[36]   See Osip Brik, "Zvukovye povtory", *Poètika* (Petrograd, 1919).

Opojaz studies, but with the connections between rhythm and syntax. In many poems, argued Brik in his paper "Ritm i sintaksis" [37] (Rhythm and Syntax), the rhythmical movement hinges not only on strictly prosodic factors, for example, stress distribution, but on the word order as well. Syntax takes its cue here from rhythm. The tendency toward regular ordering of the verbal material finds its additional expression in the parallelism of sentence structures occurring in contiguous or otherwise correlated verse lines.

Brik labeled this phenomenon "rhythmico-syntactical parallelism" and proceeded to trace it through Russian poetry of the Puškin era. He found in Russian iambic tetrameter, the most 'canonic' of Russian metrical patterns, a number of persistent rhythmico-syntactical 'figures'. These were such sequences as noun plus adjective plus noun (e.g. 'Krasa polunočnoj prirody') or personal pronoun plus adjective plus noun (e.g., Moi studenčeskie gody').[38]

As a comparable English example one could cite Robert Burns' famous stanza:

> "O my luve is like a red, red rose
> That's newly sprung in June.
> O my luve is like a melody
> That's sweetly played in tune." [39]

In his provocative article, "Verbal Style: Logical and Counterlogical",[40] W. K. Wimsatt, Jr., has also touched upon the problem of the relation between rhythm and syntax in verse. "The equalities of meter", wrote Wimsatt, "do not march with but across the parallels of sense. Shakespeare's line 'Of hand, of foot, of lip, of eye, of brow' and Milton's 'And swims or sinks, or wades, or creeps, or flies' . . . are pronounced exceptions to the rule." [41] One wonders whether Wimsatt's conclusion is not too hasty. As Brik has demonstrated, there are periods or schools in the history of poetry for which the approximate coextensiveness of

[37] Osip Brik, "Ritm i sintaksis", *Novyj lef,* 1927, No. 3–6.
[38] In some instances cited by Brik the parallel segments are half-lines. Brik quoted such examples as *'bez upoenij, bez želanij'* where each half-line consists of the preposition *'bez'* and a noun in the genitive.
[39] I have chiefly in mind the rhythmico-syntactical parallelism between the second and fourth line of Burns' stanza; the partial correspondence between the first and third line is a by-product of a repetition.
[40] W. K. Wimsatt, Jr., "Verbal Style: Logical and Counterlogical", *Publications of Modern Language Association,* Vol. LXV, No. 2 (March 1950), pp. 5–20.
[41] *Ibid.,* p. 10.

rhythmical and syntactical units is the rule rather than an exception.

This rule, the Formalists would hasten to add, does permit of many exceptions. The interaction between 'sense' and 'meter' never takes on the aspect of an idyllic harmony. The verse line is a resultant of two distinct forces – the rhythmical impulse and the syntactical pattern. Even in a poem in which these are supposed to converge, discrepancies between the two systems are inevitable: a sentence may stop short of the end of the line or, more frequently still, overlap it. The *enjambement* thus produced, asserted Tynjanov, throws into relief the potential tension between rhythm and syntax, and thus performs a function similar to that fulfilled by rhythmical variations.[42]

The importance of syntax as a rhythmical factor was insisted upon still more strongly by Ejxenbaum in his study *The Melodics of Verse*.[43] Brik tried to show that syntactical parallelism can participate in the total effect of the poem when it assists the meter in emphasizing the organized character of verse language. Ejxenbaum went Brik one better in a spirited attempt to prove that such a syntactical phenomenon as phrase melody can, in a certain type of verse, become not merely a contributing factor, but the 'dominant' element – the formative principle.

The concept of the 'dominant quality' proved doubly useful to the Formalist student of verse. This notion was invoked both in delimiting verse from prose and in establishing distinctions between various types of poetry. When poetry *in toto* was juxtaposed to prose, rhythm was found the differentia and the organizing principle of the poet's language. But rhythm, especially in the broader Formalist interpretation of the term, was admittedly a heterogeneous notion. As was shown above,[44] this term encompassed both the organization of the quantitative elements (pitch, stress, length), and the use made of the quality of the individual speech-sounds, or verbal orchestration, as well as, one may add, the utilization of phrase melody. The hierarchy of these factors, asserted Ejxenbaum, varies from one type of verse writing to another. Indeed, depending on the esthetic 'orientation' of the poem, each of the three elements of rhythm can assume the status of the underlying principle of verse structure.

Starting from his assumption, Ejxenbaum set out to examine the relative importance of phrase melody in three styles which he discerned in Russian lyrical poetry – the rhetorical or declamatory, the conversa-

---

[42]   Jurij Tynjanov, *Problema stixotvornogo jazyka*.
[43]   Boris Ejxenbaum, *Melodika stixa* (Petrograd, 1922).
[44]   See section I of this chapter, p. 215.

tional, and the melodic or 'singable' *(napevnyj)* styles. In the first type of verse, argued Ejxenbaum, as exemplified by Lomonosov's odes, phrase melody is clearly a secondary phenomenon, an "accompaniment to, or a by-product of, the logical canon". In the second, e.g. in Axmatova's lyrics, Ejxenbaum noted a tendency to emulate the variety and mobility of colloquial intonations. But it is only in the 'singable' verse, asserted the critic, that we have to do with a consistent artistic exploitation of phrase melody – a "full-fledged system of intonation *(intonirovanie),* comprising the phenomena of melodic symmetry, repetition, crescendo, cadence, etc." [45]

To substantiate this thesis Ejxenbaum drew liberally upon the Russian Romantic lyricists, Žukovskij, Fet, and, to a lesser degree, Lermontov. The Russian meditative elegy, he maintained in a well documented, if not always fully convincing, analysis,[46] made deliberate use of interrogative and exclamatory intonations. These intonational patterns were emphasized by means of such devices as inversion, lyrical repetition or refrain, the *'reprise'* (the repeating of a question within a stanza), or the 'crescendo' [47] (making a question overlap a line or a stanza).[48]

Phonemic prosody, 'rhythmico-syntactical parallelism,' 'melodics of verse', all this was a far cry from the traditional concerns of metrics – from the mechanical count of long and short, of accented and unaccented, syllables. With the concepts of 'phoneme', 'word' and 'sentence' overshadowing those of 'syllable' or 'foot', attention was called to the ways in which the 'artificial' organization of the sound of verse is involved with, and makes use of, the 'natural' organization of meaning inherent in language. From the 'relational' aspect of the problem it was but one step to what might be called its 'qualitative' phase, i.e. the impact of poetic euphony on the semantic value of the individual words or word-combinations employed by the poet.

It has already been indicated that the Formalist position is far removed from the theory of 'correspondences' between auditory and emotive responses.[49] In their early studies the Formalists paid their due to the belief in the 'potential expressiveness of phonemes'. Subsequently

---

[45] Boris Ejxenbaum, *Melodika stixa,* p. 10.

[46] Ejxenbaum's thesis was contested in an interesting paper by Žirmunskij, 'Melodika stixa' (*Voprosy teorii literatury,* Leningrad, 1928, pp. 89–153).

[47] As a rule the Formalists were wary of borrowing concepts from the study of other arts, but in discussing "singable' verse Ejxenbaum drew lavishly on musical terms, such as 'cadence,' 'reprise' and the like.

[48] These methodological insights were applied by Ejxenbaum to the verse of Lermontov and partly Axmatova.

[49] See above, chapters II and X, pp. 35–36 and 182 respectively.

they became highly sceptical of ascribing evocative power or definite emotional coloring to individual speech-sounds. They doubted whether vowels or consonants could be legitimately characterized as 'sad' or 'gay' and refused to set too much store by sound-imitative devices. According to the Formalists, onomatopoeia was a marginal phenomenon in poetry. Many poetic effects, argued Ejxenbaum,[50] which some critics attribute to sheer sound-imitation are actually dependent on the meaning of the words used.[51]

Generally speaking, the Formalists were distrustful of all theories predicated upon an 'organic' kinship between the sign and the referent. To correlate sound and meaning meant to them to establish a correspondence not between the music of verse and 'reality', but between different strata of poetic language.[52]

It is true, the Formalist theoreticians were not altogether averse to talking about 'phonetic gestures' (zvukovye žesty) in verse. But this term, when used by Tynjanov or Ejxenbaum,[53] did not necessarily imply an intrinsic suggestiveness of certain acoustic effects. 'Sound-gesture' in Opojaz parlance connoted more often than not an approximate analogy between the articulatory activity underlying a given sound-repetition – the process involved in producing a speech-sound – and a physical gesture. Thus the triple repetition of the rounded u (oo) in the first line of Puškin's poem Ruslan i Ljudmila ('U lukomor'ja dub zelënyj') is cited by Tynjanov as a "case of a phonetic gesture which suggests with an extreme power of persuasion a real gesture; one ought to add that what is suggested here are not specific or unequivocal gestures".[54]

A procedure much more frequent in Formalist writings was referring to a 'sound-repetition' – whether rime or some non-metrical alliterative device – as a sui generis 'rhythmical metaphor' or 'auditory simile'.[55] Again, it must be said that these concepts as interpreted by Jakobson or Tynjanov did not indicate any affinity between the sound-pattern and the aspect of reality allegedly evoked by it – a landscape, an emotion,

---

[50] Boris Ejxenbaum, "O zvukax v stixe", Skvoz' literaturu (Leningrad, 1924).

[51] As Wellek and Warren have pointed out (see Theory of Literature, p. 163), J. C. Ransom recently advanced a similar thesis.

[52] The above position was clearly a corollary of the Formalist notion of 'meaning' as a verbal phenomenon rather than a part of extra-linguistic reality (see above, chapter X, pp. 184–185).

[53] Jurij Tynjanov, Problema stixotvornogo jazyka; Boris Ejxenbaum, Anna Axmatova (Petrograd, 1923).

[54] Problema stixotvornogo jazyka, p. 104.

[55] Ibid., p. 117.

or a frame of mind. What was emphasized here was the similarity between two sets of devices, two levels of literary craft – poetic euphony and poetic imagery. This was a typically Formalist way of posing the problem. The terms of reference were 'intrinsic', and verse was approached as a self-contained entity. Moreover, the bracketing of rime with metaphor was closely traceable to Šklovskij's fundamental tenet that juxtaposition on the basis of partial similarity of two otherwise dissimilar notions is the omnipresent principle of poetic creation.[56]

Still more crucial to the Formalist approach to poetic semantics was the assumption that rhythm as the organizing factor of verse language modifies and 'deforms' meaning. The most outstanding characteristic of this 'deformed semantics' was said to reside in the 'orientation toward the neighboring word'. The tight organization of the sound-stratum of verse, or, as Tynjanov put it, 'the unity and compression of the verse line',[57] brings words closer to each other, makes them interact, overlap, crisscross, and in so doing, reveal the wealth of their 'lateral', potential meanings. "The play with these lateral meanings", asserted Ejxenbaum, "running afoul as it does of habitual verbal associations, is the principal feature of poetic semantics."[58] Primary meanings tend to give way to subsidiary 'oscillating' characteristics of the word, brought to the fore by the impact of the rhythmical pattern.[59] The unexpected 'crisscrossing of meanings', typical of poetic speech, confers upon the words used by the poet new semantic nuances or revives long-forgotten connotations.

With the poem poised precariously between various levels of meaning, the poet's word tends to take its cue from the context to a much greater extent than is the case with ordinary speech. This is not only true of the poetic neologism, the approximate 'meaning' of which can be deduced from the semantic aura of the passage and from the constituent morphemes. Also familiar words 'transferred into verse' and linked with logically dissimilar notions on the basis of affective or phonetic kinship may virtually surrender their denotative value for the sake of a 'subsidiary characteristic', such as an intense emotional coloring imposed by the general atmosphere of the line or a passage. Tynjanov illustrated this point by quoting some telling examples from Aleksandr Blok. In Symbolist poetry, he observed, where words are brought together by virtue of emotive rather than logical affinity and where the

[56] Viktor Šklovskij, "Svjaz' priëmov sjužetosloženija s obščimi priëmami stilja", *Poètika* (Petrograd, 1919).
[57] Jurij Tynjanov, *Problema stixotvornogo jazyka*, chapter I.
[58] Boris Ejxenbaum, *Anna Axmatova*, p. 108.
[59] Jurij Tynjanov, *Problema stixotvornogo jazyka*, chapter II.

outlines of objects are blurred, the verbal sign is not a reference, but a 'lexical tone'.[60]

Indeed, continued Tynjanov, the intensity of the 'lexical coloring' (*leksičeskaja okraska*) of the word is usually in inverse ratio to the strength of its 'primary characteristic' – to its denotative precision. Thus, barbarisms, dialectisms, archaisms, words with no recognizable 'referent' and with an only approximate 'meaning', not infrequently set the tone of a passage and transmit their 'coloring' to more intelligible components of the line or stanza. A similar phenomenon, noted Tynjanov, can be observed in 'expressive' speech: in a charged, intensely derogatory context even an emotionally neutral word is apt to be perceived as an expletive.[61]

The paramount impact of the whole upon the part is only one facet of what Mukařovský called the "semantic dynamics of the poetic context".[62] The other aspect, inseparable from the former, is the influence of a part upon a part. By gathering up the energy of speech into the rigorous discipline of rhythm, by deliberately manipulating the medium, verse underscores multiple interrelationships between words and sets off the tensions between various levels of the verbal sign.

The Formalist discussions of rime are a good case in point. Like every element of poetic structure, Žirmunskij argued in his study "The Aims of Poetics", rime is a complex phenomenon. As a canonized type of 'sound-repetition', he continued, rime is a euphonic factor, a matter of 'verbal orchestration'. At the same time signalizing as it does the end of the line, it is a pivotal element of metrical composition.[63]

This, however, Žirmunskij insisted, does not tell the whole story. Rime has also its morphological and lexical aspects. Thus, we must inquire whether the rime involves the entire word or only a part of the word, and should the latter be the case, whether the phonetic convergence is based on the root or on the affix. The student of verse can further inquire if words brought togther by rime belong to the same linguistic category, say, a feminine noun with a soft consonantal ending (*krov'-ljubov'*) or a third person plural of the present tense (*idut-vedut*), or if, on the contrary, they are drawn from disparate morphological and semantic spheres.[64]

[60] *Ibid.*, p. 57 *et al.*
[61] *Ibid.*
[62] Jan Mukařovský, *Kapitoly z české poetiky* (Prague, 1941), I, 133–134.
[63] Viktor Žirmunskij, "Zadači poètiki", *Voprosy teorii literatury* (Leningrad, 1928), pp. 49–50.
[64] *Ibid.*

It is in the latter type of rime that the Formalist students of verse were chiefly interested. Rime, it was maintained, is hardly ever a matter of sheer congruence or flat homogeneity. Phonetic similarity becomes 'perceptible' or esthetically satisfying only when thrown against the background of morphological or semantic incongruity.

This thesis was bolstered by many relevant examples drawn from modern Russian poetry. Emphasis was laid on the fact that the bulk of contemporary Russian poets steered clear of so-called grammatical rimes, where phonetic congruence was a by-product of identical inflections, and veered increasingly toward 'difficult rimes' and morphological asymmetry.

Whether or not the general conclusions were fully justified, the historical observation was valid. That modern verse writing has shunned grammatical rimes is an indubitable fact. Moreover, as the Formalists were well aware, this trend was not unrelated to the modernist insistence on the autonomy of the verbal device.[65] Where the rime appears to be a secondary factor, a mere corollary of such extra-esthetic factors as grammatical symmetry or syntactical parallelism, the 'device' is scarcely perceptible *qua* device. It is where the inexact rime pits a gerund against a noun (e.g., Majakovskij's *vrezyvajas'-trezvost'*) or two word-units against one, that the 'organized violence' committed by verse on ordinary speech is sharply underlined.

Such composite or punning rimes, which often cause a "redistribution of the substantive and formal characteristics of the word" [66] (Tynjanov), i.e., a change in the relation between the root and the affix, have been for centuries a stock-in-trade of humorist poetry.[67] The outstanding feature of modern experimental verse, the Formalists pointed out, is that it often makes use of this technique without any comic motivation for the sole purpose of "laying bare the device".[68]

What is true of rime was also found applicable to other types of verbal orchestration. A "homophonic relation" (K. W. Wimsatt's term) gravitates inevitably toward word-play.

Formalist dissections of modern poetry indicated various possibilities inherent in word-play. The poetic context, it was noted, seems to encourage punning effects and toying with homonyms. The compactness

---

[65] Jurij Tynjanov, *Problema stixotvornogo jazyka,* chapter II.
[66] *Ibid.*
[67] In American poetry many examples of punning rime are found in the verses of Ogden Nash, e.g., 'a depot'—'heap o' (The Ogden Nash *Pocket Book,* 1944, p. 6.)
[68] Roman Jakobson, *Novejšaja russkaja poèzija* (Prague, 1921).

of the verse line, invoked by Tynjanov, can create the semblance of common origin or semantic kinship where neither obtains. "If you will line up in formation", Tynjanov wrote, "disparate, but like-sounding words, they will become cognates." [69] Jakobson analyzed provocatively Xlebnikov's 'false etymology': by juxtaposing such phonetically similar words as '*meč*' (sword) and '*mjač*' (ball), the Russian Futurist made them sound like modifications of the same root.[70]

"Making unrelated words akin to each other" (Tynjanov) [71] was only one aspect of the problem. An equally effective technique was that of reviving the real etymology of the word, or, more broadly speaking, toying with actual rather than seeming cognates.

As was indicated above, an extreme example of this device was found by Jakobson in Xlebnikov's experimental poem, "Incantation by Laughter",[72] which consist solely of derivatives from '*smex*' (Russian for 'laughter'). The poetic play with formants, the critic pointed out, 'actualizes' the morpheme both by focusing sharply on the recurrent stem and by underlining the fine semantic distinctions between individual affixes.

The Formalist approach to verse structure was, on the whole, a distinct improvement over the methods of traditional rhythmics. Jakobson was on safe ground, when in 1935 [73] he credited the Russian Formalist movement with "having correlated prosody with linguistics, sound with meaning, rhythmics and melodics with syntax . . . as well as having discarded normative approach to verse and the rigid antinomy of meter versus rhythm".[74]

Perhaps, the most significant of the achievements listed by Jakobson was the correlation of sound with meaning. The *Gestalt* theory of verse language made it possible for the Formalists to grasp what Mukařovský called the peculiar 'semantic dynamics' – or, to use Empson's favorite term, the fundamental ambiguity, of the poetic context.

This crucial insight was put to good advantage in numerous studies and papers, especially in those written during the later 'Structuralist' period. Suffice it to cite Jakobson's observations on the semantic 'flexibility' of Puškin's imagery and Mukařovský's inquiry into the levels of

[69] Jurij Tynjanov, *Arxaisty i novatory*, p. 560.
[70] Roman Jakobson, *Novejšaja russkaja poèzija*, pp. 49–50.
[71] Jurij Tynjanov, *Arxaisty i novatory*, p. 560.
[72] See above, chapter II, p. 46.
[73] See Jakobson's review of M. P. Stockmar's bibliography of Russian studies in versification (*Slavia*, XIII, 1935, pp. 416–431).
[74] *Ibid.*, p. 417.

meaning in Mácha's poetry. It is true that the Formalist school cannot boast any full-length dissection of poetic ambiguities comparable to Empson's ingenious study. But the methodological principles set forth by Jakobson, Mukařovský, and Tynjanov provided a future Russian or Czech Empson with a workable set of conceptual tools.

XIII. STYLE AND COMPOSITION

1

Working our way upward from euphony to semantics, from 'outward form' to 'inward form', we have entered almost imperceptibly the realm usually assigned to stylistics. In this field, too, the Formalist efforts proved rewarding, though not always sustained. They could scarcely be accused of a lack of interest in the lexical and phraseological aspects of poetic language, but they kept rather aloof from some of the areas of investigations usually associated with the study of style. Their anti-psychological bias made the Formalists well-nigh immune to the 'neo-idealistic' school of Karl Vossler and Leo Spitzer, who analyzed the styles of individual writers and schools of poetry as a manifestation of personality or group ethos.[1] The procedures of older stylistics, such as the cataloguing of 'tropes,' held little attraction for the *Opojaz* theorists. So did run-of-the-mill stylistic analysis, where glittering generalities about the beauty and richness of the poet's language were coupled with a mechanical enumeration of the rhetorical 'figures' used by the poet.

The absence in the Formalist writings of impressionistic chatter or the rhetorician's traditional claptrap is not to be deplored. One wishes, however, that the Formalists had addressed themselves to the more rewarding task undertaken by some of the Anglo-American 'New Critics' – that of tracing pervasive patterns of imagery and relating them to the total structure of meaning embodied in a given work or series of works.[2]

This relative lack of concern with 'tropes' could be undoubtedly at-

---

[1] Cf. Karl Vossler, *Frankreichs Kultur im Spiegel seiner Sprachentwicklung* (Heidelberg, 1913); *Gesammelte Aufsätze zur Sprachphilosophie* (Munich, 1923); *Positivismus und Idealismus in der Sprachwissenschaft* (Heidelberg, 1904); Leo Spitzer, *Linguistics and Literary History; Essays in Stylistics* (Princeton, 1948); *Stilstudien*, 2 vols. (Munich, 1928).

[2] See for example, Cleanth Brooks' discussion of the 'cloaking images' in *Macbeth* (Cleanth Brooks, *The Well Wrought Urn*, New York, 1947, pp. 21–46).

tributed to the Formalist's unwillingness to see the image as the differentia of poetic language.[3] It should be added that the early Formalist position on 'images', as set forth in Šklovskij's essay 'Art as a Device', was modified. In the later Formalist writings the crucial importance of the metaphor was partly reasserted.

This is clearly evidenced by Žirmunskij's attempt at a typology of literary styles. In his paper "On Classic and Romantic Poetry",[4] the distinguished literary historian posited metaphor and metonymy as the chief earmarks of the Romantic and Classic styles respectively.

In Jakobson's essay on Pasternak's prose [5] the dichotomy of 'figures of similarity' versus 'figures of contiguity' [6] serves as a basis for still more fundamental distinctions. In a challenging theoretical digression Jakobson argues that verse gravitates naturally toward metaphor, while prose favors metonymy. His reasoning parallels, or complements, Tynjanov's notion of rime as an auditory metaphor.[7] "Verse", wrote Jakobson, "rests upon association by similarity; the rhythmical affinity of individual lines is an indispensable prerequisite for our perception of verse. The rhythmical parallelism is further strengthened whenever it is accompanied by the sense of similarity on the level of imagery." [8]

Not so narrative prose. Here the motive force is not similarity, but association by contiguity, which lies at the core of metonymy. "As the narrative unfolds, its focus shifts from an object to its neighbor (in terms of physical space – time or of causality, that is)." "Consequently", Jakobson concluded, "for verse the line of least resistance is metaphor; for artistic prose, metonymy." [9]

The above argument is fairly typical of the maturer Formalist approach to the problem of imagery in creative writing. Jakobson's theory, which raises the metaphor to a commanding height in the realm of poetic semantics, may sound like a reversal of Šklovskij's attack on the 'thinking in images' doctrine. Actually, we have to do here not with a self-repudiation, but with a shift of emphasis.

In refusing to regard imagery as the touchstone of poetic art and in

[3] See above, chapter X, pp. 175–176.
[4] See Viktor Žirmunskij, *Voprosy teorii literatury* (Leningrad, 1928), pp. 175–182.
[5] Roman Jakobson, "Randbemerkungen zur Prosa des Dichters Pasternak", *Slavische Rundschau*, VII (1935).
[6] Cf. René Wellek and Austin Warren, *Theory of Literature* (New York, 1949), p. 199.
[7] See above, chapter XII, p. 224.
[8] *Slavische Rundschau*, VII, 366.
[9] *Ibid.*

suggesting that the 'trope' is but one of numerous devices at the poet's disposal, Šklovskij seems to have underestimated the role of the image. But at the same time it must be remembered that Šklovskij's esthetics enthroned the principle, which presumably underlies the poetic image, that of 'semantic shift', as the general law of literary creation. Fundamentally, Šklovskij's view of poetic art was not as prejudicial to imagery as it may have seemed on the surface. Stripped of deliberate overstatements and polemical irrelevancies, the orthodox Formalist position would boil down to the notion of the metaphor as the prime exponent of the Poetic Principle on the level of lexical meaning.

This latter qualification must be insisted upon. Ultimately the Formalist-Structuralist opposition to the traditional emphasis on 'figures of speech' was not a matter of hostility toward metaphor – nothing could please the Formalist critic more than a 'unification of disparate ideas' [10] – but of reluctance to define poetic speech in purely lexical terms.

It was already indicated that the Formalists viewed the poet's job as an 'actualization' of *all* elements of linguistic structure. The tendency toward 'semantic shift', it was argued, asserts itself on various levels of the poetic idiom. The trope, however 'strategic' its role in the sphere of poetic vocabulary, represents only one of these strata.

This is essentially what Jakobson had in mind when he invoked Puškin's 'non-figurative' poem, "I Loved You Once", as a proof that verse can dispense with images.[11] By insisting that the effectiveness of the lyric rested on the skilful use made of phrase melody and of morphological oppositions,[12] Jakobson suggested that grammatical meanings can be as readily utilized by the poet as lexical ones.

The Formalist search for the unifying esthetic principle posed in its entirety the problem of the nature and scope of poetic *style*. Here was another key term of literary criticism. This time the Formalist treatment of this much-abused critical concept was not as rigorous as was the case with 'rhythm', but, on the whole, the discussion was far from fruitless.

Again one seems to be faced here with what was on an earlier occasion called 'maximum' and 'minimum' definitions. An example of the

[10]   Ezra Pound's definition of the image, quoted by Wellek and Warren (*Theory of Literature,* p. 192).

[11]   See above, chapter X, p. 175.

[12]   The devices referred to by Jakobson include repeating the crucial phrase "Ja vas ljubil" (I loved you once) in three different keys and placing subsidiary parts of the sentence, e.g., adverbial constructions, in metrically strategic positions, notably at the end of the verse lines.

former can be found in Žirmunskij's paper "The Aims of Poetics",[13] where style is defined as the totality of devices employed in the work of poetry, the underlying esthetic principle which insures the unity of the whole and determines the function of each individual part. Such a broad conception of 'style' would obviously include non-verbal strata of the work of literature. Indeed, stylistics, as interpreted by Žirmunskij, encompasses the problems of 'composition' and 'thematology' (tematika).

Most of the Formalist spokesmen were somewhat more specific than that. In his study of Anna Axmatova,[14] Ejxenbaum joined Žirmunskij in construing style as a 'teleological unity' of devices geared to an esthetic effect, but he wisely restricted the range of his stylistic analysis to verbal devices – to the poetic utilization of linguistic resources.

This approach stood Ejxenbaum in good stead in dissecting Axmatova's 'poetics.' The notion of dominanta was invoked again, as Axmatova's poetic style was found to be 'dominated' by a tendency toward compactness and energy of expression, constrasting sharply with the grandiloquence, if not verbosity, of the poet's Symbolist predecessors.[15] Having posited thus the stylistic Gestaltqualität, Ejxenbaum proceeded to demonstrate its impact upon the poet's syntax (laconic phrases, abrupt syntactical transitions), euphony (strenuous 'articulatory gestures' rather than smooth acoustic effects) and her vocabulary, sparse, matter-of-fact, and almost 'prosaic'.

Some Formalist or near-Formalist students of style felt that Ejxenbaum's terms of reference were dangerously broad. Viktor Vinogradov decried attempts at reconstructing the literary artist's total 'poetics' as premature and unscientific. The study of style, he asserted, ought to focus on specific aspects of the poet's vocabulary, preferably, on pervasive verbal 'motifs', that is, on words and word-combinations favored by the given poets or schools of poetry. For Vinogradov, as for Ejxenbaum, Axmatova's closely wrought lyrics provided the test-case. In an early discussion of Axmatova's style,[16] Vinogradov set out to trace her characteristic 'semantic nests' – word-clusters revolving around certain key terms.

Ejxenbaum was unimpressed. He accused Vinogradov of ignoring the esthetic function of verbal devices. "The application of linguistic

13 Viktor Žirmunskij, "Zadači poètiki", Voprosy teorii literatury, pp. 17–88.
14 Boris Ejxenbaum, Anna Axmatova (Petrograd, 1923).
15 Ibid.
16 See Viktor Vinogradov, "O simvolike Anny Axmatovoj", Literaturnaja mysl' (Petrograd, 1922), I, pp. 91–138.

methods", he wrote, "which isolate individual words as semantic centers of attraction is too mechanical a procedure, as it does not take full account of the poetic context. Ordinary 'linguistic consciousness' (Vinogradov's term) and the language of the poet, which is shaped by *sui generis* artistic laws and traditions, must be recognized as two fundamentally disparate phenomena." "The weakness of Vinogradov's approach", continued Ejxenbaum, "stands revealed in a trivial but significant error: in discussing an alleged semantic cluster found in Axmatova – a group of words revolving around the notion of singing – Vinogradov mistook the 'crane (*žuravl'*) at an old dilapidated well' for the bird which whoops." [17]

Regardless of whether the emphasis of the given *Opojaz* theorist was extensive or intensive, 'linguistic' or 'esthetic', it was recognized at a rather early stage that the notion of literary style, as the underlying artistic principle of a work, was only one aspect of the problem. It became clear that the style of a literary artist could and should be discussed not only in 'intrinsic' terms, that is, with reference to other literary traditions, but also with regard to non-poetic modes of discourse. Vinogradov put it thus: the stylistic apparatus of a work of literature ought to be seen "in two contexts: (a) the context of the artistic forms of the literary language, (b) the context of social linguistic systems which can be discerned within the written and spoken language of the educated classes".[18]

That the latter context is no less essential than the former, no *Opojaz* theoretician could fail to realize. Formalist esthetics, as stated by Šklovskij and Tynjanov, attributed the satisfaction to be derived from artistic devices to the sense of divergence from the norm *(Differenzqualität)*.[19] Now one of the crucial elements of this quality is deviation from the general linguistic usage of the time. According to the Formalists, poetic language is perceived against the background of ordinary speech. We cannot appreciate, indeed, be aware of, the poet's artful deviation from the norm unless the norm is firmly embedded in our consciousness. In other words, an adequate response to, or description of, a literary style must take into account not only the type of creative deformation, but also the nature of what is being deformed or deviated from.

[17]   Boris Ejxenbaum, *Anna Axmatova*, p. 102.
[18]   Viktor Vinogradov, *O xudožestvennoj proze* (Moscow-Leningrad, 1930).
[19]   See Viktor Šklovskij, "Iskusstvo kak priëm", *Poètika* (Petrograd, 1919); Jurij Tynjanov, *Arxaisty i novatory* (Leningrad, 1929).

This assumption opened up a score of problems to which traditional stylistics had paid but little heed. The distinction between poetic and 'practical' language did not seem to tell the whole story, since the latter clearly was not a homogeneous phenomenon. Close cooperation with modern linguistics made the Formalist keenly aware of the functional differentiation of language, of numerous subdivisions within 'practical' language.

"Man's speech-activity", wrote Jakubinskij, "is a complex phenomenon. This complexity finds expression not only in the existence of various languages and lingoes, down to the dialects of social groups and individual idiosyncrasies, but, likewise, in functional differences within each of these linguistic systems." [20] Chronological, geographical or social considerations, continued Jakubinskij, are not the only differentiating factors. No less important is the aim of the utterance in question. One may inquire as to whether it purports to convey information or arouse emotional response, whether or not it is destined for oral delivery, and if it aims at a large audience or at a select group.[21]

The methodological moral to be drawn from the above was clear enough. In addition to defining the esthetic principle underlying a given set of deviations from general usage, it is necessary to ascertain the level of nonliterary discourse to which the given work of literature is geared. Stylistic analysis must show what is in each given case the extra-literary point of reference – the comparable type of 'practical' language.

This led directly to the problem of what Tynjanov called the 'speech orientation' (*rečevaja ustanovka*) of various poetic genres.[22] In his essay on eighteenth-century Russian poetry,[23] Tynjanov made use of this concept in defining the ode as an oratorical genre, i.e., one marked by an 'orientation toward oral delivery'. Ejxenbaum, too, came close to applying Tynjanov's criterion; in a study quoted above[24] he discriminated between three styles in Russian lyrical poetry – the oratorical, the conversational and the 'singable' ones.

Linguistic categories seemed especially pertinent in dealing with the style of the seventeenth- or eighteenth-century Russian writers. This

---

[20]   Lev Jakubinskij, "O dialogičeskoj reči", *Russkaja reč'* (Petrograd, 1923), p. 36.
[21]   *Ibid.*, p. 99.
[22]   See above, chapter VII, pp. 121–122.
[23]   Jurij Tynjanov, "Oda kak oratorskij žanr", *Arxaisty i novatory*.
[24]   Boris Ejxenbaum, *Melodika stixa* (Petrograd, 1922) (see above, chapter XII, pp. 222–223).

was a period in the history of Russian letters when phonetic or morphological differences could easily become matters of style.

Russian literary language as we know it is a hybrid creation. It originated from a fusion of the Russian vernacular with certain elements of Church Slavonic – the chief literary medium of pre-Petrine Russia. These two linguistic elements, closely akin and yet different, corresponded roughly to two distinct areas of discourse – the 'higher', more learned, and the 'lower', more colloquial one.

As Trubetzkoy has pointed out, this dual origin of literary Russian is reflected in a wealth of synonyms, or more exactly, of 'correlations of shades in meaning'. "A whole series of concepts in Russian admits of two verbal expressions: one of Church Slavonic, the other of Russian origin. The two words are differentiated in meaning: the Church Slavonic word has acquired a solemn and poetic overtone which is absent in the corresponding Russian term – or else the Church Slavonic word has a metaphoric or abstract meaning, while the Russian has a more concrete significance." [25]

Even while it contributes to the synonymic richness of the present-day Russian vocabulary, this dichotomy does not loom too large in contemporary Russian. During the last two centuries many 'Church Slavisms' have become completely unintelligible to an educated Russian and have been gradually dropped. In certain instances the affinity between the Russian and the Church Slavonic variants is no longer perceived, e.g. *strana, storona*. Or else the Russian form is dropped and the Church Slavonic variant becomes vernacularized, e.g. *sladkij*. But at the formative stage of literary Russian the interaction between current Great Russian forms and their archaic counterparts was a paramount stylistic factor; the use of an old verbal form or an antiquated sentence structure was not infrequently an act of esthetic choice.

Vinogradov demonstrated this conclusively in an acute study of *The Life of Arch-Presbyter Avvakum*,[26] one of the most colorful works of seventeenth-century Russian literature. In discussing the expressive use of language in Avvakum's autobiography, Vinogradov had no trouble establishing a clear-cut correlation between verbal texture and stylistic intent. He showed how the interplay between Church Slavisms and colloquialisms in the hybrid style of *The Life* corresponded to the rapid

---

[25]   N. S. Trubetzkoy, *The Common Slavic Element in Russian Culture* (New York, Department of Slavic Languages, Columbia University, 1949), p. 38.
[26]   Viktor Vinogradov, "O zadačax stilistiki. (Nabljudenija nad stilem žitija protopopa Avvakuma", *Russkaja reč'*, I (1923), 195–293.

transitions from the Biblical grandiloquence of religious polemics to the homely realism of the narrative passages.

Essentially the same method was applied, on a larger scale if somewhat less successfully, in Vinogradov's full-length study of Puškin's style.[27] The verbal substratum of Puškin' poetry was analyzed here into such ingredients as Church Slavisms, elements of popular speech, Gallicisms, and Teutonisms.

Vinogradov adopted a similar procedure in his close linguistic analysis of Dostotoevskij's *The Double*. The critic discerned in the highly stylized speech of Goljadkin, the novel's half-crazed hero, several 'horizontal' layers – the 'lowbrow', substandard expressions, along with stilted and somewhat archaic bureaucratic phraseology, and often misplaced 'big words' of foreign origin.[28]

The Formalist's interest in the 'speech orientation' of imaginative literature and his awareness of the stylistic potentialities inherent in various types of speech-activity found expression in a frequent tendency to examine the style of a literary work as an alternation of various types of monologue and dialogue.[29]

In his provocative article "On the Dialogue" (*O dialogičeskoj reči*) [30] Jakubinskij called attention to crucial stylistic differences between monologue and dialogue by juxtaposing the extended and coherent structure of the former to the elliptical 'sloppiness' and 'automatism' of the latter. Jakobson posed the problem in terms more directly relevant to literary art in a structural analysis of a Czech medieval poem, "A Debate Between the Soul and the Body".[31] He inquired into the artistic utilization of a form of dialogue traditional in medieval literature, the theological debate – a verbal showdown, the outcome of which is determined *a priori*. He noted the see-saw composition of the poem, its 'dramatized antithetic parallelism', the intense emotional coloring of the exchange between the protagonists, as well as a distinct 'orientation' toward pungent colloquialisms. The latter, continued Jakobson, is clearly a corollary of the dialogue situation. "Since here it is the protagonists who are responsible for the vocabulary, the author can afford occasionally to deviate from the conventions of standard language." [32]

With the exception of drama and works of narrative fiction which

27 Id., *Jazyk Puškina* (Leningrad, 1937).
28 Id., *Èvoljucija russkogo naturalizma (Gogol'-Dostoevskij)* (Leningrad, 1929).
29 Viktor Vinogradov, *O xudožestvennoj proze*.
30 See above, footnote 20.
31 Roman Jakobson (ed.), *Dvě staročeské skladby o smrti* (Prague, 1927).
32 *Ibid.*, p. 23.

employ what Henry James calls the 'scenic method', the monologue is the predominant type of utterance in imaginative literature. As Vinogradov put it, "the linguistic forms of the subjective monologue constitute the basic architectonic categories of a work of literature".[33]

But, as some Formalist theoreticians pointed out, a further subdivision may be in order here. If the bulk of expository prose, say that of Turgenev, James, or Flaubert, is couched in polished, highly literary monologue, there are works of literature which exhibit a tendency toward what might be called 'oral' monologue. Not infrequently, especially in cases where we have to do with a 'narrator' mediating between the author and the audience, the story is told in such a manner as to emulate the phonetic, grammatical and lexical patterns of actual speech and produce the 'illusion of oral narration'.[34]

This narrative manner, known in Russian literary theory as *skaz,* attracted the attention of Formalist students of style, occupied as they were with the use of sound in imaginative literature and alert to all devices of stylization. Ejxenbaum and Vinogradov traced the vicissitudes of the grotesque or 'colorful' *skaz* in Russian literature, from Gogol''s Ukrainian tales and "The Overcoat", through Dostoevskij and Leskov to the contemporary masters of the technique, such as A. Belyj, A. Remizov, E. Zamjatin, and M. Zoščenko. A parallel was drawn between Gogol''s uncanny skill in conveying the pathetic inarticulateness of Akakij Akakievič in "The Overcoat" and Zoščenko's adeptness at imitating the lingo of a bewildered Soviet Philistine.[35]

Similar developments are noticeable in recent Polish stylistics. In the earlier part of this century Kazimierz Wóycicki, one of the pioneers of scientific poetics in Poland 'rediscovered' recently by the young Polish Formalists,[36] sought to reach beyond the atomistic enumeration of rhetorical 'figures' toward larger verbal constructions, such as "direct, indirect, and seemingly indirect speech".[37] About fifteen years later D. Hopensztand brought Wóycicki's categories, especially that of the

---

[33]   Viktor Vinogradov, *O xudožestvennoj proze.*
[34]   Cf. Boris Ejxenbaum, "Kak sdelana *'Šinel' '* Gogolja", *Poètika,* 1919; "Illjuzija skaza", *Skvoz' literaturu* (Leningrad, 1924); Viktor Vinogradov, "Problema skaza v stilistike", *Poètika,* I (Leningrad, 1926).
[35]   See footnote 34; also Viktor Vinogradov, "Jazyk Zoščenki (Zametki o leksike)" in a symposium entitled *Mixail Zoščenko. Stat'i i materialy* (Leningrad, 1928); *Èvoljucija russkogo naturalizma* (Leningrad, 1929).
[36]   *Prace ofiarowane Kazimierzowi Wóycickiemu* (Wilno, 1937) (= Z *zagadnień poetyki,* VI).
[37]   Kazimierz Wóycicki, "Z pogranicza stylistyki (Mowa zależna, niezależna i pozornie zależna)", *Przegląd Humanistyczny,* I (1922), 75–100.

"seemingly indirect speech",[38] to bear on a stylistic analysis of a contemporary Polish novel.[39]

2

The concern of Formalist stylistics with larger verbal structures and with narrative techniques like the *skaz* pointed clearly toward a higher level of structural analysis. Just as metrics crossed over into stylistics, so did Formalist study of 'diction' bring into play problems of composition which are traditionally the province of the theory of prose.

The Formalist performance in this latter field is, on the whole, somewhat less substantial or methodologically satisfying than was the case with the study of verse. For one thing, narrative fiction did not become an object of systematic investigation until the later stage of *Opojaz*. For another, the chief *Opojaz* authorities on prose fiction, notably, Šklovskij and Ejxenbaum, never quite succeeded in overcoming the philosophical immaturity of 'pure' Formalism. In their discussions of the novel and the short story, one finds, along with many acute insights and apt formulations, a great deal that is far-fetched and one-sided.

The Formalist approach to prose fiction, both written and popular,[40] had many points of contact with Veselovskij's "historical poetics".[41] Veselovskij's studies in narrative art, focussing on the collective literary tradition rather than on the 'creative will' of the individual artist, were bound to hold considerable appeal for the Formalist theoreticians. Moreover, the 'morphological' analysis of fiction advocated by *Opojaz* was ostensibly furthered by the discrimination introduced by Veselovskij in his unfinished *Poetics of Plots* – that between the 'motif', as the basic narrative unit, and the 'plot', as the cluster of individual motifs.

In spite of this indebtedness, the Formalist attitude toward Veselovskij's heritage was far from uncritical. Veselovskij's valuable structural insights, asserted the Formalists, were vitiated by his 'ethnographism',

---

[38] By "seemingly indirect speech" (*mowa pozornie zależna*) both Wóycicki and Hopensztand meant a narrative manner whereby the utterances or the internal monologue or a character were stated in his own vocabulary, and yet the semblance of 'indirect speech' was maintained through such syntactical devices as the use of the conjunction 'that' (cf. German 'die erlebte Rede', French 'le style indirect libre').

[39] Dawid Hopensztand "Mova pozornie zależna w kontekscie *Czarynch skrzydeł* Kadena-Bandrowskiego", *Prace ofiarowane Kazimierzowi Wóycickiemu*.

[40] See especially Viktor Šklovskij, *O teorii prozy* (Moscow, 1929); Boris Ejxenbaum, "O. Genri i teorija novelly", *Literatura* (Leningrad, 1927); V. Propp, *Morfologija skazki* (Leningrad, 1928) (= *Voprosy poètiki*, XII).

[41] See above, chapter I, pp. 28–31.

that is, a tendency to regard fictional incidents as a direct reflection of social mores. This extrinsic emphasis, it was argued, made for a certain inconsistency in Veselovskij's treatment of his key concepts. While he tended increasingly to view plot as a compositional rather than purely thematic category, he interpreted its constituent part, the 'motif', whether that of the chase, a homecoming or a mistaken identity, as an element of extra-literary reality, something to be accounted for in ethnographic or anthropological terms.

The Formalist theory of prose suggested a way out of this quandary. The motif, or the archetypal literary situation, was seen not as a reflection of the actual, but as a conventional deformation of it. The notion of the 'plot', too, was reinterpreted: to an *Opojaz* critic it was not a mere sum-total, but an artistically ordered presentation of motifs.

The basic distinction between the external 'referent' of the literary work and its intrinsic 'meaning' stood the Formalists in good stead in revising Veselovskij's conceptual frame. According to Šklovskij and Ejxenbaum, 'plot', which is usually considered a part of the 'content', is as much "an element of form as rime".[42] In what was clearly an application to the problems of narrative fiction of the dynamic dichotomy between 'device' and "materials",[43] the Formalists differentiated between 'fable' (*fabula*) and 'plot' (*sjužet*). In *Opojaz* parlance the 'fable' stood for the basic story stuff, the sum-total of events to be related in the work of fiction, in a word, the "material for narrative construction".[44] Conversely, 'plot' meant the story as actually told or the way in which the events are linked together. In order to become part of esthetic structure the raw materials of the 'fable' have to be built into the 'plot'. Naturally, it is the latter which holds the center of the stage in the *Opojaz* theory of prose. The theme alone, apart from, or prior to, its artistic embodiment, can never account for the esthetic efficacy of a novel or a short story. The 'fable' of *Anna Karenina,* for example, can be stated in one brief sentence: this paraphrase, however, would not even hint at the richness and complexity of the novel. Art in general, and art of fiction in particular, stands or falls with organization.

The Formalist critics were only too glad to note that a similar opinion had been expressed by the author of *Anna Karenina* himself, who could scarcely be accused of Formalist leanings. Šklovskij and Ejxenbaum quoted on several occasions Tolstoj's sarcastic dig at his critics who

---

[42]   Viktor Šklovskij, *O teorii prozy,* p. 60.
[43]   See above, chapter X, pp. 188 ff.
[44]   Viktor Šklovskij, *Literatura i kinematograf* (Berlin, 1923).

managed to sum up in a few sentences the 'meaning' of *Anna Karenina.* *"Ils en savent plus que moi"*, wrote Tolstoj about his brash 'paraphrasers' in a letter to A. Straxov.[45] "As for me", he continued, "if I were asked what *Anna Karenina* was about, I would have to write the book all over again." [46]

The Formalists were ostensibly gratified by this challenge to what Cleanth Brooks recently called the "heresy of paraphrase".[47] They were also quick to spot and only too eager to cite another 'Formalist' assertion of Tolstoj, namely, his remark that the prime task of the literary critic was to inquire into "the laws governing that *labyrinth of linkages* (*labirint sceplenij*) which is literary art".[48]

The overriding concern with 'linkages' meant in terms of fiction the primacy of composition over thematology. Šklovskij's theory of prose focussed on 'convention', that is, the narrative schemes rather than on the 'life' allegedly reflected or deflected in fiction. With verisimilitude brushed aside as a delusion, with psychological or social factors relegated to the status of mere 'motivations' of compositional devices, 'character' was bound to be subordinated to 'plot'.[49] Indeed, as already indicated,[50] Formalist poetics assigned to the literary hero a very modest part: he is merely a by-product of the narrative structure, and as such, a compositional rather than a psychological entity. In a loosely constructed novel such a *Don Quixote,* the principal character is merely a thread on which heterogeneous episodes are 'strung' *(nanizany),* a 'pretext for the unfolding of the action'. The development of art, declared Šklovskij, is propelled by the needs of its technique. Thus, the technique of the novel gave rise to the 'type'.[51] And crossing over into the realm of drama, the critic added brashly: "Hamlet was created by the technique of the stage." [52]

[45] Viktor Šklovskij, *O teorii prozy,* p. 60.
[46] *Ibid.*
[47] Cf. Cleanth Brooks, *The Well Wrought Urn* (New York, 1947).
[48] Cf. *Russkie pisateli o literature* (Leningrad, 1939), II, 138 (also V. Šklovskij, *Literatura i kinematograf,* p. 16).
[49] One is reminded here of Aristotle's dictum that in a tragedy Character 'holds the second place' by comparison with the Plot (*Criticism,* New York, 1948, p. 202). But, as will be shown below, Šklovskij's notion of the plot is somewhat different from Aristotle's.
[50] See above, chapter XI, pp. 196–197.
[51] Viktor Šklovskij, *Sentimental'noe putešestvie* (Moscow-Berlin, 1923), p. 132.
[52] The above was one of the few Formalist utterances bearing on the art of drama. The only full-length study in this field made along Formalist or near-Formalist lines, was S. D. Baluxatyj's analysis of Čexov's plays, *Problemy dramaturgičeskogo analiza (Čexov)* (Leningrad, 1927) (= *Voprosy poètiki,* IX).

The hegemony of narrative techniques did not necessarily imply the pitting of 'action' against 'problems' in the manner of some Anglo-Saxon critics who insist that the main job of the fiction writer is to tell a 'good story'. It is true that Šklovskij, and even more so, some of his younger disciples like Lev Lunc [53] made a spirited attempt to revive the *roman d'aventures*. But on the other side of the ledger one finds Šklovskij's passionate interest in documentary literature and his lavish praise for *Tristram Shandy* – a novel where 'plot' in the habitual sense of the word is virtually non-existent.

To blame this apparent contradiction on Šklovskij's congenital inconsistency would be to miss the point. The fact of the matter is that Šklovskij's notion of 'plot' was somewhat different from Aristotle's. To the Formalist theoretician *'sjužet'* was not exactly a "structure of incidents".[54]

There is no question but that in Šklovskij's scheme, too, the sequence of events or, in other words, the treatment of time in a work of fiction was of crucial importance. In his *Theory of Prose* Šklovskij emphasized on several occasions the conventional character of literary time.[55] The difference between 'plot' and 'fable', he pointed out, lies often in artful deviations from the natural chronological sequence, in temporal displacements. To corroborate this thesis, Šklovskij dwelt lovingly on such techniques as beginning the narrative in the middle or at the end, occasional retrospective flashes, or constant shuttling between various planes of action – devices equally germane to highly sophisticated works of fiction, like *Tristram Shandy* and to mystery stories.

But to Šklovskij the treatment of time, however crucial, was only one part of the problem. What Šklovskij meant by *sjužet* was apparently not merely the artistic arrangement of the story stuff, but the totality of 'devices' employed in the process of telling the story. This includes elements of esthetic structure like digressions irrelevant to the narration. "The plot of *Eugene Onegin'* ", wrote Šklovskij, "is not Onegin's love affair with Tatjana, but the artistic treatment of the fable, achieved by means of interpolating digressions." [56] The detours from the story

[53] See above, chapter VIII, p. 149.
[54] See *Criticism,* p. 202.
[55] "Literary time", wrote Šklovskij, "is pure convention. Its law do not coincide with the laws of time in 'real life' " (*O teorii prozy,* p. 186). To illustrate his thesis about the arbitrariness of literary time, Šklovskij cited the fact that in *Don Quixote,* in the scenes at the 'literary tavern', a number of lengthy stories are told within one night.
[56] Viktor Šklovskij, *O teorii prozy,* p. 204.

were found as integral a part of the 'plot' as the story itself. Working on this assumption, Šklovskij endorsed wholeheartedly a suggestion made by a recent painter that Puškin's famous tirade about the 'adorable little feet' ('*o nožki, nožki! gde vy nyne?*') be illustrated on a par with the scene of Onegin's last encounter with Tatjana.[57]

The traditional hierarchy of values was thus overhauled. Not only was the hero reduced to the status of a pretext for the 'unfolding of the action', but the action itself was frequently regarded as a pretext for what Šklovskij called the 'unfolding of the verbal material' (*razvertyvanie slovesnogo materiala*).

This latter notion testified both to the Formalist's concern with language and to his insistence on the organic connection between the "devices of plot-construction and the general stylistic devices".[58] The narrative techniques were seen as illustrating on the level of composition the formative power of literary art in the same way in which the metaphor was the agency of 'literariness' in the realm of poetic vocabulary.

What are, according to Šklovskij, these immanent laws of composition, these 'devices of construction' operative in the novel, the short story and the folktale?

Challenging directly Potebnja's esthetics [59] and indirectly Aristotle's, Šklovskij wrote: "Art does not strive for generalizations. In 'its urge for concreteness' (Carlyle), art seeks to atomize even that which (in actual experience? V.E.) appears as generalized and unified." [60] In imaginative literature, Šklovskij argued, "an object is bifurcated through the medium of its multiple reflections and juxtapositions".[61]

This law of 'bifurcation' finds expression in what Šklovskij dubs the 'staircase-like structure' (*stupenčatoe postroenie*) of narrative fiction. 'Architectonic tautology,' the recurrence of the same episode in a novel, a ballad, or a folk song,[62] serves the same esthetic purpose as 'verbal tautology' – alliteration, refrain, rhythmical parallelism. In either case what could have been a straightforward statement is twisted by artful detours into a bizarre, multi-storied edifice. This, Šklovskij asserted, is the function of compositional parallelism, the favorite device of Lev

---

[57] *Ibid.*

[58] Cf. Viktor Šklovskij, "Svjaz' priëmov sjužetosloženija a obščimi priëmami stilja' ", *Poètika*, 1919.

[59] See above, chapter I, pp. 25–26.

[60] Viktor Šklovskij, *O teorii prozy*, p. 33.

[61] Id., *Xod konja* (Moscow-Berlin, 1923), p. 116.

[62] Id., "Svjaz' priëmov sjužetosloženija . . .".

Tolstoj. In "Xolstomer" Tolstoj juxtaposes the cosmos of the horse to
that of human beings; in "Three Deaths" he portrays the process of
dying on three parallel planes. In Tolstoj's short novel *Xadzhi Murat*
the image of the crushed weed in the opening passage parallels and
anticipates the fate of the hero.[63]

The principle of juxtaposition, Šklovskij asserted, is especially pertinent to the short story, the most 'artful' fictional genre. In short stories
and novelettes the esthetic effect rests more often than not upon deliberate exploitation of various types of contrast and incongruity. These
range from a 'realization' of a pun in terms of narrative structure [64]
through a motif of misunderstanding to that of a collision between
two codes of morals.

This parallelism, continued Šklovskij, is not always so explicit as it is
in Čexov's story "Tolstyj i tonkij" (The Fat Man and the Thin Man) or
in Tolstoj's "Xolstomer". Sometimes the 'other member of the parallel'
is conspicuously absent. This often happens, says Šklovskij, in
Maupassant's short stories, where instead of the anticipated *pointe* we
find what the Formalist critic aptly calls a 'zero ending'.[65] The climax
never comes off, the story is left hanging in the air. The esthetic effect
thus achieved is attributed by Šklovskij to the contrast between what
actually happens, or does not happen, in the story and the 'real' ending
which a reader familiar with the traditional pattern of the short story
has every reason to expect.[66]

Nor is the novel, this allegedly 'sluggish' [67] and structurally loose
genre, exempt from the law of staircase-like construction. Tolstoj was
invoked again, as his major novels seemed to exhibit many parallels
between two individual characters or two groups of characters. "In
War and Peace", observed Šklovskij, "one can clearly discern the following juxtapositions: (1) Napoleon versus Kutuzov, (2) Pierre Bezu-
khov versus Andrej Bolkonskij, with Nikolaj Rostov serving as an external point of reference for both parties. In *Anna Karenina* the group
Anna – Vronskij is juxtaposed with the group Levin – Kitty." [68]

---

[63]   Id., *Xod konja*, pp. 119–120.
[64]   Unfortunately, Šklovskij's treatment of this challenging concept is extremely
sketchy. He alludes, for instance, to a folk tale in which the plot provides a vehicle, or 'motivation' for a pun (*O teorii prozy*, p. 57).
[65]   Viktor Šklovskij, "Stroenie rasskaza i romana", *op. cit.*
[66]   Id., *Xod konja*, pp. 119–120.
[67]   Cf. José Ortega y Gasset, *The Dehumanization of Art and Notes on the Novel*
(Princeton University Press, 1948), p. 65.
[68]   Viktor Šklovskij, *Xod konja*, p. 123.

Ostensibly, the critic remarked, the co-existence of these two groups is 'motivated' by kinship. Šklovskij did not take this 'motivation' too seriously. He insisted, moreover – apparently not without justification – that neither did Tolstoj. Šklovskij quoted Tolstoj as saying, in a letter to a reader, that he decided to make the old Bolkonskij the father of the brilliant young man (Andrej) "since it is awkward to introduce a character totally unrelated to the story". Thus, concluded Šklovskij, kinship was here merely a contrivance. "The ostensible connection between the two members of the parallel is so tenuous that the real bond must lie in artistic necessity, i.e., the exigencies of the plot." [69]

These 'reflections and gradations', whereby the object depicted is seen simultaneously on several levels, inevitably delay the climax and thus serve as a 'brake' on the action. 'Staircase-like construction' is closely bound up with another fundamental technique of narrative fiction – that of 'retardation'. This latter principle was found to be operative in all types of narrative prose.

Šklovskij drew some of his most telling examples from the early period in the history of fiction when the novel was not yet far removed from a collection of short stories of the *Decameron* variety. *Don Quixote* was cited as a case in point. The principal plot of Cervantes' novel, he claimed, is 'flexible' enough to provide a framework for a string of interpolated short stories (*vstavnye novelly*). Šklovskij described the second part of *Don Quixote* as a 'loose mosaic of anecdotes', told at the 'literary tavern'. Viewed from the standpoint of the enveloping plot or 'frame story', he argued, these anecdotes can be construed as an effective means of slowing down the action.[70]

The same phenomenon, Šklovskij reminds us, is noticeable at the opposite pole of narrative art – in tightly knit narratives, designed to build up suspense. The device of epic retardation is crucial to the structure of the folktale, especially the archetypal tale of the quest or the difficult assignment, where the incessant piling up of obstacles to be surmounted or seemingly superhuman tasks to be performed keeps dealying the climax almost indefinitely. Likewise, in the modern detective story, for example, in Conan Doyle,[71] false solutions of the 'riddle', unfailingly supplied by the 'professional fool' Watson, postpone the real solution, and thus serve as a brake on the action. A similar function is

[69]   *Ibid.*, pp. 123–125.
[70]   Viktor Šklovskij, *O teorii prozy*, p. 120.
[71]   See Viktor Šklovskij, "Novella tajn", *O teorii prozy*.

performed by the constant overlapping of contiguous plots in E. T. A. Hoffmann, as well as by the accumulation of riddles to be solved in *Little Dorrit*.[72]

Šklovskij's single-minded concern with compositional patterns at the expense of psychological and philosophical 'motivations' resulted in some rather questionable statements. Thus, he went so far as to maintain that the discursive passages in *Crime and Punishment* – for example, the dialogue between Raskol'nikov and Svidrigajlov about the immortality of the soul – were fundamentally delaying devices, interpolated into the narrative for the sake of suspense. Even if one sees some merit in Šklovskij's unorthodox notion of *Crime and Punishment* as a mystery story 'complicated by philosophical materials'[73] one must insist that in the process of this 'complication' philosophical problems acquired in Dostoevskij's novel a status much more central than that of mere 'interpolations'.

A similar, if somewhat subtler operation was performed on *Little Dorrit*. Here, too, Šklovskij tended to play down the ideological implications of the novel. He suggested that the scenes in the debtors' prison were needed chiefly in order to delay the solution of the riddles inherent in the plot. And yet Šklovskij was vaguely aware that these elements of social criticism were more than a compositional expedient. The description of the milieu, he conceded, while originally designed as a brake on the action, "yielded to the pressure of the plot and became an integral element of the work of art". What was extraneous material from the viewpoint of a 'Gothic' novel – a tradition of which *Little Dorrit* was presumably an offshoot – has shifted from the periphery to the center. The early Romantic novel, with its elaborate pattern of intrigue, had exhausted its potentialities and reached an impasse: "its narrative schemes were utilized by the nascent social novel".[74]

The method of approach applied by Ejxenbaum and Šklovskij to individual works of fiction was brought to bear also upon their discussions of fictional genres. To Ejxenbaum, Šklovskij, and Tomaševskij the genre was fundamentally a matter of architecture, a "cluster of compositional devices" (*priëmy postroenija*).[75]

---

[72] It may be noted that Dickens' novel is discussed in Šklovskij's *Theory of Prose* under the heading of the 'mystery novel' (*roman tajn*).
[73] We shall revert to this thesis in the next chapter, p. 260.
[74] Viktor Šklovskij, *O teorii prozy*, p. 175.
[75] See especially Boris Tomaševskij, *Teorija literatury* (Moscow-Leningrad, 1925), p. 159.

Critics who set more store than did the Formalists by the 'ethos'
of literature tend to define the genres in terms of their major themes.
In his perceptive essay "The Novel of Manners and Morals",[76] Lionel
Trilling indicates as the distinctive feature of the novel its concern
with the problem of reality and appearance. The Formalists by-passed
thematology and focussed on purely architectonic criteria, such as size
or dimensions. The novel, Ejxenbaum argued, is a syncretic genre;
the short story, a homogeneous and streamlined one. "The novel has
its source in history or in travelogue; the short story, in fairy tales or
anecdotes." [77] Roughly, the difference between the two genres was seen
as that between a 'large and a small form'.

This latter set of terms occurs frequently in Formalist writings. Notions of 'large form' and 'small form' figure prominently in Ejxenbaum's
statements about Tolstoj's shift from stories and short novels to the
broad epic canvases of *War and Peace* and the large-scale family novel,[78] as well as in Tynjanov's diagnosis of the contemporary crisis in
prose fiction. In his essay, "The Literature of Today",[79] Tynjanov
termed one of the symptoms of this crisis the atrophy of the 'sense of
genre' (*oščuščenie žanra*) – the clear-cut distinction between the small
and the large form. This 'sense of genre', he argued, is essential to the
reader as well as the writer of fiction. Where the perception of the
whole is lacking, the relative weight of the part cannot be assessed.
Without a mental image of the total dimensions of the work "words
have no resonator, action develops wastefully, gropingly (*vslepuju*)".[80]

The Formalists were well advised to focus on the immanent exigencies of plot, on narrative conventions. They were on solid ground in
maintaining that "no power outside the narrative structure can increase the potency of a work of fiction": [81] indeed, a 'message' not assimilated into the literary work – however 'relevant' it may be otherwise – is more likely to impair than to enhance the total effect. But
Opojaz criticism erred grievously in its apparent reluctance to admit
that an idea could be 'assimilated' so successfully as to become one
of the pivotal elements of esthetic structure. Because of this fallacy
Šklovskij's theory of prose proves a very unreliable guide with regard

[76] Lionel Trilling, *The Liberal Imagination* (New York, 1950).
[77] Boris Ejxenbaum, *Literatura* (Leningrad, 1927), pp. 171–172.
[78] Boris Ejxenbaum, *Molodoj Tolstoj* (Petrograd-Berlin, 1922); *Lev Tolstoj*, Vol.
I (Leningrad, 1928).
[79] Jurij Tynjanov, "Literaturnoe segodnja", *Russkij sovremennik*, 1924, No. 1.
[80] *Ibid.*, p. 292.
[81] Viktor Šklovskij, *Xod konja*, p. 177.

to works of fiction in which the causation hinges upon psychological probability or intellectual coherence.

By the same token, the Formalist students were at their best in dealing with what might be called quotation mark techniques – with parody and stylization, 'laying bare' the artifice and destroying the illusion of reality. Šklovskij's spirited discussion of *Tristram Shandy* has already been mentioned.[82] Equally characteristic – and somewhat more tightly reasoned – were Ejxenbaum's observations on O. Henry's literary craft.

In his essay "O. Henry and the Theory of Short Story",[83] displaying, incidentally, a thorough familiarity with American prose fiction, Ejxenbaum maintained that this seemingly 'easy' story-teller was actually a highly sophisticated and form-conscious writer. O. Henry's form-consciousness, asserted the critic, his keen insight into the laws of the short story, was attested to by his Sterne-like debunking of narrative conventions and his "ironical attitude toward the reader, indeed, toward the very art of fiction".[84] Starting from this assumption, Ejxenbaum embarked upon an interpretation of O. Henry's novel, *Cabbages and Kings,* a work which most serious critics would consider too lightweight to serve as a touchstone of critical theory. He noted the loose structure, reminiscent of an earlier phase in the history of the novel – the string of unrelated episodes injected into the 'frame' plot. These interpolated stories, Ejxenbaum argued, are designed to delay the solution of the riddle underlying the main plot, as well as to disorient the reader by putting him on the 'wrong track'.[85]

So congenial seemed O. Henry's literary irony to the *Opojaz* critic that he virtually conferred on the popular American writer the title of an honorary Formalist. "His narrative art", wrote Ejxenbaum, "is based on incessant ironizing and 'laying bare' of the devices employed, as if O. Henry had studied the Formalist method in Russia and had often talked with Viktor Šklovskij. Actually, he was successively a pharmacist, a cowboy, a cashier, spent three years in jail, in other words, had every reason to become an honest-to-God realist (*bytovik*), writing straightforward case studies of social injustice." [86] "Yes", added

[82] See above, chapter XI, pp. 193–194.
[83] Boris Ejxenbaum, "O. Genri i teorija novelly", *Literatura,* pp. 166–209.
[84] *Ibid.,* p. 202.
[85] Ejxenbaum called attention to the quizzical opening passage of *Cabbages and Kings*. This 'proem,' observed the critic, 'lays bare' the conventions of the mystery novel by pointing explicitly to the riddle as the idea behind a baffling and incongruous plot.
[86] *Ibid.,* p. 196.

Ejxenbaum somewhat belligerently, "O. Henry must have cared more about art than about the compliments of Theodore Roosevelt." [87]

If the Formalist critic felt at home in parody, indeed in any brand of literary indirection or sophistication, the Formalist method proved equally applicable to what may seem on the surface the opposite pole of literary endeavor. One of the most valid Formalist contributions to the theory of fiction was V. I. Propp's study in the morphology of the fairy tale.[88]

Actually, there is nothing surprising about this. For one thing, in spite of its apparent 'simplicity', the fairy tale, with its migratory stock situations and its indispensable *loci communes,* is one of the most thoroughly formalized literary genres. For another, it is one of the least psychology-minded types of fiction. While in many modern novels action serves as a means of revealing or unfolding character, in the fairy tale, not unlike the adventure story, character is usually the tool of the plot. Thus, in dealing with the fairy tale, the orthodox Formalist's supreme disregard of 'motivations' was no more a handicap than it proved in examining the whimsical art of O. Henry or Sterne.

The emphasis on compositional patterns paid handsome dividends in Propp's terse study. His method was that of 'morphological analysis' – that is, of separating the fairy tale structure into its constituent parts. The scholar's professed aim was "to reduce the seeming multiplicity of fairy tale plots to a limited number of basic types".

What was the basis for this typology? The Formalist authority on folklore was skeptical of the numerous attempts at classification which were predicated upon the nature of the milieu depicted or the characteristics of the protagonists. Such criteria, he maintained, are unworkable, since they introduce a virtually unlimited number of variables.

From the standpoint of structural analysis, Propp insisted, the basic unit of the fairy tale is not the 'character', but his 'function', the part which he plays in the plot.[89] While the *dramatis personae* often change from one version of the same tale to the other, the 'functions' remain the same. In other words, the 'predicate' of the fairy tale, what the protagonist 'does', is the constant element; its subject – the name and

---

[87] Theodore Roosevelt is credited with a remark that some of the social legislation which he introduced was motivated by O. Henry's stories describing the plight of the New York shop-girls. Ejxenbaum was highly skeptical: he felt apparently that O. Henry's ironical, tongue-in-cheek manner was neither intended nor likely to 'move' a practical politician and thereby induce constructive action.
[88] V. Propp, *Morfologija skazki* (Leningrad, 1928) (= *Voprosy poètiki,* XII).
[89] *Ibid.,* pp. 26–27.

the attributes of the character – the variable. "The fairy tale", wrote Propp, "ascribes not infrequently the same action to various persons." [90] Depending on the period or ethnic milieu, the role of the grim foe can be played by a monster, a serpent, a wicked giant, or a Tatar chief; the function of the obstacle placed in the hero's path can be performed by a witch, an evil sorcerer, a storm, or a beast of prey.

Surveying in the light of this working hypothesis the entire field of international folklore, Propp noted that the number of 'functions' recurring in migratory fairy tale plots was 'exceedingly small', while the number of characters was 'extremely large'. Moreover, the 'sequence of these functions is always the same'.[91] In other words, to use the terminology inherited by the Formalists from Veselovskij, the striking similarities between the fairy tales of various countries and ages lie not only in individual 'motifs', but also in 'plots', that is, in the organization of these motifs. Rigorous application of architectonic categories made it possible for Propp to resolve the chaos of crisscrossing types and subtypes into an 'amazing uniformity'. "All fairy tales", Propp concluded, "are structurally homogeneous (*odnotipny*)." [92]

[90]   *Ibid.*, p. 29.
[91]   *Ibid.*, pp. 30–31.
[92]   *Ibid.*, p. 33.

XIV. LITERARY DYNAMICS

1

The method of morphological analysis used by Propp was a typical Formalist strategem. The *Opojaz* critics firmly believed that before trying to explain anything, one should find out what it is.[1] Now description *per se* is a static procedure, but it need not necessarily imply a static approach to the object of inquiry.

It is true that at first the Formalists came dangerously close to this fallacy,[2] but they mended their methodological fences at a rather early stage. With Tynjanov redefining the literary work as an esthetic 'system' rather than a 'sum-total of literary devices',[3] the notion of the mere co-existence of various elements in a literary whole gave way to that of dynamic integration. This in turn implied periodical shifts in the hierarchy of components, "continuous changes in the esthetic function of the literary devices".[4]

Not unlike Structuralist linguistics, with which it had so much in common, Formalist criticism sought to bridge the gap between what Ferdinand de Saussure had called the 'synchronic' and 'diachronic' approaches to language,[5] i.e. between descriptive and historical studies. While isolating a certain phase of a cultural process for the purposes of analysis, the investigator ought to be aware that in actuality his object of inquiry is never stationary. By the same token, the historical approach cannot dispense with the notion of 'system'. The nature

---

[1] See especially Skaftymov's study, *Poètika i genezis bylin* (Saratov, 1924), discussed above, in chapter XI, pp. 204–206.
[2] See above, chapter V, p. 90.
[3] The latter formula was coined by Šklovskij (cf. Viktor Šklovskij, *Rozanov*, Petrograd, 1921).
[4] Boris Tomaševskij, "La nouvelle école d'histoire littéraire en Russie", *Revue des études slaves*, VII (1928).
[5] Ferdinand de Saussure, *Cours de linguistique générale* (Lausanne, 1916).

of change, whether linguistic or literary, cannot be profitably discussed without reference to a hierarchy of values typical of the given cultural 'series'. In other words, the Formalist theoreticians argued, the 'descriptivist' must not forget that the 'system' *changes* all the time, while the historian should remember that the changes into which he is inquiring take place within a *system*.

If the functional notion of the 'literary fact' stimulated interest in 'literary evolution', the improvised *Opojaz* philosophy of art, as formulated by Šklovskij and Tynjanov, pointed in the same direction. As spokesmen for the literary avant-garde, the Formalists were bound to set much store by the violation of artistic canons and by novelty in general. As estheticians they saw the core of esthetic perception and the source of artistic values in the 'quality of divergence' (*Differenzqualität*).[6] This concept seems to have meant to the Formalist theoreticians three different things: on the level of the representation of reality, *Differenzqualität* stood for the 'divergence' from the actual, i.e., for creative deformation. On the level of language it meant a departure from current linguistic usage. Finally, on the plane of literary dynamics, this catch-all term would imply a deviation from, or modification of, the prevailing artistic norm.

The case for innovation was strengthned by Šklovskij's doctrine of automatism versus 'perceptibility', which was found as germane to our esthetic responses as it was, presumably, to our perception of reality. "Each art form", wrote Šklovskij, "travels down the inevitable road from birth to death; from seeing and sensory perception, when every detail in the object is savored and relished, to mere recognition, when the object or form becomes a dull epigone which our senses register mechanically, a piece of merchandise not visible even to the buyer." [7]

Literary creation is not immune to the inexorable passage of time or the pull of habit. But art, the chief purpose of which, according to Šklovskij, is to counteract this deadening impact, cannot afford routine. This is what makes literary change so crucial. "The value of literature", wrote Tomaševskij, "lies in its novelty and originality. Depending on the way in which the attention of the evaluating literary public responds to individual devices, these can be classified as perceptible or imperceptible. In order to be perceptible, a device must be either very old or very novel." [8]

---

[6]   See above, chapters X, XI, pp. 178, 200.
[7]   Viktor Šklovskij, *Xod konja* (Moscow-Berlin, 1923), p. 88.
[8]   Boris Tomaševskij, *Teorija literatury*, p. 157.

The 'canonization' of change made the Russian Formalists much more history-minded than was the case with the bulk of their Western counterparts. Not all the Anglo-American 'New Critics' may share T. S. Eliot's notion of literature as a simultaneous order.[9] But most of them are ostensibly less concerned with literary change than with what remains unchanged. The Slavic Formalists had, if anything, too much historical sense. G. O. Vinokur, a rather sympathetic critic, claimed that the *Opojaz* literary historians were obsessed with the sheer process of motion, with divergences between different literary schools, to the extent of having virtually given up critical standards applicable to more than one period.[10]

Vinokur's strictures were not wholly unjustified. As will be mentioned below,[11] the Formalist cult of novelty was a very inadequate basis for esthetics. But whatever its other disadvantages, this attitude resulted in a number of valuable insights into literary dynamics, or, as the Formalists themselves would put it, into the laws of literary evolution.

This latter formulation indicates a belief in the regularity or 'lawfulness' of the historical process. Indeed, as already indicated, the Formalist view of literary history did have a strong deterministic tinge. *Opojaz* 'historical poetics', like Veselovskij's, was concerned with literary genres and devices rather than with creative personalities. In this Formalist scheme of literary history the genius did not figure as a major variable; he was reduced to the status of an agent of impersonal forces. "Art", said Šklovskij, "is not created by the individual will, by the genius. The creator is simply the geometrical point of intersection of forces operative outside of him." [12]

Not all Formalists would concur in Brik's dictum that if Puškin had been never born, *Evgenij Onegin* would have been written just the same.[13] However, this absurd proposition [14] was merely a grotesquely exaggerated statement of the *Opojaz* tenet that the poet is not a free agent and that in order to survive, to make his work count, the imaginative writer must fulfill the 'literary demand' of his epoch. The problems with which an author grapples, is was argued, are imposed upon him by his time, i.e., the phase in literary evolution into which he is

[9] T. S. Eliot, *Selected Essays* (New York, 1932).
[10] G. A. Vinokur, "Poèzija i nauka", *Čët i nečet* (Moscow, 1925).
[11] See below, chapter XV, pp. 279–283.
[12] Viktor Šklovskij, *Xod konja*, p. 22.
[13] Cf. Osip Brik, "T. n. formal'nyj metod", *Lef*, 1923, pp. 213–215.
[14] There is a good reason to assume that the astute Brik, given to deliberately extravagant formulations, realized himself the absurdity of his claim.

born. Likewise, the way in which he seeks to solve these problems is determined in the last analysis not by his sensibility or temperament but by the character of the literary tradition within which he operates or, more often than not, by the overriding necessity for modifying this tradition. Ejxenbaum paraphrased, perhaps unwittingly, Engels' famous phrase when he wrote: "The freedom of the individual writer lies in his capacity to be timely, to hear the voice of history." [15] "In general", he continued, "creation is an act of historical self-awareness, of locating oneself in the stream of history." [16]

What are, according to the Formalists, the driving forces of literary history 'operative outside the writer'? Is literary evolution a self-propelled or an externally determined process or, perhaps, a combination of both? Militant Formalism had little doubts on this score. Taking a leaf from Kručënyx's book,[17] it insisted on the chronological primacy of form over content. "We Futurists", declared Šklovskij in one of his most frankly partisan pronouncements, "entered literature with a new banner: 'New form gives rise to new content.' " [18] "A new form", he said elsewhere, "arises not in order to express a new content, but because the old form has exhausted its potentialies." [19] Art can grow stale like anything else. But when it does, it loses its *raison d'être;* in fact, it hardly exists at all. "It is impossible to create within forms which have been discovered, because creation means change. . . . The so-called old art does not exist, objectively does not exist, and thus it is impossible to produce a work in accordance with its canons." [20] The 'petrified" art forms are supplanted by new artistic configurations which, in view of their 'decisive novelty', are capable of restoring freshness to our perception, until these in turn wither away and go down in another literary upheaval.

The above scheme of literary change suffered from the same fallacy which vitiated the early *Opojaz* conception of the literary work. Šklovskij was again guilty of esthetic 'purism', the tendency to tear art out of its social context. The Formalists were perfectly justified in pointing to the inner dynamism of the literary process, insisting that artistic trends cannot be mechanically deduced from or reduced to data of

[15] Boris Ejxenbaum, *Skvoz' literaturu* (Leningrad, 1924), p. 236.
[16] *Ibid.*
[17] See above, chapter II, pp. 44–45.
[18] Viktor Šklovskij, *Xod konja*, p. 38.
[19] Viktor Šklovskij, "Svjaz' priëmov sjužetosloženija s obščimi priëmami stilja", *Poètika* (Petrograd, 1919), p. 120.
[20] *Xod konja*, p. 86.

other cultural 'series'. But they apparently mistook autonomy for separatism when, in an extravagant reaction against the Reductive Fallacy, they seemed to deny any interaction between the various parts of the social fabric and to construe literary evolution as a wholly self-contained proces.

Some of the independent sympathizers of the Formalist School took exception to the one-sidedness of the *Opojaz* theory of literary history. One of them was Viktor Žirmunskij, whose polemic with Šklovskij's slogan "Art is a device" was discussed above.[21] He admitted the relevance of Šklovskij's 'automatization' doctrine, but found it inadequate as an explanation of the succession of literary schools.

Since literature, Žirmunskij argued, is closely bound up with other human activities, its evolution cannot be accounted for in purely literary terms. It is impossible, he asserted, to evade the problem of the relation between the development of art forms and other aspects of culture.[22] Moreover, the principle of contrast or esthetic variation is too negative a factor to explain fully the growth of literature. The theory of the gradual withering away of art forms can account for the reaction against the old, but not for the nature of the new; it can explain the necessity of change, but not its direction. The latter is determined by the total cultural atmosphere of the period, the temper of the age, which finds its expression in literature as well as in other domains of culture. Thus the revolt against Classicism at the end of the eighteenth century may have been due to the 'petrification' of the Classicist style. But the fact that this revolt took the form of Romanticism is to be attributed to the rise of a new world-view which clamored for expression in art as well as in other cultural spheres.[23]

In his thoughtful study of Formalist methodology Engelhardt put the case in similar terms: "The theory of automatization can explain only the fact of 'movement' in literature, the inner necessity for its evolution, but not the nature or the forms of this development." [24]

The above position exhibits undoubtedly more caution and common sense than that of the militant Formalists. And yet Žirmunskij's reasonable compromise between esthetic criticism and Dilthey's *Geistesgeschichte* sounds a bit mechanistic. The thesis that literary evolution cannot be fully understood in 'immanent' terms was a much needed

---

21 See above, chapter V, pp. 96–98.
22 Viktor Žirmunskij, *Voprosy teorii literatury* (Leningrad, 1928).
23 *Ibid.*, pp. 162–165.
24 Boris Engelhardt, *Formal'nyj metod v istorii literatury* (Leningrad, 1928).

reminder. But the division of labor in Žirmunskij's scheme, whereby internal development generates a stimulus for change while the response is determined by external factors, was too neat to do full justice to the problem. That literature is inseparable from the *Zeitgeist* can hardly be denied. But the relation between art and philosophy is not a matter of ideal harmony or of point-to-point correspondences. Moreover, if one admits, as Žirmunskij did, that literature has a certain internal dynamism of its own, there is hardly any reason to assume that whenever a crisis in art arises, the solution has always to be 'borrowed' from the outside.

Ejxenbaum may not have been wide of the mark when, in his study of Axmatova, he suggested that the chief issue at stake in the transition from Symbolism to Acmeism and Futurism was the use of language rather than the outlook on life. "It became necessary", he wrote, "to change the attitude toward poetic speech, which had turned into a lifeless idiom, incapable of further growth or free play. It became necessary to create a new, inarticulate, uncouth speech, to emancipate the tradition of poetic diction from the shackles of Symbolism, and thus to restore the equilibrium between verse and language." [25]

By the same token, as Jakobson has pointed out, the fact that the widespread revulsion against positivism which set in at the beginning of this century took on in art the aspect of non-representative symbolism, was not merely a by-product of the intellectual atmosphere. This attempt at the "liberation of the sign from the object" (Jakobson),[26] while undoubtedly a part of the general cultural situation, had at least as much to do with the state of the poet's medium as it had with the prevalent state of mind.

Perhaps in tackling such phenomena as modern art one had better invoke Mukařovský's formula which is in a sense the reverse of Žirmunskij's. "Each change in artistic structure", wrote Mukařovský, "is induced from the outside, either directly, under the immediate impact of social change, or indirectly, under the influence of a development in one of the parallel cultural domains, such as science, economics, politics, language, etc. The way, however, in which the given external challenge is met and the form to which it gives rise depend on the factors inherent in the artistic structure." [27]

---

[25] Boris Ejxenbaum, *Anna Axmatova* (Petrograd, 1923), p. 66.
[26] Cf. Roman Jakobson, "Randbemerkungen zur Prosa des Dichters Pasternak", *Slavische Rundschau*, VII (1935).
[27] Jan Mukařovský, *Kapitoly z české poetiki* (Prague, 1941), I, 22.

As a general statement of the relation between art and society Mukařovský's formulation, too, is far from definitive or exhaustive. On the whole, however, the Structuralist critique of the *Opojaz* theory of literary history strikes one as methodologically more astute than Žirmunskij's eclectic scheme. The Structuralist theorists were at one with Žirmunskij in emphasizing the fundamental unity of culture and the organic connection between literature and other human activities. Indeed, both Trubetzkoy and Jakobson posited the inquiry into the nature and mechanism of this 'interrelatedness' [28] as one of the most pressing tasks of the humanist. But the spokesmen of the Prague Circle seemed more keenly aware than was Žirmunskij of the complexity of the problem. The thesis of the dialectical tension between art and society [29] allows for the temporal lags as well as the inner dynamism *(Selbstbewegung)* of individual cultural domains, and by so doing avoids the pitfalls of both separatism and reductivism.

Jakobson's and Mukařovský's theories seem to foreshadow a more mature and flexible sociology of art. I say 'foreshadow', since the Structuralist attempts a correlating art with social change never left the stage of blueprints, or of general methodological directives.

It is not in these broad generalizations, however sound and promising, that one should seek the core of the Formalist contribution to the theory of literary history. Nor is it to be found in the mere emphasis on the dramatic character of the literary process, the incessant struggle between the old and the new. That each literary school is or purports to be a reaction against its predecessors, has been said on many occasions. The Formalists may have said this more often and with greater gusto than the critics who did not set so much store by innovation. But clearly the distinguishing feature of the Formalist notion of literary history lay not so much in the insistence on the 'struggle between fathers and sons', as in the insight into the peculiar mechanism of this struggle.

The 'functional' approach to literary evolution proved very helpful indeed. The *Opojaz* researchers realized that literary continuity was neither a matter of a smooth transition from the master to the disciple, nor that of rigid antinomies. Obviously, the motivating force of literary motion is conflict, but this means, in Tynjanov's words, a reshuffling

[28]   N. S. Trubetzkoy, *Principes de phonologie* (Paris, 1949); Roman Jakobson, *K xarakteristike evrazijskogo jazykovogo sojuza* (Paris, 1931).
[29]   Roman Jakobson, "Randbemerkungen zur Prosa des Dichters Pasternak".

rather than wanton destruction, a shift in the function of the esthetic device rather than its elimination.

The Formalist observations on the role of parody cast an interesting light on the mechanics of literary change. In his acute study, *Dostoevskij and Gogol'*,[30] Tynjanov demonstrated that the relationship between these two writers was a much more complex phenomenon than was generally understood. Dostoevskij's indebtedness to Gogol', he observed, is undeniable, attested as it is by a wealth of Gogolian echoes in Dostoevskij's early novels, e.g., *Poor Folk, The Double, Netočka Nezvanova*. But, according to Tynjanov, there is also another aspect, unnoticed by most literary historians: in his novel *The Friend of the Family* (Selo Stepančikovo) Dostoevskij was parodying the ponderous rhetoric of Gogol''s *Correspondence with Friends*. Now parody, continued Tynjanov, is a sign of emancipation, indeed an act of literary 'warfare'. If *Poor Folk* and *The Double* are a proof that Dostoevskij evolved out of Gogol', *The Friend of the Family* clearly indicates that its author was moving beyond Gogol'. Dostoevskij's literary art, concluded Tynjanov, was both a product of, and a challenge to, Gogol''s 'romantic naturalism'.

Similar is the case of Nekrasov, as seen by Ejxenbaum and Tynjanov.[31] It has often been noted that Nekrasov derived some of his themes and meters from Lermontov. At the same time it was clear that on many counts Nekrasov's poetry diverged widely from the Romantic pattern. Here, too, the Formalists claimed, it is the use of parody that throws into focus the dual nature of literary continuity. This time the case in point was a bitter, sarcastic paraphrase by Nekrasov of Lermontov's popular lullaby "Spi mladenec moj prekrasnyj" (Sleep, my beautiful baby). With the shabby figure of the petty offficial substituted for the would-be proud warrior as the image of what the infant would become, the spell of the rhythm was broken and a *coup de grâce* given to the romantic cliché which Nekrasov sought to dislodge.

This is, the Formalist critic implies, how literary change comes about. The old is presented, as it were, in a new key. The obsolete device is not thrown overboard, but repeated in a new, incongruous context, and thus either rendered absurd through the agency of mechanization or made 'perceptible' again. In other words, a new art is not an anti-

---

[30] Jurij Tynjanov, *Dostoevskij i Gogol'. K teorii parodii* (Opojaz, Petrograd, 1921) (reprinted in Tynjanov's collection of essays, *Arxaisty i novatory*, Leningrad, 1928, pp. 412–455).

[31] See Boris Ejxenbaum, "Nekrasov", *Skvoz' literaturu* (Leningrad, 1924); Jurij Tynjanov, "Poètičeskie formy Nekrasova", *Arxaisty i novatory*.

thesis of the preceding one, but its reorganization, a "regrouping of the old elements".[32]

Iconoclastic gestures, the Formalists warned, ought not to be taken seriously. Even while they reject unqualifiedly the heritage of the 'fathers', the rebellious 'sons' cannot help but include in their equipment some of the techniques developed or perfected by the 'enemy'. Jakobson shrewdly observed [33] that in his cosmic élan the Russian Futurist Majakovskij had much more in common with his much-abused Symbolist predecessors than he would care to admit.

The general conclusion to be drawn from all this was clear: literary evolution is not a unilinear process; it is a twisted path, full of detours, of zigs and zags. Every literary trend represents a crisscrossing, a complex interplay between elements of tradition and innovation.

It was this awareness of the fluidity of the literary process, along with a healthy distrust of rigid definitions and official hierarchies which made the Formalists alive to literary affinities and cross-connections undreamt of by the textbook writers. Tynjanov and Ejxenbaum knew that literary conflict, like politics, makes strange bedfellows and that a great writer may not be above borrowing from, or being stimulated by, a hack. They realized, too, that a modern poet may, in his recoil from the conventions of the recent past, fall back consciously or unconsciously on the pattern of a more remote age. "In the struggle with his father the grandson turns out to resemble his grandfather".[34]

Reaching backwards toward an older literary tradition is one possible response to the artistic crises which periodically beset imaginative literature. Another way out of the stalemate might be for literature to reach beyond itself, to delve into 'mores' (byt), to seek new blood in raw materials of life.[35] Hence the popularity enjoyed in Russia by hybrid, non-fictional genres – memoirs, letters, reportage, feuilletons – at such critical junctures as the late eighteenth century and, *mutatis mutandis,* the 1920's.[36]

Frequently, the Formalists asserted, the search for a new form combines, as it were, lateral motion with a retrospective glance. An emerging literary movement can derive its stimulus from the preceding era. But more often than not the cue would be taken not from the 'fathers',

[32] Jurij Tynjanov, *Arxaisty i novatory,* p. 413.
[33] Roman Jakobson, "O pokolenii, rastrativšem svoix poètov", *Smert' Vladimira Majakovskogo* (Berlin, 1930), pp. 7–45.
[34] Jurij Tynjanov, *Arxaisty i novatory,* p. 562.
[35] See above, chapter VII, pp. 121–122.
[36] Jurij Tynjanov, *Arxaisty i novatory,* p. 15.

whose authority is being professedly defied, but, as Šklovskij graphically put it, from the 'uncles'.

"According to the law", wrote Šklovskij proudly, "which, as far as I know, I was the first to formulate, in the history of art the legacy is transmitted not from father to son, but from uncle to nephew." [37]

The 'law' which Šklovskij boasted of having discovered was known in Formalist writings as that of the 'canonization of the junior branch'. "When the 'canonized' art forms reach an impasse, the way is paved for the infiltration of the elements of non-canonized art, which by this time have managed to evolve new artistic devices." [38] In order to renew itself literature draws upon motifs and devices of sub-literary genres. Products of popular culture, leading a precarious existence on the periphery of literature, are thus admitted into the parlor, raised to the status of *bona fide* literary art, or, as Šklovskij put it, 'canonized'.

According to the Formalists, Russian literature affords many examples of such a 'canonization'. Puškin's lyrics, it was argued, emerged from the late eighteenth-century album verses, so-called *'poesie fugitive'*. Nekrasov's poetry, replete as it was with 'lowbrow' prosaisms, owed much of its tenor, rhythmical pattern, and vocabulary to journalism and vaudeville. "Blok", said Šklovskij, "canonizes the themes and cadences of the gypsy song. Čexov introduces into Russian literature elements of low farce and the feuilleton. Dostoevskij raises to the dignity of a literary norm the devices of the detective story." [39]

Once again it was not the presence of an individual component, but the use to which it is being put that was found to be the central problem of literary criticism. If an 'inferior' genre could provide a model for some of the most profound philosophical novels in world literature, if the facile rhythm of the gypsy romance could acquire emotional potency in Blok's harrowingly intense love lyrics, clearly, the prime concern of the literary scholar was function and context.

2

The Formalist conception of literary dynamics as brought to bear on the Russian literary scene gave rise to many drastic revisions of traditional notions, to many significant shifts in historical perspective. The total picture of Russian literary evolution which has emerged from

[37] Viktor Šklovskij, *Literatura i kinematograf* (Berlin, 1923), p. 27.
[38] *Ibid.,* p. 29.
[39] Viktor Šklovskij, *Rozanov* (quoted by Boris Ejxenbaum, *Literatura,* Leningrad, 1927, p. 144).

these reexamninations was at once more complex and better integrated than the one known from the textbooks of literary history. The unity of focus was due to the fact that the Formalists viewed the history of literature as an evolution of genres and styles rather than a loose mosaic of literary figures or a by-product of intellectual or social change.

If the Formalist researchers tended at the earlier stage to slight extra-literary determinants, they were appreciably more catholic than their predecessors or rivals with regard to 'immanent' literary factors. Spurning the traditional preoccupation with the 'literary generals' (Brik),[40] *Opojaz* extended the scope of historical investigation to include marginal phenomena – obscure or half-forgotten writers, mass production, and sub-literary genres. Literature, the Formalists argued, is not a succession of masterpieces. One cannot understand the evolution of literature or assess any period in its history without taking note of the second- and third-rate. For on thing, masterpieces can be recognized as such only against the background of mediocrity. For another, failure can sometimes be as important a factor in literary dynamics as success. Abortive or premature thrusts in the 'right' direection, while unimpressive in themselves, often foreshadow or pave the way for resounding triumphs and thus are of crucial importance to the literary historian.

Perhaps the most conspicuous shift in historical perspective effected by the Formalist research was one which had to do with Puškin's place in the history of Russian literature – a problem which stood in the foreground of several provocative studies by Ejxenbaum, Šklovskij, Tomaševskij, Tynjanov, and Žirmunskij.[41] The Formalists challenged the traditional notion of Puškin as a leading figure of Russian Romanticism and the demiurge of nineteenth-century Russian poetry. Approaching the heritage of the great poet from the standpoint of his attitude to language, style, and genre rather than in terms of Puškin's philosophy of life, they arrived at a highly unorthodox conclusion: Puškin was fundamentally an heir to the Classicist era rather than a forerunner of Romanticism. The poetic achievements of Lomonosov and Deržavin had come in Puškin to a supreme fruition, making possible the seemingly effortless command of the medium, the ideal equilibrium between verse and language.

---

[40] Osip Brik, "T. n. formal'nyj metod", *Lef,* I (1923).
[41] Boris Ejxenbaum, "Put' Puškina k proze", *Literatura*; Viktor Šklovskij, "Evgenij Onegin (Puškin i Sterne)", *Očerki po poètike Puškina* (Berlin, 1923); Jurij Tynjanov, *Arxaisty i novatory*; Boris Tomaševskij, *Puškin*; Viktor Žirmunskij, *Bajron i Puškin (Iz istorii romantičeskoj poèmy)* (Leningrad, 1924).

The Formalists freely admitted that Puškin had appreciably modified or transcended the Classicist heritage. He loosened up the rigidity of Lomonosov's canon by 'canonizing' the whimsical and conversational rhythms of 'light poetry' (*vers de société*). Moreover, he drew upon many themes and artistic methods of the Romantic age. But the core of Puškin's poetics remained Classicist.[42]

Perhaps, the most judicious statement of this position is found in Jakobson's essay written in 1936.[43] "The esthetic basis of Puškin's lyrics", wrote Jakobson, "is Classicism, but it is Classicism informed by Romanticism, in the same way in which the Romanticism of such late Romantics as Baudelaire, Lautréamont and Dostoevskij could not help but be influenced by the fact that they lived in the age of Realism." [44]

In his scholarly studies of Puškin and his times,[45] Tynjanov went so far as to question the applicability of the dichotomy of Romanticism and Classicism to the Russian literary scene. The Formalist critic did not deny the impact of these Western European trends on Russian literature. But he seemed to feel that the struggle between Classicism and Romanticism was not the central problem of the Puškin era. The elements of 'Romanticism' and 'Classicism', Tynjanov continued, were in Russia intermingled in such a bizarre fashion that the boundary line between the two movements was here much more blurred than, say, in France.

According to Tynjanov, the literary battles of early nineteenth-century Russia were fought around a purely Russian, and a more specifically literary,[46] issue. The debate between the so-called archaists and innovators focussed on the verbal texture of the Russian literary language. The archaists advocated a return to the Lomonosov tradition with its clear-cut distinction between genres and levels of discourse and its predominance of a 'high' style permeated with 'Church Slavicisms'. The innovators took their cue from Karamzin's urbane prose and ar-

[42] It can be argued that much of the above had been anticipated by Symbolist critics, especially, Valerij Brjusov (cf. *Moj Puškin*). But, if the Formalists cannot be given full credit for this reassessment of Puškin's historical role, they certainly did yeoman's work in developing and systematically articulating this view.

[43] Roman Jakobson, "Na okraj lyrických básní Puškinových", *Vybrané spisy A. S. Puškina* (Prague, 1936), pp. 259–267.

[44] *Ibid.,* p. 262.

[45] Jurij Tynjanov, "Arxaisty i Puškin", *Arxaisty i novatory*.

[46] Perhaps one of the reasons for Tynjanov's distrust of the traditional dichotomy was the tendency of the run-of-the-mill literary historian to designate by 'Classicism' and 'Romanticism' schools of thought rather than clearly definable literary movements.

gued for the 'middle' style, geared to the spoken language of the educated classes and free from stilted archaisms. The controversy, the most active protagonists of which were such lesser known figures of the Puškin era as Griboedov, Küchelbecker, Šiškov, Vjazemskij, etc., was complicated by a division of both camps into more conservative ('older') and more progressive ('younger') factions.

The Formalist literary historians had considerable trouble placing Puškin in the literary life of his time. Tynjanov tended to locate Puškin in the vicinity of the younger archaists,[47] while Tomaševskij seemed to lay more emphasis on Puškin's temporary association with the 'left-wing' innovators.[48] Both critics would agree that Puškin was too complex a phenomenon to admit of unequivocal classification. His creative practive, marked as it was by an interplay between 'Slavisms' and colloquialisms, light poetry and epic grandeur, as well as his astute critical pronouncements, which eschewed definite commitments, defy categorical labelling.

But the Formalists insisted that if Puškin seemed to transcend all the schools of his age – as he indeed transcend his entire epoch – this did not mean that he kept aloof from the battle. In the course of his literary career he 'overlapped' with several factions, espoused several current viewpoints, without ever becoming finally identified with any one of them. Thus, Tynjanov argued, Puškin's historical role cannot be understood without taking into account various literary cross-currents of the epoch and the activities of his lesser contemporaries.

All this allegedly pointed to the necessity for examing Puškin, or any other 'classic' for that matter, within the context of his time. Puškin's achievement, the Formalists insisted, and his place in the total scheme of Russian literature should be studied *historically*. The *Opojaz* critics were ostensibly impatient with the impressionist's 'ahistorical' notion of the masters as "eternal companions",[49] and with critical hero-worship in general. "It is time", wrote Tomaševskij, "to discard the traditional messianism of Puškin scholarship which divides Russian literature into the Old Testament (before Puškin) and the New Testament (after Puškin)." [50] The Formalists took exception to the popular notion of Puškin as the 'great divide', the shaping power of nineteenth-century Russian poetry. They did not deny Puškin's decisive impact on the for-

[47]   Jurij Tynjanov, "Arxaisty i Puškin".
[48]   See Boris Tomaševskij, *Puškin* (Moscow, 1925).
[49]   Reference is made to the collection of essays by D. S. Merežkovskij, *Večnye sputniki* (Eternal Companions).
[50]   Boris Tomaševskij, *Puškin*, p. 74.

mation of modern literary Russian; [51] they conceded that in his work he encompassed a wealth of themes and problems which were to haunt Russian writers for years to come. But Puškin's style and verse structure, they argued, found few if any successful imitators, not only because perfection is inimitable, but also because in Puškin's poetic art the literary tradition of the previous age had found its ultimate consummation. Since Puškin made the fullest use of the resources accumulated by his predecessors, after his death it became impossible to create anything worthwhile or novel along the same lines. A new departure was necessary. According to Tynjanov this is indeed what happened.

Contrary to the widely held view, he maintained, Puškin's younger contemporaries and immediate successors in Russian verse writing, Lermontov and Tjutčev, can scarcely be regarded as Puškin's disciples. "After Puškin's death", wrote Tynjanov, "poetry moved neither forwards nor backwards but sideways, toward the complex formations or Lermontov, Tjutčev, and Benediktov",[52] combining in various ratios some ingredients of Puškin's poetics with esthetic formulae of Western European Romanticism and with elements of the eighteenth-century grand style. As for the subsequent literary generations, it is toward the mellifluent and elegiac Žukovskij and partly toward Lermontov that the late Russian Romantics and Symbolists turned in search for emotional suggestiveness and for the ineffable music of verse.[53]

The periodical 'revivals' of Puškin, the Formalists warned, need not be taken too literally. A distinction should be made between the 'real', historical Puškin and his double, the "Puškin living in the ages".[54] The latter is all too often a projection of the critic's own esthetic set of values. Šklovskij argued that a work of literature is always perceived against the background of the literary norms prevailing at the given period; thus, it can be turned "upside down".[55] In the 1880's, for example, the great poet's name was invoked to uphold 'a culture totally different' from Puškin's. When in his famous anniversary speech Dostoevskij hailed Puškin as an apostle of Christian humility, the portrait emerging from this eloquent statement bore greater resemblance to Dostoevskij than to Puškin.

Perhaps the only attempt at reviving the 'real' Puškin and recap-

---

[51] Viktor Vinogradov, *Jazyk Puškina* (Moscow-Leningrad, 1934); *Očerki po istorii russkogo literaturnogo jazyka XVII-XIX vekov* (Moscow, 1934).
[52] Jurij Tynjanov, *Arxaisty i novatory*, p. 361.
[53] Boris Ejxenbaum, *Lermontov* (Leningrad, 1924).
[54] Jurij Tynjanov, *Arxaisty i novatory*, p. 291.
[55] Viktor Šklovskij, "Evgenij Onegin (Puškin i Sterne)".

turing the 'Apollonian' limpidity of his poetic style was made by the Acmeists, the immediate heirs to, and dissidents from, the Symbolist movement.[56] But Acmeism was a brief episode in the history of modern Russian poetry. The Neo-Classicist poise of Gumilëv and Mandelstam was soon overshadowed by the raucous Futurist rebellion.

In their exuberant manifestoes [57] the Futurists advertised their poetry as the complete antithesis of everything that had been written before, and as a challenge to any and all literary traditions. But their sympathetic critics knew better. They pointed out that literature does not admit of totally new departures. Even extreme innovators cannot completely dispense with tradition. The Futurist movement was seen as an illustration of the law of literary evolution, whereby reaction against the 'fathers' brings about a partial return to the 'grandfathers'.[58] "Russian Futurism", Tynjanov wrote, "was a recoil from the 'middle-style" poetic culture of the nineteenth century. In its fierce militancy and in its achievement it is akin to the eighteenth century." [59] According to Tynjanov, Xlebnikov's passionate concern with the problems of language and his quest for the epic provide a link between this Futurist explorer of poetic idiom and the eighteenth-century lawmaker of Russian poetry, Lomonosov. By the same token, Majakovskij's proclivity for the 'larger' poetic forms, such as the ode or satire, as resonators for his impassioned rhetoric, brought him back unwittingly to Russian Classicism, especially to Deržavin, with whom he shared the tendency to mix the grandiloquent with the burlesque.

This unexpected parallel between the bard of the October Revolution and the courtier of Catherine the Great was typical of the unorthodox literary genealogies established by the Formalists. The use of the eighteenth century as a point of reference was quite symptomatic, too. Many Russian literary historians, unduly impressed with Belinskij's provocative but immature essay, "Literary Reveries", tend to discount the eighteenth century and work on the assumption that Russian literature started from Puškin. *Opojaz* research, however, was keenly conscious of the formative era of Russian letters. The Formalists seem to have been strongly drawn toward the Lomonosov period. Its concern with language and style and its pioneering spirit must have struck them as more congenial than the somewhat derivative smoothness of the mid-

---

[56] Cf. Boris Ejxenbaum, *Anna Axmatova*.
[57] See above, chapter II, pp. 42–43.
[58] See above, section 1 of this chapter, p. 259.
[59] Jurij Tynjanov, *Arxaisty i novatory,* p. 553.

nineteenth-century Russian prose. Moreover, the juxtaposition of such ideologically disparate phenomena as Deržavin and Majakovskij was another proof that the Formalists, while duly aware of the differences in the over-all cultural context, chose to base their analogies upon literary criteria.

Similar revisions were undertaken with regard to the history of Russian prose. Here, too, Formalist research revealed some hitherto unnoticed connections, though no comprehensive evolutionary scheme was attempted. A number of studies and papers dealing with the formative stage of Russian prose fiction shed interesting light on some minor and half-forgotten but 'eventful' writers, such as Weltmann, presumably a forerunner of Gogol' and Dostoevskij.[60]

Still more significant were Ejxenbaum's inquiries into the literary genealogy of Lev Tolstoj.[61] We have mentioned above [62] the Formalist thesis that the narrative manner of the early Tolstoj, with its minute psychological analysis, its rationalistic discursiveness (generalizacija) and its homely 'simplicity,' was fundamentally a challenge to the Romantic canon. To Ejxenbaum Tolstoj is primarily an artist-innovator, frantically seeking a way out of the crisis of artistic prose – a notion which may incidentally partly explain the Opojaz critic's fascination with Tolstoj.

If one is to believe Ejxenbaum, Tolstoj too was obliged in his struggle against his immediate predecessors to fall back on the 'grandfathers', that is, on the eighteenth century. But, in contradistinction to Xlebnikov and Majakovskij, Tolstoj's models were Occidental rather than native.

According to Ejxenbaum, Tolstoj's tendency to break up personality into a series of individual sensations or states of mind was a late echo of the eighteenth-century Sensualist philosophy as embodied in Condillac and the Encyclopédistes. The wealth of physical detail as well as the personal tone which mark Tolstoj's autobiographical works, such as Childhood and Youth, were traced to Western European Sentimentalism, to Laurence Sterne, and to the 'plotless novel' (handlungsarmer Roman) of the Swiss writer Töpffer. The debunking of the Romantic myth about war in the Sevastopol' Stories was likened to the battle scenes in Stendhal. To the Formalist critic this relentlessly logical ana-

---

[60] See especially the collection of studies, edited by Ejxenbaum and Tynjanov, Russkaja proza (Leningrad, 1926) (= Voprosy poètiki, VIII).
[61] Boris Ejxenbaum, Molodoj Tolstoj (Petrograd-Berlin, 1922); Lev Tolstoj, I (1928), II (1931).
[62] See above, chapter XI, p. 196.

lyst of human passions was fundamentally a man of the eighteenth century born a hundred years too late.

Ejxenbaum's thesis about the impact of the Western novel on Tolstoj was bolstered by conclusive evidence of Tolstoj's familitarity with, and vivid interest in, the writers mentioned above. In other words, the critic postulated here not mere affinity, but actual literary influence. Now the problem of literary influences and borrowings has been for years one of the favorite preoccupations of academic literary history. The Formalists did not avoid this area of inquiry as they did some other traditional concerns of *Academia*. Since they insisted, especially in their earlier stage, on an intrinsic approach to literary evolution, it was only natural that they should proclaim, with F. Brunetière, "the influence of a work upon a work" [63] as a more potent factor than all extra-literary determinants.[64]

Fortunately, their wholesome emphasis on function and context prevented the Formalists from bogging down in sterile parallel- and source-hunting, from juxtaposing mechanically similar or identical 'motifs' without attempting to ascertain their place in the given esthetic 'system'.

The Formalist approach to the problem was best stated by Žirmunskij. In establishing a conceptual frame for a reexamination of Puškin's Byronism, Žirmunskij asserted that a literary influence has to do with *literary* motifs and devices rather than with temperamental or ideological affinity. "Puškin", continued Žirmunskij, "was influenced by Byron *qua* poet. Now what did he learn from Byron in this respect? What did he 'borrow' from the poetic works of his teacher and how did he adapt the borrowed elements to the individual peculiarities of his taste and talent?" [65]

It is this latter aspect of Žirmunskij's query, that of the 'adaptation' or, figuratively speaking, naturalization of a foreign motif which was of particular interest to the Formalist researchers. They knew that literary borrowing, especially if resorted to by a great poet, is always a transformation rather than a mere exchange. Literary influence, they insisted, should be viewed in terms of an interrelationship between

[63] Quoted by Viktor Šklovskij in his essay "Svjaz' priëmov sjužetosloženija s obščimi priëmami stilja", *Poètika*.

[64] Whether the Formalists shared fuly Brunetière's preoccupation with literary influences can very well be doubted. What Šklovskij wanted to emphasize in quoting the distinguished French scholar was not so much the importance of the actual literary borrowings as the fact that works of literature are perceived against the background of other works rather than of heterogenous non-literary objects.

[65] Viktor Žirmunskij, "Bajronizm Puškina kak istoriko-literaturnaja problema", *Puškinskij sbornik* (Petrograd, 1922), p. 299.

two autonomous artistic systems. Thus, even where an act of borrowing
can be clearly established, the critic's prime concern ought to be not
with the 'where from', but with the 'what for'; not with the source
of the 'motif', but with the use to which it is put in the new 'system.'
In order to be successfully assimilated, the 'foreign' element must be
adapted to its new soil. Moreover, it must meet the internal needs of
the structure into which it is incorporated. Consequently, the borrowed
motif is usually not what the 'lender' does best, but what the 'borrower'
needs most.[66]

The basic need satisfied by Byron's impact on Puškin was apparently
that for a new type of poetic narrative that could replace the obsolete
Classicist epic. Žirmunskij was careful to point out that this appraisal
of Russian Byronism was shared by some of Puškin's most perceptive
contemporaries. Vjazemskij, a gifted poet and critic, saw Byron's main
contribution to Puškin's 'poetics' in that he provided his Russian 'disciple' with a 'syncretic' genre marked by lyrical incoherence and fragmentary composition known as the 'poetic tale'.[67]

In his discussion of foreign influences on Lermontov,[68] Ejxenbaum
posed the problem in similar terms. In Ejxenbaum's argument the frame
of reference is somewhat broader: the interacting systems are not creative personalities, but two national literatures. "A foreign writer alone",
Ejxenbaum asserted, cannot give rise to a new trend, since each literature develops in accordance with its own laws and traditions. Entering
a foreign literature, an author becomes transformed and forced to yield
not what he has, or what he is noted for in his native literature, but
what is expected of him in his new sphere of influence. "Actually",
concluded Ejxenbaum, "influence is a very inadequate term. Whenever an author strikes roots in a foreign soil, he does so not of his own
volition, but *by request (po vyzovu)*." [69]

The re-examinations discussed above affected, to quote a recent discrimination, the 'elucidatory' rather than the 'judicial' aspects of literary
scholarship. Indeed, it was in the former sphere that the *Opojaz* critics
felt most at home. Anxious to avoid the pitfalls of dogmatism and subjectivism, they shied away from explicit value judgements. More exactly,
the sought to confine evaluation to what Austin Warren has called

[66]   *Ibid.*
[67]   *Ibid.*
[68]   Boris Ejxenbaum, *Lermontov* (Leningrad, 1924).
[69]   *Ibid.*, p. 28.

the "historic estimate". [70] Rather than judge the author's esthetic worth in the light of a single, if flexible, critical standard, they would address themselves to his historical role – his place in a 'closed past sequence'.

We shall attempt below [71] to indicate the limitations of such an approach. At this point it may be emphasized that the ultra-historicism of *Opojaz* was a blessing as well as a curse. While it may have inhibited the Formalists's capacity for a total critical judgement, it served them well when the task at hand was 'placing' the artist in the literary flux. A keen sense of the historical-literary context and adeptness at reconstructing the 'poetics' of an author or a literary school made it possible for the Formalists to appraise a poet's success in terms of what he actually tried to do, rather than in terms of what the critic would like him to have done.

A valuable aspect of the Formalist methodology was a determination to do away with esthetic egocentrism. Nineteenth-century European scholarship was all too prone to claim for its idiosyncrasies universal validity. The rise of cultural anthropology has counteracted his tendency by focussing on the multiplicity of cultural patterns. A similar function has been performed by modern art criticism: it has vindicated some periods in the history of art which had been found inferior in the last century.

One of the chief beneficiaries of the new critical climate was medieval art, which had been frowned upon until recently for not conforming to the standards or nineteenth-century realism. It is worth noting that both Jakobson and Trubetzkoy attacked vigorously this popular attitude as an antihistorical fallacy. In his introduction to a critical edition of two Czech medieval poems,[72] Jakobson pointed out that medieval art managed to find an adequate solution to some crucial problems of form which were subsequently relegated to the background. He suggested that the answer to the query whether medieval art was a success or a failure hinges on how well it solved *its own* problems, not on whether it did justice to ours.

"Nothing is more erroneous", Jakobson continued, "than the widely held opinion that the relation between modern poetry and medieval poetry is the same as between the machine-gun and the bow." [73] This

---

[70] Cf. Austin Warren, "Literary Criticism", *Literary Scholarship. Its Aims and Methods* (University of Northern Carolina Press, 1941), p. 170.

[71] See next chapter, pp. 279–283.

[72] R. Jakobson (ed.), *Spor duše s tělem, O nebezpečném času smrti* (Prague, 1927).

[73] *Ibid.*, p. 10.

false analogy presupposes an even development of the various spheres of human activity. Actually, no such correspondence exists. Art can and did flourish during periods of technological regression and political reaction; conversely, social progress is known to have gone hand in hand with mediocrity in art. Two Formalist tenets – the notion of art as an autonomous 'order' and the belief in the relativity of esthetic norms – were thus restated.

Another example of Formalist contextualism at its best was the re-evaluation of Nekrasov, a poet who both during his lifetime and after his death was the subject of vehement controversy among Russian critics. This father of Russian civic poetry, widely acclaimed by the socially-minded, was scorned by the esthetes as an uncouth pamphleteer in verse. However, there was one thing most of his admirers and de-tractors had agreed on: it was an 'incontrovertible fact' that Nekrasov was no wizard in matters of form. The social critics, with the partial exception of Plexanov,[74] had deemed these formal deficiencies inconse-quential, while the esthetes had made much of them. But the diagnosis itself hardly ever doubted.

The Formalist literary historians took issue with this time-honored axiom.[75] They maintained that the traditional view of Nekrasov as a civic-minded poet who did not quite make his mark as an artist was a misconception. When Turgenev complained that Nekrasov's poetry was coarse and 'prosaic', he apparently applied to it standards derived from Romantic poetry. But these, the critic argued, were clearly mis-placed criteria: it is both unfair and misleading to judge the poet's per-formance in terms of a canon which he is deliberately violating.

Nekrasov wrote 'uncouth' poetry, not because he was unable to com-pose smooth, mellifluous verse, emulating the Puškin-Lermontov pat-tern, but because he did not want to do so. That Nekrasov was keenly aware of formal considerations, he proved, according to Ejxenbaum, in his article on Tjutčev. That he could write well in Puškin's or Ler-montov's 'tradition', he showed in some of his early derivative poems. But, Ejxenbaum insisted, little could be accomplished along these lines, since the norm established by the masters had hardened into a cliché. In order to give Russian poetic language a new lease on life, Nekrasov had to move boldly beyond the Romantic tradition. Out of an unorthodox mixture of certain elements of Puškin's and Lermon-

---

[74] Georgij Plexanov, *Za dvadcat' let* (Petersburg, 1905).
[75] Boris Ejxenbaum, "Nekrasov", *Skvoz' literaturu* (Leningrad, 1924); Jurij Tynjanov, "Poètičeskie formy Nekrasova", *Arxaisty i novatory* (Leningrad, 1928).

tov's verse with motifs and rhythms of vaudeville, folk-songs and pamphleteering, he forged a new style which Turgenev, a Romantic 'epigone', found much too spicy for his palate.[76]

Many form-conscious Russian critics had taken their cue from Turgenev's derogatory remarks. Ejxenbaum and Tynjanov approached Nekrasov's literary art without prejudice, indeed, if anything, with a favorable bias, which the usually displayed toward 'hybrid' genres and poet-innovators. In contradistinction to more esoteric 'esthetes', they did not expect good poetry to be 'pure'. Moreover, they knew full well that in a dynamic poetic context 'prosaisms' can be assimilated as successfully, that is, put to as good an esthetic use as any other ingredient of ordinary speech.

Having thus given Nekrasov the benefit of the doubt, and more important still, having ascertained the nature of his 'poetics', the Formalists found him a mature and deliberate craftsman, a poet not only 'relevant', but esthetically effective. They praised Nekrasov's command of language and verse and his adeptness at utilizing in his hybrid poems the stylistic potentialities inherent in various linguistic layers.[77]

The first phase of the critical judgment was thus consummated. Ejxenbaum's vindication of Nekrasov proved once more that, in order to assay the degree of success achieved by a poet in realizing his intent, it is necessary to define this intent.

The above strictures represent only a fraction of the literary research which emanated from the Russian Formalist movement. These frankly controversial re-examinations were at times over-ingenious, often one-sided, and invariably provocative. The method of investigating the literary materials at close range, in addition to a complex and flexible scheme of literary dynamics, yielded insights of more than passing interest. None of these appraisals can be considered definitive, but few can be easily disregarded. It is, perhaps, the best measure of the critical achievement of *Opojaz* that ever since the 1920's no serious study of Puškin or Lermontov, Nekrasov or Tolstoj, Majakovskij or Axmatova could be undertaken without paying heed to the Formalist contributions.

---

[76] Boris Ejxenbaum, *Skvoz' literaturu*.
[77] This is not to imply that the Formalists were completely alone in vindicating Nekrasov's artistry. Similar views were voiced by the Symbolists, V. Brjusov and A. Belyj, and, in the 'twenties, by a free-lancing impressionist critic K. Čukovskij, although the latter disagreed sharply with Ejxenbaum and Tynjanov on some specific problems of Nekrasov's poetic craft.

XV. STOCK-TAKING

In the historical section of this study the Russian Formalist movement was examined as a largely, if not wholly, indigenous phenomenon. However, in the course of the subsequent review of the Formalist tenets we could not help but note a striking affinity between some of the Formalist pronouncements and those of a Jean Cocteau or a Cleanth Brooks, a William Empson or T. S. Eliot.

These analogies cannot be ascribed to actual cross-fertilization. If the evidence of an Occidental impact upon the Russian Formalists is very scanty, the Formalist influence on Western criticism was until recently almost nil. Linguistic barriers, as well as the cultural isolation of the Soviet Union, have prevented most Western literary scholars from taking cognizance of the achievements of the Russian Formalist School, indeed of its very existence.

The reports on the Russian Formalist School which over the period of the last twenty-five years have appeared in Western European or American publications have been scarce, brief, and more often than not addressed to specialized audiences. Three Russian literary scholars associated directly or indirectly with the Formalist movement, Tomaševskij, Voznesenskij and Žirmunskij, told the story briefly in respectively French, German and English scholarly reviews devoted to Slavic studies.[1] A Franco-Russian critic, Nina Gourfinkel, who was strongly influenced by *Opojaz*,[2] tried to sum up the Formalist methodology in

[1] Viktor Žirmunskij, "Formprobleme in der russischen Literaturwissenschaft", *Zeitschrift für slavische Philologie,* I (1925), pp. 117–152; A. N. Voznesenskij, "Die Methodologie der russischen Literaturforschung in den Jahren 1910–1925", *Zeitschrift für slavische Philologie,* IV (1927), pp. 145–162, and V (1928), pp. 175–199; A. N. Voznesenskij, "Problems of Method in the Study of Literature in Russia", *Slavonic Review,* VI (1927), pp. 168–177; Boris Tomaševskij, "La nouvelle école d'histoire littéraire en Russie", *Revue des études slaves,* VIII (1928), pp. 226–240.
[2] The interesting book of Nina Gourfinkel, *Tolstoï sans Tolstoïsme* (Paris, 1945) owes a great deal to Ejxenbaum's and Šklovskij's studies of Tolstoj.

Le Monde Slave.[3] Shortly afterwards, Mrs. Gourfinkel's account was condensed in a somewhat garbled fashion by a noted French comparatist, Philippe van Tieghem.[4] Brief references to Formalist studies in versification are found in the work of a Dutch linguist and metrist, A. W. de Groot, as well as in Henry Lanz' study *The Physical Basis of Rime* and, more recently, in an interesting paper of a Belgian student of verse, M. Rutten.[5]

In the United States basic data on Russian Formalism were provided by Manfred Kridl's informative article, published in 1944 in *The American Bookman*,[6] and lately, in a paper by William E. Harkins in *Word*.[7] The authoritative *Theory of Literature* by Wellek and Warren (1949) was the first full-fledged study to appear in the United States which attests to a thorough familiarity, as well as a substantial agreement, with the Formalist-Structuralist methodology.

The similarities of approach and formulation between Tynjanov and Ejxenbaum on the one hand and Cleanth Brooks or W. K. Wimsatt Jr. on the other are thus a matter of convergence rather than of influence. In fact, the work just mentioned – a product of collaboration between two mature scholars, differing markedly in background and training – is a good example of this. That René Wellek, whose approach to literature was shaped by Prague Structuralism, and Austin Warren, a distinguished representative of American 'New Criticism,' could register upon their meeting in 1939 a "large agreement in literary theory and methodology" [8] is a testimony to the affinity between two parallel critical movements, as well as to the fundamental universality of scholarship.

Contrary to the militantly parochial 'line' now prevailing in the cradle of the Formalist movement, both the problems confronting the scholar and the solutions at which he arrives are international in scope. Seen as a part of the Russian cultural scene – a reaction against Symbolist metaphysics and crude sociologism, or a theoretical mouthpiece of the

---

[3] Nina Gourfinkel, "Les nouvelles méthodes d'histoire littéraire en Russie", *Le Monde Slave*, VI (1929), pp. 234–263.
[4] Philippe van Tieghem, "Tendances nouvelles en histoire littéraire", *Études Françaises*, No. 22 (1930).
[5] Henry Lanz, *The Physical Basis of Rime* (Stanford University Press, 1931); M. Rutten, "Dichtkunst en Phonologie", *Revue Belge de Philologie et d'histoire*, XXVIII, No. 3–4 (Brussels, 1950).
[6] Manfred Kridl, "Russian Formalism", *The American Bookman*, I (1944), pp. 19–30.
[7] William E. Harkins, "Slavic Formalist Theories in Literary Scholarship", *Word*, VII (August 1951), 177–185.
[8] René Wellek and Austin Warren, *Theory of Literature*, p. vi.

Futurist movement – Formalism was, or seemed to be, a specifically Russian phenomenon. But, while fighting his local critical battles, the Formalist, often without knowing it, found himself asking the same questions and giving practically the same answers as did some of his confrères in Germany, France, England, and the United States. As an organized movement, Formalism was fundamentally a native response to a native challenge. But, as a body of critical thought, it was part and parcel of that trend toward the reexamination of aim and method which during the first quarter of this century became discernible in European literary scholarship.

In this sense Russian Formalism is not necessarily a thing of the past. 'Formalist' activities in Russia, and subsequently in other Slavic countries, could be prohibited by bureaucratic fiat. But many Formalist insights outlasted the totalitarian purge as they found a new lease on life in kindred movements on the other side of the 'Marxist-Leninist' iron curtain.

Viewed in a broader perspective, Russian Formalism appears as one of the most vigorous manifestations of the recent trend toward close analysis of literature and art – a development, which, as was mentioned above,[9] found early expression in the work of Hanslick, Woelfflin, Walzel and in the French *explication des textes,* and which in the last two decades has made substantial inroads in English and American literary study.

The points of contact between the Formalist School and the Anglo-American 'New Criticism' are especially worth exploring. Indeed, many illuminating parallels could be drawn between Russian Formalism and the movement which, with T. S. Eliot, shifted emphasis from the poet to poetry,[10] which, with John Crowe Ransom, focussed on the "esthetic and characteristic values of literature",[11] and which, with Cleanth Brooks and I. A. Richards, promoted the rigorous discipline of close reading.[12]

Not that the differences are any less instructive than the similarities. The 'New Criticism' developed in a social and philosophical climate vastly different from that which had given rise to Russian Formalism or Prague Structuralism. Hence the wide divergencies in manner and

[9]   See above, chapter III, pp. 58–60.
[10]   T. S. Eliot, *Selected Essays* (New York, 1932), p. 11.
[11]   J. C. Ransom, *The World's Body* (New York, 1938), p. 332.
[12]   Cleanth Brooks and Robert Penn Warren, *Understanding Poetry* (New York, 1938); I. A. Richards, *Practical Criticism* (London, 1929).

ideological leanings of the two movements. The typical Formalist was a radical Bohemian, a rebel against authority, seeking to avoid a total commitment in favor of the new regime, but little concerned with the old. The 'New Critic', especially his American variant, is more often than not a conservative intellectual, distrustful of the 'mass-man', repelled by industrial civilization, looking back nostalgically toward a more stable society and a more binding set of values. For Jakobson and Šklovskij, the watchword was innovation, for Tate and Ransom, tradition. Anti-academic in the extreme, the Russian Formalists would have little use for Ransom's attempt to confine professional criticism within the walls of *Academia*.[13] Their esthetic 'purism', which they eventually renounced, had more to do with Bohemian extravagance and provocative bravado than with aristocratic aloofness from the *profanum vulgus*.

William Elton distinguished recently between several quite disparate schools of thought, usually bracketed together under the heading of New Criticism.[14] If we accept tentatively Elton's subdivisions, we find that the version of New Criticism which comes closest to the Formalist-Structuralist methodology is the trend represented by Cleanth Brooks and Robert Penn Warren. This approach, which is often described as 'organistic' – less ideology-ridden than Tate's or Ransom's and more systematic or rigorous than R. P. Blackmur's or T. S. Eliot's – parallels in many crucial respects the later phase of Slavic Formalist theorizing. The emphasis on the organic unity of a work of literature, with the concomitant warning against the "heresy of paraphrase",[15] keen aware-ness of the 'ambiguity' of poetic idiom and the 'conflict-structures' resulting from this ambiguity, such as irony and paradox – all this re-minds one of Tynjanov and Jakobson in their later phases and of the Prague Linguistic Circle.

This affinity, one might add, has to do with analytical procedures rather than with criteria of evaluation. While Brooks and Warren postu-late the possibility of some flexible yet absolute standards applicable to poetry of various ages, the Formalists frankly espoused critical relativism. Where the American 'organicists' along with other branches or the New Criticism searched for an esthetic norm, their Slavic counterparts tended to locate the source of esthetic value in deviations from the norm. The latter position was not merely Bohemian anti-

---

13 See especially J. C. Ransom, "Criticism, Inc", *The World's Body*.
14 William Elton, *Glossary of the New Criticism* (Chicago, 1948).
15 Cleanth Brooks, *The Well Wrought Urn* (New York, 1947), pp. 176–196.

academicism with a vengeance; it was also a by-product of the Formalist's association with modern art.

Literary scholarship, as the Formalists so often insisted, is or ought to be an autonomous discipline. But each dramatic shift in its methodology, while always necessitated by an internal crisis, bears a definable relation to parallel trends in relevant fields of intellectual endeavor, such as the philosophy of culture or theory of knowledge. Moreover, the critic's conception of literature cannot help but be affected by the current trends in the field which constitutes the object of his inquiry, that is, by the type of art prevailing at the time.

Russian Formalism was no exception in this respect. Thus, any attempt to place the Formalist School within a broader cultural context must take note of three closely interrelated developments. One of these has already been mentioned: the trend toward structural analysis in the study of literature. The other two tendencies were the 'modern' movement in the arts and the epistemological crisis.

Let us give a specific example. When the *Opojaz* theoretician posited the 'orientation toward the medium' as the differentia of poetry, he arrived at this insight because freed from the blinkers of extrinsic criticism, he could addres himself to the literary work and its structural qualities. But there is hardly any doubt that the Formalist's interest in the structural properties of literary art was stimulated by the growing emphasis on structure and function which in the first decades of this century made itself felt in various branches of science and scholarship. By the same token, it could be plausibly argued that the early Formalist's concern with the verbal texture of poetry owed some of its single-mindedness to the non-objective tendency of modern art. Jakobson's definition of 'literariness' called attention to what is a crucial element of *any* poetic structure. But it was especially pertinent to a literary situation, where the poet's professed aim was manipulation of the medium rather than representation of reality.

The last half-century has seen a virtual upheaval in our ways of thinking and methods of inquiry. This methodological reorientation has been directed chiefly against two fallacies inherited from the nineteenth century — the extreme empiricism which recognizes as real only the immediately 'given', and crude monism, which seeks, as a contemporary writer put it, to "reduce heterogeneous levels to homogeneous laws".[16]

[16] Arthur Koestler, *The Yogi and the Commissar* (New York, 1945), p. 238.

On the level of epistemology, to quote Susanne Langer, the "problem of observation is all but eclipsed by the problem of meaning".[17] The positivist's concern with sense-data was overshadowed by the 'philosophy of symbolic forms' – the view of man as an *animal symbolicum* (Cassirer).[18]

In the general methodology of scholarship the new orientation meant, in the phrase of Skaftymov,[19] "primacy of structural description over genetic study". It was realized that each level of experience has its own 'laws' or organizing principles which cannot be deduced from other levels. Consequently, the scholar, whether linguist, psychologist, or art critic, was urged to inquire first into the structural properties of the given domain and only later attempt to correlate the data thus obtained with those of other spheres.

The revolt against the Reductive Fallacy made itself felt in disciplines as disparate as linguistics and biology. But it was, perhaps, best illustrated by the *Gestalt* psychologist's closely reasoned polemics with Behaviorism. When Koehler, Wertheimer, and Koffka introduced the concept of 'organized whole' and pointed to forces operating within the field of visual perception, they made, whether they knew it or not, an iron-clad case for a structuralist approach to all cultural phenomena.

As ought to be clear from the previous discussions, Russian Formalism paid its due to both these tendencies of modern scholarship – the preoccupation with symbolism and the *Gestalt* approach. Even in their early stages the Formalists tended to state the problem of poetic language in terms of the dichotomy between sign and referent. And in the later 'structuralist' phase they made an explicit, if somewhat inconclusive, attempt to make poetics a part of semiotics. More important still, the Formalist theorizing went a long way toward evolving a *Gestalt* scheme of literary creation, especially of poetry. It is sufficient to cite the later *Opojaz* notions of 'system' and of 'dominanta' and the Prague concept of esthetic 'structure'.

It was the Formalist's good fortune to have been able to participate in, and profit from, one of the most vital achievements of modern thought. In his inquiry into the nature of the 'literary fact' and of 'literary evolution', the new methodological insights stood him in good stead. Moreover, this involvement with what Susanne Langer calls the 'genera-

[17] Susanne K. Langer, *Philosophy in a New Key* (Harvard University Press, 1942), p. 16.
[18] Ernst Cassirer, *An Essay on Man* (Yale University Press, 1944), p. 26.
[19] See above, pp. 204–206.

tive ideas' of our age [20] may serve as a proof that Formalism was much more than a minor intellectual fad, some of its 'Marxist' critics notwithstanding.[21]

If its organic relation to the intellectual *Zeitgeist* was an indubitable asset, the militant 'modernism' of *Opojaz* seems in retrospect to have been a mixed blessing. The alliance with the literary advance-guard enhanced the vitality and the striking power of Formalist criticism. Indeed, nothing is more stimulating for a critical movement than interaction with creative writing. It was this excitement of participation which accounts for the vigor of Šklovskij's best essays, for the brilliance of Jakobson's and Tynjanov's studies in Russian Futurism, where critical acumen was assisted by sympathetic immersion into the poet's search for a new vision.

If this esthetic commitment enriched and enlivened much of the Formalist's critical practice, it often handicapped his theorizing about literature. Not infrequently what was intended as an objective description of the poetic quality would turn into an impassioned 'defense' of poetry, more specifically of the type of poetry of which the theorist happened to approve.

We live in an era when 'new verse' can become obsolete in a matter of years and when schools in art age faster than methodological principles (not that the latter last too long either!). Thus, theoretical pronouncements made consciously or unconsciously with a view to justifying a 'modern' trend in poetry or in painting, be it Futurism or Dadaism, Surrealism or Cubism, two or three decades later may strike one as period pieces. This is apparently the price to be paid for timeliness.

A good case in point is Ortega y Gasset's study on *The Dehumanization of Art*.[22] This able and still partly relevant challenge to realistic esthetics is patently vitiated by some extreme formulations which bear too strong an imprint of the twenties to sound fully convincing in 1950. The same is true of Šklovskij's criticism. His early writings were infinitely more provocative and rewarding than anything he has written after 1930. But some of his hasty generalizations which were so obviously geared to Futurist or 'Constructivist' experiments at that time, in the somewhat different esthetic climate of today seem to have lost their relevance.

---

[20]   Susanne K. Langer, *op. cit.*
[21]   See above, chapter VI, pp. 99–100.
[22]   José Ortega y Gasset, *The Dehumanization of Art and Notes on the Novel* (Princeton University Press, 1948).

Another effect of the close association with the literary Bohemia of the time was the petulant and often needlessly belligerent tone of the Formalist publications.[23] On an earlier occasion it was pointed out that many *Opojaz* pronouncements made in the heat of polemics ought not to be taken literally. While one would do well to heed this warning, at times one cannot help but be annoyed by the constant 'tactical' overstatements and wish that the Formalists had said just what they meant and no more. As one watches the *Opojaz* spokesmen briskly disengaging art from society and from its creators, one may long for a little less exuberance and more 'academic' decorum.

However, viewed in the light of Formalism's total contribution, these early excesses do not loom too large. The tiresome exaggerations and the harping on the 'device' as the only concern of the literary scholar these were merely the growing pains of a vital and dynamic movement. From the long-range point of view some of the extravagances of *Opojaz* proved more fruitful than many a safe statement of conservative critics. The very narrowness of focus, as suggested above, may have been useful in that it helped to dramatize crucial problems which had been so long ignored. And when pure Formalism reached an impasse, the Czech Structuralists suggested a viable alternative course toning down the initial claims and placing the problem of art versus society in a more plausible perspective.

It may be argued that although relevant social considerations eventually received their due, the problem of the creative personality was still largely neglected. But some of the later contributions, such as Jakobson's oft-quoted eassay on Pasternak's prose,[24] seem to indicate that this much-abused and yet indispensable critical concept was also gradually finding its way into the Structuralist scheme of literary dialectics.

More important were the inadequacies of Formalist thinking on the level of evaluation. The extreme relativism which had characterized the *Opojaz* writings was not discarded by the Structuralist revision. In 1923 Šklovskij had described esthetic canons as layers of heresies superimposed upon each other.[25] A decade later Mukařovský claimed

[23] As was indicated above, Bohemianism was only one of the factors involved. Formalist aggressiveness could be blamed in part on the shrill tenor of the Russian critical controversy in the post-1917 period.
[24] Roman Jakobson, "Randbemerkungen zur Prosa des Dichters Pasternak", *Slavische Rundschau,* VII (1935).
[25] Viktor Šklovskij, *Xod konja* (Moscow-Berlin, 1923), p. 73.

that for the literary historian there are no esthetic norms, as it is the essence of the esthetic norm to be broken.' [26]

This was a peculiarly slanted way of stating the problem. That today's canon is yesterday's heresy is unquestionably true. Esthetic norms change, but it is not this susceptibility to change which is their chief characteristic. It is indeed a curious theory which locates the essence of the esthetic norm in its capacity for being discarded, rather than in the binding force which it has while it prevails. Esthetic values, like any other values, are 'relative' in that their content varies from period to period. But this empirical fact does not make a norm any less 'absolute' in the eyes of those who abide by it.

Perhaps one should not blame it all on 'modernism'. The debunking of 'norms', while obviously reinforced by the cult of novelty, may have had something to do with the ultra-empiricist strain in Formalist thinking, with the instinctive distrust of anything that smacked of absolutes. From this standpoint the 'historic estimate' seemed to be a much safer and more scientific procedure than 'esthetic judgment'.

In his study of Lermontov, after a less than enthusiastic reference to the poet's 'eclecticism', Ejxenbaum hastened to add: "This is not an esthetic judgment, but a historic judgment, the only emotion behind which is that of establishing facts." [27]

As Wellek has pointed out,[28] a hard-and-fast distinction between facts and values is hardly feasible in literary scholarship, where all relevant 'facts' – the works of literature – are themselves systems of values and where the object of inquiry becomes accessible to the literary historian only by a "response . . . involving the kind of activity that produces value-judgments".[29]

The Formalists were well advised in planting critical evaluation on the firm ground of ascertainable historical fact. They were very adept at assessing the role of an author in the literary process, at determining how boldly moved beyond the canon inherited from his immediate predecessors. Now this was undoubtedly an important inquiry, but it is not the only question which the literary historian has the right and duty to ask. Historic estimate is an indispensable phase of total critical judgment, but not a substitute for it. While it is essential to know how

[26]   Jan Mukařovský, "Estetická funkce, norma a hodnota jako sociální fakt", Prague, 1936 (quoted in *Theory of Literature,* p. 341).
[27]   Boris Ejxenbaum, *Lermontov* (Leningrad, 1924), p. 20.
[28]   René Wellek, "Literary History", *Literary Scholarship, Its Aims and Methods* (University of North Carolina Press, 1941).
[29]   *Ibid.,* p. 100.

successfully a historical 'assignment' has been performed, it can be plausibly argued that some assignments are esthetically more rewarding or more exacting than others. While it is entirely possible – and at a certain phase of the argument imperative – to gauge the poet's perform- ance in his own terms, the critic should try to place it ultimately on a scale of values transcending the 'poetics' of the given period. Rather than rejoice in the very process of moving away from the old, the stu- dent of literature ought to assay the quality of the 'new'.

Alexander Romm wrote in a caustic review of Ejxenbaum's study of Lermontov: "To the Formalist literary historian Puškin's greatness seems to lie in the fact that he paved the way for Poležaev." [30] Since Poležaev was a second-rate poet of the second quarter of the nineteenth century, the ironic intent was unmistakable. The Formalists, it was implied, were so obsessed with the sheer process of breaking new ground, that they hardly cared whether it was a mediocre poet who paved the way for a genius or *vice versa*.

Romm's irony is obviously far-fetched (the Formalists were getting a taste of their own medicine!), but not altogether unwarranted. It would be ludicrous to assume that Ejxenbaum, one of the most culti- vated and sensitive modern Russian critics, did not realize or appreciate the difference between Puškin and Poležaev. What was at issue, how- ever, was not 'sensibility', the individual critic's capacity for discrimi- nating between greatness and mediocrity, but definable standards whereby such discriminations could lay claim to supra-personal validity. In shying away from critical judgments other than 'historic', the For- malist came dangerously close to the ultra-historicism which can size up the literary work as an event or a cause of events but fail to do justice to it as a value.

The paradox of esthetic relativism lies in the fact that the harder it tries to avoid dogmatism and subjectivism, the less likely it is to steer clear of this twin danger. Literary history, as Wellek has said, "is ut- terly inconceivable without some value-judgments", just as no theorizing of any kind, as Mukařovský knew and Ejxenbaum did not, can dispense with philosophical premises. Where there is no clear awareness of the underlying principles, philosophy gets in just the same, but it does so through the back door – in an 'implicit', that is, in undigested, form. By the same token, where a critical movement lacks clear-cut criteria of evaluation, the inevitable value judgments are more often than not

---

[30]   Aleksander Romm, "B. Ejxenbaum, *Lermontov*," *Čët i nečet* (Moscow, 1925), p. 44.

projections of the critic's personal taste, or of the particular 'poetics' which he happens to favor.

This law is clearly applicable to whatever judgments the Formalists did allow themselves to make. Their enthusiasm for non-objective art found expression in lavish praise of Xlebnikov, the early Majakovskij, and Sterne. Their preoccupation with novelty and experiments made them responsive to the unorthodox, hybrid art of Nekrasov, but somewhat less than fair to the 'eclectic' Lermontov or the 'epigone' Turgenev. Now one does not need to be a Formalist to admit that Tolstoj was a greater writer than Turgenev. But this difference in stature was not necessarily due to the fact that Tolstoj made a break with the Romantic tradition, while Turgenev worked within its limits. Ejxenbaum's study of Lermontov is an acute piece of analytical groundbreaking. But the critic's ill-concealed impatience with Lermontov's poetic 'eclecticism' strikes one as a bit doctrinaire. It is a critical commonplace that a great poet always says something 'new' and makes a dramatic contribution to the store of artistic values. But what the Formalists seemed to forget all too often – perhaps because they lived in a revolutionary atmosphere – is that this new word can sometimes be uttered within the given literary tradition or traditions, and that literary progress could be attained by means of evolution as well as revolution. They seemed all too often neglectful of the fact that pure novelty would make esthetic experience impossible. "Men's pleasure in a literary work", says Austin Warren, "is compounded of the sense of novelty and the sense of recognition." [31]

This raises the question of esthetic experience. The fascination with the notion of change played havoc not only with the Formalist's specific critical judgments, but also with his sporadic attempts to define esthetic quality. Whenever a Formalist theorist, for instance, Šklovskij, left the firmer ground of linguistic or semasiological concepts for uncharted if exciting flights into the philosophy of art, divergence from a given standard would be invoked as the ultimate touchstone of esthetic judgment. With the esthetician's sights set on the new art, which as Ortega y Gasset put it, "consists almost solely of protests against the old", [32] it was only natural, to quote the same writer, that this "negative mood of mocking aggressiveness be made into a factor of esthetic pleasure". [33]

[31] René Wellek and Austin Warren, *Theory of Literature*, p. 296.
[32] José Ortega y Gasset, *The Dehumanization of Art and Notes on the Novel*, p. 25.
[33] *Ibid.*, p. 44.

It is significant that B. Christiansen's notion of *Differenzqualität* [34] loomed so large in Formalist thinking. Šklovskij and Tynjanov were undoubtedly saying something both important and helpful, when, in elaborating the German esthetician's concept, they focussed on deviation from ordinary usage and on deformation of reality as essential ingredients of the esthetic satisfaction to be derived from imaginative literature. But the cumulative effect of playing up the principle of contrast or shift was somewhat less than satisfactory. Some of Šklovskij's ventures into esthetics bogged down in a tautological proposition: the differentiating feature of literature lies in its quality of divergence, in its being different. On the whole, too much intellectual energy and enthusiasm seems to have been lavished on a purely negative statement of the problem. The idiosyncratic character of art was insisted upon so strenuously that the precise nature of this idiosyncrasy was too often left unexplored. [35]

All this seems to indicate that Formalism had no clear-cut esthetics; it failed to solve, indeed to face squarely, such crucial problems as the mode of existence of the literary work or critical standards.

Perhaps, it is this deficiency, along with the technological emphasis of *Opojaz,* which gave rise to the widespread view that Formalist theorizing was a series of isolated technical insights, of methodological pointers, but not a *bona fide* body of literary theory.

If by 'literary theory' one means a comprehensive scheme of literary creation, grounded in a coherent esthetics, and integrated into a full-blown philosophy of culture, one must concede that Formalism was much less than this. But, while granting this point, it would be only fair to add that no critical movement has come anywhere near this objective.

With few exceptions, philosophizing about art has been a singularly barren pastime. It is enough to glance at the *Foundations of Aesthetics* by Richards and Ogden, a sketchy and popular but on the whole reliable survey of the chief esthetic theories, to see that Šklovskij at his worst was scarcely more tautological than most speculations about beauty, esthetic pleasure, or form.

If the Formalists failed to evolve a well-rounded theory of literature, they can be credited with having worked out some of its most essential aspects. They did not attempt to formulate what S. C. Pepper calls a

---

[34] See above, chapters X, XI, and XIV, pp. 178, 200, and 252 respectively.
[35] I am referring here to generalizations bearing on the function of art or on esthetic experience rather than to the more specific and more rewarding discussions of the poetic differentia.

'quantitative criterion' of criticism, that is, some standard of 'determining the amount of esthetic value' inherent in the given literary object.[36] But they were much more rewarding in discussing what the same
esthetician labels the 'qualitative criterion,' that is, in delimiting literature from other modes of human endeavor.

The end-product of the Formalist search for the differentia of imaginative writing was far from sterile. When they did not try to shock
the public by dogmatic slogans of the variety that "Art is nothing
but . . ." or did not generalize too recklessly, the Formalists provided
the student of literature with some immensely helpful definitions. Poetry
as a unique mode of discourse, the 'actualization' of the sign as the
distinguishing feature of poetic speech, 'semantic dynamics of the poetic
context', 'literariness' as *Gestaltqualität,* literary work as a 'structure' –
all these were fruitful concepts. Not all, it is true, could be fully utilized
during the brief period of time which history allotted to the Formalist-
Structuralist movement. Thus, the Jakobson-Mukařovský attempt to in-
corporate poetics into the nascent philosophy of symbolic forms has
remained a methodological postulate to be acted upon. But, perhaps,
it is not too much to say that here is an auspicious beginning of what
may yet become a significant new departure in esthetics; many problems
of literary ontology could be profitably restated, if not solved, in categories of semiotics, and in terms of the tension between sign and referent.

To be sure, the above generalizations are not an end in themselves.
They are useful insofar as they illuminate the discussion of more specific problems of historical and theoretical poetics or the analyses of concrete works of literature.

Measured by this yardstick, the key Formalist concepts seem to fare
well enough. While the brevity of the preceding three chapters has made
it impossible to do justice to the scope and ingenuity of the Formalist
analyses, it is clear, I hope, that the Formalist theoreticians did not
labor in vain. The application of the notions of *dominanta,* 'structure',
and 'perceptibility' to problems of versification, style, composition, and
literary history, made it possible in many instances to substitute precision
and logical rigor for impressionistic metaphors. At the same time the
sense of the whole prevented most technical dissections of poetry
from lapsing into the atomistic detail-hunting of the old- school textual
criticism. Formalist theorizing went a long way toward bringing down
to earth some of those 'mystic beings' of traditional esthetics, such as

---

[36]   Cf. S. C. Pepper, *Basis of Criticism* (Cambridge, 1945), p. 3.

'Construction', 'Design', 'Form', 'Rhythm', 'Expression', whose elusiveness was recently deplored by I. A. Richards.[37]

But, one could rejoin, though all this may well be of great use in describing and classifying literary forms, how about the broader frame of reference? How about determining the function of literary art and relating it to other modes of human activity?

The above is a legitimate question, provided that it does not reduce **the problems of literary craft to the status of** 'technical trivia' and that the 'broader frame of reference' is not a rigid monistic scheme into which literature has to be forced, whatever the cost. The record of crude sociological criticism in Russia and outside Russia is proof enough that certain 'broader frameworks' are more dangerous than none.

This is not to say that the study of literature can dispense with a wider social context. As Jakobson and Tynjanov pointed out in their 1928 theses,[38] determining the 'immanent' laws, that is, the internal dynamism of an individual 'system', is only a part of the theorist's job. His other duty is to inquire into the 'transcendent' laws, to examine the nature of the interrelationship between the given field and other cultural domains.

Obviously, in the latter, 'transcendent' realm the Formalist contribution was on the whole less impressive than in the 'immanent' one. For one thing, the Formalists did not become aware of this aspect of literary theory until rather late. For another, the task of correlating various spheres of human culture could not be undertaken by the study of literature alone. It is a job which calls for a rigorous interdisciplinary effort, and a philosophy of culture more flexible than nineteenth-century monism and better integrated than purely 'descriptive' electicism.

The Formalist theoreticians can hardly be blamed for not having evolved single-handed such a philosophy. What is worth emphasizing is that at the later stage they did their best to dramatize the necessity of it. Thus, the movement which in the early twenties attempted to 'free' art from society, in the thirties saw in the interrelationship between various parts of the social fabric the humanist's most vital concern.[39]

In our final judgment of Russian Formalism we need not take our cue either from the frankly partisan apologists or the vociferous detractors. We would do better to turn toward a fair-minded opponent, Efimov,

[37] I. A. Richards, *Principles of Literary Criticism* (London, 1948), p. 20.
[38] See above, chapter VII, pp. 134–135.
[39] See above, chapter XIV, p. 257.

who in his study on the Formalist School summed up its achievement thus:

"The contribution of the Formalist School to our literary scholarship lies . . . in the fact that it has focussed sharply on the basic problems of literary study, first of all on the specificity of its object; that it modified our conception of the literary work and broke it down into its component parts; that it opened up new areas of inquiry, vastly enriched our knowledge of literary technology, raised the standards of our literary research and our theorizing about literature . . . effected, in a sense, a Europeanization of our literary scholarship." "Poetics", Efimov continued, "once a sphere of unbridled impressionism, became an object of scientific analysis, a concrete problem of literary scholarship." [40] Coming from an adversary, this was a telling and, on the whole, a well deserved tribute.

In the course of their brief and turbulent career, the Formalists laid themselves open to many attacks. They could be irritatingly flippant or unnecessarily abstruse; they were often extravagant, far-fetched, over-ingenious. But they were never dull or derivative, irrelevant or stuffy. Their hardboiled, technical lingo notwithstanding, they were motivated by a genuine devotion to literature and a deep-seated respect for the integrity of artistic vision. In the face of the trend toward bureaucratic regimentation, they tried to cultivate such untimely virtues as ingenuity, wit, and critical intransigence. It was hardly their fault that they did not succeed.

Today, when Soviet criticism is in the grip of tame mediocrity and humorless dogmatism, it is a refreshing experience to look back on the irreverence, the gaiety, and the acumen of the Formalist writings. For all its shortcomings and inconsistencies, the heritage of this brilliant team will remain one of the highpoints of modern critical thought.

[40] N. I. Efimov, "Formalizm v russkom literaturovedenii", *Naučnye izvestija Smolenskogo Gosudarstvennogo Universiteta*, III (1929), p. 106.

BIBLIOGRAPHY

I. FORMALIST-STRUCTURALIST PUBLICATIONS [1]

1. Russian

Ars Poetica, Trudy Gosudarstvennoj Akademii Xudožestvennyx Nauk. Literaturnaja sekcija, Vol. I (Moscow, 1927). M. Petrovskij, ed. Articles by B. Jarxo, A. Peškovskij, M. Petrovskij, R. Šor, M. Stoljarov.

Ars Poetica, v. II (Moscow, 1928). M. Petrovskij and B. Jarxo, ed. Articles by B. Jarxo, M. Stockmar, L. Timofeev.

Baluxatyj, S. D., *Problemy dramaturgičeskogo analiza (Čexov)* (= *Voprosy poètiki,* IX) (Leningrad, 1927).

Bogatyrëv, Pëtr, and Jakobson, Roman, *Slavjanskaja filologija v Rossii za gody vojny i revoljucii* (Berlin, 1923).

Bogatyrëv, Pëtr, and Jakobson, Roman, "Die Folklore als eine besondere Form des Schaffens", *Donum Natalicium Schrijnen* (Nijmegen-Utrecht, 1929), pp. 900—913.

Bogatyrëv, Pëtr, and Jakobson, Roman, "K probleme razmeževanija fol'kloristiki i literaturovedenija", *Lud Słowiański,* II, 2 (Cracow, 1931), pp. 230-233.

Brik, Lili, "Iz vospominanij", *Al'manax s Majakovskim* (Moscow, 1934).

Brik, Osip, "Zvukovye povtory" (1917), *Poètika* (Petrograd, 1919) (see below). Reprinted in *Michigan Slavic Materials.*

—, "T.n.formal'nyj metod", *Lef,* 1923, No. 1, pp. 213-15.

—, "Ritm i sintaksis (materialy po izučeniju stixotvornoj reči)", *Novyj lef,* No. 3-6: Reprinted in *Michigan Slavic Materials* (see below).

Ejxenbaum, Boris, "Kak sdelana 'Šinel' Gogolja", *Poètika* (Petrograd,

---

[1] I include under this heading some of the more significant critical studies written along semi-Formalist lines as well as several works of imaginative literature which emanated from the Formalist movement.

1919) (see below). Reprinted in *Michigan Slavic Materials*.

—, "Melodika stixa", *Letopis' Doma Literatorov,* 1921, No. 4 (reprinted in 1922 under the title *Melodika russkogo liričeskogo stixa).*

—, *Molodoj Tolstoj* (Petrograd-Berlin, 1922).

—, *Anna Axmatova (Opyt analiza)* (Petrograd, 1923).

—, *Lermontov (Opyt istoriko-literaturnoj ocenki)* (Leningrad, 1924).

—, "Vokrug voprosa o formalistax", *Pečat' i revoljucija,* 1924, No. 5, pp. 1-12.

—, *Skvoz' literaturu* (= *Voprosy poètiki,* IV) (Leningrad, 1924) (Reprinted The Hague, 1962, *Slavistic Printings and Reprintings,* XXVI).

—, "Nužna kritika", *Žizn' iskusstva,* IV (1924).

—, "O. Genri i teorija novelly", *Zvezda,* 1925, No. 6, pp. 291-308 (later reprinted in *Literatura).*

—, *Literatura (Teorija, kritika, polemika)* (Leningrad, 1927).

—, "Literatura i pisatel' ", *Zvezda,* 1927, later reprinted in *Moj vremennik* (see below).

—, "Literatura i literaturnyj byt", *Na literaturnom postu,* 1927, later in *Moj vremennik.*

—, *Lev Tolstoj,* Vol. I (Leningrad, 1928).

—, "Poèt-žurnalist", *Nekrasov* (a collection of articles on Nekrasov, published on the 50th anniversary of his death) (Leningrad, 1928), pp. 25-33.

—, *Moj vremennik* (Leningrad, 1929).

—, *Lev Tolstoj,* Vol. II (Leningrad, 1931).

Gric, T., Nikitin, N., Trenin, V., *Slovesnost' i kommercija* (Moscow, 1927).

Gruzdëv, Il'ja, *Utilitarnost' i samocel'* (Petrograd, 1923).

Gukovskij, G., *Russkaja poèzija 18-go veka* (Leningrad, 1927).

Jakobson, Roman, *Novejšaja russkaja poèzija (Nabrosok pervyj). Viktor Xlebnikov* (Prague, 1921).

— (with P. Bogatyrëv), *Slavjanskaja filologija v Rossii za gody vojny i revoljucii,* see above.

—, "Brjusovskaja stixologija i nauka o stixe", *Naučnye izvestija,* II (Moscow, 1922), pp. 222-240.

—, *O češskom stixe preimuščestvenno v sopostavlenii s russkim* (Berlin, 1923).

— (ed.), *Spor duše s tělem; O nebezpečném času smrti* (Prague, 1927).

— (with Ju. Tynjanov), "Problemy izučenija literatury i jazyka", *Novyj lef,* 1928, No. 12, pp. 36-37.

— (with P. Bogatyrëv), "Die Folklore als eine besondere Form des Schaffens" (see above).

—, "Über die heutigen Voraussetzungen der russischen Slavistik", *Slavische Rundschau,* I (1929), 682-684.

—, "O pokolenii rastrativšem svoix poètov", *Smert' Vladimira Majakovskogo* (Berlin, 1931), 7-45.

— (with P. Bogatyrëv), "K probleme razmeževanija fol'kloristiki i literaturovedenija" (see above).

—, "Bolgarskij pjatistopnyj jamb v sopostavlenii s russkim", *Sbornik Miletič* (Sofia, 1933), 108-117.

—, "Co je poesie?", *Volné směry* (Prague, 1933-34), 229-239.

—, "M. P. Stockmar: Bibliografija rabot po stixosloženiju", *Slavia,* XIII (1934), 416-431.

—, "Staročeský verš", *Československá vlastivěda,* III, *Jazyk* (Prague, 1934), 429-459.

—, "Randbemerkungen zur Prosa des Dichters Pasternak", *Slavische Rundschau,* VII (1935), 357-374.

—, "Na okraj lyrických básní Puškinových", *Vybrané spisy A. S. Puškina,* I (Prague, 1936), 259-267 (also found in the Czech literary review *Listy pro umění a kritiku,* IV, 1936, 389-392).

—, "Socha v symbolice Puškinově", *Slovo a slovesnost,* III (1937), 2-24.

—, "Z zagadnień prozodji starogreckiej", *Prace ofiarowane Kazimierzowi Wóycickiemu* (Wilno, 1937), 73-88 (see below, section 3).

—, "Na okraj Eugena Oněgina", *Vybrané spisy A. S. Puškina,* III (1937), 257-265.

—, "K popisu Máchova verše" (1938), *Torso a tajemství Máchova díla,* see below, section 2.

— (with Marc Szeftel), "The Vseslav Epos", *Russian Epic Studies,* ed. edited by Roman Jakobson and Ernest J. Simmons (Philadelphia, 1949).

—, "Studies in Russian Philology", *Michigan Slavic Materials,* No. 1 (1963).

Jakubinskij, Lev, "O zvukax poètičeskogo jazyka" (1916), *Poètika. Sborniki po teorii poètičeskogo jazyka* (Petrograd, 1919) (see above).

—, "Skoplenie odinakovyx plavnyx v praktičeskom i poètičeskom jazykax" (1917), *op. cit.*

—, "O poètičeskom glossemosočetanii" (1919), *op. cit.*

—, "O dialogičeskoj reči", *Russkaja reč',* I (Petrograd, 1923).

Jarxo, B. I., "Granicy naučnogo literaturovedenija", *Iskusstvo,* 1925, No. 2, 46-60; 1927, I, 3, 16-38.

—, "Obščie principy formal'nogo analiza", *Ars Poetica,* I (Moscow, 1927).

Kaverin, Ven'jamin, *Skandalist ili večera na Vasil'evskom ostrove* (Leningrad, 1928).

—, *Xudožnik neizvesten* (Leningrad, 1931).

Lunc, Lev, "Počemu my Serapionovy brat'ja", *Literaturnye zapiski,* III (1922).

—, "Na zapad!", *Beseda,* September-October 1923.

Michigan Slavic Materials, No. 2, "Readings in Russian Poetics", (Ann Arbor, 1963). Articles by M. M. Bakhtin, B. M. Eichenbaum, R. Jakobson, Ju. Tynjanov, V. V. Vinogradov, V. N. Voloshinov.

Očerki po poètike Puškina (Berlin, 1923). Articles by Pëtr Bogatyrëv, Viktor Šklovskij, Boris Tomaševskij.

Petrovskij, M. A., "Kompozicija novelly u Maupassanta", *Načala,* 1921, 106-127.

—, "Morfologija novelly", *Ars Poetica,* I (see above).

Petrovskij, M., "Poètika i iskusstvovedenie", *Iskusstvo,* 1927, Nos. 2-3, pp. 119-139.

Poètika. Sborniki po teorii poètičeskogo jazyka (Petrograd, 1919). Articles by Osip Brik, Boris Ejxenbaum, Lev Jakubinskij, E. D. Polivanov, Viktor Šklovskij.

Poètika, I (Leningrad, 1926) (= Publication of the Division of the Verbal Arts at the Petrograd State Institute of Art History). Articles by A. Astaxova, S. Baluxatyj, S. Bernstein, G. Gukovskij, B. Kazan-skij, N. Kolpakova, R. Tomaševskaja, Ju. Tynjanov, L. Vindt, V. Vi-nogradov.

Poètika, II (Leningrad, 1927). Articles by A. Fëdorov, L. Ginzburg, B. Larin, K. Šimkevič, B. Tomaševskij, V. Žirmunskij.

Poètika, III (Leningrad, 1927). Articles by S. Baluxatyj, S. Bernstein, G. Gukovskij, N. Kolpakova, N. Surina, L. Vindt, V. Vinogradov, S. Vyšeslavceva.

Poètika, IV (Leningrad, 1928). Articles by A. Fëdorov, G. Gukovskij, N. Kovarskij, V. Propp, B. Tomaševskij, V. Vinogradov, V. Žirmun-skij.

Propp, V. I., *Morfologija skazki* (= *Voprosy poètiki,* XII) (Leningrad, 1928).

Russkaja proza (Leningrad, 1926) (= *Voprosy poètiki,* VIII) (Re-printed The Hague, 1963, Slavistic Printings and Reprintings,

XLVIII). Boris Ejxenbaum and Jurij Tynjanov, ed. Articles by B. Buxstab, L. Ginsburg, V. Hoffmann, N. Kovarskij, T. Roboli, N. Stepanov, V. Silber.

Russkaja reč', I (Petrograd, 1923). Lev Ščerba, ed. Articles by L. Jakubinskij, B. Larin, L. Ščerba, V. Vinogradov.

Russkaja reč' (Leningrad, 1927). Lev Ščerba, ed. Articles by S. Bernstein, B. Larin, V. Vinogradov.

Sborniki po teorii poètičeskogo jazyka, I (Petersburg, 1916).

Sborniki po teorii poètičeskogo jazyka, II (Petersburg, 1917).

Skaftymov, A., *Poètika i genezis bylin* (Saratov, 1924).

Šklovskij, Viktor, *Voskrešenie slova* (Petersburg, 1914).

—, "O poèzii i zaumnom jazyke" (1916), *Poètika,* 1919 (see above).

—, "Iskusstvo kak priëm" (1917), *op. cit.*

—, "O psixologičeskoj rampe", *Žizn' iskusstva,* 1920, No. 445.

—, *Razvertyvanie sjužeta* (Petrograd, 1921) (later included in the collection of essays *O teorii prozy,* see below).

—, "Sjužet u Dostoevskogo", *Letopis' Doma Literatorov,* 1921, No. 4

—, *Tristram Shandy Sterne'a i teorija romana* (Petrograd, 1921), reprinted in *O teorii prozy.*

—, *Rozanov* (Petrograd, 1921).

—, *Xod konja* (Moscow-Berlin, 1923).

—, *Literatura i kinematograf* (Berlin, 1923).

—, *Sentimental'noe putešestvie* (Moscow-Berlin, 1923).

—, "Andrej Belyj", *Russkij sovremennik,* 1924, No. 2, 231-245. See also next item.

—, *O teorii prozy* (Moscow, 1925); 2nd edition (Moscow, 1929).

—, "V zaščitu sociologičeskogo metoda", *Novyj lef,* 1927, No. 3 (later reprinted in *Gamburgskij ščët,* see below).

—, *Tret'ja fabrika* (Moscow, 1926).

—, *Texnika pisatel'skogo remesla* (Moscow-Leningrad, 1927).

—, *Gamburgskij ščët* (Moscow, 1928).

—, *"Vojna i mir* L'va Tolstogo (Formal'no-sociologičeskoe issledovanie)", *Novyj lef,* 1928, No. 1.

—, *Material i stil' v romane L. N. Tolstogo Vojna i mir* (Moscow, 1928).

—, "Pamjatnik naučnoj ošibke", *Literaturnaja gazeta,* 27.I.1930.

—, "Suxoplavcy ili uravnenie s odnim neizvestnym", *Literaturnaja gazeta,* 13.III.1930.

—, *O Majakovskom* (Moscow, 1940).

Stepanov, N., "V zaščitu izobretatel'stva", *Zvezda,* VI (1929).

Tomaševskij, Boris, "Andrej Belyj i xudožestvennaja proza", *Žizn' is-kusstva,* 1920, Nos. 454, 458-9, 460.

—— "Literatura i biografija", *Kniga i revoljucija,* IV (1923).

——, "Problema stixotvornogo ritma", *Literaturnaja mysl',* II (1923), 124-140 (later reprinted in the collection of studies, *O stixe,* see below).

——, *Russkoe stixosloženie. Metrika* (Petrograd, 1923) (= *Voprosy poètiki,* II).

——, "O dramatičeskoj literature", *Žizn' iskusstva,* 1924, No. 13.

——, "Pjatistopnyj jamb Puškina", *Očerki po poètike Puškina* (see above).

——, *Puškin* (Moscow, 1925).

——, *Teorija literatury (Poètika)* (Moscow-Leningrad, 1925), 6th ed. Moscow, 1931).

——, *O stixe* (stat'i) (Leningrad, 1929).

Trubetzkoy, N. S., *"Xoženie za tri morja* Afanasija Nikitina kak litera-turnyj pamjatnik", *Vёrsty* (Paris, 1926), I, 164-186.

——, "R. Jakobson, *O češskom stixe", Slavia,* II (1923-24), 452-460.

——, "O metrike častuški", *Vёrsty* (Paris, 1927), 11, 205-223. Reprinted in *Three Philological Studies* (see below).

——, "K voprosu o stixe 'Pesen zapadnyx slavjan Puškina,' " *Belgradskij puškinskij sbornik* (Belgrad, 1937).

——, "O metode izučenija Dostoevskogo", *Novyj Žurnal,* vol. 48 (New York, 1957), pp. 109-121.

——, O dvux romanax Dostoevskogo", *Novyj Žurnal,* vol. 60 (New York, 1960), pp. 116-137.

——, "Rannij Dostoevskij", *Novyj Žurnal,* vol. 71 (New York, 1963), pp. 101-127.

——, "Three Philological Studies", *Michigan Slavic Materials,* No. 3 (Ann Arbor, 1963).

Tynjanov, Jurij, "Stixovye formy Nekrasova", *Letopis' Doma Literato-rov,* 1921 (later reprinted in *Arxaisty i novatory,* see below).

——, *Dostoevskij i Gogol' (K teorii parodii)* (Petrograd, 1921) (see also below: *Arxaisty i novatory).*

——, "Literaturnoe segodnja", *Russkij sovremennik,* I (1924).

——, *Problema stixotvornogo jazyka* (Leningrad, 1924) (Reprinted The Hague, 1963, *Slavistic Printings and Reprintings,* XLVII).

——, "O literaturnom fakte", *Lef,* 1924, No. 2, 100-116 (see also *Arxaisty i novatory,* Leningrad, 1929).

——, "Arxaisty i Puškin", *Puškin v mirovoj literature* (symposium) (Leningrad, 1926), 215-286, later reprinted in *Arxaisty i novatory.*

—, "O literaturnoj èvoljucii", *Na literaturnom postu,* 1927, No. 4 (see also *Arxaisty i novatory).*

—, (with R. Jakobson), "Voprosy izučenija literatury i jazyka", see above.

—, *Arxaisty i novatory* (Leningrad, 1929).

Vinogradov, Viktor, "Sjužet i kompozicija povesti Gogolja 'Nos' ", *Načala,* 1921, 82-105 (later reprinted in Vinogradov's collection of studies, *Èvoljucija russkogo naturalizma,* see below).

—, "Stil' peterburgskoj poèmy 'Dvojnik", *Dostoevskij,* I (symposium) (Petrograd, 1922), 211-257.

—, "O simvolike Anny Axmatovoj", *Literaturnaja mysl',* I (Petrograd, 1922), I, pp. 91-138.

—, "O zadačax stilistiki (Nabljudenija nad stilem žitija protopopa Avvakuma)". *Russkaja reč,'* 1923 (see above).

—, "Sjužet i arxitektonika romana Dostoevskogo *Bednye ljudi* v svjazi s voprosom o poètike natural'noj školy", *Tvorčeskij put' Dostoevskogo* (symposium) (Leningrad, 1924) (also *Èvoljucija russkogo naturalizma,* see below).

—, *O poèzii Anny Axmatovoj (Stilističeskie nabroski)* (Leningrad, 1925).

—, *Gogol' i natural'naja škola* (Leningrad, 1925).

—, "Jules Janin i Gogol' ", *Literaturnaja mysl',* III (1925), 342-365 (see also *Èvoljucija . . .).*

—, *Ètjudy o stile Gogolja* (=*Voprosy poètiki,* VII) (Leningrad, 1926).

—, "Jazyk Zoščenki (zametki o leksike)", *Mixail Zoščenko, stat'i i materialy* (Leningrad, 1928).

—, *Èvoljucija russkogo naturalizma (Gogol'-Dostoevskij)* (Leningrad, 1929).

—, *O xudožestvennoj proze* (Moscow-Leningrad, 1930).

—, *Očerki po istorii russkogo literaturnogo jazyka 17-19-go vekov* (Moscow, 1934).

—, *Jazyk Puškina (Puškin i istorija russkogo literaturnogo jazyka)* (Moscow-Leningrad, 1935).

—, "Jazyk Gogolja", *N. V. Gogol'. Materialy i issledovanija,* II (Moscow-Leningrad, 1936).

—, *Stil' Puškina* (Moscow, 1941).

Vinokur, G. O., "Novaja literatura po poètike (obzor)", *Lef,* 1923. No. 1, 239-243.

—, "Poètika. Lingvistika. Sociologija (Metodologičeskaja spravka)", *Lef,* 1923, No. 3, 104-113.

—, *Kul'tura jazyka. Očerki lingivističeskoj texnologii* (Moscow, 1925).

—, "Poèzija i nauka", *Čët i nečet* (Moscow, 1925).

—, *Biografija i kul'tura* (Moscow, 1927).

—, *Kritika poètičeskogo teksta* (Moscow, 1927).

Zadači i metody izučenija iskusstv (a symposium published by the Petrograd Institute of Art History) (Petrograd, 1924).

Žirmunskij, Viktor, *Kompozicija liričeskix stixotvorenij* (Petrograd, 1921).

—, "Poèzija Aleksandra Bloka", cf. symposium *O Aleksandre Bloke* (Petrograd, 1921), pp. 65-165 (later reprinted in Žirmunskij's collection of studies *Voprosy teorii literatury,* see below).

—, "Zadači poètiki", *Načala,* 1921, No. 1, 51-81 (see also *Voprosy ...*).

—, *Valerij Brjusov i nasledie Puškina (Opyt sravnitel'no-stilističeskogo issledovanija)* (Petrograd, 1922).

—, "Melodika stixa (Po povodu knigi B. M. Ejxenbauma *Melodika stixa)", Mysl',* 1922, No. 5, 109-139 (also in *Voprosy teorii literatury).*

—, "K voprosu o formal'nom metode" (introduction to the Russian translation of Walzel's book, *Problema formy v poèzii)* (Petrograd, 1923), pp. 3-23; also found in *Voprosy teorii literatury.*

—, *Rifma, eë istorija i teorija (= Voprosy poètiki,* III) (Leningrad, 1923).

—, *Bajron i Puškin (Iz istorii romantičeskoj poèmy)* (Leningrad, 1924).

—, *Vvedenie v metriku. Teorija stixa (= Voprosy poètiki,* VI) (Leningrad, 1925) (An English translation, *Introduction to Metrics,* was recently published in The Hague, *Slavistic Printings and Reprintings,* LVIII).

—, *Voprosy teorii literatury* (Leningrad, 1928) (Reprinted The Hague, 1962, *Slavistic Printings and Reprintings,* XXXIV).

—, "Puškin i zapadnye literatury", cf. *Puškin* (a publication of the Puškin Committee of the Academy of Sciences), III (Moscow, 1937).

2. *Czech and Slovak*

Bakoš, M., and K. Simončič, "O 'úpadku' literatúry", *Slovenské smery,* II (1934-35), 179-196.

Bakoš, Mikuláš, "K vývinu a situacii slovenskéj literatúry", *Slovenské smery,* V (1937-38), 250-262.

—, *Vývin slovenského verša* (Turč. Sv. Martin, 1939).

— (ed.), *Teória literatúry* (anthology of Russian Formalism) (Trnava, 1941).

Čyževs'kyj (Čiževskij), Dmytro, "Příspěvek k symbolice českého básnictví náboženského", *Slovo a slovesnost,* II (1936), 98-105.

—, "Puškin medzi romantizmom a klasicizmom", *Slovenské pohl'ady,* 1937, 53, pp. 36-41, 75-82.

—, "K Máchovemu světovému názoru", cf. *Torso a tajemství Máchova díla,* see below.

Havránek, B., "Máchov jázyk", *Torso a tajemství Máchova díla.*

Hrabák, Josef, *Staropolský verš ve srovnání se staročeským (= Studie Pražského linguistického kroužku,* 1) (Prague, 1937).

—, *Smilova škola (Rozbor básnické struktury) (=* Studie Pražského linguistického kroužku, 3) (Prague, 1941).

Isačenko, A. V., "Der slovenische fünffüssige Jambus", *Slavia,* XIV (1935-36), 45-47.

—, *Slovenski verz* (Ljubljana, 1939).

—, and M. Bakoš, "Literatúra a jej skúmanie", *Ve dne a v noci* (Bratislava, 19 . . .), 121-124.

Mathesius, Vilém, "Deset let pražského linguistického kroužku", *Slovo a slovesnost,* 1936, No. 2.

Mukařovský, Jan, *Máchov 'Máj.' Estetická studie* (Prague, 1928).

—, "K českému překladu Šklovského *Teorie prozy", Čin,* VI (1934), 123-130 (later reprinted in *Kapitoly z české poetiky,* see below).

— (ed.), *Torso a tajemství Máchova díla* (Prague, 1938). Articles by D. Čiževskij, O. Fischer, B. Havránek, R. Jakobson, J. Mukařovský, F. X. Šalda, B. Václavek, R. Wellek.

—, *Kapitoly z české poetiky* (Prague, 1941). Vol. 1: *Obecní věci básnictví* (General Problems of Poetry). Vol. II: *K. vývoji české poesie a prozy* (On the Evolution of Czech Poetry and Prose).

—, "O básnickom jázyku", *Vo dne a v noci* (Bratislava, 1941), 129-133.

Thèses sur la langue poétique. Tézy Pražského linguistického kroužku, cf. *Mélanges linguistiques dédiés au Premier Congrès de Philologues Slaves (= Travaux du Cercle Linguistique de Prague, I)* (Prague, 1929), 17-21.

Wellek, René, "K. H. Mácha a anglická literatura", *Torso a tajemství Máchova díla.*

3. *Polish*

Budzyk, Kazimierz, *Stylistyka teoretyczna w Polsce* (Warsaw, 1946) (Z zagadnień poetyki).

Hopensztand, David, "Mowa pozornie zależna w kontekście *Czarnych*

Skrzydeł Kadena-Bandrowskiego", *Prace ofiarowane Kazimierzowi Wóycickiemu* (see below).

Ingarden, Roman, *Das literarische Kunstwerk (Eine Untersuchung aus dem Grenzgebiet der Ontologie, Logik und Literaturwissenschaft)* (Halle, 1931).

—, *O poznawaniu dziela literackiego* (Lwow, 1937).

Kridl, Manfred, *Wstęp do badań nad dziełem literackiem (= Z zagadnień poetyki,* I) (Wilno, 1936).

Prace ofiarowane Kazimierzowi Wóycickiemu (= Z zagadnień poetyki, 6) (Wilno, 1937). A symposium dedicated to the pioneer of Polish poetics, Kazimierz Wóycicki. Articles by W. Borowy, K. Budzyk, H. Elsenberg, H. Felczak, M. Grzędzielska, S. Hopensztand, J. Hrabák, R. Jakobson, K. Kaplan, St. Krispel, J. Kreczmar, M. Kridl, J. Kuryłowicz, Z. Łempicki, L. Podhorski-Okołów, M. Rzeuska, F. Siedlecki, St. Skwarczyńska, N. Trubetzkoy, K. W. Zawodziński, St. Żółkiewski.

Putrament, Jerzy, *Struktura nowel Prusa (= Z zagadnień poetyki,* 2) (Wilno, 1935).

Rosyjska szkola formalna, 1914-1934 (= *Archiwum tłumarczeń,* 3) (Warsaw, 1939). A selection from the Russian Formalists, e.g. Ejxenbaum, Jakobson, Šklovskij, Tomaševskij, Tynjanov, Žirmunskij, prepared for publication on the eve of the War.

Siedlecki, Franciszek, "Sprawy wersyfikacji polskiej", *Wiadomości Literackie,* 1934.

—, "O rytmie i metrze", *Skamander,* IX (1935), 420-436.

—, "Jeszcze o sprawach wiersza polskiego", *Przegląd Współczesny,* 1936, pp. 370-388.

—, *Studja z metryki polskiej,* 2 vols. (= *Z zagadnień poetyki,* 4, 5) (Wilno, 1937).

—, "O swobodę wiersza polskiego", *Skamander,* II (1938), Nos. 13—14.

Troczyński, Konstanty, *Elementy form literackich* (Poznań, 1936).

Wóycicki, Kazimierz, *Rytm w liczbach* (= Z zagadnień poetyki, 3) (Wilno, 1938).

Žirmunskij, Viktor, *Wstęp do poetyki (= Archiwum tłumaczeń,* 1) (1934). Polish translation of the study by Žirmunskij "Zadači poètiki", see above, section 1.

Z zagadnień stylistyki (= Archiwum tłumaczeń, 2) (Warsaw, 1937). Selections from Leo Spitzer, Karl Vossler and Viktor Vinogradov. Introduction by Zygmunt Łempicki.

II. DISCUSSIONS OF THE FORMALIST MOVEMENT

1. In Russian

Arvatov, Boris, "Jazyk poètičeskij i jazyk praktičeskij", *Pečat' i revoljucija*, VII (1923), 58-67.

—, *Iskusstvo i proizvodstvo* (Moscow, 1926).

—, "O formal'no-sociologičeskom metode", *Pečat' i revoljucija*, III (1927), 54-64.

Breitburg, S., "Sdvig v formalizme", *Literatura i marksizm*, Vol. I (Moscow, 1929).

Buxarin, Nikolaj, "O formal'nom metode v iskusstve", *Krasnaja nov'*, III (1925).

Efimov, N. I., "Formalizm v russkom literaturovedenii", *Naučnye Izvestija Smolenskogo Gosudarstvennogo Universiteta*, V (1929), p. III.

Engelhardt, Boris, *Formal'nyj metod v istorii literatury* (= *Voprosy poètiki*, XI) (Leningrad, 1927).

Foxt, U., "Problematika sovremennoj markistskoj literatury", *Pečat' i revoljucija*, 1927, No. 2.

Gel'fand, M., "Deklaracija carja Midasa ili čto slučilos' s Viktorom Šklovskim," *Pečat' i revoljucija*, 1930, No. 2.

Gorbačëv, G., "My ešče ne načinali drat'sja", *Zvezda*, 1930, No. 5.

Gornfel'd, A. G., "Formalisty i ix protivniki", *Literaturnye zapiski*, 1922, No. 3.

Gukovskij, G., "Viktor Šklovskij kak istorik literatury", *Zvezda*, 1930, No. 1.

Kogan, P. S., "O formal'nom metode", *Pečat' i revoljucija*, V (1924).

Lunačarskij, A. V., "Formalizm v iskusstvovedenii", *Pečat' i revoljucija*, V (1924).

Medvedev, Pavel, *Formal'nyj metod v literaturovedenii* (Leningrad, 1928).

Mustangova, E., "Put' naibol'šego soprotivlenija", *Zvezda*, 1928, No. 3.

Piksanov, N. K., "Novyj put' literaturnoj nauki", *Iskusstvo*, 1923, No. 1.

Poljanskij, V., "Po povodu B. Ejxenbauma", *Pečat' i revoljucia*, V (1924).

Sakulin, Pavel, "Iz pervoistočnika", *Pečat' i revoljucija*, V (1924).

—, "K voprosu o postroenii poètiki", *Iskusstvo*, 1923, No. 1.

Trockij, Lev, *Literatura i revoljucija* (Moscow, 1924) (cf. English translation: Trotsky, Leo, *Literature and Revolution*, New York, 1925).

Vinogradov, Ivan, *Bor'ba za stil'* (Leningrad, 1937), pp. 387-448.

Voznesenskij, A. N., "Poiski ob'ekta (K voprosu ob otnošenii metoda sociologičeskogo k formal'nomu)", *Novyj mir,* 1926, No. 6, 116-28.

Zeitlin (Cejtlin), A., "Marksisty i formal'nyj metod", *Lef,* III (1923).

2. *In Languages other than Russian*

Gourfinkel, Nina, "Les nouvelles méthodes d'histore littéraire en Russie", *Le Monde Slave,* VI (1929), 234-263).

Harkins, William E., "Slavic Formalist Theories in Literary Scholarship", *Word,* Vol. 7, No. 2 (August, 1951), 177-185.

Kridl, Manfred, "Russian Formalism", *The American Bookman,* I (1944), 19-30.

Rutten, M., "Dichtkunst en phonologie", *Revue Belge de Philologie et d'Histore,* XXVIII (1950), No. 3-4.

Tomaševskij, Boris, "La nouvelle école d'histoire littéraire en Russie", *Revue des études slaves,* VIII (1928), 226-240.

Voznesenskij, A. N., "Die Methodologie der russischen Literaturwissenschaft", *Zeitschrift für slavische Philologie,* IV (1927), 145-162, and V(1928), 175-199.

—, "Problems of Method in the Study of Literature in Russia", *Slavonic Review,* VI (1927), 168-177.

Žirmunskij, Viktor, "Formprobleme in der russische Literaturwissenschaft", *Zeitschrift für slavische Philologie,* I (1925), 117-152.

III. BACKGROUND MATERIAL

Abercrombie, Lascelles, *Poetry: Its Music and Meaning* (London, 1932).

Andreevskij, S., *Istoričeskie očerki* (St. Petersburg, 1902).

Aristotle, *'Poetics,'* cf. *Criticism,* ed. by Mark Schorer, Josephine Miles, Gordon McKenzie (New York, 1948), 199-217.

Bal'mont, Konstantin, *Poèzija kak volšebstvo* (Moscow, 1915).

Belyj, Andrej, *Simvolizm* (Moscow, 1910).

—, *Lug zelënyj* (Moscow, 1910).

—, *Ritm kak dialektika i Mednyj vsadnik* (Moscow, 1929).

—, *Masterstvo Gogolja* (Moscow, 1934).

Blok, Aleksandr, "O sovremennom položenii russkogo simvolizma", *Apollon,* 1910, No. 8.

Brodskij, N., and L'vov-Rogačevskij, V., *Literaturnye manifesty* (Moscow, 1929).

Brjusov, Valerij, *Kratkij kurs nauki o stixe* (Moscow, 1919).
—, "Ob odnom voprose ritma", *Apollon,* 1910, Nr. 11.
—, "O rifme", *Pečat' i revoljucija,* 1 (1924).
—, *Osnovy stixovedenija* (Moscow, 1924).
Brooks, Cleanth, *The Well Wrought Urn* (New York, 1947).
Brooks, Cleanth, and Robert Penn Warren, *Understanding Poetry* (New York, 1938).
Burljuk, David, *Galdjaščie Benoit i novoe russkoe nacional'noe iskusstvo* (Petersburg, 1913).
Cassirer, Ernst, *An Essay on Man* (Yale University Press, 1944).
—, *Die Philosophie der symbolischen Formen* (Berlin, 1923-29).
—, *Language and Myth* (New York and London, 1946).
—, "Structuralism in Modern Linguistics", *Word,* Vol. 1, No. 2 (1945), 99-120.
Cocteau, Jean, "Le Secret Professionel", *Le Rappel à l'Ordre* (Paris, 1926).
Coleridge, Samuel Taylor, "Occasion of the Lyrical Ballads", cf. *Criticism,* (New York, 1948), 249-257.
Eastman, Mac, *Artists in Uniform* (New York, 1934).
—, *Art and the Life of Action* (London, 1935).
Eliot, T. S., *Selected Essays* (New York, 1932).
—, *The Use of Poetry and the Use of Criticism* (Cambridge, Mass., 1933).
Elton, William, *Glossary of the New Criticism* (Chicago, 1948).
Empson, William, *Seven Types of Ambiguity* (London, 1930).
Engelhardt, Boris, *Aleksandr Nikolaevič Veselovskij* (Petrograd, 1924).
Evlaxov, A., *Vvedenie v filosofiju xudožestvennogo tvorčestva* (Warsaw, 1910-12).
Farrell, James T., *Literature and Morality* (New York, 1947).
Fedin, Konstantin, *Gor'kij sredi nas* (Moscow, 1943).
Friče, V. M., *Novejšaja evropejskaja literatura* (Moscow, 1919).
Geršenzon, Mixail, *Mudrost' Puškina* (Moscow, 1919).
—, "Videnie poèta", *Mysl' i slovo,* Moscow, II (1918), 76-84.
Hanslick, Eduard, *Vom Musikalisch-Schönen* (Leipzig, 1885) (English translation: *The Beautiful in Music,* London and New York, 1941).
Hildebrandt, Adolf, *Das Problem der Form in der bildenden Kunst* (Strassburg, 1893).
Husserl, Edmund, *Logische Untersuchungen,* 2 vols. (Halle, 1913).
Ivanov, Vjačeslav, *Borozdy i meži* (Moscow, 1916).
Jakobson, Roman, *Remarques sur l'évolution phonologique du russe*

comparée à celle des autres langues slaves (= *Travaux du Cercle Linguistique de Prague,* II) (1929).

—, *K xarakteristike evrazijskogo jazykovogo sojuza* (Paris, 1931).

Kaun, Alexander, *Soviet Poets and Poetry* (Berkeley and Los Angeles, 1943).

Kazin, Alfred, *On Native Grounds* (New York, 1942).

Koehler, Wolfgang, *Gestaltpsychology* (New York, 1929).

Korš, Fëdor, "Plan issledovanija o stixosloženii Puškina i slovarja Puškinskix rifm", *Puškin i ego sovremenniki,* III (1905), 111-134.

—, *Slovo o polku Igoreve* (Petersburg, 1909).

Kručënyx, A., *Troe* (Moscow, 1914).

Langer, Susanne K., *Philosophy in a New Key* (Cambridge, Mass., 1942).

Lanz, Henry, *The Physical Basis of Rime* (Stanford University Press, 1931).

Levin, Harry, "Notes on Convention", *Perspectives of Criticism,* ed. by H. Levin (Harvard University Press, 1950).

Literary Scholarship, Its Aims and Methods, ed. by Norman Foerster (University of Northern Carolina Press, 1941).

Majakovskij, Vladimir, "Kak delat' stixi", *Sobranie sočinenij,* V (Moscow, 1928-1933), 381-428.

V. Majakovskij. Materialy i issledovanija (Moscow, 1940). Symposium on the tenth anniversary of Majakovskij's death; see especially the paper by V. Xardžiev on Majakovskij and painting.

Marty, Anton, *Psyche und Sprachstruktur, Nachgelassene Schriften* (Bern, 1940).

Merežkovskij, D. S., *Tolstoj and Dostoevskij* (Petersburg, 1914).

Mirsky, D. S., *Contemporary Russian Literature* (New York, 1926).

Ogden, R., and Richards, I. A., *The Meaning of Meaning* (New York, 1936).

Ortega y Gasset, José, *The Dehumanization of Art and Notes on the Novel* (Princeton University Press, 1948).

Ovsjaniko-Kulikovskij, D., *Istorija russkoj intelligencii* (Moscow, 1908).

—, *Istorija russkoj literatury 19-go veka* (Moscow, 1908), 5 vols.

Pepper, Stephen C., *The Basis of Criticism in the Arts* (Cambridge, Mass., 1945).

Pereverzev, F., *Tvorčestvo Gogolja* (Leningrad, 1926).

Peretc, V. N., *Iz lekcij po metodologii istorii russkoj literatury* (Kiev, 1914).

Plexanov, Georgij, "Pis'ma bez adresa", *Sočinenija,* XIV (Moscow, 1923-27).

Plekhanov, George, *Art and Society* (New York, 1937).

Potebnja, Aleksandr, *Iz lekcij po teorii slovesnosti* (Xar'kov, 1894).

—, *Iz zapisok po teorii slovesnosti* (Xar'kov, 1905).

—, *O nekotoryx simvolax v slavjanskoj poèzii* (Xar'kov, 1860).

—, *Jazyk i mysl',* 1st ed. (Xar'kov, 1862); 3er ed. (Xar'kov, 1926).

Puškin i ego sovremenniki (series of studies in the Puškin age) (St Petersburg-Petrograd-Leningrad, 1903-1930).

Pypin, A. N., *Istorija russkoj literatury* (St. Petersburg, 1913).

Ransom, John Crowe, *The New Criticism* (Norfolk, Conn., 1941).

—, *The World's Body* (New York, 1938).

Read, Herbert, "Surrealism and the Romantic Principle", *Criticism* (New York, 1948).

Reavey, George, *Soviet Literature To-Day* (London, 1946).

Richards, I. A., *Practical Criticism* (Londen, 1929).

—, *Principles of Literary Criticism* (Londen 1924).

Sakulin, Pavel, *Sociologičeskij metod v literaturovedenii* (Leningrad, 1925).

Sapir, E., *Language* (New York, 1921).

Saran, Franz, *Deutsche Verslehre* (Munich, 1907).

Saussure, de, Ferdinand, *Cours de linguistique générale* (Lausanne, 1916).

Sievers, Wlihelm, *Rhythmisch-melodische Studien* (Heidelberg, 1912).

Simmons, Ernest J., *Leo Tolstoy* (Boston, Mass., 1946).

Špet, Gustav, *Estetičeskie fragmenty,* 2 vols. (Petrograd, 1922).

—, *Vnutrennjaja forma slova* (Moscow, 1927).

Spitzer, Leo, *Linguistics and Literary History; Essays in Stylistics (Princeton, 1948).

Straxov, N., *Zametki o Puškine i drugix poètax* (Kiev, 1897).

Struve, Gleb, *Soviet Russian Literature* (University of Oklahoma Press, Norman, 1951).

Timofeev, L., *Teorija literatury* (Moscow, 1945).

Trilling, Lionel, *The Liberal Imagination* (New York, 1950).

Trubetzkoy, N. S., *Principes de phonologie* (Paris, 1949).

Tynjanov, Jurij, *Kjuxlja* (Leningrad, 1925).

—, *Puškin* (Leningrad, 1936).

—, *Smert' Vazir-Muxtara* (Leningrad, 1927).

Verrier, Paul, *Essai sur les principes de la métrique anglaise,* 3 vols. (Paris, 1909).

Veselovskij, Aleksandr, *Istoričeskaja poètika* (Leningrad, 1940) (with an introduction by V. Žirmunskij).

—, *Izbrannye stat'i* (Leningrad, 1939).

Vossler, Karl, *Frankreichs Kultur im Spiegel seiner Sprachentwicklung* (Heidelberg, 1913).

—, *Gesammelte Aufsätze zur Sprachphilosophie* (Munich, 1923).

—, *Positivismus und Idealismus in der Sprachwissenschaft* (Heidelberg, 1904).

Walzel, Oscar, *Gehalt und Gestalt im Kunstwerk des Dichters* (Berlin, 1923).

—, *Wechselseitige Erhellung der Künste* (Berlin, 1917).

Warren, Austin, "Literary Criticism", *Literary Scholarship, Its Aims and Methods,* see above.

Wellek, René, "Literary History", *Literary Scholarship . . . ,* see above.

—, "The Revolt against Positivism in Recent European Literary Scholarship", *Twentieth Century English* (New York, 19 . . .), 67-89.

—, "The Theory of Literary History", *Travaux du Cercle Linguistique de Prague,* VI (1936), 173-191.

Wellek, René and Austin Warren, *Theory of Literature* (New York, 1949).

Wimsatt, W. K. Jr., "Verbal Style: Logical and Counterlogical", *Publications of the Modern Language Association of America,* LXV, Nov. 2 (1950), 5-20.

Wölfflin, Heinrich, *Kunstgeschichtliche Grundbegriffe,* 5th ed. (Munich, 1921).

—, *Renaissance und Barock,* Munich, 1888.

Worringer, Wilhelm, *Formprobleme der Gotik* (Munich, 1911).

Xlebnikov, Velemir, *Sobranie proizvedenij* (Leningrad, 1923).

Zieliński, Tadeusz, "Ritm xudožestvennoj reči i ego psixologičeskie osnovanija", *Vestnik psixologii, kriminal'noj antropologii i gipnotizma.* 1906, Nos. II, IV.

—, "Die Behandlung der gleichzeitigen Ereignisse im antiken Epos", *Philologus,* Supplementband 8 (1899-1900).

INDEX

*   This index includes the notes, but does not include the Bibliography. The italicized numbers indicate the most important discussions of the concepts in question.